# The *Ultimate* FRENCH VERB
## Review and Practice

### Second Edition

David M. Stillman, PhD, and Ronni L. Gordon, PhD

New York   Chicago   San Francisco   Lisbon   London   Madrid   Mexico City
Milan   New Delhi   San Juan   Seoul   Singapore   Sydney   Toronto

**Online Audio Exercises**
Recordings for the Oral Exercises for each chapter (see pages 260–268) are available at www.audiostudyplayer.com.

# Contents

# Preface

> The Verb was the storm-center. This discovery made plain the right
> and wise course to pursue in order to acquire certainty and exactness
> in understanding the statements which the newspaper was daily
> endeavoring to convey to me: I must catch a Verb and tame it.
>
> —Mark Twain, "Italian With Grammar"

**The Ultimate French Verb Review and Practice: Mastering Verbs and Sentence Building for Confident Communication, Second Edition** is designed to provide advanced beginners through advanced learners of French with a powerful tool for reviewing and mastering French verb forms and turning these forms into the building blocks of meaningful sentences. We present the forms of French verbs through verb paradigms in the seven simple tenses and seven compound tenses, and proceed to show how these verb forms function in phrases, clauses, and sentences. This highly productive sentence-building feature, unique to our book, moves the learner effectively from verb forms to communication.

We use a contrastive approach in presenting grammar, comparing French verb tenses and structures to the usage of their English counterparts. Grammar explanations of verb formation and usage are clear, concise, and well-organized. Copious examples, many presented in dialogue format, reflect authentic, everyday language usage. Charts and tables are clear and easy to read. Verb lists are presented in structural and semantic groupings and include the latest additions to the lexicon, as in the case of verbs related to the computer and technology.

All French tenses and moods are presented in the 12 efficiently organized chapters of **The Ultimate French Verb Review and Practice, Second Edition**. Each chapter treats one or more tenses, such as the passé composé, or type of verb, such as irregular verbs. Following the presentation of verb paradigms and tenses is a section called *Building Sentences,* in which the chapter material is functionally expanded. As learners master each tense, they learn to expand the forms of that tense into real sentences that can be used for communication through the addition of different elements, such as other verbs, objects, and subordinate clauses, and the transformation of statements into questions. The flexible organization of the chapters permits the learner to study them in any order.

**The Ultimate French Verb Review and Practice, Second Edition** provides a large number of varied exercises that are designed to facilitate the learner's mastery of the French verb system and sentence building. Exercise types include writing verb forms and dialogue exchanges, translation into French and English, building sentences, replacement, expansion, and identifying types of sentences and verb endings. Useful current vocabulary is incorporated in the exercises. **The Ultimate French Verb Review and Practice, Second Edition** gives extensive treatment to the complexities of linguistic register in French, and thus helps learners select the forms and structures appropriate for different social and professional settings. The Answer Key at the end of the book allows learners to monitor their progress as they work through the exercises.

Several chapters have *language boxes* that present information about interesting lexical, historical, and cultural aspects of the French language. These brief language notes are designed to enhance the learner's knowledge and appreciation of the language by presenting etymology, borrowing, punctuation, verb and tense formation, and other features.

In this second edition, we have added an oral component to help learners make the crucial leap from written practice to oral control of forms and patterns. Recorded by native speakers of French, the oral exercises to be practiced in each chapter are based on topics and material presented in the chapter. These structures, the building blocks of communication, will help learners progress to the next level of language skills development—listening and speaking. Many of the exercises are contextual, offering the learner practice in authentic settings, such as home and office. Instruction lines and *Modèles* for the oral exercises can be found on pages 260–268, and responses can be found on pages 313–324 of the Answer Key; to make these pages easy to find, a gray band is printed on their outer edges. The audio material is easily accessible on McGraw-Hill's website (www.audiostudy player.com).

Our acclaimed grammar review and workbook, **The Ultimate French Review and Practice: Mastering French Grammar for Confident Communication**, provides learners with a highly effective tool for review and progress in the French language. We use the same successful pedagogy in **The Ultimate French Verb Review and Practice, Second Edition**, with the knowledge that learners will benefit measurably from its application. This book is ideal for learners working on their own and as an ancillary for students using a textbook in a classroom setting.

We have every confidence that with **The Ultimate French Verb Review and Practice, Second Edition**, you too will be able to catch a Verb and tame it!

$\sim$

We want to express our deepest gratitude to Christopher Brown, our editor and publisher par excellence, for sharing our pedagogical vision and making it a reality in this book and all the others we have written for McGraw-Hill. We are fortunate to have him not only as an expert guide and professional supporter, but also as a most cherished friend.

We dedicate this book to our children, Alex and Mimi, whose brilliance, love, and laughter inspire every word we write.

David M. Stillman, PhD
Ronni L. Gordon, PhD

# Introduction

Verbs are presented in conjugation paradigms that summarize the forms of a verb in each tense. French verbs change their form for person and number. Verbs are said to have three persons: the speaker, the person spoken to, and the third person, referring neither to the speaker nor the person spoken to. French, like English, has two numbers: singular and plural.

The persons of the verb and their corresponding subject pronouns in English are as follows.

|  | SINGULAR | PLURAL |
| --- | --- | --- |
| FIRST PERSON | *I* | *we* |
| SECOND PERSON | *you* | *you* |
| THIRD PERSON | *he, she, it* | *they* |

The persons of the verb and their corresponding subject pronouns in French are as follows.

|  | SINGULAR | PLURAL |
| --- | --- | --- |
| FIRST PERSON | je | nous |
| SECOND PERSON | tu | vous |
| THIRD PERSON | il/elle/on | ils/elles |

## Differences Between English and French

- English has only one form for *you*; French has two. **Tu** is a singular form and is informal. The **tu** form of the verb is used to address one person with whom you have an informal relationship: a family member, a close friend, a fellow student, etc. **Vous** is both the plural of **tu** and a formal singular form. The **vous** form of the verb is used to address one person with whom you have a formal relationship: a stranger, a customer, a colleague at work, etc., or more than one person in either a formal or an informal relationship.

  | | |
  | --- | --- |
  | Papa, **tu** peux m'aider? | *Dad, can you help me?* |
  | Papa, maman, **vous** pouvez m'aider? | *Dad, Mom, can you help me?* |
  | Madame, **vous** pouvez m'aider? | *Ma'am, can you help me?* |

- French has no subject pronoun for *it*. All nouns, whether animate or inanimate, are referred to as either **il** or **elle**. Thus, masculine nouns such as **le jeune homme** and **le crayon** are referred to as **il**, while feminine nouns such as **la femme** and **la ville** are referred to as **elle**.

- French makes a gender distinction in the third-person plural. (Note that English *they* does not.) **Ils** refers to masculine plural nouns, while **elles** refers to feminine plural nouns. **Ils** also refers to groups of males and females, while **elles** refers to groups consisting of females only.

  | | |
  |---|---|
  | —Où sont Luc et Marie? | *"Where are Luc and Marie?"* |
  | —**Ils** sont là. | *"They're here."* |
  | —Où sont Christine et Marie? | *"Where are Christine and Marie?"* |
  | —**Elles** sont là. | *"They're here."* |

- The pronoun **on** has two main uses in French.

  It is used as a general subject similar to English *one, people, you, they* or the passive voice.

  | | |
  |---|---|
  | Ici **on parle** français. | *French is spoken here.* |
  | **On s'amuse** bien à Paris. | *People have a good time in Paris.* |

  In contemporary French, **on** replaces **nous** in everyday speech and writing. Note that even when **on** is used to mean *we*, it takes a third-person singular verb form.

  | | |
  |---|---|
  | —Toi et ta famille, vous restez en ville? | *"Are you and your family staying in town?"* |
  | —Non, **on part** en vacances. | *"No, we're leaving on vacation."* |

- French subject pronouns are frequently accompanied by the corresponding disjunctive or stress pronoun. The disjunctive pronoun serves to focus on the subject.

  | SINGULAR | PLURAL |
  |---|---|
  | **moi**, je | **nous**, nous / **nous**, on |
  | **toi**, tu | **vous**, vous |
  | **lui**, il | **eux**, ils |
  | **elle**, elle | **elles**, elles |

  | | |
  |---|---|
  | Odile regarde la télé, mais **moi, je** fais mes devoirs. | *Odile is watching TV, but I'm doing my homework.* |

  The disjunctive pronouns **nous autres**, **vous autres** are common in informal language. Note that **vous autres** can refer only to groups of two or more, while **vous** can be either singular or plural.

# The Present Tense of Regular Verbs

**BUILDING SENTENCES**

**Subject + verb, subject + verb + direct object**
**(transitive and intransitive verbs)**
**Disjunctive pronoun + subject + verb,**
**disjunctive pronoun + subject + verb + direct object**

Regular verbs in French are divided into three broad classes called conjugations. The ending of the infinitive tells which conjugation a verb belongs to.

## INFINITIVE

The infinitive is a form of the verb unmarked for person or tense. English infinitives have the word *to* before the verb: *to speak, to finish, to sell.*

French infinitives end in **-er**, **-ir**, **-re**, or **-oir**. When you remove the infinitive ending, you are left with the *stem* of the verb.

## Conjugation of **-er** Verbs

French verbs of the first conjugation have infinitives ending in **-er**. **-Er** verbs are conjugated as follows.

**parler** (STEM **parl-**) *to speak*

| | |
|---|---|
| je parle | nous parl**ons** |
| tu parl**es** | vous parl**ez** |
| il/elle/on parle | ils/elles parl**ent** |

**NOTES**

1 · All of the singular forms and the third-person plural form are pronounced alike, in spite of the spelling differences.

2 · The mute **e** endings in the first conjugation (**-e**, **-es**, **-ent**) should be interpreted as orthographic signals indicating that the preceding consonant is pronounced.

3 · The full stem **parl-** is pronounced in all forms.

## Common -er verbs

| | |
|---|---|
| **accepter** *to accept* | **hésiter** *to hesitate* |
| **accompagner** *to accompany* | **imprimer** *to print* |
| **adorer** *to adore, love* | **installer** *to install* |
| **aider** *to help* | **inviter** *to invite* |
| **aimer** *to like, love* | **jouer** *to play* |
| **allumer** *to light, turn on* (appliance) | **laisser** *to leave, let* |
| **apporter** *to bring* | **laver** *to wash* |
| **apprécier** *to appreciate* (rate highly) | **marcher** *to walk* |
| **arriver** *to arrive* | **monter** *to go up, go upstairs* |
| **bavarder** *to chat* | **montrer** *to show* |
| **casser** *to break* | **naviguer (sur Internet)** *to surf (the Web)* |
| **cesser** *to stop* | **organiser** *to organize* |
| **chanter** *to sing* | **oublier** *to forget* |
| **chercher** *to look for* | **parler** *to speak* |
| **cliquer** *to click* (computer) | **passer** *to pass; to spend* (time) |
| **continuer** *to continue* | **penser** *to think* |
| **copier** *to copy* | **photocopier** *to photocopy; to xerox* |
| **créer** *to create* | **porter** *to carry, wear* |
| **danser** *to dance* | **pousser** *to push* |
| **décider** *to decide* | **pratiquer** *to practice* |
| **déjeuner** *to have lunch* | **préparer** *to prepare* |
| **demander** *to ask, ask for* | **présenter** *to present* |
| **dépenser** *to spend* (money) | **prêter** *to lend* |
| **désirer** *to desire, want* | **quitter** *to leave* (a person or place) |
| **dessiner** *to draw* | **raconter** *to tell, tell about, relate* |
| **détester** *to hate* | **refuser** *to refuse* |
| **dîner** *to have dinner* | **regarder** *to look at* |
| **discuter** *to discuss* | **remercier** *to thank* |
| **donner** *to give* | **rencontrer** *to meet* (by chance) |
| **écouter** *to listen to* | **rentrer** *to return, go back* |
| **éditer** *to edit* | **retourner** *to return, come/go back* |
| **emporter** *to carry/take away, carry off* | **retrouver** *to meet* (by appointment) |
| **emprunter** *to borrow* | **rouler** *to move, travel* (of a vehicle) |
| **enseigner** *to teach* | **saluer** *to greet* |
| **entrer** *to go/come in, enter* | **sauvegarder** *to save* (computer file) |
| **étudier** *to study* | **supporter** *to bear, stand* |
| **fermer** *to close* | **surfer (sur le Web)** *to surf (the Web)* |
| **fonder** *to found* | **téléphoner** *to phone* |
| **formater** *to format* | **tourner** *to turn* |
| **frapper** *to strike, hit* | **travailler** *to work* |
| **gagner** *to earn, win* | **traverser** *to cross* |
| **garder** *to keep* | **trouver** *to find* |
| **habiter** *to live* (reside) | **voler** *to fly* |

**A** *Practice the forms of regular -er verbs by completing each sentence with the correct form of the verb in parentheses.*

1. (retrouver)     Je _____ mes amis en ville.

2. (étudier)       Elle _____ la géographie.

3. (retourner)     Mes cousins _____ demain.

4. (passer)        Nous _____ l'été au Québec.

5. (aider)         Vous _____ vos enfants.

6. (aimer)         Tu _____ les tartes au citron?

7. (sauvegarder)   Ils _____ leurs fichiers.

8. (rentrer)       Je _____ en métro.

9. (téléphoner)    Il _____ à tout le monde.

10. (saluer)       Vous _____ vos copains.

11. (rouler)       L'autobus _____ vite.

12. (voler)        Les oiseaux _____ vers le sud.

13. (marcher)      Vous _____ lentement.

14. (donner)       Il _____ de bons conseils.

15. (dépenser)     Tu _____ une fortune.

16. (fermer)       Nous _____ les fenêtres.

17. (jouer)        Les enfants _____ sur le trottoir.

18. (dessiner)     Tu _____ au crayon.

19. (gagner)       Ils _____ beaucoup d'argent.

20. (oublier)      On _____ toujours son adresse.

**B** *Answer the questions, using the verb from the question along with the cues provided. Include the disjunctive pronoun when it is given.*

MODÈLE     Qu'est-ce qu'ils apportent?

toi, tu / des bonbons     *Toi, tu apportes des bonbons.*

nous, nous / du vin     *Nous, nous apportons du vin.*

elle, elle / des fleurs     *Elle, elle apporte des fleurs.*

1. Qu'est-ce qu'ils acceptent?

   a. moi, je / l'invitation _____

   b. eux, ils / le paquet _____

   c. nous, nous / le cadeau _____

   2.  Qui est-ce qu'ils remercient?

       a.  les étudiants / leur professeur _____

       b.  l'enfant / ses parents _____

       c.  toi, tu / ton ami _____

   3.  Où est-ce qu'ils travaillent?

       a.  vous, vous / en ville _____

       b.  lui, il / au bureau _____

       c.  les voisines / à la maison _____

   4.  Qui est-ce qu'ils invitent?

       a.  elle, elle / son fiancé _____

       b.  vous autres, vous / toute la famille _____

       c.  eux, ils / les voisins _____

   5.  Qu'est-ce qu'ils organisent?

       a.  moi, je / un dîner d'affaires _____

       b.  toi, tu / une réunion _____

       c.  mon chef / une réception _____

# Conjugation of **-ir** and **-re** Verbs

**-Ir** and **-re** verbs share some important features.

**-Ir** verbs are conjugated as follows.

| **finir** (STEM **finiss-**)  *to finish* | |
| --- | --- |
| je fini**s** | nous finiss**ons** |
| tu fini**s** | vous finiss**ez** |
| il/elle/on fini**t** | ils/elles finiss**ent** |

**-Re** verbs are conjugated as follows.

| **vendre** (STEM **vend-**)  *to sell* | |
| --- | --- |
| je vend**s** | nous vend**ons** |
| tu vend**s** | vous vend**ez** |
| il/elle/on vend | ils/elles vend**ent** |

**NOTES**

1 ·  The singular endings for **-ir** and **-re** verbs are **-s, -s, -t.** (The ending **-t** is not written if the verb stem ends in **-d**, as in **il vend.**) All the singular forms of any **-ir** or **-re** verbs are pronounced alike.

2 · In the plural forms of **-ir** and **-re** verbs, the final consonant of the stem is pronounced before the ending. This consonant is *not* pronounced in the singular forms. The final consonant of the stem of **finir** is /s/, spelled **ss**. The final consonant of the stem of **vendre** is /d/. This /d/ is heard in the plural forms, but—in spite of the spelling—it is not pronounced in the singular.

3 · The third-person singular and the third-person plural of **-ir** and **-re** verbs are therefore *not* pronounced alike. The third-person singular form ends in a vowel in spoken French, while the third-person plural form ends in a consonant.[1]

## Common -ir verbs

| | |
|---|---|
| **agir** *to act* | **guérir** *to cure, make better* |
| **applaudir** *to applaud* | **maigrir** *to get thin* |
| **atterrir** *to land* | **mincir** *to get thin* |
| **avertir** *to warn* | **obéir** *to obey* |
| **bâtir** *to build* | **périr** *to perish* |
| **choisir** *to choose* | **réfléchir** *to think, reflect* |
| **désobéir** *to disobey* | **remplir** *to fill* |
| **établir** *to establish* | **réussir** *to succeed* |
| **finir** *to finish* | **rougir** *to blush* |
| **gémir** *to moan* | **salir** *to make dirty* |
| **grossir** *to get fat* | |

## Common -re verbs

| | |
|---|---|
| **attendre** *to wait for* | **rendre** *to give back* |
| **confondre** *to confuse* | **répondre** *to answer* |
| **défendre** *to forbid* | **rompre** *to break, break off* (especially |
| **descendre** *to go down(stairs)* | figuratively) |
| **entendre** *to hear* | **tendre** *to stretch out; to extend an offer;* |
| **interrompre** *to interrupt* | *to tend to* |
| **mordre** *to bite* | **tordre** *to twist* |
| **perdre** *to lose* | **vendre** *to sell* |
| **prétendre** *to claim* | |

**C** *Practice the forms of regular* **-ir** *and* **-re** *verbs by completing each sentence with the correct form of the verb in parentheses.*

1. (interrompre) Vous _____ le professeur.

2. (descendre) Qui _____ faire les courses?

3. (réussir) Mes sœurs _____ au lycée.

4. (mordre) Ce chien _____ les gens.

5. (entendre) J'_____ un bruit.

6. (obéir) Nous _____ toujours.

---

[1] The forms **vends**, **vend** are pronounced /vã/. They end in a nasal vowel.

7. (réfléchir)    Toi, tu _____ avant d'agir.

8. (agir)    Jean-Claude _____ avant de réfléchir.

9. (attendre)    Nous _____ l'autobus.

10. (vendre)    Mes voisins _____ leur appartement.

11. (choisir)    Quel dessert est-ce que vous _____?

12. (rendre)    Nous _____ les livres à la bibliothèque.

13. (confondre)    Je _____ toujours ces deux mots.

14. (perdre)    Tu _____ toujours ton cahier.

15. (remplir)    Je _____ mes valises.

16. (répondre)    Je _____ en français.

17. (guérir)    Les bons médecins _____ les malades.

18. (rougir)    Vous _____, mademoiselle.

19. (applaudir)    Nous _____ les acteurs.

20. (bâtir)    Elle _____ son avenir.

## Verbs with Spelling Changes

First-conjugation verbs ending in **-cer** and **-ger** are regular, but they have a spelling change. The letter **c** changes to **ç** and the letter **g** changes to **ge** before **a** and **o**. In the present tense, this change appears in the **nous** form.

**placer**  *to place, put*

| | |
|---|---|
| je place | nous plaçons |
| tu places | vous placez |
| il/elle/on place | ils/elles placent |

**manger**  *to eat*

| | |
|---|---|
| je mange | nous mangeons |
| tu manges | vous mangez |
| il/elle/on mange | ils/elles mangent |

Verbs whose stems end in **-y**, such as **employer** *to use,* change the **y** to **i** before a silent **e** in all the singular forms and in the third-person plural.[1]

**employer**  *to use*

| | |
|---|---|
| j'emploie | nous employons |
| tu emploies | vous employez |
| il/elle/on emploie | ils/elles emploient |

---

[1]Verbs ending in **-ayer** may either make the above change or keep the **y** in all forms: **je paie** or **je paye**. Verbs ending in **-oyer** and **-uyer** must change **y** to **i** before a silent **e**.

### Common **-er** verbs ending in **-cer**

| | |
|---|---|
| **annoncer** *to announce* | **lancer** *to launch* |
| **avancer** *to advance* | **menacer** *to threaten* |
| **commencer** *to begin* | **placer** *to place, put; to invest* |
| **devancer** *to get ahead of* | **prononcer** *to pronounce* |
| **divorcer** *to divorce* | **remplacer** *to replace* |
| **effacer** *to erase* | **renoncer** *to resign, quit* |

### Common **-er** verbs ending in **-ger**

| | |
|---|---|
| **aménager** *to fix up, convert, modernize* | **loger** *to house, put someone up* |
| **arranger** *to arrange* | **longer** *to walk along, go along* |
| **changer** *to change* | **manger** *to eat* |
| **corriger** *to correct* | **nager** *to swim* |
| **décourager** *to discourage* | **partager** *to share* |
| **déménager** *to move* (change residence) | **plonger** *to dive* |
| **déranger** *to bother* | **ranger** *to put away* |
| **diriger** *to direct* | **rédiger** *to draft, write* |
| **encourager** *to encourage* | **télécharger** *to download* |
| **engager** *to hire* | **voyager** *to travel* |

### Common verbs whose stems end in **-y**

| | |
|---|---|
| **appuyer** *to support* | **nettoyer** *to clean* |
| **balayer** *to sweep* | **noyer** *to drown* |
| **broyer** *to grind, make into powder* | **payer** *to pay* |
| **effrayer** *to frighten* | **rayer** *to cross out* |
| **employer** *to use* | **renvoyer** *to send back, dismiss* |
| **ennuyer** *to bore* | **tutoyer** *to use the **tu** form to address someone* |
| **envoyer** *to send* | |
| **essayer** *to try, try on* | **vouvoyer** *to use the **vous** form to address someone* |
| **essuyer** *to wipe* | |

**D**   *Answer the following questions affirmatively, using the **nous** form.*

MODÈLE   Vous prononcez le vocabulaire?

      *Oui, nous prononçons le vocabulaire.*

1. Vous aménagez la cuisine? _____

2. Vous renoncez à ce voyage? _____

3. Vous tutoyez les amis? _____

4. Vous placez cet argent? _____

5. Vous nagez tous les jours? _____

6. Vous balayez la maison? _____

7. Vous partagez ces opinions? _____

8. Vous changez de route? _____

9. Vous lancez un projet? _____

10. Vous appuyez ce candidat? _____

11. Vous remplacez cet employé? _____

12. Vous mangez en ville? _____

13. Vous téléchargez des programmes? _____

14. Vous payez la facture? _____

15. Vous rédigez des lettres? _____

**E** *M. Sampy describes how he and his staff operate his restaurant. Rewrite the following sentences in a more informal style by changing* **nous** *to* **on**.

MODÈLE    Nous préparons notre restaurant.

_____*On prépare notre restaurant.*_____

1. Nous balayons le parquet. _____

2. Nous nettoyons les tables. _____

3. Nous appuyons les chaises contre le mur.

   _____

4. Nous essuyons les verres. _____

5. Nous broyons le poivre. _____

6. Nous employons des ingrédients de qualité.

   _____

7. Nous essayons la viande. _____

8. Nous payons les serveurs. _____

9. Nous tutoyons nos amis. _____

10. Nous rayons les fautes. _____

**F** *Review the forms of* **-er**, **-ir**, *and* **-re** *verbs by writing the correct verb form for the subject and infinitive given.*

1. tu / parler _____

2. je / réussir _____

3. vous / vendre _____

4. nous / voyager _____

5. elle / monter _____

6. ils / descendre _____

7. nous / remplacer _____

8. on / retourner _____

9.  vous / fermer  _____

10. nous / aménager  _____

11. tu / fournir  _____

12. il / ennuyer  _____

13. vous / mincir  _____

14. tu / répondre  _____

15. ils / choisir  _____

16. elles / payer  _____

17. je / perdre  _____

18. ils / jouer  _____

19. vous / étudier  _____

20. tu / nettoyer  _____

21. nous / partager  _____

22. il / demander  _____

23. nous / lancer  _____

24. on / tutoyer  _____

25. je / envoyer  _____

26. nous / télécharger  _____

## First-Conjugation (-er) Verbs with Mute e as the Stem Vowel

In first-conjugation verbs that have mute **e** as their stem vowel (**acheter**, **appeler**, **jeter**, **mener**, etc.), the mute **e** of the stem is pronounced as **è** in those forms where the ending also has a mute **e**. In the present tense, this includes all singular forms and the third-person plural. This change in sound is shown in French spelling in one of two ways.

### Verbs that change mute e to è in the stem before an ending with a mute e

Verbs such as **acheter** *to buy* and **mener** *to lead* change the stem vowel **e** to **è** before an ending with a mute **e** to indicate this pronunciation change.

| **acheter**  *to buy* | |
| --- | --- |
| j'achète | nous achetons |
| tu achètes | vous achetez |
| il/elle/on achète | ils/elles achètent |

| **mener**  *to lead* | |
| --- | --- |
| je mène | nous menons |
| tu mènes | vous menez |
| il/elle/on mène | ils/elles mènent |

### Other verbs that change mute e to è in the stem before an ending with a mute e

**amener**  *to bring (someone)*
**démener** (reflexive **se démener**)  *to thrash about, make a strenuous effort*
**emmener**  *to take (someone)*
**enlever**  *to remove, take off*
**geler**  *to freeze*
**lever**  *to pick up, raise*
**peler**  *to peel*

**peser**  *to weigh*
**promener**  *to walk*
**racheter**  *to buy back, redeem*
**ramener**  *to bring (someone) back*
**relever**  *to pick up again, put something back on its feet*
**semer**  *to sow*

## Verbs that double the consonant after mute e in the stem before an ending with a mute e

The verbs **appeler** *to call* and **jeter** *to throw* double the consonant after the mute **e** to show the pronunciation change of mute **e** to **è**.

**appeler**  *to call*

| | |
|---|---|
| j'app**elle** | nous appelons |
| tu app**elle**s | vous appelez |
| il/elle/on app**elle** | ils/elles app**elle**nt |

**jeter**  *to throw*

| | |
|---|---|
| je j**ett**e | nous jetons |
| tu j**ett**es | vous jetez |
| il/elle/on j**ett**e | ils/elles j**ett**ent |

### Other verbs that double the consonant after mute e in the stem before an ending with a mute e

**épeler**  *to spell*
**épousseter**  *to dust*
**feuilleter**  *to leaf through*
**projeter**  *to project*

**rappeler**  *to call back*
**rejeter**  *to reject*
**renouveler**  *to renew*

## First-Conjugation (-er) Verbs with é as the Stem Vowel

First-conjugation verbs that have **é** as their stem vowel (**espérer** *to hope*, **compléter** *to complete*, etc.) change **é** to **è** when the ending has a mute **e**. In the present tense, this includes all singular forms and the third-person plural. The spelling change reflects a change in pronunciation.

**espérer**  *to hope*

| | |
|---|---|
| j'esp**è**re | nous espérons |
| tu esp**è**res | vous espérez |
| il/elle/on esp**è**re | ils/elles esp**è**rent |

In verbs such as **préférer** *to prefer* and **répéter** *to repeat,* the stem vowel is the **é** in the next-to-last syllable. That is the vowel that changes to **è**, not the **é** of the prefixes **pré** and **ré**.

| **préférer** *to prefer* | |
| --- | --- |
| je préf**è**re | nous préférons |
| tu préf**è**res | vous préférez |
| il/elle/on préf**è**re | ils/elles préf**è**rent |

**Other verbs that change é to è in the stem before endings with mute e**

| | |
| --- | --- |
| **céder** *to yield* | **posséder** *to possess* |
| **célébrer** *to celebrate* | **protéger** *to protect* |
| **compléter** *to complete* | **refléter** *to reflect* |
| **dépoussiérer** *to dust* | **répéter** *to repeat* |
| **pénétrer** *to penetrate* | **révéler** *to reveal* |

**G**   *Rewrite each phrase, replacing* **nous** *with* **on**. *Remember to use third-person singular verb forms.*

1. nous complétons _____
2. nous renouvelons _____
3. nous ramenons _____
4. nous achetons _____
5. nous révélons _____
6. nous promenons _____
7. nous jetons _____
8. nous préférons _____
9. nous répétons _____
10. nous levons _____
11. nous rappelons _____
12. nous pelons _____
13. nous pénétrons _____
14. nous enlevons _____
15. nous semons _____
16. nous célébrons _____
17. nous amenons _____
18. nous projetons _____

**H** *Rewrite each question in the **tu** form. Change the possessives **votre** and **vos** to agree with the new subject.*

1. Quand est-ce que vous préférez prendre vos vacances?

   _____

2. Qu'est-ce que vous espérez faire cet été?

   _____

3. Combien est-ce que vous pesez?

   _____

4. Comment est-ce que vous épelez votre nom?

   _____

5. Est-ce que vous rejetez les idées extrémistes?

   _____

6. Où est-ce que vous achetez vos vêtements?

   _____

7. Quand est-ce que vous nous ramenez?

   _____

8. Est-ce que vous répétez les nouveaux mots?

   _____

9. Comment est-ce que vous célébrez votre anniversaire?

   _____

10. Comment est-ce que vous relevez votre entreprise?

    _____

11. Quelle revue feuilletez-vous là?

    _____

12. Où est-ce que vous promenez votre chien?

    _____

## Uses of the Present Tense

The French present tense is used to express general actions or states.

—Où est-ce que ta sœur travaille?           *"Where does your sister work?"*
—Elle enseigne les mathématiques           *"She teaches math at the university."*
à l'université.

It can also express actions going on at the present time, a function for which English usually prefers the present progressive tense.

| | |
|---|---|
| —Le consultant parle avec les cadres? | *"Is the consultant speaking with the managerial staff?"* |
| —Non, il prépare le compte rendu. | *"No, he's preparing the report."* |

Note that French has no equivalent for the English auxiliary *do, does* in questions or negative sentences.

| | |
|---|---|
| —Quelle langue étudiez-vous? L'allemand? | *"What language do you study? German?"* |
| —Non, je n'étudie pas l'allemand. J'apprends le français. | *"No, I don't study German. I'm learning French."* |

French can use the present tense to express future time when another element of the sentence makes it clear that the verb is referring to the future. Note that English often uses the present progressive for this function.

| | |
|---|---|
| —**Vous arrivez** à quelle heure demain? | *"At what time **are you arriving** tomorrow?"* |
| —**On arrive** à dix heures. **Nous vous appelons** tout de suite après notre arrivée. | *"**We're getting in** at ten o'clock. **We will call** you immediately after we arrive."* |

The present tense can be used to express past actions once the conversation makes clear that the past is being referred to. This may occur in speech and in writing, and it has parallels in English. This use of the present to refer to the past is called the *historical present*.

| | |
|---|---|
| Écoute ce qui est arrivé hier soir. J'entre dans la salle du théâtre, je trouve ma place, je m'assieds et je regarde autour de moi. Et qui est-ce que je vois, assis à côté de moi? Mon ancien petit ami Lucien et ma meilleure amie! Tu te rends compte? | *Listen to what happened last night. I go into the theater, I find my seat, I sit down, and I look around. And whom do I see sitting next to me? Lucien, my ex-boyfriend, and my best friend! Can you imagine?* |

French uses the present tense to refer to actions that began in the past but are continuing into the present. English uses a *have/has been doing something* construction for this function. The French construction consists of the following elements.

- **depuis combien de temps** + verb in present tense? OR
  **ça fait combien que** + verb in present tense? (more colloquial) OR
  **il y a combien de temps que** + verb in present tense? (more colloquial)

These patterns are used to ask a question about how long something has been going on.

| | |
|---|---|
| **Depuis combien de temps** est-ce que vous habitez ce quartier? | |
| **Ça fait combien que** vous habitez ce quartier? | *How long have you been living in this neighborhood?* |
| **Il y a combien de temps que** vous habitez ce quartier? | |

- verb in present tense + **depuis** + time expression. OR
  **ça fait** + time expression + verb in present tense. (more colloquial) OR
  **il y a** + time expression + verb in present tense. (more colloquial) OR
  **voilà** + time expression + verb in present tense. (more colloquial)

  These patterns are used to tell how long something has been going on.

  **J'habite** ce quartier **depuis un an.**
  **Ça fait un an que j'habite** ce quartier.      *I've been living in this neighborhood*
  **Il y a un an que j'habite** ce quartier.            *for a year.*
  **Voilà un an que j'habite** ce quartier.

- **Depuis quand** is used in a question to specify the starting point of an action that began in the past and continues into the present. **Depuis** is used in the answer to such a question.

  **Depuis quand** est-ce que vous attendez        *Since when* have you been waiting for
     le train?                                                                *the train?*
  J'attends **depuis** midi.                                        *I've been waiting **since** noon.*

**I**  *How long has this been going on?* Create conversational exchanges in formal style, using the elements given. Use the constructions **depuis combien de temps est-ce que** + verb in present tense *and* verb in present tense + **depuis** + time expression.

MODÈLE    vous / attendre le bus  (vingt minutes)

—  *Depuis combien de temps est-ce que vous attendez le bus?*

—  *J'attends le bus depuis vingt minutes.*

1. Raoul / travailler à la banque  (trois ans)

   —  _____

   —  _____

2. vous / discuter de politique  (une heure)

   —  _____

   —  _____

3. ils / télécharger des programmes  (trois heures)

   —  _____

   —  _____

4. les vieilles dames / bavarder  (deux heures)

   —  _____

   —  _____

5. vous et votre mari / chercher un appartement  (trois mois)

   —  _____

   —  _____

6. tu / regarder cette émission (*TV program*)  (dix minutes)

   — _____

   — _____

7. vous autres les professeurs / enseigner dans ce lycée  (deux ans)

   — _____

   — _____

8. cet enfant / agir comme ça  (trois semaines)

   — _____

   — _____

9. les fermiers / semer du maïs  (des siècles)

   — _____

   — _____

10. toi et ton frère, vous / nettoyer la maison  (une heure et demie)

    — _____

    — _____

11. vous autres / rédiger le compte rendu  (une semaine)

    — _____

    — _____

12. ils / photocopier des documents  (vingt minutes)

    — _____

    — _____

**J**  *Rewrite each formal sentence about how long things have been going on, using the structure given in parentheses.*

MODÈLE    J'étudie à Lyon depuis trois ans.  (voilà)
          *Voilà trois ans que j'étudie à Lyon.*_____

1. Nos voisins habitent à côté depuis dix ans.  (il y a)

   _____

2. Vous attendez l'avion depuis deux heures.  (ça fait)

   _____

3. Ils étudient l'anglais depuis cinq ans.  (voilà)

   _____

4. Depuis combien de temps est-ce qu'ils rédigent le compte rendu?  (ça fait)

   _____

5. Elle promène son chien depuis une demi-heure. (il y a)

_____

6. Il feuillette le magazine depuis quarante minutes. (voilà)

_____

7. Depuis combien de temps est-ce que vous logez des étudiants étrangers? (il y a)

_____

_____

8. Le public applaudit depuis deux minutes déjà. (ça fait)

_____

_____

**K** *Create conversational exchanges about the starting point of the following actions.*

MODÈLE    Marc / chercher du travail / le mois de septembre

     — *Depuis quand est-ce que Marc cherche du travail?*

     — *Il cherche du travail depuis le mois de septembre.*

1. Suzanne / étudier en Allemagne / 2005

  — _____

  — _____

2. cette famille / habiter en France / le début de l'été

  — _____

  — _____

3. tu / acheter tes légumes chez ce marchand / l'année dernière

  — _____

  — _____

4. vous / ranger la chambre / hier

  — _____

  — _____

5. les élèves / répondre en français / la semaine dernière

  — _____

  — _____

6. ils / passer leurs vacances en Bretagne / 1999

  — _____

  — _____

7. vous / voyager pour affaires / 2003

— _____

— _____

8. tu / tutoyer le chef / l'été

— _____

— _____

9. ton ami / fumer / janvier

— _____

— _____

10. ce conseiller / organiser des réunions / le mois d'août

— _____

— _____

| BUILDING SENTENCES | **Subject + verb, subject + verb + direct object (transitive and intransitive verbs)** |
|---|---|

The subject is the element of the sentence that determines the ending of the verb. In the following sentences, **nous** and **ils** are subjects.

**Nous** nageons souvent.     *We swim often.*

**Ils** réussissent.     *They're succeeding.*

The idea or action expressed by the verb may affect or be directed at a person or thing. That person or thing is the object of the verb. If the object follows the verb directly without a preposition, it is called a *direct object*. In the sentences below the direct objects are in boldface.

| | |
|---|---|
| Nous aménageons **notre cuisine**. | *We're fixing up our kitchen.* |
| Je vends **mes livres**. | *I'm selling my books.* |
| Elle perd **ses clés**. | *She loses her keys.* |

Most French verbs must have a direct object. These verbs are called *transitive verbs*. In the verb lists in this book, transitive verbs that take a direct object are followed by **qqn** (**quelqu'un** *someone*) to show that they must have a person as direct object or by **qqch** (**quelque chose** *something*) to show that they must have an inanimate object as direct object. Verbs followed by **qqn/qqch** may have either an animate or inanimate direct object.

Some French verbs cannot be followed by a direct object. These are called *intransitive verbs* and they are usually verbs of motion.

| | |
|---|---|
| Elle **monte**. | *She is going upstairs.* |
| Tu **nages** bien. | *You swim well.* |
| Vous **retournez** demain. | *You're coming back tomorrow.* |

Sometimes transitive verbs appear without an expressed direct object, but they have an implied direct object that is understood from context.

| | |
|---|---|
| On ferme à six heures. | *We close at six. (= We close the store at six.)* |

Here are some transitive verbs in French that do not take a direct object in English. Note that the English verbs have a preposition (*for, over, to, along, at*) before the object.

**attendre qqn/qqch**  *to wait for someone/something*
**chercher qqn/qqch**  *to look for someone/something*
**demander qqch**  *to ask for something*
**écouter qqn/qqch**  *to listen to someone/something*
**escalader qqch**  *to climb over something*
**espérer qqch**  *to hope for something*
**longer qqch**  *to walk/go along something*
**payer qqch**  *to pay for something*
**regarder qqn/qqch**  *to look at someone/something*
**viser qqn/qqch**  *to aim at someone/something*

| | |
|---|---|
| Il attend ses amis. | *He's waiting for his friends.* |
| Nous espérons une bonne récompense. | *We're hoping for a good reward.* |
| La route longe le fleuve. | *The road runs along the river.* |
| Ses remarques visent ses collègues. | *His remarks are directed at his colleagues.* |

There are also English transitive verbs whose cognates or equivalents do not take a direct object in French. These verbs have a preposition (most frequently **à** or **de**, depending on the verb) linking them to their objects.

**abuser de qqch**  *to take (unfair) advantage of something*
**discuter d'un sujet**  *to discuss a subject*
**échapper à qqch**  *to evade something*
**échouer à un examen**  *to fail an exam*
**jouer à un jeu**  *to play a game*
**jouer d'un instrument de musique**  *to play a musical instrument*
**renoncer à qqch**  *to resign from something, quit something*
**ressembler à qqn/qqch**  *to look like someone/something*
**téléphoner à qqn**  *to call/phone someone*
**toucher à qqch**  *to mess around with something*

| | |
|---|---|
| N'**abusez** pas **de** sa bonté. | *Don't take advantage of his kindness.* |
| Ils ont **discuté d'**économie. | *They discussed economics.* |
| Elle **ressemble à** son père. | *She looks like her father.* |
| Ne **touche** pas **à** mes cahiers. | *Keep your hands off my notebooks.* |

**L** *Yves tells about going to the stadium with his friends to see their team compete in a soccer match. Identify each of his sentences as having a transitive or intransitive verb.*

|  | | TRANSITIVE | INTRANSITIVE |
|---|---|:---:|:---:|
| 1. | Mon équipe joue cet après-midi. | ☐ | ☐ |
| 2. | Je cherche le stade. | ☐ | ☐ |
| 3. | Je regarde le plan de la ville. | ☐ | ☐ |
| 4. | Je traverse la rue. | ☐ | ☐ |
| 5. | Je cherche l'arrêt d'autobus. | ☐ | ☐ |
| 6. | J'attends le bus. | ☐ | ☐ |
| 7. | Je retrouve mes copains dans le bus. | ☐ | ☐ |
| 8. | Le bus tourne à gauche. | ☐ | ☐ |
| 9. | Il roule vite. | ☐ | ☐ |
| 10. | Nous arrivons au stade. | ☐ | ☐ |
| 11. | Nous descendons de l'autobus. | ☐ | ☐ |
| 12. | On entre dans le stade. | ☐ | ☐ |
| 13. | Nous trouvons nos places. | ☐ | ☐ |
| 14. | Nous regardons le match. | ☐ | ☐ |
| 15. | Notre équipe gagne! | ☐ | ☐ |

**M** *Subject + verb + direct object. Write sentences using the transitive verbs and direct objects given in the following strings.*

1. Marc / fermer / la porte _____

2. tu / attendre / le train _____

3. nous / finir / notre projet _____

4. vous / vendre / votre maison _____

5. je / étudier / la leçon _____

6. elle / choisir / une université _____

7. il / entendre / un bruit _____

8. ils / trouver / un appartement _____

9. Christine / chercher / un travail _____

10. nous / placer / notre argent _____

11. les enfants / regarder / un film _____

12. les piétons / traverser / la rue _____

13. vous / nettoyer / les tables _____

14. tu / écouter / la radio _____

15. nous / ranger / nos livres _____

16. les étudiants / vouvoyer / le professeur _____

**N** **Subject + verb.** *Write sentences using the intransitive verbs and other elements given in the following strings. Tell when or how the action happens.*

1. nous / nager / bien _____

2. tu / monter / vite _____

3. elle / retourner / demain _____

4. je / descendre / bientôt _____

5. vous / travailler / tous les jours _____

6. elles / réussir / toujours _____

7. ils / jouer / constamment _____

8. je / marcher / dans la neige _____

9. la voiture / rouler / lentement _____

10. vous / danser / très bien _____

11. nous / voyager / en été _____

12. il / réfléchir / beaucoup _____

| BUILDING SENTENCES | Disjunctive pronoun + subject + verb, disjunctive pronoun + subject + verb + direct object |
| --- | --- |

French subject pronouns are frequently accompanied by the corresponding disjunctive or stress pronoun. The disjunctive pronoun serves to focus on the subject. This is especially common in spoken French. A list of the disjunctive pronouns with their corresponding subject pronouns follows.

| SINGULAR | PLURAL |
| --- | --- |
| **moi**, je | **nous**, nous / **nous**, on |
| **toi**, tu | **vous**, vous |
| **lui**, il | **eux**, ils |
| **elle**, elle | **elles**, elles |

Note that **nous** is the disjunctive pronoun for **on** when **on** means **nous**. In informal speech, **nous autres** and **vous autres** are also used as disjunctive pronouns.[1]

---

[1]**Vous autres** is used only when **vous** refers to more than one person.

The disjunctive pronouns must be used when two different subjects are set off in contrast. When the English equivalents of the examples below are read aloud, the main stress of the sentence moves to the subject pronoun.

**Moi, je** cherche un appartement, mais **toi, tu** cherches un travail.
*I'm looking for an apartment, but **you're** looking for a job.*

**Elle, elle** chante bien, mais **eux, ils** chantent mal.
**She** *sings well, but **they** sing badly.*

**Nous, on** voyage beaucoup, mais **lui, il** reste à la maison.
*We travel a lot, but **he** stays home.*

The disjunctive pronoun usually precedes the subject pronoun, although in colloquial French it may appear at the end of the sentence. In spoken French, this construction is used even when there is no particular focus on the subject.

**Je** travaille beaucoup, **moi.**
*I work hard.*

**Tu** rentres, **toi?**
*Are you going home?*

**Vous** regardez le match, **vous autres?**
*Are you watching the game?*

---

### LA LANGUE FRANÇAISE  written and spoken French

French is characterized by a wide gap between the written and the spoken language. The written language makes much less use of the disjunctive pronoun than the spoken language. Sometimes there are grammatical differences between the written and spoken language, especially in the formation of negative sentences and questions.

| FORMAL FRENCH | COLLOQUIAL FRENCH |
|---|---|
| Je ne sais pas. | J'sais pas. |
| Le connais-tu? | Tu le connais, toi? |

---

**O** *Write sentences with contrasting subjects, using the elements given. Use the appropriate disjunctive pronoun in each part of the sentence. Note that these sentences contain both transitive and intransitive verbs.*

MODÈLE   on / dîner / mais / elle / travailler

_Nous, on dîne, mais elle, elle travaille._

1. tu / descendre / mais / je / rester ici

   _____

2. il / retrouver ses amis / et / on / rentrer

   _____

3. vous / quitter le restaurant / tandis que / elle / rester à table

   _____

4. ils / finir leur travail / tandis que / vous / commencer votre projet

   _____

5. je / monter / mais / elles / continuer leur promenade

_____

6. on / ranger nos livres / et / elle / nettoyer les meubles

_____

7. ils / écouter des cédés / tandis que / tu / regarder la télé

_____

8. vous / chercher un restaurant / et / je / visiter les monuments

_____

_____

9. nous autres / télécharger des programmes / tandis que / tu / sauvegarder tes fichiers

_____

_____

10. ils / rédiger un contrat / et / nous / corriger leur prose

_____

**P** *Create sentences in colloquial style, using the elements given. Add the appropriate disjunctive pronoun at the end of the sentence.*

MODÈLE    ils / interrompre le professeur

_Ils interrompent le professeur, eux._

1. je / descendre _____

2. il / rougir _____

3. ils / effacer leurs fautes _____

4. on / répondre aux lettres _____

5. tu / commencer ton nouveau travail

_____

6. elle / quitter le bureau _____

7. vous / manger au restaurant _____

8. nous / attendre l'autobus _____

9. il / escalader la montagne _____

10. elles / perdre leurs papiers _____

**Q**  **Translation.**  *Express the following sentences in French.*

1. *He is waiting for the bus.* _____

2. *She is leaving the house.* _____

3. *I am listening to the song.* _____

4. *You* (vous) *are taking advantage of my kindness.*

   _____

5. *We are looking for a hotel.* _____

6. *I am answering the letter.* _____

7. *You* (tu) *play the piano.* _____

8. *They are playing soccer.* _____

9. *I am paying for the apartment.* _____

10. *They are discussing politics.* _____

11. *She looks like her mother.* _____

12. *He is asking for money.* _____

**2**

# Irregular Verbs (Part I)

Many French verbs do not follow the conjugation patterns presented in Chapter 1. These are called *irregular verbs*.

## Aller, avoir, être, faire, prendre

### Aller

Most irregular verbs have infinitives ending in **-ir**, **-re**, or **-oir**. The only irregular verb with an infinitive ending in **-er** is **aller** *to go*.

| aller *to go* | |
| --- | --- |
| je **vais** | nous **allons** |
| tu **vas** | vous **allez** |
| il/elle/on **va** | ils/elles **vont** |

**Aller** is frequently followed by a phrase of place that begins with **à** or **en**.

| Expressions with **aller** |
| --- |
| **aller à la campagne/à la montagne** *to go to the country/to the mountains* |
| **aller à Paris/à New York/à Londres** *to go to Paris/to New York/to London* |
| **aller au bord de la mer** *to go to the seashore* |
| **aller au cinéma/au théâtre/au match** *to go to the movies/to the theater/to the game* |
| **aller au lycée/au bureau/au travail** *to go to high school/to the office/to work* |
| **aller aux États-Unis/au Canada** *to go to the United States/to Canada* |
| **aller en classe/en ville** *to go to class/downtown* |
| **aller en France/en Suisse/en Belgique** *to go to France/to Switzerland/to Belgium* |

Note the variety of prepositions used with geographical names.

French does not distinguish between *location* and *motion toward* with geographical names.

| | |
| --- | --- |
| Je suis **à** Paris. | *I'm **in** Paris.* |
| Je vais **à** Paris. | *I'm going **to** Paris.* |

Note that the same preposition is used for both.

## NOTES

1 · Use **en** before feminine names of countries: **en France**, **en Angleterre**, **en Allemagne**, **en Russie**, **en Chine**.

2 · Use **à** + the definite article before masculine and plural names of countries: **aux États-Unis**, **au Canada**, **au Mexique**, **au Portugal**, **au Danemark**, **aux Pays-Bas** *Netherlands*.

3 · Use **à** before names of cities: **à Paris**, **à New York**, **à Londres**, **à Berlin**, **à Moscou**, **à Madrid**, **à Mexico**.

4 · Use **à** + the definite article before names of cities that have a definite article as part of their name: **au Havre**, **au Caire**, **à la Nouvelle-Orléans**.

5 · For a full treatment of this topic, consult a reference grammar.

**A**   ***En vacances.*** *Create sentences using the verb* **aller** *and the correct preposition to tell where these people are going on vacation.*

> MODÈLE   Louis / Espagne
>
>       *Louis va en Espagne.*

1. je / Paris _____

2. tu / Mexique _____

3. mes parents / bord de la mer _____

4. vous / montagne _____

5. nous / Moscou _____

6. Christine et Paulette / Portugal _____

7. Samuel / campagne _____

8. Albert et Joseph / Jérusalem _____

## Avoir and être

The most common irregular verbs in French are **avoir** *to have* and **être** *to be*.

| **avoir** *to have* | |
| --- | --- |
| j'**ai** | nous **avons** |
| tu **as** | vous **avez** |
| il/elle/on **a** | ils/elles **ont** |

| **être** *to be* | |
| --- | --- |
| je **suis** | nous **sommes** |
| tu **es** | vous **êtes** |
| il/elle/on **est** | ils/elles **sont** |

In addition to their basic meanings, the verbs **avoir** and **être** are used as auxiliary verbs to form the compound tenses, and they appear in numerous phrases and idioms.

**Avoir** is used with nouns to express many physical and emotional sensations that are expressed with *to be* + an adjective in English.

### Expressions with avoir

**avoir faim**  *to be hungry*
**avoir soif**  *to be thirsty*
**avoir chaud**  *to be warm*
**avoir froid**  *to be cold*
**avoir de la chance**  *to be lucky*
**avoir peur (de qqch, de qqn)**  *to be afraid (of something, of someone)*
**avoir raison**  *to be right*
**avoir sommeil**  *to be sleepy*
**avoir tort**  *to be wrong*
**avoir besoin de qqch**  *to need something*
**avoir envie de qqch**  *to feel like something* (a food item)
**avoir envie de faire qqch**  *to feel like doing something*
**avoir du cran**  *to have guts, be gutsy* (colloquial)

**Avoir** is used to express age.

—Tu **as** quel âge?                              *"How old are you?"*
—J'**ai** vingt-neuf ans.                         *"I'm twenty-nine."*

**Être** appears in many expressions followed by a prepositional phrase, an adjective, or a past participle.

### Expressions with être

**être à bout de forces**  *to be exhausted*
**être à bout de souffle**  *to be out of breath*
**être à l'heure**  *to be on time*
**être à la maison**  *to be at home*
**être à qqn**  *to belong to someone*
**être chez moi/toi/lui/elle/soi**  *to be at my/your/his/her/one's place/home*
**être de retour**  *to be back*
**être en avance**  *to be early*
**être en retard**  *to be late*
**être en vacances**  *to be on vacation*
**être pressé(e)**  *to be in a hurry*
**être sorti(e)**  *to be out*

**B** *Complete each sentence with the correct form of the present tense of* **avoir** *to tell how people are feeling.*

1. Marc _____ soif.

2. Moi, j'_____ faim.

3. Les enfants _____ sommeil.

4. Toi, tu _____ du cran.

5. Nous, nous _____ froid.

6. Vous _____ chaud.

7. Notre chien _____ peur.

8. On _____ envie de manger.

**C** *Complete each sentence with the correct form of the present tense of* **être** *to talk about these people's locations and schedules.*

1. Nous _____ en retard.

2. Vous _____ en avance.

3. Nos amis _____ sortis.

4. Moi, je _____ à la maison.

5. Toi, tu _____ à l'heure.

6. Marie-Laure _____ chez elle.

7. On _____ de retour.

8. Vous _____ en vacances.

9. Mes parents _____ à Paris.

10. Ma femme et moi, nous _____ aux États-Unis.

**D** *Complete each sentence with the correct form of* **avoir** *or* **être***.*

1. Le chat _____ faim.

2. Je/J'_____ sommeil, moi.

3. Est-ce que tes parents _____ sortis?

4. Nous _____ besoin d'un guide.

5. Tu _____ envie d'une glace?

6. Il _____ à bout de forces.

7. Elle _____ du cran.

8. Les clés USB _____ à moi.

9. Ma chambre _____ en haut.

10. Vous _____ soif?

11. Nous _____ pressés.

12. Je/J'_____ de retour.

13. Tu _____ peur?

14. Vous _____ tort.

15. Vous _____ chez vous?

## Faire

The verb **faire** *to do, make* is one of the most common verbs in French.

| **faire** *to do, make* | |
| --- | --- |
| je **fais** | nous **faisons** |
| tu **fais** | vous **faites** |
| il/elle/on **fait** | ils/elles **font** |

### Expressions with **faire: à l'école**

**faire de la chimie**  *to take/study chemistry*
**faire des fautes d'orthographe**  *to make spelling mistakes*
**faire des progrès en géométrie**  *to be doing well in geometry*
**faire du français**  *to take French*
**faire l'école buissonnière**  *to play hooky*
**faire sa médecine**  *to be studying medicine*
**faire son droit**  *to be studying law*

### Expressions with **faire: à la maison**

**faire la cuisine**  *to do the cooking*
**faire la vaisselle**  *to do the dishes*
**faire le linge / la lessive**  *to do the laundry*
**faire le ménage**  *to do the housework*
**faire le parquet**  *to do the floor*
**faire les carreaux**  *to wash the windows*

### Expressions with **faire: les loisirs**

**faire de la varappe**  *to go rock climbing*
**faire du foot**  *to play soccer*
**faire du piano / du violon / de l'alto / de la flûte / de la clarinette / du saxophone**
  *to take piano/violin/viola/flute/clarinet/saxophone lessons*
**faire du vélo / de la bicyclette**  *to go bike riding*
**faire l'Amérique**  *to take a trip around America*
**faire la grasse matinée**  *to sleep late, oversleep*
**faire un voyage**  *to take a trip*
**faire une promenade / un tour**  *to go for a walk*
**faire une promenade en voiture**  *to go for a ride*
**faire une randonnée**  *to go on a hike*

### Expressions with **faire: le temps qu'il fait**

**Quel temps fait-il?**  *What's the weather like?*
**Il fait beau/mauvais.**  *The weather is nice/bad.*
**Il fait chaud/froid.**  *It's warm/cold out.*
**Il fait (du) soleil.**  *The sun is out.*
**Il fait du vent.**  *It's windy.*
**Il fait un sale temps.**  *The weather is lousy.*

**Il fait un froid de canard.** *It's bitter cold.*
**Il fait jour.** *It's light out.*
**Il fait nuit.** *It's dark out.*

## Expressions with **faire: d'autres expressions**

**faire acte de présence** *to put in an appearance*
**faire attention à** *to pay attention to, watch out for*
**faire l'idiot** *to act like an idiot*
**faire la moue** *to pout*
**faire le singe** *to clown around*
**faire semblant de faire qqch** *to pretend to do something*
**faire une fugue** *to run away from home*
**faire une gaffe** *to blunder*
**faire une tête** *to make a face*

**E** *On est libre aujourd'hui. Using the elements given, create sentences with the correct form of the present tense of the verb* **faire** *to tell what these people are doing for fun.*

1. nous / de la varappe _____

2. Claude / de l'alto _____

3. vous / une randonnée _____

4. les enfants / du foot _____

5. tu / un voyage _____

6. je / une promenade _____

7. on / de la bicyclette _____

8. vous / un petit tour _____

9. mes amis / la grasse matinée _____

**F** *Le même sens. Using an expression with* **faire**, *create a sentence with the same meaning as the sentence given. Keep the same subject.*

MODÈLE    Je nettoie la maison.
    *Je fais le ménage.* _____

1. Tu dors jusqu'à onze heures du matin. _____

2. Elles marchent pendant trois heures dans le bois.

    _____

3. Je n'écris pas bien les mots. _____

4. Nous écoutons le professeur. _____

5. Vous arrivez et vous restez cinq minutes.

    _____

6. Ma mère lave les vêtements. _____

7. Mon frère et ma sœur lavent les fenêtres.

_____

## Prendre

Learn the forms of the verb **prendre** *to take*. **Prendre** looks like a regular -**re** verb by its infinitive, but its conjugation is irregular. Note that its singular forms resemble those of regular -**re** verbs.

| **prendre** *to take* | |
| --- | --- |
| je prends | nous **prenons** |
| tu prends | vous **prenez** |
| il/elle/on prend | ils/elles **prennent** |

**Prendre** translates most meanings of English *take*.

**prendre des médicaments** *to take medicine*
**prendre l'autoroute** *to take the superhighway*
**prendre le bus / le train / l'avion** *to take the bus / the train / the plane*
**prendre ses affaires** *to take one's things*
**prendre son temps** *to take one's time*
**prendre un raccourci** *to take a shortcut*

**Prendre** expresses the consumption of food and drink. English uses *have* for this meaning, but French does not use **avoir** in this sense. Compare the following sentences.

| | |
| --- | --- |
| J'ai du jus d'orange. | *I have orange juice. (e.g., in the refrigerator)* |
| Je prends du jus d'orange. | *I'm having/drinking orange juice.* |

**Prendre** is also used with the names of meals.

| | |
| --- | --- |
| —Où est-ce que **tu prends le petit déjeuner**? | *"Where do you have breakfast?"* |
| —**Je prends le petit déjeuner** chez moi, mais **je prends le déjeuner** au restaurant. | *"I have breakfast at home, but I have lunch out."* |

**Prendre** can also mean *to buy,* especially with food.

| | |
| --- | --- |
| Elle prend son pain chez ce boulanger-là. | *She buys her bread at that baker's.* |
| Je descends prendre du pain. | *I'm going out to buy some bread.* |
| Nous prenons des billets de théâtre. | *We're buying theater tickets.* |

**Prendre** is used in giving directions.

| | |
| --- | --- |
| **Prenez** la deuxième rue à droite jusqu'à la place et là, **prenez** à gauche. | *Turn right on the second street and keep on going up to the square. There, turn left.* |

**G** *Using the elements given, create sentences with the correct form of the present tense of the verb* **prendre** *to tell what these people are having at the café.*

MODÈLE   Jean / un café

_Jean prend un café._

1. je / un thé _____

2. les enfants / une glace _____

3. ma mère / un citron pressé _____

4. mon père / une bière _____

5. tu / de l'eau minérale _____

6. nous / du vin _____

7. vous / un dessert _____

8. on / un jus de pomme _____

The following compound verbs are conjugated like **prendre**.

**apprendre**  *to learn*
**comprendre**  *to understand*
**entreprendre**  *to begin, undertake*
**reprendre**  *to start again*
**surprendre**  *to surprise*

## Expressions with **prendre** and its compounds

**apprendre la nouvelle**  *to hear the news*
**apprendre une langue étrangère**  *to learn a foreign language*
**comprendre le français**  *to understand French*
**comprendre le problème**  *to understand the problem*
**comprendre le sens d'une expression**  *to understand the meaning of an expression*
**comprendre les choses**  *to understand things*
**comprendre une plaisanterie**  *to understand a joke*
**entreprendre un voyage / un projet**  *to begin a trip / a project*
**entreprendre une étude de la situation**  *to undertake a study of the situation*
**prendre du poids**  *to gain weight*
**prendre qqn dans ses bras**  *to take someone in one's arms, hug someone*
**prendre un rhume / prendre froid**  *to catch a cold*
**reprendre l'histoire**  *to start the story over again*
**reprendre sa place**  *to take one's seat again*
**reprendre son travail**  *to go back to work*
**surprendre qqn**  *to surprise someone*
**surprendre une conversation**  *to overhear a conversation*

**H** *Complete each sentence with the correct present tense form of the appropriate verb, using* **prendre** *or one of its compounds.*

1. Nous _____ un nouveau projet.

2. Ils _____ un raccourci.

3. Je/J'_____ une langue étrangère en ligne.

4. Elle _____ sa place.

5. Tu _____ du poids.

6. Quand est-ce que vous _____ votre travail après les vacances?

7. Il _____ des conversations au bureau.

8. Tu _____ la plaisanterie?

9. Vous _____ votre temps.

10. Ils _____ une étude du problème.

11. Elle _____ du café le matin.

## -Ir Verbs Conjugated Like -er Verbs

There is a small group of verbs that have an infinitive ending in **-ir** but are conjugated like **-er** verbs.

**ouvrir**  *to open*
**couvrir**  *to cover*
**découvrir**  *to discover*
**rouvrir**  *to open again*
**offrir**  *to offer*
**souffrir**  *to suffer*
**cueillir**  *to gather, pick*
**accueillir**  *to welcome, receive*

| **ouvrir** *to open* | |
| --- | --- |
| j'ouvre | nous ouvrons |
| tu ouvres | vous ouvrez |
| il/elle/on ouvre | ils/elles ouvrent |

| **offrir** *to offer* | |
| --- | --- |
| j'offre | nous offrons |
| tu offres | vous offrez |
| il/elle/on offre | ils/elles offrent |

| **souffrir** *to suffer* | |
| --- | --- |
| je souffre | nous souffrons |
| tu souffres | vous souffrez |
| il/elle/on souffre | ils/elles souffrent |

| **accueillir** *to welcome, receive* | |
| --- | --- |
| j'accueille | nous accueillons |
| tu accueilles | vous accueillez |
| il/elle/on accueille | ils/elles accueillent |

The verb **offrir** often means to give something as a gift.

Elle offre toujours des livres à ses amis.          *She always gives her friends books as gifts.*

**I**　*Complete each sentence with the correct present tense form of the verb in parentheses.*

1. (souffrir)　Elle _____ de migraines.

2. (ouvrir)　Nous _____ la boutique à neuf heures.

3. (offrir)　J'_____ des billets de théâtre à mes parents.

4. (couvrir)　Vous _____ la casserole.

5. (rouvrir)　On _____ le bureau en septembre.

6. (découvrir)　Ils _____ la cause du problème.

7. (souffrir)　Les malades _____ beaucoup.

8. (ouvrir)　Tu _____ ton livre.

9. (découvrir)　Nous _____ des quartiers charmants dans cette ville.

10. (cueillir)　Elle _____ des fleurs dans le jardin.

11. (offrir)　Tu _____ de beaux cadeaux à tout le monde.

12. (accueillir)　Vous _____ des étudiants étrangers.

13. (couvrir)　La neige _____ la ville.

14. (ouvrir)　Pourquoi est-ce que vous n'_____ pas les fenêtres?

15. (cueillir)　Les paysans _____ les fruits en automne.

## -Ir Verbs Conjugated Like -re Verbs

Some -**ir** verbs are conjugated like -**re** verbs.

> **dormir**　*to sleep*
> **mentir**　*to lie*
> **partir**　*to leave, depart*
> **repartir**　*to leave again*
> **sentir**　*to feel*
> **servir**　*to serve*
> **sortir**　*to go out*

The final consonant of the stem is neither written nor pronounced in the singular forms of the following verbs.

| **dormir** *to sleep* | |
| --- | --- |
| je dors | nous dormons |
| tu dors | vous dormez |
| il/elle/on dort | ils/elles dorment |

| **mentir** *to lie* | |
| --- | --- |
| je mens | nous mentons |
| tu mens | vous mentez |
| il/elle/on ment | ils/elles mentent |

| **partir** *to leave, depart* | |
| --- | --- |
| je pars | nous partons |
| tu pars | vous partez |
| il/elle/on part | ils/elles partent |

| **sentir** *to feel* | |
| --- | --- |
| je sens | nous sentons |
| tu sens | vous sentez |
| il/elle/on sent | ils/elles sentent |

| **servir** _to serve_ | | **sortir** _to go out_ | |
|---|---|---|---|
| je sers | nous servons | je sors | nous sortons |
| tu sers | vous servez | tu sors | vous sortez |
| il/elle/on sert | ils/elles servent | il/elle/on sort | ils/elles sortent |

**J**  _Complete each sentence with the correct present tense form of the verb in parentheses._

1. (sortir)      Je _____ ce soir.

2. (partir)      Le train _____ du quai numéro cinq.

3. (sentir)      Nous _____ la chaleur.

4. (dormir)      Est-ce que les enfants _____ dehors?

5. (servir)      Vous _____ toujours un bon repas.

6. (mentir)      Cet enfant _____ trop.

7. (repartir)    Tu _____ demain?

8. (servir)      Ce restaurant _____ des plats végétariens.

9. (dormir)      Je _____ dans ma chambre.

10. (sentir)     Vous _____ un courant d'air?

11. (sortir)     Ils _____ ensemble.

12. (partir)     Nous _____ jeudi.

13. (repartir)   Je _____ tout de suite.

14. (mentir)     Mais tu _____!

15. (sortir)     Vous _____ souvent?

16. (servir)     Je _____ du vin à mes invités.

17. (dormir)     Nous _____ mal dans cette chambre.

18. (mentir)     Elle ne _____ jamais.

**K**  _Practice the forms of regular and irregular_ **-ir** _verbs by completing each sentence with the correct present tense form of the verb in parentheses._

1. (finir)       Je _____ mon travail.

2. (souffrir)    Ils _____ de la chaleur.

3. (sentir)      Vous _____ le froid?

4. (partir)      Nous _____ pour le Canada.

5. (choisir)     Nous _____ un hôtel.

6. (ouvrir)      Ils _____ la porte.

7. (applaudir)   Ils _____ après le spectacle.

8. (réfléchir)   Tu _____ à tes vacances.

9. (dormir)     Tu _____ à la campagne.

10. (découvrir)     Tu _____ un joli village.

11. (avertir)     Elle _____ les voisins.

12. (servir)     Elle _____ l'apéritif.

13. (offrir)     Elle _____ des hors-d'œuvre.

14. (grossir)     Je _____!

15. (sortir)     Je _____ maintenant.

16. (repartir)     Vous _____.

17. (réussir)     Vous _____ à vos examens.

18. (rougir)     La jeune fille _____.

19. (atterrir)     Les avions _____ sur la piste.

20. (mincir)     Ils _____ rapidement et sans peine.

21. (désobéir)     Un bon enfant ne _____ pas.

## Verbs with Stems in **-gn-** and Infinitives in **-indre**

There is a group of French verbs with stems ending in **-gn-** and infinitives ending in **-indre**. The **-gn-** disappears in the singular where the stem ends in **-n** in written French. In spoken French, the singular forms of these verbs end in a nasal vowel.

**craindre** *to fear*

| | |
|---|---|
| je crains | nous craignons |
| tu crains | vous craignez |
| il/elle/on craint | ils/elles craignent |

The verbs **contraindre** *to force, constrain* and **plaindre** *to pity, feel sorry for* are conjugated like **craindre**.

**atteindre** *to reach*

| | |
|---|---|
| j'atteins | nous atteignons |
| tu atteins | vous atteignez |
| il/elle/on atteint | ils/elles atteignent |

The verbs **éteindre** *to extinguish*, **étreindre** *to embrace*, **feindre** *to feign*, **peindre** *to paint*, and **teindre** *to dye* are conjugated like **atteindre**.

**joindre** *to join*

| | |
|---|---|
| je joins | nous joignons |
| tu joins | vous joignez |
| il/elle/on joint | ils/elles joignent |

The verb **rejoindre** *to rejoin* is conjugated like **joindre**.

**L** *Complete each sentence with the present tense form of an appropriate verb ending in -indre so that the French sentence matches the English sentence.*

1. *She dyes her shoes.*

   Elle _____ ses chaussures.

2. *They meet up with their friends again.*

   Ils _____ leurs amis.

3. *I'm painting my room.*

   Je _____ ma chambre.

4. *We fear the worst.*

   Nous _____ le pire.

5. *You put out the light.*

   Tu _____ la lumière.

6. *You attain your goals.*

   Vous _____ vos buts.

7. *People feel sorry for the sick.*

   On _____ les malades.

8. *We don't force anyone.*

   Nous ne _____ personne.

9. *He pretends to be interested.*

   Il _____ l'intérêt.

10. *They embrace their children.*

    Ils _____ leurs enfants.

## Battre and mettre

The verbs **battre** *to hit, beat* and **mettre** *to put* have stems ending in the sound /t/ in spoken French, represented in the written language by **tt**. This /t/ drops in the singular in speech, but a single **t** appears in the written language.

**battre** *to hit, beat*

| | |
|---|---|
| je bats | nous battons |
| tu bats | vous battez |
| il/elle/on bat | ils/elles battent |

**mettre** *to put*

| | |
|---|---|
| je mets | nous mettons |
| tu mets | vous mettez |
| il/elle/on met | ils/elles mettent |

Compounds of these verbs are conjugated in the same way.

**abattre**  *to knock down*
**combattre**  *to fight*
**débattre**  *to debate*
**rebattre**  *to hit again*
**commettre**  *to commit*
**omettre**  *to omit*
**permettre**  *to permit*
**remettre**  *to hand in*
**soumettre**  *to submit*

## Expressions with **battre**

**battre des mains**  *to clap hands*
**battre des œufs**  *to beat eggs*
**battre du tambour**  *to beat the drum*
**battre l'autre équipe**  *to beat the other team*
**battre les cartes**  *to shuffle the cards*
**battre un enfant**  *to hit a child*

## Expressions with **mettre**

**mettre de l'argent à côté**  *to put some money aside*
**mettre la famille avant tout**  *to put the family first*
**mettre la table**  *to set the table*
**mettre la télé**  *to turn on the TV*
**mettre qqn à la porte**  *to fire someone*
**mettre sa veste / ses chaussures**  *to put on one's jacket / one's shoes*

**M**  *Rewrite each of the following sentences in the plural.*

1. Elle ne bat pas le chat. _____

2. Je mets la table. _____

3. Tu mets la télé? _____

4. Il abat un arbre. _____

5. Tu permets ça? _____

6. Je remets le compte rendu. _____

7. Le soldat combat. _____

8. Elle met de l'argent à côté. _____

**N**  *Rewrite each of the following sentences in the singular.*

1. Les médecins combattent les maladies. _____

2. Les enfants battent des mains. _____

3. Nous mettons la famille avant tout. _____

4. Ils mettent les employés à la porte. _____

5. Vous mettez un imperméable. _____

6. Nous battons des œufs. _____

7. Ils débattent la question. _____

8. Vous battez les cartes. _____

**O** *Complete each sentence by selecting the correct verb from the three given, and writing its correct form.*

1. (finir | mettre | ouvrir)            Nous _____ la porte.

2. (partir | mettre | dormir)           Elle _____ pour la Suisse.

3. (étreindre | éteindre | atteindre)   Nous _____ la lumière.

4. (abattre | remettre | combattre)     Les soldats _____ pour la patrie.

5. (mettre | sortir | être)             Tu ne _____ pas ton imperméable?

6. (aller | venir | faire)              Il _____ l'école buissonnière aujourd'hui.

7. (sortir | aller | mettre)            L'année prochaine je _____ en France.

8. (être | faire | avoir)               Est-ce que tu _____ froid?

9. (faire | prendre | battre)           On va arriver plus vite si on _____ le raccourci.

10. (être | avoir | aller)              Je/J'_____ pressé aujourd'hui.

11. (faire | avoir | prendre)           Il _____ l'idiot.

12. (abattre | reprendre | craindre)    Ils _____ un désastre.

13. (être | sortir | avoir)             Tu _____ à bout de souffle.

14. (mettre | joindre | faire)          Ils _____ semblant de comprendre.

---

**BUILDING SENTENCES**    **Negative sentences**

The negative in French consists of two parts. The word **ne** is placed before the verb and the word **pas** is placed after it. The word **ne** is elided to **n'** before a vowel or a silent **h**.

| | |
|---|---|
| Elle **ne** va **pas** à Genève. | *She's not going to Geneva.* |
| Je **ne** prends **pas** le métro. | *I'm not taking the subway.* |
| Ils **n'**habitent **pas** ce quartier. | *They don't live in this neighborhood.* |
| Nous **n'**avons **pas** soif. | *We're not thirsty.* |

The indefinite articles (**un, une, des**) and the partitive articles (**du, de la, de l'**) become **de** (elided to **d'** before a vowel) after negative words such as **pas**. The definite articles (**le, la, l', les**) do not change.

—Tu n'as pas **d'**argent suisse?      *"Don't you have any Swiss money?"*

—Non, j'ai des euros, mais je n'ai pas **de** francs.      *"No, I have euros, but I don't have any francs."*

—Vous ne prenez pas **de** café?      *"Aren't you having any coffee?"*

—Merci, je n'aime pas le café.      *"No, thank you, I don't like coffee."*

—Trois œufs durs, s'il vous plaît.      *"Three hard-boiled eggs, please."*

—Je regrette, mais nous n'avons pas **d'**œufs durs aujourd'hui.      *"I'm sorry, but we don't have any hard-boiled eggs today."*

---

## LA LANGUE FRANÇAISE   ne and pas

In the everyday speech of people of all educational levels, there is a marked tendency to drop **ne** in negatives, thus making **pas** the word that negates the verb. In writing, however, the word **ne** cannot be omitted.

---

**P**   *Create two sentences from the elements given—one affirmative, one negative.* **Attention!** *Make sure to change any indefinite articles or partitive articles to* **de** *in negative sentences.*

MODÈLE    Luc / manger / des frites

     *Luc mange des frites.*

     *Luc ne mange pas de frites.*

1. Philippe / mettre / une veste

   _____

   _____

2. ils / abattre / des arbres

   _____

   _____

3. ma sœur / faire / son déjeuner

   _____

   _____

4. nous / prendre / le raccourci

   _____

   _____

5. tu / apprendre / le nouveau vocabulaire

   _____

   _____

6. les étudiants / faire / des langues

_____

_____

7. notre équipe / battre / son rival

_____

_____

8. je / entreprendre / un projet

_____

_____

9. les enfants / cueillir / des fleurs

_____

_____

10. elle / reprendre / son travail

_____

_____

11. nous / découvrir / des quartiers intéressants

_____

_____

12. ils / finir / leur travail

_____

_____

13. tu / ouvrir / les fenêtres

_____

_____

14. vous / accueillir / des étudiants étrangers

_____

_____

15. il / offrir / des cadeaux

_____

_____

16. je / surprendre / des conversations

_____

_____

There are other negative words that can replace **pas** in negative sentences. Here is a list of the most common ones with their affirmative counterparts.

| NEGATIVE WORDS AND EXPRESSIONS | AFFIRMATIVE WORDS AND EXPRESSIONS |
|---|---|
| **jamais** *never* | { **quelquefois** *sometimes* <br> **souvent** *often* |
| **rien** *nothing* | **quelque chose** *something* |
| **personne** *no one, nobody* | **quelqu'un** *someone, somebody* |
| **plus** *no more* | **toujours, encore** *still* |
| **nulle part** *nowhere* | **quelque part** *somewhere* |

—Il va souvent en France?      *"Does he often go to France?"*
—Non, il ne va jamais en France.      *"No, he never goes to France."*

—Tu prends quelque chose?      *"Are you having anything?"*
—Non, je ne prends rien.      *"No, I'm not having anything."*

—Elle cherche quelqu'un?      *"Is she looking for someone?"*
—Non, elle ne cherche personne.      *"No, she isn't looking for anybody."*

—Monsieur Durand est là?      *"Is Mr. Durand in?"*
—Non, il ne travaille plus ici.      *"No, he doesn't work here anymore."*

—Vous partez en vacances cet été?      *"Are you going on vacation this summer?"*
—Non, nous n'allons nulle part.      *"No, we're not going anywhere."*

**Personne** and **rien** can also be used as subjects of a sentence. When they are used as subjects, the verb is preceded by **ne**, but **pas** is not used.

Personne n'ouvre la porte.      *No one is opening the door.*
Rien ne permet de croire cela.      *Nothing makes that believable.*

**Q**   *Quelle soirée! Rewrite each sentence in the negative to tell what people are **not** doing to prepare for the party.*

1. Marie-Claire invite ses amis. _____

2. Moi, j'appelle le traiteur (*caterer*). _____

3. Christine prépare des hors-d'œuvre. _____

4. Luc achète du café. _____

5. Nos amis font une pizza. _____

6. Nous cherchons des CD. _____

7. Vous apportez du pain. _____

8. Moi, je lave la nappe (*tablecloth*). _____

9. Toi, tu laves les verres. _____

10. Albertine ouvre une bouteille de vin. _____

11. Nous, on sert des bonbons. _____

12. Toi, tu sors les gobelets en papier. _____

**R**  *Answer each question in the negative. Use the appropriate negative word where necessary.*

1. Est-ce que tu vas souvent au théâtre?

   _____

2. Est-ce que tu vas quelque part cet été?

   _____

3. Est-ce qu'ils ont une voiture? _____

4. Est-qu'elle va à la banque? _____

5. Est-ce que tu travailles aujourd'hui? _____

6. Est-ce que tu as de l'argent sur toi? _____

7. Est-ce que Valérie sort avec Vincent? _____

8. Est-ce vous cherchez quelqu'un? _____

9. Est-ce que tu fais quelque chose maintenant?

   _____

10. Est-ce qu'il y a encore du vin? _____

**S**  **Translation.**  *Express the following sentences in French.*

1. *They need an apartment.* _____

2. *He's not on vacation.* _____

3. *She's not serving any cake.* _____

4. *He never turns off the light.* _____

5. *They rejoin their families.* _____

6. *Nobody is cleaning the house.* _____

7. *He's not taking a shortcut.* _____

8. *No one understands the teacher.* _____

9. *She's beating eggs for the cake.* _____

10. *I'm not thirsty anymore.* _____

11. *They're shuffling the cards.* _____

12. *She overhears their conversation.* _____

# Irregular Verbs (Part II)

**BUILDING SENTENCES**

Verb + infinitive construction
Questions: yes/no questions

## Verbs with Stems Ending in -v: **boire, écrire, suivre, vivre**

The irregular verbs **boire** *to drink*, **écrire** *to write*, **suivre** *to follow*, and **vivre** *to live* all have stems ending in **-v**.

### **boire**  *to drink*

| je bois | nous buvons |
|---|---|
| tu bois | vous buvez |
| il/elle/on boit | ils/elles boivent |

### **écrire**  *to write*

| j'écris | nous écrivons |
|---|---|
| tu écris | vous écrivez |
| il/elle/on écrit | ils/elles écrivent |

### **suivre**  *to follow*

| je suis | nous suivons |
|---|---|
| tu suis | vous suivez |
| il/elle/on suit | ils/elles suivent |

### **vivre**  *to live*

| je vis | nous vivons |
|---|---|
| tu vis | vous vivez |
| il/elle/on vit | ils/elles vivent |

### Expressions with **boire, écrire, suivre, vivre**

**boire à la réussite de qqn**  *to drink to someone's success*
**boire du vin à table**  *to drink wine with one's meals*
**boire un coup**  *to have a drink* (colloquial)
**boire un verre**  *to have a drink*
**écrire au crayon / à l'encre**  *to write in pencil / in ink*
**écrire au tableau**  *to write on the chalkboard*
**écrire sa thèse**  *to write one's thesis*
**écrire un mot**  *to write a word; to drop a line*

**suivre bien à l'école**  *to be a good student*
**suivre un cours**  *to take a course*
**vivre au jour le jour**  *to live from hand to mouth*
**vivre sa vie**  *to live one's life*

**A**  *Complete each sentence with the correct present tense form of* **boire**, **écrire**, **suivre**, *or* **vivre**.

1.  Vous _____ des cours cette année?

2.  Les élèves _____ au tableau.

3.  Elle _____ un coup avec nous.

4.  Je/J'_____ un mot à mes amis.

5.  Elle _____ sa vie.

6.  Nous _____ du vin à table.

7.  Ces familles _____ au jour le jour.

8.  Ils _____ un verre avec eux.

9.  Cet enfant ne _____ pas bien à l'école.

10.  Vous _____ dans votre cahier.

## Verbs with Stems Ending in -s: dire, lire

The verbs **dire** *to say, tell* and **lire** *to read* have stems ending in **-s**. The second-person plural form (**vous** form) of **dire** is irregular.

| dire *to say, tell* | | lire *to read* | |
|---|---|---|---|
| je dis | nous disons | je lis | nous lisons |
| tu dis | vous **dites** | tu lis | vous lisez |
| il/elle/on dit | ils/elles disent | il/elle/on lit | ils/elles lisent |

## Verbs with Stems Ending in -r: courir, mourir

The verbs **courir** *to run* and **mourir** *to die* have stems ending in **-r**. The **r** is retained in both writing and speech in the singular.

| courir *to run* | |
|---|---|
| je cours | nous courons |
| tu cours | vous courez |
| il/elle/on court | ils/elles courent |

| mourir *to die* | |
|---|---|
| je meurs | nous mourons |
| tu meurs | vous mourez |
| il/elle/on meurt | ils/elles meurent |

**B** *Rewrite each sentence, changing all singular forms to plural and all plural forms to singular.*

1. Il lit. _____

2. Nous courons. _____

3. Elle meurt. _____

4. Tu dis. _____

5. Vous lisez. _____

6. Nous mourons. _____

7. Vous courez. _____

8. Il dit. _____

**C** *Complete each sentence with the correct form of* **dire**, **lire**, **courir**, *or* **mourir**.

1. Ils _____ cinq kilomètres par jour.

2. Je veux boire quelque chose. Je _____ de soif.

3. Nous _____ le journal tous les jours.

4. Je _____ quelques mots en anglais, mais on ne me comprend pas.

5. Allons manger. Nous _____ de faim.

6. Nous _____ la vérité.

7. Elle _____ parce qu'elle est pressée.

8. Je _____ un article.

## Verbs Ending in **-duire, -uire: conduire, nuire**

Verbs ending in **-duire** and **-uire** have a stem ending in **-s**.

| **conduire**  *to drive, lead* | | **nuire**  *to harm* | |
|---|---|---|---|
| je conduis | nous conduisons | je nuis | nous nuisons |
| tu conduis | vous conduisez | tu nuis | vous nuisez |
| il/elle/on conduit | ils/elles conduisent | il/elle/on nuit | ils/elles nuisent |

Most French verbs ending in **-duire** or **-uire** are cognates of English verbs that end in -**duce**, -**duct**, or -**struct**. They are all conjugated like **conduire**.

| | |
|---|---|
| **construire**  *to build, construct* | **produire**  *to produce* |
| **déduire**  *to deduce; to deduct* | **reconduire**  *to drive someone back* |
| **détruire**  *to destroy* | **réduire**  *to reduce* |
| **enduire**  *to put a coating on* | **reproduire**  *to reproduce* |
| **instruire**  *to instruct* | **séduire**  *to seduce; to charm* |
| **introduire**  *to introduce* | **traduire**  *to translate* |

**D**  *Complete each sentence with the correct form of the verb in parentheses.*

1.  (reconduire)     Ils _____ leurs amis après le dîner.

2.  (détruire)       La tempête _____ les arbres.

3.  (instruire)      Nous _____ nos enfants.

4.  (traduire)       Tu _____ les documents en anglais.

5.  (introduire)     Elle _____ une idée nouvelle dans la discussion.

6.  (déduire)        Je _____ que vous n'aimez pas cette situation.

7.  (nuire)          Vous _____ à mon succès.

8.  (construire)     Ils _____ un pont.

## Verbs Ending in -cevoir: recevoir

Verbs ending in **-cevoir** have a distinctive pattern. The stem ends in **-v**, but the vowels of the singular and the third-person plural forms are **oi**. The letter **ç** (**c** cedilla) is used before the **oi** in these forms.

**recevoir**  *to receive; to see customers or clients; to have company*

| | |
|---|---|
| je reçois | nous recevons |
| tu reçois | vous recevez |
| il/elle/on reçoit | ils/elles reçoivent |

**Verbs conjugated like recevoir**

**apercevoir**  *to notice*
**concevoir**  *to conceive*
**décevoir**  *to disappoint*

## Vaincre, convaincre

The verb **vaincre** *to conquer* and its compound **convaincre** *to convince* have no **t** in the third-person singular, and they have **qu** instead of **c** in the plural.

**vaincre**  *to conquer*

| | |
|---|---|
| je vaincs | nous vainquons |
| tu vaincs | vous vainquez |
| il/elle/on vainc | ils/elles vainquent |

**convaincre**  *to convince*

| | |
|---|---|
| je convaincs | nous convainquons |
| tu convaincs | vous convainquez |
| il/elle/on convainc | ils/elles convainquent |

# Voir, croire, fuir

The verbs **voir** *to see*, **croire** *to believe*, and **fuir** *to flee* have stems ending in a vowel. The final letter of the stem is spelled **i** in the singular and third-person plural forms, but **y** in the first- and second-person plural forms (**nous** and **vous** forms).

**voir** *to see*

| | |
|---|---|
| je vois | nous voyons |
| tu vois | vous voyez |
| il/elle/on voit | ils/elles voient |

**croire** *to believe*

| | |
|---|---|
| je crois | nous croyons |
| tu crois | vous croyez |
| il/elle/on croit | ils/elles croient |

**fuir** *to flee*

| | |
|---|---|
| je fuis | nous fuyons |
| tu fuis | vous fuyez |
| il/elle/on fuit | ils/elles fuient |

## Expressions with **voir, croire, fuir**

**voir qqch** *to see something*
**voir qqn** *to see someone*
**croire qqch** *to believe something*
**croire qqn** *to believe someone*
**croire que non** *not to think so*
**croire que oui** *to think so*
**fuir devant le danger** *to flee in the face of danger*
**fuir devant ses responsabilités** *to run away from one's responsibilities*
**fuir qqn** *to avoid someone*

**E** *Rewrite each sentence, changing all singular forms to plural and all plural forms to singular.*

1. Elle croit. _____

2. Vous voyez. _____

3. Nous recevons. _____

4. Tu fuis. _____

5. Elles convainquent. _____

6. Ils aperçoivent. _____

7. Je vaincs. _____

8. Il conçoit. _____

9. Ils voient. _____

10. Vous convainquez. _____

11. Tu reçois. _____

12. Nous voyons. _____

**F**　*Complete each sentence by selecting the correct verb from the two given, and writing its correct present tense form.*

1. (recevoir | fuir)　　　　Ils _____ beaucoup de paquets.

2. (vaincre | croire)　　　Je _____ que oui.

3. (décevoir | apercevoir)　Cet auteur ne _____ jamais.

4. (fuir | convaincre)　　　Vous _____ devant vos responsabilités.

5. (croire | voir)　　　　　Tu _____ beaucoup de bons films.

6. (vaincre | concevoir)　　Nos soldats _____ l'ennemi.

7. (concevoir | fuir)　　　Ils _____ un plan formidable.

8. (voir | convaincre)　　　Ses idées ne me _____ pas.

9. (recevoir | croire)　　　Nous ne _____ pas ce qu'il dit.

10. (apercevoir | recevoir)　Il _____ le danger.

**G**　*Complete each sentence with the correct form of the verb in parentheses.*

1. (décevoir)　　Ce film _____ tout le monde.

2. (fuir)　　　　Vous _____ les problèmes.

3. (conduire)　　Je _____ un Peugeot.

4. (voir)　　　　Nous _____ beaucoup de films.

5. (boire)　　　Elle _____ trop de café.

6. (écrire)　　　Je n'_____ pas de lettres.

7. (lire)　　　　Ils _____ le journal.

8. (séduire)　　Ce village _____ les touristes.

9. (traduire)　　Tu _____ les phrases françaises.

10. (croire)　　　Vous _____ les politiciens?

11. (convaincre)　Nous _____ nos amis.

12. (recevoir)　　Tu _____ beaucoup de courriels.

13. (produire)　　La France _____ beaucoup de fromage.

14. (suivre)　　　Elles _____ le guide.

15. (mourir)　　　Ils _____ de faim.

16. (boire)　　　Vous _____ du vin?

17. (écrire)　　　Ils _____ une dissertation.

18. (réduire)　　Le gouvernement _____ le budget.

19. (fuir)　　　　Je _____ le danger.

20. (dire)　　　　Vous ne _____ pas la vérité.

21. (lire)        Tu _____ des articles.

22. (mourir)      Je _____ de froid.

23. (fuir)        Cette actrice _____ devant la presse.

24. (voir)        Ils _____ leurs amis.

25. (convaincre)  Elle _____ les autres.

26. (boire)       Je _____ à votre réussite.

27. (écrire)      Pourquoi est-ce que vous _____ au crayon?

28. (dire)        Les enfants _____ des bêtises.

29. (vaincre)     Notre armée _____ les terroristes.

30. (suivre)      Cet enfant _____ bien à l'école.

## Savoir and connaître

The verbs **savoir** and **connaître** both mean *to know*. Both verbs are irregular in the present tense.

### savoir

| | |
|---|---|
| je sais | nous savons |
| tu sais | vous savez |
| il/elle/on sait | ils/elles savent |

### connaître

| | |
|---|---|
| je connais | nous connaissons |
| tu connais | vous connaissez |
| il/elle/on connaît | ils/elles connaissent |

The verb **reconnaître** *to recognize* is conjugated like **connaître**.

Although **savoir** and **connaître** both mean *to know,* they are not interchangeable. **Savoir** means to know facts, to know something that you can state or repeat. It is used in cases of learned knowledge.

| | |
|---|---|
| Tu sais l'heure? | *Do you know what time it is?* |
| Elle sait l'allemand. | *She knows German.* |
| Nous savons les formules. | *We know the formulas.* |
| Il sait son rôle par cœur. | *He knows his part by heart.* |

**Savoir**, not **connaître**, is used before subordinate clauses and indirect questions.

| | |
|---|---|
| Je ne sais pas si tu as envie de sortir. | *I don't know if you feel like going out.* |
| Vous savez quand ils partent? | *Do you know when they are leaving?* |
| Nous ne savons pas comment il réussit à travailler comme ça. | *We don't know how he manages to work like that.* |
| Tu sais où elle habite? | *Do you know where she lives?* |

**Connaître** means to be familiar with a person or place. It is used before direct object nouns referring to both people and things.

—Tu connais son nom?                          *"Do you know his name?"*
—Oui, et je connais son adresse.              *"Yes, and I know his address."*

Sometimes the choice between **savoir** and **connaître** seems arbitrary to English speakers. In the following sentences, the English verb is *to know* in both examples, but the French verb is **connaître** in one and **savoir** in the other.

Je connais son adresse.                       *I know his address.*

BUT

Je sais l'heure.                              *I know the time.*

When the object is a person or a place, **connaître** must be used because the idea is familiarity, not knowledge acquired by learning. **Savoir** cannot be used in the sentences below.

—Nous connaissons un bon restaurant          *"We know a good restaurant in the*
dans le quartier.                             *neighborhood."*
—Est-ce que vous connaissez le               *"Do you know the owner of the*
propriétaire du restaurant?                   *restaurant?"*

**Connaître** is frequently used before geographical names to express familiarity or acquaintance with the place. **Savoir** cannot be used in such cases.

—Elle connaît la Belgique?                    *"Has she been to Belgium?"*
—Elle connaît Bruxelles, c'est tout.          *"She knows Brussels, that's all."*

**Connaître** designates knowledge acquired through experience, as opposed to study.

Ce peuple connaît la misère.                  *This people knows poverty.*

**H** *Complete each sentence with the correct present tense form of* **savoir** *or* **connaître.**

1. Vous _____ M. Durand?

2. Je ne _____ pas où elle travaille.

3. Je _____ bien Lyon.

4. Cet enfant _____ ses tables de multiplication.

5. Nous _____ combien.

6. Tu _____ un magasin de vêtements près d'ici?

7. Cette entreprise _____ des difficultés.

8. Ils ne _____ pas si le train est en retard.

9. Elles _____ notre famille.

10. Vous _____ l'heure du départ de son avion?

11. Il ne _____ pas l'adresse.

12. Tu _____ l'espagnol?

**I** *Complete each sentence by selecting the correct verb from the three given, and writing its correct present tense form.*

1. (réduire | produire | déduire)      Ce pays _____ beaucoup de fruits et de légumes.

2. (boire | suivre | écrire)      Elles _____ du thé.

3. (conduire | lire | savoir)      Il _____ une vieille voiture.

4. (savoir | reproduire | suivre)      Nous _____ la même route.

5. (vivre | suivre | dire)      Il _____ au jour le jour.

6. (lire | savoir | boire)      Je _____ un coup avec lui.

7. (croire | recevoir | introduire)      Ils _____ beaucoup de lettres.

8. (dire | voir | fuir)      Ils _____ devant leurs responsabilités.

9. (voir | lire | dire)      Vous _____ souvent des films à la télé?

10. (dire | croire | recevoir)      Elle _____ beaucoup de monde (*people*).

11. (construire | instruire | introduire)      L'instituteur _____ les élèves.

12. (connaître | reconduire | convaincre)      Elles ne _____ pas notre adresse.

13. (savoir | suivre | apercevoir)      Mes enfants _____ bien à l'école.

# Devoir, pouvoir, vouloir

The verbs **devoir** *to owe, must, ought to, should*, **pouvoir** *to be able to, can*, and **vouloir** *to want* are irregular.

**devoir** *to owe; must, ought to, should*

| | |
|---|---|
| je dois | nous devons |
| tu dois | vous devez |
| il/elle/on doit | ils/elles doivent |

**pouvoir** *to be able to; can*

| | |
|---|---|
| je peux | nous pouvons |
| tu peux | vous pouvez |
| il/elle/on peut | ils/elles peuvent |

**vouloir** *to want*

| | |
|---|---|
| je veux | nous voulons |
| tu veux | vous voulez |
| il/elle/on veut | ils/elles veulent |

**J** *Using the elements given, create sentences with the correct present tense form of* **devoir** *to tell how much money each of these people owes.*

MODÈLE    Paulette / trois euros

_Paulette doit trois euros._

1. je / cent euros _____

2. vous / dix dollars _____

3. nous / mille francs suisses _____

4. on / beaucoup d'argent _____

5. tu / trois cents dollars _____

6. Marc / mille euros _____

7. les voisins / trois mille francs suisses _____

8. Christine / deux cents dollars canadiens

_____

**K** *Complete each sentence with the correct present tense form of* **vouloir** *to tell what these people want to have to eat or drink.*

1. Les enfants _____ des bonbons.

2. Je _____ du champagne.

3. Nous _____ du vin rouge.

4. Elle _____ un steak frites.

5. Vous _____ des légumes.

6. Tu _____ du poisson.

7. On _____ de l'eau.

8. Les clients _____ du rosbif.

**L** ***These people are exhausted!*** *Create sentences with the expression* **n'en pouvoir plus** *not to be able to take any more.*

MODÈLE    Luc  _Luc n'en peut plus._

1. je _____

2. nous _____

3. les touristes _____

4. ma sœur _____

5. on _____

6. tu _____

7. vous _____

8. mes amis _____

# Venir, tenir

The verbs **venir** *to come* and **tenir** *to hold* end in a nasal vowel in the singular forms. In the plural, the stem-final consonant **n** is pronounced and there are no nasal vowels.

| **venir** *to come* | |
|---|---|
| je viens | nous venons |
| tu viens | vous venez |
| il/elle/on vient | ils/elles viennent |

| **tenir** *to hold* | |
|---|---|
| je tiens | nous tenons |
| tu tiens | vous tenez |
| il/elle/on tient | ils/elles tiennent |

## Expressions with **venir** and **tenir**

**en venir à** *to come to, turn to, get to*

    J'en viens à me demander si…     *I'm beginning to wonder whether . . .*
    Où voulez-vous en venir?     *What are you getting/driving at?*

**D'où vient que le moteur cale si souvent?** *How come the motor stalls so often?*
**venir de faire qqch** *to have just done something*
**tenir à faire qqch** *to be anxious to do something, insist on doing something*
**tenir à qqch, à qqn** *to cherish something, be very attached to someone*
**Qu'à cela ne tienne.** *It won't be a problem., Never mind.*
**tenir qqn au courant** *to keep someone informed/up-to-date*
**Cela ne tient qu'à vous.** *It all depends on you.*

**M**   *Complete each sentence with the correct present tense form of* **venir** *or* **tenir**, *according to the meaning.*

1. Je ne peux plus attendre. Je _____ à lui parler maintenant.

2. Vous ne le savez pas? Mais nous _____ de vous le dire.

3. Dans ce jardin il faut _____ les chiens en laisse.

4. Il pleut? Qu'à cela ne _____. Nous partirons de toute façon.

5. Vos propos ne sont pas clairs. Où voulez-vous en _____?

6. Je ne sais pas pourquoi ils _____ à inviter Solange.

7. D'où _____ qu'elle parle un français impeccable?

8. J'en _____ à me demander si elle veut vraiment travailler avec nous.

---

**BUILDING SENTENCES**   **Verb + infinitive construction**

The verbs **devoir** *must, ought to, should,* **pouvoir** *to be able to, can,* and **vouloir** *to want* frequently take an infinitive as a complement. The infinitive occupies the direct object position and may itself take a direct object. This construction, which consists of a conjugated verb + an infinitive, is called the verb + infinitive construction.

    **Je dois finir** mon projet aujourd'hui.     *I ought to finish my project today.*
    **Nos amis ne peuvent pas faire** ce voyage.     *Our friends can't take that trip.*
    **Elle ne veut pas acheter** cette voiture.     *She doesn't want to buy that car.*

In the following list, which includes other common verbs that can take an infinitive as a complement, **faire qqch** *to do something* represents any infinitive.

> **adorer faire qqch** *to love to do something*
> **aimer faire qqch** *to like to do something*
> **aimer mieux faire qqch** *to prefer to do something*
> **compter faire qqch** *to intend/plan to do something*
> **désirer faire qqch** *to want/desire to do something*
> **détester faire qqch** *to hate to do something*
> **espérer faire qqch** *to hope to do something*
> **oser faire qqch** *to dare to do something*
> **préférer faire qqch** *to prefer to do something*
> **savoir faire qqch** *to know how to do something*
> **sembler faire qqch** *to seem to do something*
> **souhaiter faire qqch** *to wish to do something*

| | |
|---|---|
| —**J'adore passer** mes vacances en Bretagne. | *"I love to spend my vacation in Brittany."* |
| —Moi, **j'aime mieux aller** à Nice. | *"I prefer to go to Nice."* |
| —Qu'est-ce que **tu aimes faire** en été? | *"What do you like to do in the summer?"* |
| —**J'aime aller** à la plage, mais **je ne sais pas nager**. | *"I like to go to the beach, but I don't know how to swim."* |
| —Quand est-ce que **vous comptez recevoir** vos amis? | *"When do you intend to invite your friends over?"* |
| —**Nous comptons voir** nos amis demain. | *"We intend to see our friends tomorrow."* |
| —**Je n'ose pas parler** avec le chef. | *"I don't dare speak with the boss."* |
| —Oui, **il semble être** fâché. | *"Yes, he seems to be angry."* |

Negative words surround the conjugated verb of a verb + infinitive construction, except for **personne**, which usually follows the infinitive.

| | |
|---|---|
| Elle ne veut pas partir. | *She doesn't want to leave.* |
| Nous ne pouvons jamais sortir. | *We can never go out.* |
| Il ne sait plus parler espagnol. | *He doesn't know how to speak Spanish anymore.* |
| Tu ne dois rien dire. | *You shouldn't say anything.* |
| Je ne veux déranger personne. | *I don't want to bother anyone.* |

**N**  *Expand each sentence by adding the correct present tense form of the verb in parentheses and changing the original verb to the infinitive. The new sentence will have a* verb + infinitive *construction.*

> MODÈLE    Claude part. (vouloir)
>
> _____*Claude veut partir.*_____

1. Mon fils réussit à ses examens.  (souhaiter)

   _____

2. Je ne viens plus.  (pouvoir) _____

3. Il sort le samedi soir. (aimer) _____

4. Je sors le vendredi. (aimer mieux) _____

5. Les étudiants ne disent pas la vérité. (oser)

_____

6. Nous finissons notre travail avant cinq heures. (espérer)

_____

7. Vous rentrez en autobus. (préférer) _____

8. Tu rédiges des lettres en allemand. (savoir)

_____

9. Robert ne comprend pas. (sembler) _____

10. Je ne vois personne. (compter) _____

11. Maryse est contente. (sembler) _____

12. Elle fait du camping. (adorer) _____

13. Cette région produit des fruits et des légumes. (pouvoir)

_____

14. Il ne fuit pas devant ses responsabilités. (devoir)

_____

15. Je convaincs les autres. (espérer) _____

16. Elles voient ce film. (vouloir) _____

17. J'écris ma thèse cet été. (compter) _____

18. Ils boivent un verre avec nous. (aimer)

_____

**O** *Answer the following questions in the negative. Use the appropriate negative word in your response.*

MODÈLE    Est-ce que les enfants veulent toujours manger des légumes?

*Non, les enfants ne veulent jamais manger des légumes.*

1. Est-ce que tu peux souvent jouer au football?

_____

2. Est-ce qu'il veut voir quelqu'un?

_____

3. Est-ce que vous devez acheter quelque chose?

_____

4. Est-ce que vous aimez faire de la varappe?

_____

5. Est-ce que les enfants veulent boire quelque chose?

_____

6. Est-ce que Paul sait piloter un avion?

_____

7. Est-ce que Marc ose inviter Christine à sortir?

_____

8. Est-ce que tu souhaites trouver un nouveau travail?

_____

9. Est-ce que Jeanne compte faire de l'informatique?

_____

10. Est-ce que tu veux encore attendre nos amis?

_____


**BUILDING SENTENCES** | **Questions: yes/no questions**

There are many ways to form questions in French. The different patterns convey differences in register (formal language, everyday language, informal language, slang). Thus, the type of question pattern that speakers select depends on the situation they are in and the relationship they have with the person to whom they are asking the question.

There are two types of questions: yes/no questions and information questions. Yes/no questions expect the answer *yes* or *no*. They do not begin with an interrogative word.

In colloquial French, statements are turned into yes/no questions most frequently by changing the intonation of the sentence from falling to rising, with no change in the word order of the original statement.

| | |
|---|---|
| Claire sait programmer? | *Does Claire know how to program?* |
| Cet enfant suit bien à l'école? | *Is this child a good student?* |
| Tu connais ce type-là? | *Do you know that guy?* |

The addition of **est-ce que** at the beginning of each of the questions above makes them appropriate in all registers.

| | |
|---|---|
| Est-ce que Claire sait programmer? | *Does Claire know how to program?* |
| Est-ce que cet enfant suit bien à l'école? | *Is this child a good student?* |
| Est-ce que tu connais ce type-là? | *Do you know that guy?* |

In formal French, a yes/no question may be formed by inverting the subject and verb if the subject is a subject pronoun. In this type of question, the subject pronoun is connected to the verb by a hyphen. Compare the following statements and the corresponding questions.

| | |
|---|---|
| Vous êtes en retard. | *You're late.* |
| Êtes-vous en retard? | *Are you late?* |

| | |
|---|---|
| Elle connaît Paris. | *She knows Paris.* |
| Connaît-elle Paris? | *Does she know Paris?* |
| Nous pouvons entrer. | *We can enter.* |
| Pouvons-nous entrer? | *Can we enter?* |
| Ils font une promenade. | *They're taking a walk.* |
| Font-ils une promenade? | *Are they taking a walk?* |

Inversion also requires a hyphen for third-person singular forms of **-er** verbs, including **aller**, where a **-t-** is added between the verb and the inverted pronoun. The **-t-** is also added between the third-person singular of **avoir** and the inverted pronoun.

| | |
|---|---|
| Arrive-t-il en voiture? | *Is he arriving by car?* |
| Parle-t-elle au téléphone mobile? | *Is she speaking on the cell phone?* |
| Trouve-t-on une solution? | *Are people finding a solution?* |
| Va-t-il en avion? | *Is he going by plane?* |
| A-t-elle soif? | *Is she thirsty?* |
| A-t-on des difficultés? | *Are people having trouble?* |

## Restrictions on Inversion

There are some restrictions on inversion, however.

- In French, only a pronoun can be inverted.

  If the sentence has a noun subject and inversion is selected to convey formal register, then the pronoun corresponding to the noun subject is added after the verb and connected to it by a hyphen or **-t-**. Compare the following statements and the corresponding questions.

| | |
|---|---|
| Cet immigré parle français. | *That immigrant speaks French.* |
| Cet immigré parle-t-il français? | *Does that immigrant speak French?* |
| Cette ville a des industries. | *That city has industry.* |
| Cette ville a-t-elle des industries? | *Does that city have industry?* |
| Maurice va en Italie. | *Maurice is going to Italy.* |
| Maurice va-t-il en Italie? | *Is Maurice going to Italy?* |

- The pronoun **je** is rarely inverted in modern French.

  **Est-ce que** can be used to make a question with the subject **je suis** for formal speech or writing. However, inversion of **je** with the monosyllabic verb forms **je suis**, **j'ai**, **je puis** (**je puis** is a literary variant of **je peux**) is still occasionally found in very formal speech and formal writing.

| | |
|---|---|
| Suis-je l'homme que vous cherchez? | *Am I the man you are looking for?* |
| Ai-je le droit de dire cela? | *Do I have the right to say that?* |
| Puis-je vous demander un service? | *May I ask a favor of you?* |

**P** *Using inversion, rewrite each statement as a question.*

1. Il arrive à l'heure. _____

2. Nous allons en France. _____

3. Vous comprenez ce texte. _____

4. Ils voient leurs collègues. _____

5. Il neige aujourd'hui. _____

6. Elle va en avion. _____

7. Tu sais nager. _____

8. On va en Amérique. _____

9. Elle a un bon travail. _____

10. Nous rédigeons la lettre. _____

11. Il mange au restaurant. _____

12. Ils réduisent leurs frais (*expenses*). _____

13. On sauvegarde les archives. _____

14. Il retourne en Afrique. _____

15. On reçoit un message. _____

16. Elles répondent en français. _____

17. On télécharge des documents. _____

18. Il renvoie ses employés. _____

19. Elle voyage en Asie. _____

20. Il prononce correctement. _____

**Q** *Rewrite the following informal questions as formal questions. Remember that simple inversion is not possible in all cases.*

1. Nous encourageons les étudiants? _____

2. Ce pays a besoin de notre aide? _____

3. Le PDG (*CEO*) renonce à son poste? _____

4. Je travaille dans une entreprise internationale?

_____

5. On arrive en avance? _____

6. Elle fait de la flûte? _____

7. Les touristes prennent un raccourci? _____

8. Mes amis appuient ce candidat? _____

9. L'autocar roule vite? _____

10. Je présente les résultats? _____

11. La bonne (*maid*) fait les carreaux? _____

12. Les ouvriers quittent l'usine à cinq heures?

   _____

13. Ces agences dépensent trop? _____

14. La compagnie emprunte trop d'argent?

   _____

15. Nous discutons constamment? _____

16. Vous habitez à la campagne? _____

17. Je téléphone à nos fournisseurs (*suppliers*)?

   _____

18. Le public va applaudir? _____

19. La direction (*management*) annonce la fusion (*merger*) des entreprises?

   _____

20. Cette famille loge des étudiants étrangers?

   _____

**R**   **Translation.** *Express the following sentences in French. There may be more than one way to express these sentences.*

1. *They drink wine with their meals.* _____

2. *We drink to your* (vous) *success.* _____

3. *Are you* (tu) *reading the documents?* _____

4. *She lives near the mall.* _____

5. *He runs very quickly.* _____

6. *I think so. And what about you* (tu)? _____

7. *I don't think so.* _____

8. *Do you* (vous) *see the Internet café?* _____

9. *Do you* (tu) *get many e-mails?* _____

10. *We know New York.* _____

11. *I don't know when they're arriving.* _____

12. *Do you* (vous) *know what time it is?* _____

13. *We don't want to wait any longer.* _____

14. *She can go with me.* _____

15. *He intends to begin the project.* _____

16. *Is she going to England?* _____

17. *Are people hungry?* _____

18. *I like to sing, but I prefer to dance.* _____

# 4

# The Imperative

**BUILDING SENTENCES**

Sentences with indirect objects
Sentences with direct object pronouns
Sentences with indirect object pronouns
Object pronouns with the imperative

The imperative, or command, forms of the verb are used to tell someone to do something or not to do something.

The imperative of almost all French verbs is easy to form. You simply drop the subject pronoun (**tu**, **vous**, or **nous**) of present tense forms. This is true for both affirmative and negative commands. Note that the **nous** command is the equivalent of *let's (not) do something* in English.

| | |
|---|---|
| **Réfléchis** avant d'agir. **N'agis pas** sans réfléchir. | *Think before you act. Don't act without thinking.* |
| **Ne m'interrompez pas. Ne dites** rien. | *Don't interrupt me. Don't say anything.* |
| **N'attendons** plus. **Choisissons** un cadeau pour Annie aujourd'hui. | *Let's not wait any longer. Let's choose a gift for Annie today.* |

Most imperatives are regular in speech. However, the written forms have one orthographic change. The informal imperative (**tu** form) of **-er** verbs loses the final **s** of the present tense ending. The **s** is also lost in the informal imperative of **aller** and of **-ir** verbs conjugated like **-er** verbs, such as **ouvrir**, **souffrir**, etc.

| | |
|---|---|
| **N'ouvre pas** la porte. **Demande** qui c'est d'abord. | *Don't open the door. Ask who it is first.* |
| **Va** au bureau et **donne** cette lettre à la secrétaire. | *Go to the office and give this letter to the secretary.* |

Some verbs have irregular imperative forms.

| | COMMAND FORM | | | |
|---|---|---|---|---|
| PERSON | **être** | **avoir** | **savoir** | **vouloir** |
| tu | sois | aie | sache | veuille[1] |
| nous | soyons | ayons | sachons | — |
| vous | soyez | ayez | sachez | veuillez[1] |

---

[1]Sometimes **veux** and **voulez** are used as command forms for **vouloir**.

**Veuillez** + an infinitive is used to add a polite note to a request, rather like English *please*.

| | |
|---|---|
| **Veuillez attendre** en bas. | *Please wait downstairs.* |
| **Veuillez répondre** dans les plus brefs délais. | *Please answer as soon as possible.* |

**Veuille** + an infinitive is theoretically possible, but not common, since the imperative of **vouloir** has a very formal tone.

The infinitive of the verb, rather than the command form, is often used as an imperative in written French to express commands to the general public, such as instructions for use (for example, on medicine bottles) or road signs (see Chapter 12, p. 231).

| | |
|---|---|
| **Agiter** avant d'ouvrir. | *Shake before opening.* |
| **Tenir** la droite. | *Keep right.* |

**A**  *Using the following phrases, create sentences in the form of a command to a child. Change each infinitive to the appropriate **tu** form for all verbs.*

MODÈLE    garder tes affaires    *Garde tes affaires.*

1. ramasser (*pick up*) tes vêtements _____
2. ne pas crier si fort _____
3. finir tes devoirs _____
4. téléphoner à ta tante _____
5. ne pas laisser tes livres par terre _____
6. mettre tes crayons dans le tiroir _____
7. manger tout ce qu'il y a sur ton assiette

_____

8. ne pas jouer dans le salon _____
9. ne pas inviter tes amis aujourd'hui _____
10. venir au supermarché avec moi _____
11. ne pas aller chez les voisins _____
12. ne pas allumer la télé _____
13. fermer le lecteur de cédés _____
14. lacer tes chaussures _____
15. ne pas salir la nappe (*tablecloth*) _____
16. avoir un peu de patience _____
17. ne pas embêter (*annoy* [colloquial]) le chat _____
18. être gentil avec tout le monde _____

**B** *Using the following phrases, create sentences with the imperative to tell a colleague at work what to do. Change each infinitive to the appropriate* **vous** *form for all verbs.*

1.  arriver au bureau à neuf heures _____

2.  allumer votre ordinateur _____

3.  choisir un mot de passe _____

4.  lire vos courriels (*e-mails*) _____

5.  répondre à tous les messages _____

6.  ne pas prendre de rendez-vous _____

7.  ne pas ennuyer le chef _____

8.  ne pas faire de coups de téléphone personnels

    _____

9.  ne pas commander de repas _____

10. ne pas mettre votre bureau en désordre

    _____

11. ranger toujours vos affaires _____

12. être patient avec vos collègues _____

13. ne pas avoir peur de demander de conseils

    _____

14. aider les nouveaux employés _____

15. savoir où se trouvent nos clients _____

16. réfléchir avant d'agir _____

17. finir tout votre travail avant de partir

    _____

18. ne pas sortir du bureau avant six heures

    _____

**C** *Exchanging suggestions.* *Rewrite each phrase as the* **nous** *form of an imperative to express what these friends are proposing to do.*

1.  faire quelque chose ensemble _____

2.  ne pas rester à la maison _____

3.  aller à la campagne _____

4.  prendre nos bicyclettes _____

5.  nager dans le lac _____

6.  jouer au foot _____

7. ne pas avoir peur de faire du ski nautique

   _____

8. manger au bord de l'eau _____

9. rentrer vers six heures du soir _____

10. changer de vêtements _____

11. dîner au restaurant _____

12. acheter un journal _____

13. chercher une boîte de nuit _____

14. réserver une table _____

15. être ponctuels _____

16. voir le spectacle _____

17. retourner à pied _____

18. réfléchir à nos activités pour demain

    _____

---

**BUILDING SENTENCES**   **Sentences with indirect objects**

Chapter 1 introduced recognizing objects in French. The idea or action expressed by the verb may affect or be directed at a person or thing—the object of the verb. If the object follows the verb directly without a preposition, it is called a direct object. In French, direct objects may be either persons or things. In the following sentences, the phrases in boldface are direct objects.

| | |
|---|---|
| Je vois **mon amie Lisette**. | *I see my friend Lisette.* |
| Tu connais **notre collègue**? | *Do you know our co-worker?* |
| Où achetez-vous **vos vêtements**? | *Where do you buy your clothing?* |
| Elle finit **le compte rendu**. | *She finishes the report.* |

Indirect objects in French are usually animate nouns—nouns referring to living beings. Indirect objects are joined to the verb by the preposition **à**. In the following sentences, the phrases in boldface are indirect objects. The meaning in English often includes the notion of English *to*.

| | |
|---|---|
| Il téléphone **à sa petite amie**. | *He phones his girlfriend.* |
| Vous écrivez **à vos cousins**. | *You write to your cousins.* |
| Le vendeur répond **au client**. | *The clerk answers the customer.* |

Indirect objects most often occur with an inanimate direct object. Examine the following sentences. The direct objects appear in boldface, with the indirect objects in underlined boldface.

| | |
|---|---|
| Il donne **un cadeau <u>à son frère</u>**. | *He gives his brother a gift.* |
| Je montre **les photos <u>à mes amis</u>**. | *I show my friends the pictures.* |

Here is a list of verbs that take a direct object and an indirect object. Inanimate direct objects are represented as **qqch** (**quelque chose**). Animate indirect objects are represented as **à qqn** (**à quelqu'un**).

**apporter qqch à qqn**  *to bring something to someone*
**demander qqch à qqn**  *to ask someone for something*
**dire qqch à qqn**  *to tell/say something to someone*
**donner qqch à qqn**  *to give something to someone*
**enseigner qqch à qqn**  *to teach something to someone*
**envoyer qqch à qqn**  *to send something to someone*
**expliquer qqch à qqn**  *to explain something to someone*
**laisser qqch à qqn**  *to leave something for someone*
**montrer qqch à qqn**  *to show something to someone*
**offrir qqch à qqn**  *to give something (as a gift) to someone*
**passer qqch à qqn**  *to pass something to someone*
**prêter qqch à qqn**  *to lend something to someone*
**promettre qqch à qqn**  *to promise something to someone*
**rendre qqch à qqn**  *to give something back to someone*
**vendre qqch à qqn**  *to sell something to someone*

Note that in **présenter qqn à qqn** *to introduce someone to someone*, both the direct and the indirect objects refer to people.

**Écouter, attendre**, and **recevoir** can also take a direct object of the person: **écouter qqn** *to listen to someone*, **attendre qqn** *to wait for someone*, **recevoir qqn** *to receive someone*.

The indirect object is the equivalent of English *from* with verbs that mean *to take away, borrow, steal*, etc. The indirect object is joined to the verb by the preposition **à** in these cases as well.

**acheter qqch à qqn**  *to buy something from someone*
**arracher qqch à qqn**  *to snatch something from someone*
**cacher qqch à qqn**  *to hide something from someone*
**emprunter qqch à qqn**  *to borrow something from someone*
**enlever qqch à qqn**  *to take something away from someone*
**louer qqch à qqn**  *to rent something from someone*
**prendre qqch à qqn**  *to take something from someone*
**voler qqch à qqn**  *to steal something from someone*

French verbs should be learned as underlying structures. For example, a verb listed with the underlying structure **chercher qqch/qqn** means that **chercher** takes a direct object of the person or of the thing. A verb listed with the underlying structure **répondre à qqn** is a verb that takes an indirect object of the person.

The following verbs and verb phrases take an indirect object in French (**à** + person) but varying types of objects in English.

**aller bien à qqn**  *to look nice on someone*
**convenir à qqn**  *to suit someone, be convenient for someone*
**déplaire à qqn**  *to displease someone*
**désobéir à qqn**  *to disobey someone*

**nuire à qqn** *to harm/hurt someone*
**obéir à qqn** *to obey someone*
**plaire à qqn** *to please someone*
**répondre à qqn** *to answer someone*
**ressembler à qqn** *to resemble someone*
**téléphoner à qqn** *to call/phone someone*

The verbs **plaire** and **déplaire** are often used for English *to like someone/something* and *to dislike someone/something.* In English translations of sentences with these verbs, the French subject corresponds to the English direct object, and the English subject corresponds to the French indirect object.

Ce restaurant plaît beaucoup à ma famille.　　*My family likes this restaurant a lot.*
Ces films plaisent à tout le monde.　　*Everyone likes these films.*

**D**　*Analyze the types of objects in the following French sentences. Write the direct object, the indirect object, and the underlying structure of the verb for each sentence. If there is no direct object or indirect object in the sentence, write an X on the line.*

MODÈLE　　J'envoie une lettre à mon patron.

　　a. DIRECT OBJECT　*une lettre*

　　b. INDIRECT OBJECT　*mon patron*

　　c. UNDERLYING STRUCTURE　*envoyer qqch à qqn*

1. Ils écoutent leurs cédés.

　　a. DIRECT OBJECT _____

　　b. INDIRECT OBJECT _____

　　c. UNDERLYING STRUCTURE _____

2. J'achète mes voitures à ce concessionnaire (*dealer*).

　　a. DIRECT OBJECT _____

　　b. INDIRECT OBJECT _____

　　c. UNDERLYING STRUCTURE _____

3. Nous recevons vos courriels.

　　a. DIRECT OBJECT _____

　　b. INDIRECT OBJECT _____

　　c. UNDERLYING STRUCTURE _____

4. Ces enfants obéissent à leur mère.

　　a. DIRECT OBJECT _____

　　b. INDIRECT OBJECT _____

　　c. UNDERLYING STRUCTURE _____

5. Le père prête sa voiture à son fils.

   a. DIRECT OBJECT _____

   b. INDIRECT OBJECT _____

   c. UNDERLYING STRUCTURE _____

6. Elle présente le projet à ses collègues.

   a. DIRECT OBJECT _____

   b. INDIRECT OBJECT _____

   c. UNDERLYING STRUCTURE _____

7. Nous attendons l'autobus au coin de la rue.

   a. DIRECT OBJECT _____

   b. INDIRECT OBJECT _____

   c. UNDERLYING STRUCTURE _____

8. Tu dois expliquer la situation à tes enfants.

   a. DIRECT OBJECT _____

   b. INDIRECT OBJECT _____

   c. UNDERLYING STRUCTURE _____

9. J'offre un iPod à ma fille.

   a. DIRECT OBJECT _____

   b. INDIRECT OBJECT _____

   c. UNDERLYING STRUCTURE _____

10. Son attitude déplaît au chef.

   a. DIRECT OBJECT _____

   b. INDIRECT OBJECT _____

   c. UNDERLYING STRUCTURE _____

11. Elle ressemble à sa mère.

   a. DIRECT OBJECT _____

   b. INDIRECT OBJECT _____

   c. UNDERLYING STRUCTURE _____

12. Ils disent la vérité à leurs parents.

   a. DIRECT OBJECT _____

   b. INDIRECT OBJECT _____

   c. UNDERLYING STRUCTURE _____

**E** *Create sentences from the following strings of elements. Each sentence will have a subject, a verb in the present tense, a direct object, and an indirect object.*

MODÈLE    Jean / donner / le message / les employés

*Jean donne le message aux employés.*

1. les Durand / vendre / leur appartement / les Dupont

   _____

2. le chien / apporter / le journal / son maître

   _____

3. Lucille / demander / l'argent / ses parents

   _____

4. je / rendre / les livres / Jean-Claude

   _____

5. il / laisser / sa maison / sa fille

   _____

6. tu / prêter / ta bicyclette / ton amie

   _____

7. ils / envoyer / les courriels / leurs assistants

   _____

8. vous / présenter / le compte rendu / le PDG (Président–directeur général = *CEO*)

   _____

9. le voleur / arracher / le sac / la dame

   _____

10. elle / offrir / les cédés / ses neveux

    _____

11. le professeur / dire / la réponse / les étudiants

    _____

12. je / donner / l'addition / les clients

    _____

13. nous / promettre / la voiture / notre fils

    _____

14. tu / passer / le sel / les invités

    _____

## BUILDING SENTENCES  *Sentences with direct object pronouns*

Direct object nouns can be replaced by direct object pronouns. The first and second persons have the following direct object pronouns.

|  | SINGULAR | PLURAL |
|---|---|---|
| FIRST PERSON | **me** | **nous** |
| SECOND PERSON | **te** | **vous** |

The pronouns **me** and **te** become **m'** and **t'** before a vowel.

| —Tu veux **m'**accompagner? | *"Do you want to go with me?"* |
|---|---|
| —Oui, je **t'**accompagne volontiers. | *"Yes, I'll go with you gladly."* |

Direct object pronouns in French precede the conjugated verb.

| —Vous **me** quittez maintenant? | *"Are you leaving me now?"* |
|---|---|
| —Non, je **vous** raccompagne. | *"No, I'll walk you home."* |

If there are two verbs, one conjugated and one in the infinitive form, the direct object pronoun follows the conjugated verb and precedes the infinitive.

| —Tu peux **nous** déposer en ville? | *"Can you drop us off downtown?"* |
|---|---|
| —Oui, bien sûr. Je vais **vous** laisser près de la gare. | *"Yes, of course. I'll leave you near the train station."* |

In a negative sentence, the direct object pronoun follows **ne**.

| —Vous ne **me** reconnaissez pas? | *"You don't recognize me?"* |
|---|---|
| —Non, je regrette, mais je ne **vous** reconnais pas du tout. | *"No, I'm sorry, but I don't recognize you at all."* |

In verb + infinitive constructions, direct object pronouns follow **pas** when the conjugated verb is negative.

| Ce film ne m'intéresse pas. Je ne vais pas **t'**accompagner au cinéma. | *That film doesn't interest me. I'm not going to go with you to the movies.* |
|---|---|
| Je ne sais pas pourquoi il ne veut pas **vous** contacter. | *I don't know why he doesn't want to get in touch with you.* |

In the third person, direct object pronouns are the same for people and things.

|  | SINGULAR | PLURAL |
|---|---|---|
| THIRD PERSON MASCULINE | **le (l')** | **les** |
| THIRD PERSON FEMININE | **la (l')** | **les** |

Masculine singular direct object nouns are replaced by **le**. Feminine singular direct object nouns are replaced by **la**. All plural direct object nouns are replaced by **les**. The direct object pronouns **le** and **la** become **l'** before a vowel.

| —Tu ne manges pas le yaourt? | *"Aren't you eating the yogurt?"* |
|---|---|
| —Non, je ne **le** mange pas. Il est abîmé. | *"No, I'm not eating it. It's spoiled."* |
| —Tu emmènes Daniel au cinéma? | *"Are you taking Daniel to the movies?"* |
| —Non, je **l'**emmène au cirque. | *"No, I'm taking him to the circus."* |

| | |
|---|---|
| —Voici la note. | *"Here's the bill."* |
| —Moi, je vais **la** régler. | *"I'll pay (= settle) it."* |
| —Ce cadeau est de Marianne? | *"Is this gift from Marianne?"* |
| —Oui, je dois **la** remercier. | *"Yes, I have to thank her."* |
| —Ils comprennent les exemples? | *"Do they understand the examples?"* |
| —Oui, ils **les** comprennent. | *"Yes, they understand them."* |
| —Tu vas voir tes amis aujourd'hui? | *"Are you going to see your friends today?"* |
| —Oui, je vais **les** retrouver au café. | *"Yes, I'm going to meet them at the café."* |

All direct object pronouns can be used before **voici** and **voilà**.

| | |
|---|---|
| —Tu n'as pas la photo? | *"You don't have the picture?"* |
| —Si, je l'ai. **La** voici. | *"Yes, I do have it. Here it is."* |
| —Je cherche les enfants. Tu les vois? | *"I'm looking for the children. Do you see them?"* |
| —Oui, **les** voilà, dans le jardin. | *"Yes, there they are, in the garden."* |

**F** *Answer the following questions affirmatively, changing direct object nouns to pronouns in your responses. Some items may have more than one answer.*

MODÈLE    Est-ce que toi et ton copain, vous prenez la voiture?

*Oui, nous la prenons./Oui, on la prend.*

1. Est-ce que le PDG reçoit le conseiller?

2. Est-ce que les étudiants apprennent les mots?

3. Est-ce que tu appelles tes amis?

4. Est-ce que Lucille invite Jean-Paul au bal?

5. Est-ce que les clients commandent leur dîner?

6. Est-ce que tu nettoies la cuisine?

7. Est-ce que les enfants mettent la table?

8. Est-ce que ta femme achète le vin?

9. Est-ce que Paul a les renseignements?

10. Est-ce que la petite Nicole range ses affaires?

_____

11. Est-ce que vous finissez votre travail, vous autres?

_____

12. Est-ce qu'il raccompagne sa petite amie?

_____

**G** *Answer the following questions negatively, changing direct object nouns to pronouns in your responses. Some items may have more than one answer.*

MODÈLE    Est-ce que toi et ton copain, vous prenez la voiture?
     *Non, nous ne la prenons pas. / Non, on ne la prend pas.*

1. Est-ce que ces ouvriers bâtissent cette maison?

_____

2. Est-ce que vous autres, vous écoutez la chanson?

_____

3. Est-ce que ces garçons aiment les match de foot?

_____

4. Est-ce que tu photocopies les documents?

_____

5. Est-ce que vous autres, vous téléchargez les chansons?

_____

6. Est-ce que tu paies la chambre d'hôtel?

_____

7. Est-ce qu'elle promène son chien?

_____

8. Est-ce que tu perds souvent ta clé?

_____

9. Est-ce qu'il fait le linge?

_____

10. Est-ce que les enfants mettent leurs bottes?

_____

11. Est-ce que tu avertis les autres?

_____

12. Est-ce que vous interrompez votre chef?

_____

**H** *Answer the following questions either affirmatively or negatively, according to the cue* **Oui** *or* **Non**, *and change the direct object nouns to pronouns in your responses. All of your responses will contain a* verb + infinitive *construction. Some items may have more than one answer.*

MODÈLES   Est-ce que toi et ton copain, vous allez prendre la voiture? (Oui)

   *Oui, nous allons la prendre./Oui, on va la prendre.*

   Est-ce que toi et ton copain, vous allez prendre la voiture? (Non)

   *Non, nous n'allons pas la prendre./Non, on ne va pas la prendre.*

1. Est-ce que la secrétaire va photocopier les documents? (Oui)

_____

2. Est-ce que le chef va préparer ce plat? (Non)

_____

3. Est-ce que cet enfant va casser ses jouets? (Oui)

_____

4. Est-ce que le chef peut recevoir les conseillers? (Non)

_____

5. Est-ce que je dois mettre ma cravate? (Oui)

_____

6. Est-ce qu'elle veut sauvegarder ses fichiers? (Non)

_____

7. Est-ce qu'ils savent programmer l'ordinateur? (Oui)

_____

8. Est-ce que vous comptez prendre le déjeuner avec nous? (Non)

_____

9. Est-ce qu'il peut accepter l'invitation? (Oui)

_____

10. Est-ce que tu aimes faire le ménage? (Non)

_____

11. Est-ce qu'ils vont arroser (*water*) les fleurs? (Oui)

_____

12. Est-ce que tu veux ouvrir le paquet? (Non)

_____

13. Est-ce que tu aimes lire les courriels? (Oui)

_____

14. Est-ce que nous devons fermer les fenêtres? (Non)

_____

15. Est-ce qu'elle compte remercier le professeur? (Oui)

_____

16. Est-ce que tu vas imprimer la lettre? (Non)

_____

17. Est-ce que ton petit frère veut télécharger ces jeux? (Oui)

_____

18. Est-ce que vous souhaitez quitter la ville? (Non)

_____

19. Est-ce qu'elle préfère enseigner les mathématiques? (Oui)

_____

20. Est-ce qu'il espère convaincre ses amis? (Non)

_____


**BUILDING SENTENCES** | **Sentences with indirect object pronouns**

French indirect object pronouns are the same as the corresponding direct object pronouns for the first and second persons.

|  | SINGULAR | PLURAL |
| --- | --- | --- |
| FIRST PERSON | **me** | **nous** |
| SECOND PERSON | **te** | **vous** |

In the third person, indirect object pronouns vary for number, but not for gender.

|  | SINGULAR | PLURAL |
| --- | --- | --- |
| THIRD PERSON | **lui** | **leur** |

**Lui** replaces **à** + an animate singular noun and **leur** replaces **à** + an animate plural noun. The pronoun **lui** can therefore mean both *(to) him* and *(to) her*.

Indirect object pronouns follow the same rules of placement as direct object pronouns. They precede the conjugated verb.

—Tu téléphones souvent à ta mère?　　*"Do you call your mother often?"*
—Oui, je **lui** téléphone tous les jours.　　*"Yes, I call her every day."*

In negative constructions, indirect object pronouns follow **ne** and precede the verb.

—Pourquoi est-ce que tu ne **leur** écris pas?　　*"Why don't you write to them?"*
—Parce qu'ils ne **m'**écrivent jamais.　　*"Because they never write to me."*

In verb + infinitive constructions, indirect object pronouns follow the conjugated verb and precede the infinitive.

—Je ne fais pas attention au prof.        *"I don't listen to the teacher."*
—Tu as tort. Tu dois **lui** obéir.        *"You're wrong to do that. You should*
                                                *obey him."*

When a verb + infinitive construction is negated, the negative words surround the conjugated verb. Object pronouns therefore follow the negative and precede the infinitive directly.

—Tu ne comptes pas **lui** envoyer un        *"You don't intend to send him an e-mail?"*
  courriel?
—Mon message ne va pas **lui** plaire.        *"He is not going to like my message."*

The French verb **manquer à qqn** *to miss someone* has reversed subject and object functions, like **plaire** and **déplaire**, when compared to the structures in English.

Quand je suis en voyage d'affaires, mes        *When I'm on a business trip, I miss my*
    enfants **me** manquent beaucoup.        *children a lot.*
Ses amis **lui** manquent.        *He misses his friends.*
Il manque **à ses amis**.        *His friends miss him.*

**I**    *Rewrite each sentence, replacing the indirect object noun with the corresponding indirect object pronoun.*

1. Il envoie un courriel à sa petite amie.

   _____

2. La secrétaire téléphone aux employés.

   _____

3. Je veux louer un appartement à ces messieurs.

   _____

4. Elle va demander ce produit au pharmacien.

   _____

5. Cette pièce de théâtre ne va pas plaire à votre professeur.

   _____

6. Ils cachent la vérité à leur chef.

   _____

7. Nous apportons les documents au PDG.

   _____

8. Ils écrivent un message au patron.

   _____

9. Je ne vais pas dire ce secret à cette fille.

_____

10. Vous ne pouvez pas expliquer ces résultats aux cadres.

_____

11. Elle donne des cadeaux aux enfants pauvres.

_____

12. Ce professeur ne sait pas expliquer les problèmes difficiles à ses étudiants.

_____

13. Il ne veut pas prêter sa voiture à son copain.

_____

14. Elle vend ses peintures à ses voisins.

_____

15. Nous comptons rendre l'argent à nos amis.

_____

16. J'enseigne des chansons à ma petite sœur.

_____

**J** *Answer the following questions, using an indirect object pronoun and the cue provided in parentheses.*

MODÈLE    Qu'est-ce que tu donnes à Monique? (un tableur [*spreadsheet program*])
            *Je lui donne un tableur.*

1. Qu'est-ce que vous expliquez au chef? (le projet)

_____

2. Qu'est-ce que tu vas demander à tes parents? (un lecteur de cédés)

_____

3. Qu'est-ce qu'elle va t'offrir? (une montre)

_____

4. Qu'est-ce qu'il vend à ces gens-là? (sa maison)

_____

5. Qu'est-ce que le professeur va dire à ces étudiants? (la solution)

_____

6. Qu'est-ce que je dois envoyer à ce fonctionnaire? (un formulaire)

_____

7. Qu'est-ce que vous allez nous prêter, monsieur? (mille dollars)

   _____

8. Qu'est-ce que le voleur a pris à la dame? (son sac à main)

   _____

9. Qu'est-ce que vous comptez apporter à vos amis? (un gâteau)

   _____

10. Qu'est-ce qu'ils promettent à leurs enfants? (un mois en Suisse)

    _____

---

| BUILDING SENTENCES | **Object pronouns with the imperative** |

In negative commands, object pronouns have their usual position before the verb.

| | |
|---|---|
| Ce programme antivirus n'est pas bon. Ne le télécharge pas. | *That antivirus program is no good. Don't download it.* |
| Cette carte de crédit n'est pas valable. Ne l'accepte pas. | *That credit card isn't valid. Don't accept it.* |
| Ces données sont très importantes. Ne les perdons pas. | *This data is very important. Let's not lose it.* |

In affirmative commands, however, object pronouns follow the command form and are joined to it in writing by a hyphen.

| | |
|---|---|
| Ce chapeau est joli. Essaie-**le**. | *This hat is pretty. Try it on.* |
| Cette assiette est sale. Lave-**la**. | *This plate is dirty. Wash it.* |
| Ces fichiers sont importants. Sauvegardons-**les**. | *These files are important. Let's save them.* |
| Si vous voulez ce meuble, commandez-**le**. | *If you want this piece of furniture, order it.* |
| Hélène et Marie veulent rentrer. Raccompagnez-**les**. | *Hélène and Marie want to go home. Walk them home.* |
| Dites-**lui** que nous sommes en retard. | *Tell him that we're late.* |
| Il faut les mettre au courant. Téléphonez-**leur**. | *We have to inform them. Phone them.* |

The object pronouns **me** and **te** (as both direct and indirect object pronouns) become **moi** and **toi** when they follow affirmative commands.

| | |
|---|---|
| Aide-**moi**, s'il te plaît. | *Help me, please.* |
| Envoyez-**moi** un courriel pour me tenir au courant. | *Send me an e-mail to keep me informed.* |

**Toi** as an object pronoun appears only with reflexive verbs (see Chapter 7, p. 147).

| | |
|---|---|
| Lave-**toi**. | *Wash up.* |
| Brosse-**toi** les dents. | *Brush your teeth.* |

**K** *Answer each question with an affirmative **tu** command containing the correct object pronoun.*

MODÈLE    Je dois acheter ces bloc-notes?

_Oui, achète-les._

1.  Je peux manger cette pâtisserie? _____

2.  Je peux boire ce verre de jus? _____

3.  Je dois jeter ces papiers à la corbeille (*wastebasket*)? _____

4.  Je peux lire ces courriels? _____

5.  Je dois sauvegarder ce fichier? _____

6.  Je dois t'attendre? _____

7.  Je dois chercher les enfants? _____

8.  Je peux imprimer ces documents? _____

9.  Je peux utiliser ton ordinateur? _____

10.  Je dois remercier Janine? _____

11.  Je peux te montrer ma photo? _____

12.  Je peux te déposer en ville? _____

13.  Je dois finir le compte rendu? _____

14.  Je peux enlever ma veste? _____

15.  Je dois répéter ces mots? _____

**L** *Answer each question with a negative **tu** command containing the correct object pronoun.*

MODÈLE    Je dois acheter ces bloc-notes?

_Non, ne les achète pas._

1.  Je peux manger cette pâtisserie? _____

2.  Je peux boire ce verre de jus? _____

3.  Je dois jeter ces papiers à la corbeille (*wastebasket*)?

_____

4.  Je peux lire ces courriels? _____

5.  Je dois sauvegarder ce fichier? _____

6.  Je dois t'attendre? _____

7.  Je dois chercher les enfants? _____

8.  Je peux imprimer ces documents? _____

9.  Je peux utiliser ton ordinateur? _____

10. Je dois remercier Janine? _____

11. Je peux te montrer ma photo? _____

12. Je peux te déposer en ville? _____

13. Je dois finir le compte rendu? _____

14. Je peux enlever ma veste? _____

15. Je dois répéter ces mots? _____

**M** *Answer each question with an affirmative* **vous** *command containing the correct object pronoun.*

MODÈLE    Est-ce que je dois acheter ces bloc-notes?

_Oui, achetez-les._

1. Est-ce que nous pouvons vous raccompagner? _____

2. Est-ce que je peux prendre cette barque? _____

3. Est-ce que je dois dépenser cet argent? _____

4. Est-ce que nous devons laver ces assiettes? _____

5. Est-ce que nous devons oublier cet incident? _____

6. Est-ce que je dois photocopier mon passeport? _____

7. Est-ce que nous devons traverser ce pont? _____

8. Est-ce que je dois obéir au chef? _____

9. Est-ce que nous devons répondre aux employés? _____

10. Est-ce que je dois écouter ce discours? _____

11. Est-ce que je dois annoncer leur arrivée? _____

12. Est-ce que nous devons corriger cette lettre? _____

13. Est-ce que nous devons rejeter ces idées? _____

14. Est-ce que je peux feuilleter cette revue? _____

15. Est-ce que nous devons faire les carreaux? _____

16. Est-ce que nous devons écrire à ces candidats? _____

**N** *Answer each question with a negative* **vous** *command containing the correct object pronoun.*

MODÈLE    Est-ce que je dois acheter ces bloc-notes?

_Non, ne les achetez pas._

1. Est-ce que nous pouvons vous raccompagner? _____

2. Est-ce que je peux prendre cette barque? _____

3. Est-ce que je dois dépenser cet argent? _____

4. Est-ce que nous devons laver ces assiettes? _____

5. Est-ce que nous devons oublier cet incident? _____

6. Est-ce que je dois photocopier mon passeport? _____

7. Est-ce que nous devons traverser ce pont? _____

8. Est-ce que je dois obéir au chef? _____

9. Est-ce que nous devons répondre aux employés? _____

10. Est-ce que je dois écouter ce discours? _____

11. Est-ce que je dois annoncer leur arrivée? _____

12. Est-ce que nous devons corriger cette lettre? _____

13. Est-ce que nous devons rejeter ces idées? _____

14. Est-ce que je peux feuilleter cette revue? _____

15. Est-ce que nous devons faire les carreaux? _____

16. Est-ce que nous devons écrire à ces candidats? _____

**O**  *Respond to each of the following statements with a suggestion to a group of your friends. Use the affirmative **nous** command of the verb in parentheses and the correct object pronoun in your response.*

MODÈLE    Ce livre a l'air très intéressant. (lire)

_____*Lisons-le.*_____

1. Les conseillers veulent une réponse. (répondre) _____

2. Ce programme est très bon et gratuit. (télécharger) _____

3. Ces chansons sont très jolies. (écouter) _____

4. Ces logiciels sont excellents. (commander) _____

5. Notre oncle veut avoir de nos nouvelles. (écrire un courriel) _____

6. Les enfants veulent jouer dans le parc. (emmener) _____

7. La porte est fermée. (ouvrir) _____

8. Les hors-d'œuvre sont prêts. (servir) _____

9. Cet employé ne travaille pas. (mettre à la porte) _____

10. Isabelle veut savoir à quelle heure elle doit venir. (téléphoner) _____

11. Cette nappe est usée (*worn*). (remplacer) _____

12. Ce gâteau a l'air délicieux. (manger) _____

**P** *Respond to each of the following statements with a suggestion to a group of your friends. Use the negative* **nous** *command of the verb in parentheses and the correct object pronoun in your response.*

MODÈLE   Ce livre n'a pas l'air très intéressant.  (lire)

   *Ne le lisons pas.* _____

1. Ces fenêtres doivent rester fermées.  (ouvrir) _____

2. Luc n'aime pas les fêtes.  (inviter) _____

3. Nos rideaux sont encore bons.  (remplacer) _____

4. Ces vêtements ne sont pas sales.  (laver) _____

5. Cette viande n'est pas bonne.  (manger) _____

6. Je trouve que Nicole gâche (*ruins*) toutes nos soirées.  (téléphoner)

   _____

7. Le parquet est propre.  (nettoyer) _____

8. Je crois que le chien est malade.  (promener) _____

9. Ce garçon veut réussir.  (décourager) _____

10. Marc et Paul sont déjà en retard.  (attendre) _____

**Q** *Translation.* *Express the following sentences in French.*

1. *Don't speak too softly.*  (vous) _____

2. *Speak louder.*  (vous) _____

3. *—Come eat this mushroom pizza.*  (tu) _____

4. *—Mushrooms? I hate them. Eat it yourself.*  (tu)

   _____

5. *—Are you going to see the film?*  (tu) _____

6. *—No, I don't want to see it.* _____

7. *Let's take the train to go to Paris, but let's not take it to go to Normandy.*

   _____

8. *—Let's not be late.* _____

9. *—Okay, let's leave right away.* _____

10. *—I intend to send them the files today.* _____

11. *—Save them. Then send them the files next week.*  (vous)

   _____

12. *—Can you lend me your digital camera?*  (tu)

   _____

13.   —*I don't have it. Juliette is going to return the camera to me tomorrow.*

      _____

14.   *Wait for me at Starbucks.* (tu) _____

15.   *Write him an e-mail.* (tu) _____

16.   *Pay attention.* (vous) _____

# The Passé Composé

**BUILDING SENTENCES**

**Questions: information questions, question words**
**Placement of adverbs in the passé composé**
**The passive voice**

The passé composé (literally, the compound past) is one of the two past tenses of modern French. In form, but only partially in function, it resembles the English present perfect (*have/has done something*). Both the passé composé and the English present perfect are compound tenses consisting of an auxiliary verb plus the past participle.

## The Past Participle

The past participle in French has a different ending for each conjugation.

- **-Er** verbs change the **-er** of the infinitive to **é**.
- **-Ir** verbs change the **-ir** of the infinitive to **i**.
- **-Re** verbs change the **-re** of the infinitive to **u**.

| INFINITIVE | PAST PARTICIPLE | USUAL ENGLISH TRANSLATION OF PAST PARTICIPLE |
|---|---|---|
| parler | parlé | *spoken* |
| marcher | marché | *walked* |
| finir | fini | *finished* |
| choisir | choisi | *chosen* |
| vendre | vendu | *sold* |
| interrompre | interrompu | *interrupted* |

Many common verbs have irregular past participles. As in English, these must be memorized.

| INFINITIVE | PAST PARTICIPLE |
|---|---|
| apprendre | appris |
| atteindre | atteint |
| avoir | eu |
| boire | bu |
| comprendre | compris |
| conduire | conduit |
| connaître | connu |
| construire | construit |
| courir | couru |

| INFINITIVE | PAST PARTICIPLE |
|------------|-----------------|
| couvrir | couvert |
| craindre | craint |
| croire | cru |
| cuire | cuit |
| découvrir | découvert |
| devoir | dû |
| dire | dit |
| écrire | écrit |
| être | été |
| faire | fait |
| instruire | instruit |
| joindre | joint |
| lire | lu |
| mettre | mis |
| ouvrir | ouvert |
| paraître | paru |
| peindre | peint |
| pouvoir | pu |
| prendre | pris |
| produire | produit |
| recevoir | reçu |
| savoir | su |
| souffrir | souffert |
| suivre | suivi |
| tenir | tenu |
| venir | venu |
| vivre | vécu |
| voir | vu |
| vouloir | voulu |

There are patterns in the irregular forms of past participles in French. Compounds of irregular verbs show the same irregularity in the past participle. For example, the following list shows two compounds of **prendre**.

| INFINITIVE | PAST PARTICIPLE |
|------------|-----------------|
| prendre | pris |
| apprendre | appris |
| comprendre | compris |

Most verbs ending in **-uire** have a past participle ending in **-uit**.

| INFINITIVE | PAST PARTICIPLE |
|------------|-----------------|
| conduire | conduit |
| instruire | instruit |

However, the past participle of **nuire** is **nui**.

Most verbs ending in **-indre** have a past participle ending in **-int**.

| INFINITIVE | PAST PARTICIPLE |
|------------|-----------------|
| craindre   | craint          |
| joindre    | joint           |
| peindre    | peint           |

Verbs ending in **-cevoir** replace **-cevoir** with **-çu** to form the past participle.

| INFINITIVE | PAST PARTICIPLE |
|------------|-----------------|
| décevoir   | déçu            |
| recevoir   | reçu            |

Most verbs ending in **-aître** replace **-aître** with **-u** to form the past participle.

| INFINITIVE | PAST PARTICIPLE |
|------------|-----------------|
| connaître  | connu           |
| paraître   | paru            |

**Naître** and **renaître**, however, do not follow this pattern.

| INFINITIVE | PAST PARTICIPLE |
|------------|-----------------|
| naître     | **né**          |
| renaître   | **rené**        |

Other irregular past participles are seen in **il a plu** *it rained* and the passé composé of **il y a**, which is **il y a eu**.

**A**  *Write the past participle for each of the following verbs.*

1. surprendre  _____

2. plaindre  _____

3. attendre  _____

4. atteindre  _____

5. introduire  _____

6. décevoir  _____

7. recouvrir  _____

8. promettre  _____

9. déduire  _____

10. apparaître  _____

11. relire  _____

12. craindre  _____

13. admettre  _____

14. maintenir  _____

15. revenir _____

16. défaire _____

17. apercevoir _____

18. décrire _____

19. revoir _____

20. disparaître _____

## Passé Composé with Auxiliary Verb **avoir**

Most French verbs form the passé composé with **avoir**. The past participle does *not* change to agree with the subject in gender and number.

**parler** *to speak*

| | |
|---|---|
| j'ai parlé | nous avons parlé |
| tu as parlé | vous avez parlé |
| il/elle/on a parlé | ils/elles ont parlé |

**finir** *to finish*

| | |
|---|---|
| j'ai fini | nous avons fini |
| tu as fini | vous avez fini |
| il/elle/on a fini | ils/elles ont fini |

**vendre** *to sell*

| | |
|---|---|
| j'ai vendu | nous avons vendu |
| tu as vendu | vous avez vendu |
| il/elle/on a vendu | ils/elles ont vendu |

**recevoir** *to receive*

| | |
|---|---|
| j'ai reçu | nous avons reçu |
| tu as reçu | vous avez reçu |
| il/elle/on a reçu | ils/elles ont reçu |

**mettre** *to put*

| | |
|---|---|
| j'ai mis | nous avons mis |
| tu as mis | vous avez mis |
| il/elle/on a mis | ils/elles ont mis |

—Tu as écouté la météo?    *"Did you listen to the weather forecast?"*

—Oui, et c'est pour ça que j'ai mis mon anorak.    *"Yes, and that's why I put on my ski jacket."*

—Pourquoi est-ce qu'il n'a pas réussi à entrer?    *"Why didn't he manage to get in?"*

—Je crois qu'il a perdu ses clés.    *"I think he lost his keys."*

—Ils ont reçu notre courriel?     *"Have they received our e-mail?"*
—Oui, mais ils ne l'ont pas encore lu.     *"Yes, but they haven't read it yet."*
—Vous n'avez pas vu vos amis?     *"You didn't see your friends?"*
—Non, j'ai oublié de leur téléphoner.     *"No, I forgot to call them."*

**B**    *Rewrite each sentence in the passé composé.*

1. Elles font trois kilomètres à pied. _____

2. Elles marchent avec leurs copines. _____

3. Elles mettent des baskets (*tennis shoes, sneakers*).

   _____

4. Je suis très content. _____

5. Je reçois un courriel de ma sœur. _____

6. Elle décide de venir me voir. _____

7. Elle prend son billet d'avion. _____

8. Vous lisez beaucoup d'articles. _____

9. Nous préparons le petit déjeuner. _____

10. Nous achetons des croissants. _____

11. Tu réfléchis à ton avenir. _____

12. Il attend ses amis. _____

13. Nous comprenons le professeur. _____

14. Ils rejoignent leurs amis. _____

15. Ils produisent du fromage. _____

16. Nous téléchargeons un programme. _____

17. Il recommande un logiciel. _____

18. Tu entends un bruit. _____

19. Elle finit son travail. _____

20. La police suit le taxi. _____

**C**    *Create sentences in the passé composé from the following strings of elements.*

1. ma sœur / jouer au basket-ball / au parc

   _____

2. les étudiants / étudier / toute la journée

   _____

3. le public / applaudir / après le spectacle

   _____

4. je / vendre / ma vieille voiture _____

5. nous / mettre la table / pour dîner _____

6. elle / apprendre / les théorèmes _____

7. ils / boire / un café _____

8. vous / vivre / en France _____

9. tu / écrire / un courriel _____

10. le consultant / rédiger / un document _____

11. nous / apercevoir / un changement d'attitude

_____

12. je / courir / cinq kilomètres _____

13. les soldats / détruire / la base de l'ennemi

_____

14. les citoyens / fuir / devant l'assaut _____

15. nous / voir / un très bon film _____

16. je / vouloir / sortir _____

17. le chef / pouvoir / comprendre ce problème

_____

18. elles / avoir besoin / de notre aide _____

19. tout le monde / être / en retard _____

20. je / faire / la grasse matinée _____

## Passé Composé in the Negative with avoir

In negative sentences, **ne** (elided to **n'** before a vowel) precedes the auxiliary verb, and **pas** or any other negative word follows it—except **personne**, which follows the participle. Study the placement of the negative words in the following examples of verbs conjugated with **avoir**.

| **parler** *to speak* | |
|---|---|
| je n'ai pas parlé | nous n'avons pas parlé |
| tu n'as pas parlé | vous n'avez pas parlé |
| il/elle/on n'a pas parlé | ils/elles n'ont pas parlé |

| **réussir** *to succeed* | |
|---|---|
| je n'ai jamais réussi | nous n'avons jamais réussi |
| tu n'as jamais réussi | vous n'avez jamais réussi |
| il/elle/on n'a jamais réussi | ils/elles n'ont jamais réussi |

**vendre** *to sell*

| | |
|---|---|
| je n'ai rien vendu | nous n'avons rien vendu |
| tu n'as rien vendu | vous n'avez rien vendu |
| il/elle/on n'a rien vendu | ils/elles n'ont rien vendu |

**recevoir** *to receive*

| | |
|---|---|
| je n'ai reçu personne | nous n'avons reçu personne |
| tu n'as reçu personne | vous n'avez reçu personne |
| il/elle/on n'a reçu personne | ils/elles n'ont reçu personne |

**D**  *Rewrite each negative sentence in the passé composé.* **Avoir** *is the auxiliary verb for each one.*

1. Je ne comprends pas. _____

2. Nous ne voyons personne. _____

3. Ils n'achètent rien. _____

4. Tu n'interromps jamais. _____

5. Elle ne fait jamais la grasse matinée.

   _____

6. Vous ne suivez pas la route. _____

7. Cette idée n'intéresse personne. _____

8. Elles ne lisent rien. _____

9. Tu ne télécharges jamais de programmes.

   _____

10. Elle ne mange rien. _____

11. Je ne finis pas. _____

12. Ce pays ne produit rien. _____

13. Je n'attends personne. _____

14. Ils ne promettent rien. _____

15. Vous ne conduisez jamais. _____

## Passé Composé with Auxiliary Verb **être**

Some French verbs form the passé composé with **être** rather than **avoir**. This includes a number of French intransitive verbs of motion plus a few French verbs that describe a change in state. Intransitive verbs cannot take a direct object. When the passé composé is formed with **être**, the past participle agrees in gender and number with the subject. Study the passé composé of **aller** *to go*.

| aller  *to go* | |
| --- | --- |
| je **suis** all**é(e)** | nous **sommes** all**é(e)s** |
| tu **es** all**é(e)** | vous **êtes** all**é(e)(s)** |
| il **est** all**é** | ils **sont** all**és** |
| elle **est** all**ée** | elles **sont** all**ées** |

In the conjugation above, the letters in parentheses represent possible agreements. In other words, **vous** can have four possible forms, as shown by the underlined endings below.

- If **vous** refers to one male, you write **vous êtes allé**.
- If **vous** refers to one female, you write **vous êtes allée**.
- If **vous** refers to two or more males or to a group of males and females, you write **vous êtes allés**.
- If **vous** refers to two or more females, you write **vous êtes allées**.[1]

The following verbs of motion are conjugated with **être** as the auxiliary in the passé composé.

| INFINITIVE | PASSÉ COMPOSÉ |
| --- | --- |
| arriver | je suis **arrivé(e)** |
| descendre | je suis **descendu(e)** |
| entrer | je suis **entré(e)** |
| monter | je suis **monté(e)** |
| partir | je suis **parti(e)** |
| rentrer | je suis **rentré(e)** |
| rester | je suis **resté(e)** |
| retourner | je suis **retourné(e)** |
| sortir | je suis **sorti(e)** |
| tomber | je suis **tombé(e)** |
| venir | je suis **venu(e)** |

The verbs listed above are also conjugated with **être** when a prefix is added.

| INFINITIVE | PASSÉ COMPOSÉ | ENGLISH MEANING |
| --- | --- | --- |
| redescendre | je suis **redescendu(e)** | *I went back down(stairs)* |
| remonter | je suis **remonté(e)** | *I went back up(stairs)* |
| repartir | je suis **reparti(e)** | *I left again* |
| ressortir | je suis **ressorti(e)** | *I went out again* |
| revenir | je suis **revenu(e)** | *I came back* |

Other verbs conjugated with **être** in the passé composé are the following.

| INFINITIVE | PASSÉ COMPOSÉ | ENGLISH MEANING |
| --- | --- | --- |
| devenir | il est **devenu** / elle est **devenue** | *he/she became* |
| mourir | il est **mort** / elle est **morte** | *he/she died* |
| naître | il est **né** / elle est **née** | *he/she was born* |

---

[1]In contemporary usage, the past participle is plural when the subject **on** means *we*: **On est partis tout de suite.** *We left right away.*

## Passé Composé in the Negative with **être**

The negative of the passé composé with **être** follows the same rules as the negative of the passé composé with **avoir**. Ne (elided to **n'** before a vowel) precedes the auxiliary verb, and **pas** or any other negative word follows it. Study the placement of the negative words in the following examples of verbs conjugated with **être**.

| | |
|---|---|
| Elle **n'est pas** redescendue. | *She didn't come back downstairs.* |
| Je **ne suis jamais** allé au Sénégal. | *I have never gone to Senegal.* |
| Ils **ne sont plus** venus nous voir. | *They didn't come to see us anymore.* |
| Il **n'est pas encore** reparti. | *He hasn't set out again yet.* |

# Verbs Conjugated with **avoir** or **être**

Several of the verbs conjugated with **être** in the passé composé can be used transitively as well as intransitively. When they have a direct object, they are conjugated with **avoir**, not with **être**. Note that when these verbs are used transitively, the past participle does *not* agree with the subject.

- **monter** *to go/bring up,* **descendre** *to go/bring down*

| | |
|---|---|
| —Est-ce que tu **as monté** le courrier? | *"Did you bring up the mail?"* |
| —Oui, et j'**ai descendu** les vieux journaux. | *"Yes, and I brought down the old newspapers."* |
| Le train **a monté** la pente. | *The train went up the slope.* |
| Elle **a descendu** l'escalier. | *She went down the stairs.* |

- **entrer** *to go/come in, enter,* **rentrer** *to return, go back,* **sortir** *to go out*

| | |
|---|---|
| Je **n'ai pas encore entré** les données. | *I haven't yet entered the data.* |
| Tu **n'as pas rentré** le chat? | *Didn't you bring the cat in?* |
| Nous **avons sorti** les ordures. | *We took out the garbage.* |

---

### ATTENTION! **passer**

The verb **passer** has several meanings. It is conjugated with **être** in the passé composé when it means *to come by, to stop by, to visit, to be over.*

| | |
|---|---|
| L'autobus **est** déjà **passé**. | *The bus came and went already.* |
| Je **suis passée** te voir, mais tu étais sorti. | *I stopped by to see you, but you were out.* |
| Ils **sont passés** nous prendre hier. | *They came by to pick us up yesterday.* |
| La crise **est passée**. | *The crisis is over.* |
| Le temps **est passé** lentement. | *The time passed slowly.* |
| Son angine **est passée**. | *Her throat infection is over.* |

In its other meanings, for example, *to take/pass (a test), to spend time,* or *to go past,* **passer** is conjugated with **avoir**.

| | |
|---|---|
| Elle **a passé** son permis de conduire. | *She took her driving test.* |
| J'**ai passé** un mois au Tahiti. | *I spent a month in Tahiti.* |

**E**  *Rewrite each sentence in the passé composé.* **Être** *is the auxiliary verb for each one.*

1. Jean arrive à huit heures. _____

2. Michèle ne part pas aujourd'hui. _____

3. Mes amis viennent me voir. _____

4. Qui sort? _____

5. Nous n'allons jamais en ville. _____

6. Les autres rentrent. _____

7. Ma cousine devient programmeuse. _____

8. Le train ne passe pas. _____

9. Mes tantes descendent faire le marché.

   _____

10. Mon chien meurt. _____

11. Mes copines entrent dans le restaurant.

   _____

12. Quand est-ce qu'elle revient? _____

13. Pourquoi est-ce qu'elles ne restent pas?

   _____

14. La petite fille tombe. _____

15. Vous ne ressortez pas, vous autres. _____

**F**  *Create sentences in the passé composé from the following strings of elements. For the auxiliary, some verbs are conjugated with* **être** *and some are conjugated with* **avoir**.

1. mon frère / jouer du violon / au concert

   _____

2. nos cousins / arriver / du Canada _____

3. le train / entrer / en gare _____

4. les voyageurs / attendre / sur le quai _____

5. les passagers / monter / dans le train _____

6. chacun / chercher / sa place _____

7. le train / partir / avec un quart d'heure de retard

   _____

8. ma tante / venir / me voir _____

9. elle / m'apporter / des livres _____

10. nous / manger / ensemble _____

11. je / rester / à la maison _____

12. je / lire / un livre _____

13. quelques amis / me téléphoner _____

14. ils / m'inviter / à sortir avec eux _____

15. je / ne pas pouvoir / les accompagner

    _____

16. je / ne pas quitter / mon appartement

    _____

17. je / finir / mon travail _____

18. Christine / perdre / sa montre _____

19. elle / retourner / au bureau pour la chercher

    _____

20. elle / revenir / avec sa montre _____

## Uses of the Passé Composé

The passé composé indicates that an action is complete in the past or that it happened once.

> Hier j'ai perdu un billet de cent euros.  *Yesterday I lost a one hundred euro bill.*

The passé composé, like the English present perfect, is used to express an action that happened in the past but is seen as having an effect on the present.

> Je vois que tu as acheté une nouvelle voiture.  *I see that you have bought a new car.*

English also uses the present perfect to express actions begun in the past and continuing into the present, but French uses the present tense in those cases.

> Il est à Paris depuis un an.  *He has been in Paris for a year.*

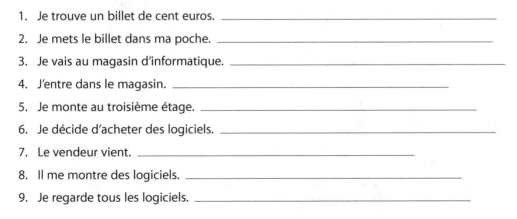

**G**  *Rewrite each sentence in the passé composé. The exercise includes both **être** and **avoir** verbs.*

1. Je trouve un billet de cent euros. _____

2. Je mets le billet dans ma poche. _____

3. Je vais au magasin d'informatique. _____

4. J'entre dans le magasin. _____

5. Je monte au troisième étage. _____

6. Je décide d'acheter des logiciels. _____

7. Le vendeur vient. _____

8. Il me montre des logiciels. _____

9. Je regarde tous les logiciels. _____

10. J'en choisis trois. _____

11. Ces logiciels coûtent 98 euros. _____

12. Avec les deux euros restants je prends un café.

_____

## Agreement of the Past Participle with **avoir**

The participles of verbs conjugated with **avoir** in the passé composé agree with the direct object, but only when the direct object *precedes* the verb. This occurs most often with a direct object pronoun.

—Est-que tu as trouvé les clés?                         *"Did you find the keys?"*
(The direct object **les clés** follows the verb; the past participle does not agree.)

—Oui, je les ai trouv**ées** au sous-sol.               *"Yes, I found them in the basement."*
(The direct object pronoun **les** precedes the verb, and the past participle agrees with the feminine plural direct object pronoun.)

—J'ai acheté une nouvelle cravate en soie.              *"I bought a new silk tie."*
(The direct object **une nouvelle cravate** follows the verb; the past participle does not agree.)

—Alors, pourquoi est-ce que tu ne l'a                   *"So then, why didn't you put it on?"*
  pas mis**e**?
(The direct object pronoun **la** precedes the verb, and the past participle agrees with the feminine singular direct object pronoun.)

The indirect object pronouns **lui** and **leur** do not cause the past participle to agree.

Nicole m'a envoyé un courriel, mais je                  *Nicole sent me an e-mail, but I haven't*
  ne lui ai pas encore répondu.                           *answered her yet.*
Je leur ai offert un cédé.                              *I gave them a CD as a gift.*

The other case where direct objects precede the verb is the relative clause.

—Est-ce qu'il a découvert une solution?                 *"Has he come up with a solution?"*
(The direct object **une solution** follows the verb; the past participle does not agree.)

—Oui, mais je n'aime pas la solution                    *"Yes, but I don't like the solution that*
  qu'il a découvert**e**.                                  *he came up with."*
(The **que** of the relative clause [elided to **qu'** before a vowel] precedes the verb, and the past participle agrees with the feminine singular relative pronoun, which replaces **la solution**.)

—Tu savais que j'ai écrit cette histoire?               *"Did you know that I wrote this story?"*
(The direct object **cette histoire** follows the verb; the past participle does not agree.)

—Prête-la-moi. Je veux lire l'histoire que              *"Lend it to me. I want to read the story*
  tu as écrit**e**.                                        *that you wrote."*
(The **que** of the relative clause precedes the verb, and the past participle agrees with the feminine singular relative pronoun, which replaces **l'histoire**.)

It is the relative pronoun **que**, not **qui**, that causes agreement of the past participle. Because the relative pronoun **qui** is the subject, not the object of its clause, it does not cause agreement of the past participle with verbs conjugated with **avoir**.

| | |
|---|---|
| Qui est la femme qui a travaillé ici? | *Who's the woman who worked here?* |
| Les étudiants qui ont réussi les examens sont très contents. | *The students who passed the exams are very happy.* |

Expressions of cost (with the verb **coûter**) and distance are not really direct objects and do not cause agreement of the past participle.

| | |
|---|---|
| les cent euros que le billet a coûté | *the one hundred euros the ticket cost* |
| les trois kilomètres que tu as couru | *the three kilometers you ran* |

Except for the relatively few past participles ending in a consonant, such as **dit, fait, mis, pris, écrit, ouvert**, etc., the agreement of the past participle is a feature of written French only. In spoken French, the agreement is heard only in the feminine singular and plural of participles ending in a consonant.

**H**  *Complete each sentence with the past participle of the verb in parentheses, paying special attention to the rules for agreement of the past participle.*

1. (ouvrir)    Voilà les fenêtres que j'ai _____.

2. (mettre)    Elle a une nouvelle robe mais elle ne l'a pas _____.

3. (connaître)    Voilà le garçon que j'ai _____ hier à la soirée.

4. (descendre)    Est-ce que les enfants sont _____?

5. (écrire)    Voici les courriels qu'elle a _____.

6. (choisir)    Tu aimes les cadeaux que j'ai _____?

7. (gagner)    Voilà la femme qui a _____ le concours.

8. (donner)    Je leur ai _____ mille euros.

9. (acheter)    Nous lui avons recommandé des actions (*stocks* [feminine]) et il les

      a _____.

10. (répondre)    Elle m'a écrit mais je ne lui ai pas encore _____.

11. (envoyer)    Est-ce que vous avez déjà _____ tous les paquets?

12. (faire)    Les fautes qu'il a _____ montrent qu'il ne parle pas très bien l'anglais.

13. (entrer)    Elle a _____ toutes les données.

14. (marcher)    Les dix kilomètres que j'ai _____ m'ont épuisé (*tired out*).

15. (découvrir)    Ces manuscrits sont intéressants et c'est Fanny qui les a

      _____.

16. (recevoir)    J'ai imprimé les courriels que j'ai _____.

# Questions in the Passé Composé

Questions in the passé composé are formed in the same way as questions in the present tense (see Chapter 3, p. 55). They may be formed by merely changing the intonation.

| | |
|---|---|
| Tu as fait le ménage? | *Have you done the housework?* |
| Tu es allé au travail aujourd'hui? | *Did you go to work today?* |

They may also be formed by the use of **est-ce que**.

| | |
|---|---|
| Est-ce que vous avez fini le projet? | *Have you finished the project?* |
| Est-ce qu'ils sont déjà arrivés? | *Have they arrived already?* |

Inversion is possible in the passé composé just as it is in the present tense. Inversion is characteristic of formal written French.

| | |
|---|---|
| As-tu fait la vaisselle? | *Have you done the dishes?* |
| Sont-ils déjà rentrés? | *Have they gotten back yet?* |

Inversion with **je** in the forms **ai-je** and **suis-je** is also possible in literary written French and in formal spoken French that imitates classical style.

| | |
|---|---|
| Ai-je compris vos mots? | *Did I understand what you said?* |
| Suis-je arrivé à temps? | *Have I arrived on time?* |

In negative questions in the passé composé using inversion, the **ne** and **pas** surround the inverted subject and verb.

| | |
|---|---|
| N'est-elle pas encore partie? | *Hasn't she left yet?* |
| N'ont-ils pas compris? | *Didn't they understand?* |

Remember that if the subject of the sentence is a noun, it cannot be placed after the verb in inversion. Instead, the corresponding pronoun is added and inverted with the verb.

| | |
|---|---|
| Le peuple n'a-t-il pas élu ce président? | *Didn't the people elect this president?* |
| Les exportations n'ont-elles pas augmenté? | *Haven't exports increased?* |
| Les prix ne sont-ils pas tombés? | *Haven't prices fallen?* |

**I**  *Rewrite each statement in two ways: first as a statement in the passé composé, then as a question in the passé composé using inversion.*

MODÈLE   Elle arrive en retard.

   *Elle est arrivée en retard.*

   *Est-elle arrivée en retard?*

1. Il vend ses actions.

   _____

   _____

2. Paulette loue un appartement.

   _____

   _____

3.  Les Chardin montent une entreprise.

    _____

    _____

4.  L'entreprise exporte des logiciels.

    _____

    _____

5.  Ils vendent leurs produits dans plusieurs pays.

    _____

    _____

6.  La compagnie ne perd pas d'argent.

    _____

    _____

7.  Les Chardin embauchent beaucoup d'employés.

    _____

    _____

8.  Les employés reçoivent des primes (*bonuses*).

    _____

    _____

9.  Je réponds à toutes vos questions.

    _____

    _____

10. Les ouvriers font grève.

    _____

    _____

11. Notre pays adopte l'euro.

    _____

    _____

12. La Pologne devient membre de l'Union Européenne.

    _____

    _____

13. Le Sénat approuve une nouvelle loi.

    _____

    _____

14. Ces trois pays signent le traité.

_____

_____

15. Les autres pays ne le signent pas.

_____

_____

---

**BUILDING SENTENCES** | **Questions: information questions, question words**

Questions beginning with question words such as *When?*, *Who?*, and *Where?* are called information questions because they ask for a piece of information, not just *yes* or *no* as an answer.

### Key question words in French

**Qui?** *Who?, Whom?*
**Qu'est-ce que?** *What?*
**Pourquoi?** *Why?*
**Comment?** *How?*
**Où?** *Where?*
**Quand?** *When?*
**Combien?** *How much?, How many?*
**Quel/Quelle** + noun**?** *Which* (noun)*?* (singular)
**Quels/Quelles** + noun**?** *Which* (noun)*?* (plural)

**Qui** can be used as either subject or object. To specify the function, **qui est-ce que** is used for the object of the verb (formal English *whom*) and **qui est-ce qui** is used for the subject of the verb (English *who*).

| | |
|---|---|
| **Qui est-ce que** vous attendez? | *Who(m) are you waiting for?* |
| **Qui est-ce qui** travaille ici? | *Who works here?* |

However, **qui est-ce qui** is not very common.

When *what* is the subject of the verb, it becomes **qu'est-ce qui**.

| | |
|---|---|
| **Qu'est-ce qui** vous tracasse? | *What is upsetting you?* |
| **Qu'est-ce qui** les intéresse? | *What interests them?* |

When *what* is the object of a preposition, it becomes **quoi**.

| | |
|---|---|
| **Sur quoi** est-ce que vous comptez? | *What are you counting on?* |
| **De quoi** est-ce qu'il s'agit? | *What's this all about?* |
| **Avec quoi** est-ce que tu as fait ça? | *What did you make that with?* |

Note that in French the preposition must *precede* the interrogative word at the beginning of the sentence. It cannot be separated from it and placed at the end of the question as it is in everyday English.

In questions where inversion is used, *what* is **que**. This question pattern is typical of formal language.

| | |
|---|---|
| **Que** voulez-vous? | *What do you want?* |
| **Qu'**a-t-il fait? | *What did he do?* |

The interrogative word **combien** is followed by **de** when it is followed by a noun.

| | |
|---|---|
| **Combien de** lait avez-vous acheté? | *How much milk did you buy?* |
| **Combien de** chèques avez-vous touchés? | *How many checks did you cash?* |

The interrogative adjective **quel** agrees in gender and number with the noun it refers to.

| | |
|---|---|
| **Quel train** avez-vous pris? | *Which train did you take?* |
| **Quels logiciels** avez-vous utilisés? | *Which software programs did you use?* |
| **Quelle route** avez-vous suivie? | *Which route did you follow?* |
| **Quelles pièces** avez-vous vues? | *What plays did you see?* |

**Quel** + a noun can be replaced by the corresponding interrogative pronoun, **lequel**, **laquelle**, **lesquels**, or **lesquelles**.

| | |
|---|---|
| —Ce cinéma passe trois films. | *"This theater is showing three films."* |
| —**Lequel** vous intéresse? | *"Which one interests you?"* |
| —J'ai essayé toutes les vestes. | *"I've tried on all the jackets."* |
| —**Laquelle** vous plaît? | *"Which one do you like?"* |
| —Il y a pas mal de musées dans cette ville. | *"There are a lot of museums in this city."* |
| —**Lesquels** méritent une visite? | *"Which ones are worth a visit?"* |
| —Ce pays a beaucoup de belles régions. | *"This country has a lot of beautiful regions."* |
| —**Lesquelles** voudriez-vous connaître? | *"Which ones would you like to visit?"* |

**J**  Using **est-ce que**, *write the information question that would have elicited each of these responses. The questions should ask about the information that is underlined.*

MODÈLE    J'ai <u>trois</u> cédéroms.

*Combien de cédéroms est-ce que tu as?*

1. Élisabeth a pris l'avion <u>de huit heures vingt</u>.

   _____

2. <u>Monsieur Tessier</u> est dans la salle d'attente.

   _____

3. Il a apporté <u>un document</u>. _____

4. Il est ici <u>parce qu'il veut vous voir</u>. _____

5. Elle travaille <u>prudemment</u>. _____

6. Les employés sont partis <u>à cinq heures et demie</u>.

   _____

7. Je fais mes études <u>en Suisse</u>. _____

8.  L'informatique l'intéresse beaucoup. _____

9.  Il y a une séance du film cet après-midi.

    _____

10. Elle reçoit beaucoup de courriels. _____

11. Il est en retard parce qu'il a manqué son train.

    _____

12. Les étudiants répondent poliment. _____

**K**  *Translation.*  *Express the following sentences in French.*

1.  *I received my airplane e-ticket by e-mail yesterday.*

    _____

2.  *We weren't able to contact them by cell phone.*

    _____

3.  *He went to the Internet café at five o'clock and she arrived at 5:30.*

    _____

    _____

4.  *You (tu) saw the Web site, didn't you?* _____

5.  *She was born in Chicago.* _____

6.  *Did you (vous) find out the flight number?*

    _____

7.  *There's all the data I entered.* _____

8.  *We wanted to play tennis.* _____

9.  *The software packages? I bought them on sale.*

    _____

10. *Did they [masculine] create a new database? [Use inversion.]*

    _____

11. *They [feminine] came to see us at the office.*

    _____

12. *Did you (tu) finish the project?* _____

## Register of Question Patterns

Information questions are complicated in French. There are several patterns that express the same question, but the register of each pattern is different. The term register refers to the social situation or level of formality of a particular sentence pattern.

The most formal way to ask an information question is with inversion.

| | |
|---|---|
| Où allez-vous cet été? | *Where are you going this summer?* |
| Quand sont-ils partis? | *When did they leave?* |

When there is a noun subject, the corresponding pronoun must be added in inversion. This structure is limited to the most formal registers of the language.

| | |
|---|---|
| Combien de cathédrales les touristes ont-ils visitées? | *How many cathedrals did the tourists visit?* |
| Pourquoi Marie n'a-t-elle pas fini son travail? | *Why didn't Marie finish her work?* |

In all registers, information questions can be formed by placing **est-ce que** after the question word.

| | |
|---|---|
| Pourquoi est-ce qu'ils ne sont pas venus? | *Why didn't they come?* |
| Comment est-ce que vous avez réussi à faire cela? | *How did you manage to do that?* |
| Quand est-ce que tu vas sortir? | *When are you going to go out?* |

In informal spoken French, **est-ce que** is often dropped when the subject is a pronoun. This usage is considered grammatically incorrect, but is very frequent in speech.

| | |
|---|---|
| Pourquoi ils ne sont pas venus? | *Why didn't they come?* |
| Comment vous avez réussi à faire cela? | *How did you manage to do that?* |
| Quand tu vas sortir? | *When are you going to go out?* |
| Où tu travailles? | *Where do you work?* |

In everyday French, the question words are often put at the end of the sentence. This pattern is increasingly frequent in speech. It can be used with either pronoun or noun subjects.

| | |
|---|---|
| Le train va partir quand? | *When is the train going to leave?* |
| Tu es allé où? | *Where did you go?* |
| Ils sont passés combien de fois? | *How many times did they come by?* |
| Il est quelle heure? | *What time is it?* |

**Quoi** is used for *what* in this pattern, as follows.

| | |
|---|---|
| Les touristes ont vu quoi? | *What did the tourists see?* |
| Tu as fait quoi aujourd'hui? | *What did you do today?* |

Note that **pourquoi** rarely appears at the end of a question.

In very informal registers, noun subjects may follow the question word, with the corresponding pronoun serving as the grammatical subject of the sentence.

| | |
|---|---|
| Ils ont vu quoi, les touristes? | *What did the tourists see?* |
| Elle est comment, ta sœur? | *What does your sister look like?* |
| Ils sont arrivés quand, les invités? | *When did the guests arrive?* |

If there is no noun subject, the disjunctive pronoun may be added.

| | |
|---|---|
| Tu es allé où, toi? | *Where did you go?* |

Let's examine one information question with a noun subject in all the registers. Study the different ways of asking *When did the guests arrive?*

| VERY FORMAL FRENCH | Quand les invités sont-ils arrivés? |
| NEUTRAL PATTERN, ACCEPTABLE IN ALL REGISTERS | Quand est-ce que les invités sont arrivés? |
| INFORMAL PATTERN, VERY COMMON BUT GRAMMATICALLY INCORRECT | Et les invités, quand ils sont arrivés? |
| COLLOQUIAL PATTERN, QUESTION WORD AT END | Les invités sont arrivés quand? |
| INFORMAL COLLOQUIAL PATTERN, QUESTION WORD AT END, NOUN SUBJECT FOLLOWING QUESTION WORD | Ils sont arrivés quand, les invités? |

**L** *Rewrite each question with* **est-ce que** *in two ways: first as a formal question with inversion, then as a colloquial question with the interrogative word after the verb and the noun subject at the end.*

MODÈLE    Quand est-ce que Serge et Antoinette sont sortis?

*Quand Serge et Antoinette sont-ils sortis?*

*Ils sont sortis quand, Serge et Antoinette?*

1. À quelle heure est-ce que leur autocar arrive à la gare routière (*bus terminal*)?

   _____

   _____

2. Dans quel immeuble est-ce que sa famille habite?

   _____

   _____

3. Où est-ce que Mme Ducros fait ses achats?

   _____

   _____

4. Combien d'heures par jour est-ce que le petit Pierre passe devant son ordinateur?

   _____

   _____

5. Qu'est-ce que tu fais pour t'amuser?

   _____

   _____

6. Quelle sorte d'emploi est-ce que Jean-Luc cherche?

   _____

   _____

7. Comment est-ce que ce mot se prononce?

   _____

   _____

8. Quel clavier (*keyboard*) est-ce que ce programmeur préfère?

   _____

   _____

9. Avec qui est-ce que Marie-Claire est sortie?

   _____

   _____

10. Sur qui est-ce que notre chef compte?

    _____

    _____

---

**BUILDING SENTENCES** | **Placement of adverbs in the passé composé**

## Adverbs of Place

We have seen that negative words except for **personne** precede the past participle in the passé composé. **Nulle part** *nowhere* also follows the past participle.

| Cet été on n'est allés **nulle part**. | *This summer we didn't go anywhere.* |

Adverbs of place such as **ici, là, là-bas, dedans, dehors**, and **partout** follow the past participle in the passé composé.

| Il a travaillé **ici**. | *He worked here.* |
| Je les ai vus **là-bas**. | *I saw them over there.* |
| Nous avons mangé **dehors**. | *We ate outside.* |
| Ils ont cherché **partout**. | *They've looked everywhere.* |

## Adverbs of Time

Adverbs of time do not all behave alike. The adverbs **aujourd'hui, hier, avant-hier, tout à l'heure, tôt, de bonne heure, avant, après, depuis**, and **il y a longtemps** follow the past participle.

| —Elle a travaillé **hier**? | *"Did she work yesterday?"* |
| —Oui, et elle a travaillé **avant-hier** aussi. | *"Yes, and she worked the day before yesterday too."* |
| —Et elle n'est pas venue **aujourd'hui**? | *"And she didn't come today?"* |
| —Si. Je l'ai croisée **tout à l'heure**. | *"Yes, she did. I ran across her a little while ago."* |

The adverbs **déjà** and **toujours** *precede* the past participle. Note that **déjà** often means *ever* in addition to *already* and **toujours** often means *still* in addition to *always*.

| | |
|---|---|
| —Est-elle **déjà** allée en Belgique? | *"Has she already gone to Belgium?"* |
| —Non, mais elle a **toujours** voulu connaître ce pays. | *"No, but she has always wanted to visit that country."* |

Other adverbs of time can either precede or follow the past participle. Among the most frequent are **aussitôt**, **d'abord**, **bientôt**, **encore**, **enfin**, **longtemps**, **maintenant**, **parfois**, **quelquefois**, **rarement**, **récemment**, **souvent**, and **tout de suite**. Note the position of these adverbs in the following examples.

| | |
|---|---|
| —Tu es **enfin** rentrée, Janine? | *"Have you finally come back, Janine?"* |
| —Oui. Je suis restée trop **longtemps** à la bibliothèque. | *"Yes, I stayed at the library too long."* |
| —Tu es **parfois** passé la voir? | *"Did you sometimes go to see her?"* |
| —Oui, je suis allé **récemment** chez elle. | *"Yes, I went to her house recently."* |
| —Tu as **souvent** conduit la voiture de ton père? | *"Have you often driven your father's car?"* |
| —Pas **souvent**. Il me l'a prêté **quelquefois**. | *"Not often. He has lent it to me sometimes."* |

## Adverbs of Quantity

Adverbs of quantity such as **beaucoup**, **tant**, and **assez** most often precede the past participle.

| | |
|---|---|
| —Moi, j'ai **beaucoup** mangé. | *"I ate a lot."* |
| —Et moi, j'ai **trop** bu. | *"And I drank too much."* |
| —Il a **tant** parlé! | *"He talked so much!"* |
| —Oui, et j'ai **assez** entendu. | *"Yes, and I have heard enough."* |

## Adverbs of Manner

The adverbs of manner **bien**, **mal**, **mieux**, **peut-être**, and **sans doute** precede the past participle in the passé composé. The adverbs **ainsi**, **plutôt**, **vite**, and **volontiers** usually precede the participle, but may follow it. Adverbs ending in **-ment** may also either precede or follow the past participle.

| | |
|---|---|
| —Elle a très **bien** expliqué le problème. | *"She has explained the problem very well."* |
| —Oui, elle a **certainement** fait un grand effort. | *"Yes, she certainly put forth a great effort."* |
| —Il est **vite** revenu. | *"He came back quickly."* |
| —Il a **peut-être** compris qu'il était trop tard. | *"He probably realized that it was too late."* |

The adverbs **n'importe comment**, **exprès** *on purpose*, and **ensemble** *together* follow the past participle.

—Les enfants ont fait un vrai gâchis **ensemble**.
    *"The children made a real mess together."*

—Ne te fâche pas. Ils ne l'ont pas fait **exprès**.
    *"Don't get angry. They didn't do it on purpose."*

Most adverbs ending in **-ment** can either stand between the auxiliary and the past participle or follow the participle.

Ils se sont **fréquemment** vus. ⎫
Ils se sont vus **fréquemment**. ⎭
    *They saw each other frequently.*

**M**   *Create sentences in the passé composé from the following strings of elements. Be sure to place each adverb correctly. There may be more than one correct placement of the adverb.*

1. les cousins / manger / ensemble _____

2. je / acheter / trop _____

3. nous / passer nos vacances / dans le Midi / récemment

_____

4. les voisins / déménager / certainement

_____

5. les enfants / le faire / exprès _____

6. vous / expliquer notre difficulté / très bien

_____

7. ils / partir / vite _____

8. elle / perdre sa clé / peut-être _____

9. je / préparer le goûter / n'importe comment

_____

10. il / refuser de nous aider / sûrement _____

11. tu / répondre / tout de suite _____

12. nous / dîner / dehors _____

13. je / ne pas le voir / ici _____

14. elles / rester / là-bas _____

15. je / travailler / assez _____

16. nous / voir / beaucoup _____

17. ils / arriver / déjà _____

18. elle / comprendre / sans doute _____

19. il / entrer / les données / souvent _____

**BUILDING SENTENCES**   **The passive voice**

The passive voice is similar in both formation and function in French and English. The passive voice serves to remove the focus from the performer of the action to the action itself. To understand this, it is helpful to see passive sentences as deriving from active ones.

ACTIVE VOICE

Paul a réparé les ordinateurs.                    *Paul repaired the computers.*

PASSIVE VOICE

Les ordinateurs ont été réparés.                  *The computers were repaired.*

Note that the performer of the action can be added to a passive sentence in a phrase beginning with **par**. This is called *the agent*.

Les ordinateurs ont été réparés **par Paul**.     *The computers were repaired by Paul.*

In the French passive voice, the past participle agrees in gender and number with the grammatical subject.

La bicyclette a été vendue.                        *The bicycle was sold.*
Les bicyclettes ont été vendues.                   *The bicycles were sold.*

The passive voice exists in all tenses.

Les ordinateurs sont réparés par Paul.             *The computers are repaired by Paul.*
Les ordinateurs vont être réparés par             *The computers are going to be repaired*
   Paul.                                              *by Paul.*

After verbs of mental activity, the agent in a passive sentence may be introduced by **de** instead of **par**.

Ce médecin est admiré **de** tous ses            *This doctor is admired by all his colleagues.*
   collègues.
Mon grand-père était aimé **de** tous les         *My grandfather was loved by all the*
   enfants du quartier.                               *children in the neighborhood.*

Although the passive voice in English is relatively frequent, the French passive voice belongs more to the written language than to everyday speech. To deemphasize the performer of the action, spoken French usually uses the pronoun **on** or **ils**. Note that in passive sentences with **on** or **ils** as the subject, an agent phrase beginning with **par** cannot be added.

Ici on parle français.                             *French is spoken here.*
Ils ont réparé les ordinateurs.                    *They've repaired the computers.*

**N**  *Rewrite the following active sentences in the passive voice, using an agent phrase.
Retain the tense of the original sentence.*

MODÈLE    Mon cousin a acheté cette tablette.

*Cette tablette a été achetée par mon cousin.*

1. La secrétaire a ouvert le bureau.

   _____

2. Le propriétaire a sauvegardé (*preserved*) cette entreprise.

   _____

3. Les commerçants étalent (*display*) les marchandises.

   _____

4. Les touristes achètent ces parfums.

   _____

5. Les consultants ont étudié le marché.

   _____

6. Cette usine fabrique des chaussures.

   _____

7. Marianne a vendu les actions.

   _____

8. Le client a réglé la note (*bill*).

   _____

9. L'employée a envoyé un chèque postal.

   _____

10. Les Poirier vont ouvrir un compte de chèques.

    _____

11. Les étrangers apprécient ce fromage.

    _____

12. Les entreprises exportent ce fromage dans le monde entier.

    _____

13. Le gouvernement a construit une nouvelle ligne de chemin de fer.

    _____

14. Les entreprises utilisent les transports routiers (*highway*).

    _____

15. L'expéditeur doit remplir une déclaration pour la douane.

    _____

16. La banque a accordé un prêt à cette entreprise.

_____

17. Le patron va embaucher cet ouvrier.

_____

18. Les spécialistes en marketing ont mené une enquête auprès du public.

_____

19. Le débiteur va acquitter cette facture.

_____

20. Nos agents ont trouvé des marchés étrangers pour nos produits.

_____

**O** _The following sentences are in the passive voice and do not contain an agent phrase beginning with_ **par.** _Rewrite each one in the active voice with_ **on** _as the subject._

MODÈLE     Le français est parlé ici.

_On parle français ici._

1. Ces journaux sont lus. _____

2. Les journalistes sont estimés. _____

3. Leurs articles sont discutés. _____

4. Votre courriel a été reçu. _____

5. Votre courriel a été imprimé. _____

6. Votre courriel a été réparti à tout le monde.

_____

7. Nos ordinateurs ont été remplacés. _____

8. De nouveaux programmes ont été installés.

_____

9. De nouveaux logiciels ont été achetés.

_____

10. Un cours de formation a été organisé. _____

11. Une succursale a été ouverte. _____

12. Un informaticien est cherché. _____

13. Des spécialistes en bureautique ont été consultés.

_____

14. Des meubles ont été achetés. _____

15. L'ouverture du bureau a été annoncé. _____

**P** **Translation.** *Express the following sentences in French.*

1. *Society has been transformed by technology.*

   _____

2. *The files are opened by the programmer* [masculine].

   _____

3. *The skyscraper is going to be designed by a noted architect.*

   _____

4. *Those pictures were painted by Manet.*

   _____

5. *Hors d'oeuvres were served at 8:00.*

   _____

6. *The money was withdrawn from the ATM* (GAB = guichet automatique de banque).
   [Use **on**.]

   _____

7. *The spy novels were translated into English by the author himself.*

   _____

8. *The use of cell phones is prohibited.*

   _____

9. *Our decision should be made tomorrow.*

   _____

10. *The report was written by the marketing consultant* [feminine].

   _____

# The Imperfect;
# The Imperfect vs.
# the Passé Composé

## The Imperfect Tense

The imperfect tense is used to describe background actions or situations in the past rather than events. Its formation is simple—the imperfect endings are the same for all verbs. The endings of the imperfect tense are added to the stem of the **nous** form of the present tense (the **nous** form minus the **-ons** ending).

Examine the imperfect stems of the following regular and irregular verbs.

| INFINITIVE | **nous** FORM PRESENT TENSE | IMPERFECT STEM |
|---|---|---|
| parler | nous parlons | parl- |
| finir | nous finissons | finiss- |
| vendre | nous vendons | vend- |
| recevoir | nous recevons | recev- |
| étudier | nous étudions | étudi- |
| boire | nous buvons | buv- |
| lire | nous lisons | lis- |
| avoir | nous avons | av- |
| craindre | nous craignons | craign- |

Study the conjugation of these sample verbs in the imperfect.

**parler** *to speak*

| je parl**ais** | nous parl**ions** |
|---|---|
| tu parl**ais** | vous parl**iez** |
| il/elle/on parl**ait** | ils/elles parl**aient** |

**finir** *to finish*

| je finiss**ais** | nous finiss**ions** |
|---|---|
| tu finiss**ais** | vous finiss**iez** |
| il/elle/on finiss**ait** | ils/elles finiss**aient** |

#### vendre  *to sell*

| | |
|---|---|
| je vend**ais** | nous vend**ions** |
| tu vend**ais** | vous vend**iez** |
| il/elle/on vend**ait** | ils/elles vend**aient** |

#### boire  *to drink*

| | |
|---|---|
| je buv**ais** | nous buv**ions** |
| tu buv**ais** | vous buv**iez** |
| il/elle/on buv**ait** | ils/elles buv**aient** |

#### craindre  *to fear*

| | |
|---|---|
| je craign**ais** | nous craign**ions** |
| tu craign**ais** | vous craign**iez** |
| il/elle/on craign**ait** | ils/elles craign**aient** |

#### faire  *to do, make*

| | |
|---|---|
| je fais**ais** | nous fais**ions** |
| tu fais**ais** | vous fais**iez** |
| il/elle/on fais**ait** | ils/elles fais**aient** |

#### prendre  *to take*

| | |
|---|---|
| je pren**ais** | nous pren**ions** |
| tu pren**ais** | vous pren**iez** |
| il/elle/on pren**ait** | ils/elles pren**aient** |

#### avoir  *to have*

| | |
|---|---|
| j'av**ais** | nous av**ions** |
| tu av**ais** | vous av**iez** |
| il/elle/on av**ait** | ils/elles av**aient** |

**-Er** verbs whose imperfect stems end in **-i** double the letter **i** in the **nous** and **vous** forms of the imperfect.

#### étudier  *to study*

| | |
|---|---|
| j'étudiais | nous étud**ii**ons |
| tu étudiais | vous étud**ii**ez |
| il/elle/on étudiait | ils/elles étudiaient |

**-Er** verbs ending in **-cer** have a **ç** before those imperfect endings that begin with **a**.

#### commencer  *to begin*

| | |
|---|---|
| je commen**ç**ais | nous commencions |
| tu commen**ç**ais | vous commenciez |
| il/elle/on commen**ç**ait | ils/elles commen**ç**aient |

**-Er** verbs ending in **-ger** have **ge** before those imperfect endings that begin with **a**.

| **manger** *to eat* | |
| --- | --- |
| je man**ge**ais | nous mangions |
| tu man**ge**ais | vous mangiez |
| il/elle/on man**ge**ait | ils/elles man**ge**aient |

The only verb in French with an irregular imperfect stem is **être**. The endings, however, are regular.

| **être** *to be* | |
| --- | --- |
| j'ét**ais** | nous ét**ions** |
| tu ét**ais** | vous ét**iez** |
| il/elle/on ét**ait** | ils/elles ét**aient** |

 *Rewrite each phrase in the imperfect.*

1. elle mange _____

2. je choisis _____

3. il reçoit _____

4. nous vendons _____

5. vous sauvegardez _____

6. tu commences _____

7. elle paie _____

8. ils nettoient _____

9. je programme _____

10. on finit _____

11. tu bois _____

12. elles prennent _____

13. vous êtes _____

14. j'ai _____

15. il sait _____

16. nous sommes _____

17. elles ont _____

18. nous étudions _____

19. ils font _____

20. elle va _____

21. tu convaincs _____

22. il croit _____

23. tu veux _____

24. ils peuvent _____

25. elle vient _____

**B** *Complete each sentence with the correct imperfect form of the verb in parentheses.*

1. (lire)      Je _____ le journal.

2. (être)      Elle _____ toujours en retard.

3. (jouer)      Vous _____ au golf en été.

4. (monter)      Les prix _____.

5. (travailler)      Ils _____ dans un magasin de musique.

6. (ranger)      Le vendredi je _____ mes affaires.

7. (remplacer)      L'entreprise _____ les ouvriers.

8. (boire)      Je _____ mon café.

9. (prendre)      Elles _____ des croissants le matin.

10. (avoir)      Tu _____ faim.

11. (devoir)      Qu'est-ce qu'il _____ faire?

12. (neiger)      Il _____ beaucoup en hiver.

13. (voir)      Je _____ mes amis après les cours.

14. (apprendre)      Nous _____ beaucoup dans la classe de Mlle Verdier.

15. (aller)      Tu _____ beaucoup au cinéma.

16. (ouvrir)      Elles _____ les fenêtres en automne.

17. (tourner)      Le régisseur _____ un film.

18. (dire)      Nous lui _____ quelque chose.

19. (être)      Vous _____ en vacances.

20. (nager)      Avant je _____ souvent.

21. (tenir)      Tu nous _____ au courant.

22. (faire)      Il _____ beau ce matin-là.

23. (savoir)      Je n'en _____ rien.

24. (attendre)      Nous _____ le bus devant le cinéma.

25. (éteindre)      Il n'_____ jamais la lumière.

26. (réussir)      Elle _____ à tous ses examens.

27. (offrir)      Mes parents m'_____ beaucoup de cadeaux.

28. (établir)      Le gouvernement _____ un nouveau règlement.

29. (produire)      Ce pays _____ beaucoup de vin dans le passé.

30. (fuir)      Il _____ ses responsabilités.

**C**  *Rewrite each sentence, changing the verb from present tense to imperfect.*

1. Je veux vous accompagner. _____

2. Qu'est-ce que vous dites? _____

3. Il fait chaud au mois de septembre. _____

4. Ils boivent du jus de pomme. _____

5. Quelque chose sent mauvais. _____

6. Il craint le rhume. _____

7. Tu achètes des logiciels. _____

8. J'écris des courriels. _____

9. Elle ne peut pas trouver un travail. _____

10. Nous allons en avion. _____

11. Tu comprends les poèmes. _____

12. Ils ont peur. _____

13. Il doit partir. _____

14. Tu songes à tes vacances. _____

15. Elle place ses affaires sur le sofa. _____

16. Cet enfant suit bien à l'école. _____

17. Tu conduis beaucoup. _____

18. Vous êtes pressé. _____

19. Nous commençons nos études. _____

20. Je dors bien. _____

## Uses of the Imperfect Tense

The imperfect tense is used to describe conditions existing in the past or past actions seen as backgrounds rather than events, actions that help set the scene. Here are some specific examples of how the imperfect is used.

### Time

The imperfect—not the passé composé—is used in clauses that tell the time at which something happened in the past. This includes not only clock time but also time words such as **tard**, **tôt**.

| | |
|---|---|
| Il **était** cinq heures quand nous sommes partis. | *It was five o'clock when we left.* |
| Il **était** tard quand je suis sorti. | *It was late when I went out.* |
| Il **faisait** déjà noir quand on a quitté le bureau. | *It was already dark when we left the office.* |

## Weather

The imperfect is usually (but not always) used to describe weather conditions existing in the past.

| | |
|---|---|
| **Il pleuvait** quand on est rentrés. | *It was raining when we got home.* |
| **Il faisait beau** quand les enfants jouaient dans le jardin. | *The weather was nice when the children were playing in the garden.* |

Weather phenomena can also be seen as events, and in those cases they are expressed in the passé composé, and do not serve as backgrounds for other actions.

| | |
|---|---|
| Hier **il a neigé**. | *It snowed yesterday.* |

**D**   *Time and weather. Rewrite each sentence, changing background verbs from the present tense to the imperfect and changing verbs telling what happened to the passé composé.*

MODÈLE     Il est une heure quand ils rentrent.

   *Il était une heure quand ils sont rentrés.*

1. Il est midi quand j'arrive. _____

2. Il fait soleil quand on part au pique-nique.

   _____

3. Quand ils viennent, il est déjà tard. _____

4. Il neige quand je sors de chez moi. _____

5. Il fait noir quand l'avion décolle. _____

6. Il y a des éclairs quand l'avion atterrit. _____

7. Il pleut à verse (*pouring*) quand la mariée arrive à l'église.

   _____

8. Le temps est couvert quand on se met en route.

   _____

9. Il fait du vent quand on quitte le parc.

   _____

10. Il est tard quand elle me téléphone. _____

11. Il est deux heures quand la séance commence.

    _____

12. Le temps est à l'orage (*it was starting to thunder*) quand la voiture tombe en panne.

    _____

13. Quand on sort du théâtre, les rues sont mouillées.

    _____

14. Il est neuf heures et quart quand le train entre en gare.

    _____

## Conditions

The imperfect is used to describe conditions in the past.

| | |
|---|---|
| Le métro **était** très bondé et je n'ai pas pu monter. | *The subway was very crowded and I couldn't get on.* |
| On a mangé à la maison parce que tous les restaurants **étaient** fermés. | *We ate at home because all the restaurants were closed.* |
| À cette époque-là, beaucoup d'immigrés **arrivaient** dans le pays. Ils **cherchaient** du travail pour améliorer leur vie. La population du pays **montait** vite. | *At that time, many immigrants were arriving in the country. They were looking for work to improve their lives. The population of the country was rising rapidly.* |

## Description

The imperfect is used to describe things and people in the past.

| | |
|---|---|
| Sa maison **était** très grande. Il y **avait** un joli jardin tout autour. | *His house was very big. There was a pretty garden surrounding it.* |
| Les étudiants **étaient** très nerveux parce que leurs cours **étaient** très difficiles. | *The students were very nervous because their courses were very difficult.* |
| Cette femme **s'appelait** Christine Duhamel. Elle **était** française et elle **travaillait** au Ministère de la Défense. | *That woman's name was Christine Duhamel. She was French and she worked at the Ministry of Defense.* |

**E**   *Rewrite each sentence in the imperfect to describe this childhood home in the past.*

1. Nous avons une maison à la campagne.

   _____

2. C'est une maison à trois étages.

   _____

3. Moi, je dors dans la mansarde (*attic*).

   _____

4. Il y a un jardin autour de la maison.

   _____

5. Ma mère y cultive des légumes.

   _____

6. Mes grand-parents habitent avec nous.

   _____

7. La maison est entourée d'une clôture (*fence*).

   _____

8. Nous gardons notre voiture dans le garage.

   _____

9. Mon père travaille dans le village.

_____

10. Ma mère reste à la maison avec les enfants.

_____

11. Nous mangeons dans la salle à manger.

_____

12. La salle à manger est au rez-de-chaussée.

_____

13. On utilise le salon seulement pour recevoir (*to have company*).

_____

14. Ma sœur et moi nous faisons nos devoirs dans nos chambres.

_____

15. Nous aimons beaucoup notre maison.

_____

## Repeated Actions

The imperfect is used to label repeated actions in the past when the focus is on the actions themselves rather than on when the actions began or ended. Adverbs and adverbial phrases such as **toujours, tous les jours/mois/ans, toutes les semaines, souvent, chaque fois, d'habitude, généralement,** etc. indicate repeated actions.

| | |
|---|---|
| Quand j'**étais** jeune ma famille et moi, nous **allions** au bord de la mer tous les étés. | *When I was young, my family and I used to go to the seashore every summer.* |
| Il me **téléphonait** souvent et il me **posait** des questions. | *He would often call me and ask me questions.* |
| Elle **oubliait** toujours ce que je lui **disais**. | *She always forgot what I would tell her.* |
| Chaque fois qu'il **venait** chez moi, il **restait** à dîner. | *Every time he would come to my house, he would stay for dinner.* |

**F**    ***Repeated actions in the imperfect.*** *Rewrite each sentence in the imperfect, using the adverbs and adverbial phrases of frequency in parentheses.*

MODÈLE    Christine m'envoie des messages électroniques. (tous les jours)

     *Christine m'envoyait des messages électroniques tous les jours.*

1. J'apporte des bonbons à mes grand-parents. (toujours)

_____

2. Tous les collègues prennent un verre. (en sortant du bureau)

_____

3.  Daniel et Françoise sortent. (le samedi)

    _____

4.  Frédéric prête sa voiture à son frère. (souvent)

    _____

5.  Tu nages en été. (tous les jours)

    _____

6.  Notre classe commence ponctuellement. (toujours)

    _____

7.  Il craint l'obscurité. (quand il était petit)

    _____

8.  Elle nettoie son appartement. (toutes les semaines)

    _____

9.  J'achète ma viande au supermarché. (avant)

    _____

10. Ils sont absents. (une fois par semaine)

    _____

## The Imperfect in Reported Speech

The imperfect usually replaces the present tense in reported speech (indirect discourse) when the main verb of the sentence is in a past tense. English works similarly. Compare the following pairs of sentences.

| | |
|---|---|
| Il **dit** qu'il le **sait**. | _He says that he knows (it)._ |
| Il **a dit** qu'il le **savait**. | _He said that he knew (it)._ |
| Il **écrit** qu'il ne **vient** pas. | _He writes that he isn't coming._ |
| Il **a écrit** qu'il ne **venait** pas. | _He wrote that he wasn't coming._ |
| Elle **affirme** qu'elle **veut** travailler. | _She insists that she wants to work._ |
| Elle **a affirmé** qu'elle **voulait** travailler. | _She insisted that she wanted to work._ |

**G**  _Rewrite each sentence, showing reported speech in the past by replacing the present tense verb in the first clause with the passé composé and the present tense verb in the second clause with the imperfect._

MODÈLE    Elles disent qu'elles veulent nous rendre visite.

_Elles ont dit qu'elles voulaient nous rendre visite._

1.  Robert m'écrit qu'il cherche du travail.

    _____

2.  Monique mentionne qu'elle part en vacances.

    _____

3. Claude et Philippe affirment qu'ils peuvent le faire.

_____

4. Je dis que je ne peux pas le faire. _____

5. Il m'assure qu'il va venir. _____

6. Elle promet que tout est prêt. _____

7. L'accusé jure qu'il est innocent. _____

8. Elle demande s'il rejoint ses amis. _____

9. Il nous répond qu'il compte nous aider.

_____

10. On annonce que l'avion arrive en retard.

_____

## Imperfect and Passé Composé Contrasted

The passé composé and imperfect both refer to past time, but express different ways of looking at past actions and events. The imperfect tense denotes an action as going on in the past without any reference to its beginning or end. The passé composé denotes an action that the speaker sees as completed in the past or as having happened once.

| | |
|---|---|
| Quand j'étais en France, **je parlais** français. | *When I was in France, **I spoke** French.* |
| Hier **j'ai parlé** français avec Nicole. | *Yesterday **I spoke** French with Nicole.* |

French speakers must select one of these two aspects—imperfect or passé composé—for every past action they refer to. English often does not distinguish between these two aspects of past time.

### Completed Action

The passé composé implies that an action is complete in the past. It also may imply that the action happened once.

| | |
|---|---|
| On **a sonné** à la porte d'en bas. | *Someone rang the downstairs doorbell.* |
| Tout à coup la porte **s'est ouverte**. | *Suddenly, the door opened.* |
| L'avion **est arrivé** en retard. | *The plane arrived late.* |
| La bombe **a éclaté**. | *The bomb exploded.* |

### Continuous or Repeated Action

The imperfect is used for actions that the speaker sees as going on in the past without reference to the beginning or the end of the action. The imperfect may convey that the action happened repeatedly.

| | |
|---|---|
| Le quartier **devenait** de plus en plus bruyant. | *The neighborhood was getting noisier and noisier.* |
| Les enfants **faisaient** leurs devoirs dans la cuisine. | *The children used to do their homework in the kitchen.* |
| Tu **te couchais** toujours tôt. | *You always went to bed early.* |

## Description in the Past

A series of imperfects may be used to describe what was going on in the past.

Il **était** six heures du matin. Tout le monde **dormait**. On **entendait** très peu de voitures dans la rue. Quelques piétons **allaient** vers l'arrêt d'autobus et **attendaient**. Le soleil **se montrait**.

*It was six in the morning. Everyone was asleep. Very few cars were heard in the street. Some pedestrians were going to the bus stop and were waiting. The sun was coming out.*

For a French speaker, the logical question to ask after hearing the above paragraph is **Et alors?** because in the imperfect, nothing really happens—the narration is not advanced at all. To make the above paragraph part of a narration, a passé composé has to be added.

Il **était** six heures du matin. Tout le monde **dormait**. On **entendait** très peu de voitures dans la rue. Quelques piétons **allaient** vers l'arrêt d'autobus et **attendaient**. Le soleil **se montrait**. Tout d'un coup, on **a entendu** le bruit d'une explosion. Les gens **ont commencé** à crier de peur.

*It was six in the morning. Everyone was asleep. Very few cars were heard in the street. Some pedestrians were going to the bus stop and were waiting. The sun was coming out. All of a sudden, people heard the noise of an explosion. People began to scream in fear.*

## Background for Past Actions or Events

The imperfect often provides the background for past actions or events that are expressed in the passé composé.

Paulette **lisait** quand ses amis **sont arrivés**.

*Paulette was reading when her friends arrived.*

Quand je **suis entré**, tout le monde **travaillait**.

*When I came in, everyone was working.*

J'**ai fermé** les fenêtres parce qu'il **pleuvait**.

*I closed the windows because it was raining.*

**H** *Complete each sentence, choosing either the imperfect or the passé composé for each verb in parentheses. Each sentence has two verbs, one of which will be imperfect and the other passé composé.*

MODÈLE   Pendant qu'il ___*attendait*___ le bus, il ___*a commencé*___ à pleuvoir. (attendre, commencer)

1. Il _____ onze heures du soir quand ils _____ à la discothèque. (être, arriver)

2. Elle _____ son diplôme quand elle _____ trente ans. (recevoir, avoir)

3. Sa femme _____ pendant que Georges _____ en voyage. (accoucher, être)

4. Moi, je/j'_____ l'addition pendant que mes amis _____ leur dessert. (demander, finir)

5. Jacques _____ à la fac quand on lui _____ un poste en Afrique. (enseigner, offrir)

6. Le chien _____ de la maison pendant que vous _____. (s'échapper, dormir)

7. Les idées de ce texte _____ difficiles, mais moi, je/j'_____ les comprendre. (être, pouvoir)

8. On _____ dans la rue quand on _____ des cris. (marcher, entendre)

9. Le village où je _____ _____ beau. (naître, être)

10. Les cambrioleurs _____ dans la maison pendant que les propriétaires _____ en vacances. (entrer, être)

## Continuing Past Action

French uses the imperfect tense to refer to past actions that are seen as continuing at another point of time in the past. English uses a *had been doing something* construction for this function. The French construction consists of the following elements.

- **depuis quand** + imperfect? OR
  **depuis combien de temps** + imperfect? OR
  **ça faisait combien de temps que** + imperfect? (more colloquial) OR
  **il y avait combien de temps que** + imperfect? (more colloquial)

  These patterns are used to ask a question about how long something had been going on.

  | | |
  |---|---|
  | **Depuis quand est-ce que tu travaillais** à Québec? | *How long had you been working in Quebec?* |
  | **Depuis combien de temps est-ce que vous étiez** à la bibliothèque quand vous avez vu votre professeur? | *How long had you been* at the library *when you saw your teacher?* |
  | **Ça faisait combien de temps qu'ils cherchaient** un logement quand on leur a offert cet appartement? | *How long had they been looking* for *a place to live when they were offered that apartment?* |
  | **Il y avait combien de temps qu'elle travaillait** dans cette entreprise quand ils lui ont donné une augmentation? | *How long had she been working at that company when they gave her a raise?* |

- imperfect + **depuis** + time expression OR
  **ça faisait** + time expression + **que** + imperfect (more colloquial) OR
  **il y avait** + time expression + **que** + imperfect (more colloquial) OR
  imperfect + **depuis** + starting point of action

  These patterns are used to tell how long something had been going on.

  | | |
  |---|---|
  | **J'habitais** ce quartier **depuis un an**. | *I'd been living in that neighborhood for a year.* |
  | **Ça faisait un an qu'ils sortaient ensemble** quand ils se sont fiancés. | *They had been going out for a year when they got engaged.* |

| | |
|---|---|
| **Il y avait une heure que nous attendions** l'autocar quand vous nous avez aperçus. | *We had been waiting for the bus for an hour when you spotted us.* |
| **Je travaillais** à Québec **depuis septembre** quand j'ai dû rentrer en Belgique. | *I had been working in Quebec since September when I had to go back to Belgium.* |

## End Point Specified for Past Action

Although the imperfect is usually used to express repeated actions in the past, when the end point of those actions is specified, the verb is in the passé composé because the speaker's focus shifts to the completion of the actions. In the sentence below, no end point is specified.

| | |
|---|---|
| Quand j'**étais** petit, j'**allais** au bord de la mer tous les étés. | *When I was a child, I went to the seashore every summer.* |

Notice the change in tense when an endpoint is specifically mentioned.

| | |
|---|---|
| Jusqu'à l'âge de douze ans, je **suis allé** au bord de la mer tous les étés. | *Until the age of twelve, I went to the seashore every summer.* |

**I**  **Translation.**  *Express the following sentences in French.*

1. *How long had you (vous) been living in New York when you bought an apartment?*

    _____

    _____

2. *We had been living there for two years.*

    _____

3. *How long had you (tu) been studying French in Paris when you decided to return to your American university?*

    _____

    _____

4. *I had been there for six weeks.*

    _____

5. *How long had Julie been using her computer when she changed brands?*

    _____

    _____

6. *She had it for three years.*

    _____

7. *Since when had Paul been working as a consultant?*

    _____

8. *Since last year when he got his degree.*

    _____

## Differences in Meaning Between the Imperfect and the Passé Composé of Some Common Verbs

Sometimes English uses entirely different verbs to express the difference between the imperfect and the passé composé of some French verbs. For example, **j'avais** means *I was in the process of having* or *I had*; **j'ai eu** means *I began to have* or *I got, I received*.

| | |
|---|---|
| **Elle avait** beaucoup d'idées. | **She had** a lot of ideas. (They were in her head.) |
| **Elle a eu** une bonne idée. | **She had** a good idea. (It popped into her head.) |
| **Je savais** qu'il habitait cet immeuble. | **I knew** that he lived in that apartment house. |
| **J'ai su** qu'il habitait cet immeuble. | **I found out** that he lived in that apartment house. |
| **On connaissait** Marie-Laure. | **We knew** Marie-Laure. |
| **On a connu** Marie-Laure. | **We met** Marie-Laure. |
| **On ne pouvait pas** sortir à cause de la neige. | **We couldn't** go out because of the snow. (It's not stated whether we went out or not, just that it was very difficult to go out.) |
| **On n'a pas pu** sortir à cause de la neige. | **We couldn't** go out because of the snow. (And we didn't go out.) |
| Jacques **ne voulait pas** aller en taxi. | Jacques **didn't want** to go by cab. (It leaves open whether he went or not.) |
| Jacques **n'a pas voulu** aller en taxi. | Jacques **didn't want** (= **refused**) to go by cab. (And he didn't go.) |

---

**BUILDING SENTENCES**    **Sentences with the pronouns y and en**

## The Pronoun y

The basic function of the French pronoun **y** is to replace complements that consist of the preposition **à** + an inanimate noun. (Remember that complements consisting of **à** + an animate noun are indirect objects and are replaced by **lui** or **leur**.) The complement consisting of the preposition **à** + a singular or plural inanimate noun may be either a phrase of location or a "notional" phrase, a phrase in which the preposition **à** is required by French structure and whose meaning is figurative.

Examine the following examples of complements that can be replaced by **y**.

### Location

| | |
|---|---|
| Nous passons nos vacances **à Chicago**. | *We're spending our vacation in Chicago.* |
| Nous **y** passons nos vacances. | *We're spending our vacation there.* |
| J'ai vu Christine **au café**. | *I saw Christine at the café.* |
| J'**y** ai vu Christine. | *I saw Christine there.* |

| L'enfant monte **à sa chambre**. | *The child is going up to his room.* |
| L'enfant **y** monte. | *The child is going up (to it).* |
| Ils vont **à la fac**. | *They are going to the university.* |
| Ils **y** vont. | *They are going there.* |

## Notional uses

| Elle ne répond pas **à mes courriels**. | *She doesn't answer my e-mails.* |
| Elle n'**y** répond pas. | *She doesn't answer them.* |
| Vous pensez **à votre travail**? | *Are you thinking about your work?* |
| Vous **y** pensez? | *Are you thinking about it?* |
| Il faut faire attention **au message**. | *You have to pay attention to the message.* |
| Il faut **y** faire attention. | *You have to pay attention (to it).* |
| Nous réfléchissons **à notre avenir**. | *We think about our future.* |
| Nous **y** réfléchissons. | *We think about it.* |
| Tu renonces **à ton travail**? | *Are you quitting your job?* |
| Tu **y** renonces? | *Are you quitting (it)?* |

Note in the examples above that **y** has many translations in English—or may not be translated at all.

French **y** also replaces other prepositions of location (**chez, en, dans, sur, sous, devant, derrière**, etc.) followed by an inanimate noun.

| J'ai laissé mon livre **sur le canapé**. | *I left my book on the sofa.* |
| J'**y** ai laissé mon livre. | *I left my book there (on it).* |
| Ils ont garé la voiture **devant l'immeuble**. | *They parked the car in front of the apartment house.* |
| Ils **y** ont garé la voiture. | *They parked the car there (in front of it).* |
| Le chat dormait **sous la table**. | *The cat used to sleep under the table.* |
| Le chat **y** dormait. | *The cat used to sleep there (under there).* |

When a preposition of location other than **à** + an inanimate noun is used in a figurative—not spatial—sense, then the phrase cannot be replaced by **y**. The phrases **là-dessus, là-dessous**, and **là-dedans** can replace **sur, sous**, and **dans**, respectively, when followed by an inanimate noun and used in a notional (not spatial) sense.

| Elle compte **sur mon appui**. | *She's counting on my support.* |
| Elle compte **là-dessus**. | *She's counting on it.* |
| Je reviendrai **sur cette idée**. | *I'll come back to this idea.* |
| Je reviendrai **là-dessus**. | *I'll come back to it.* |
| Il cache quelque chose **sous cette apparence souriante**. | *He's hiding something under that smiling appearance.* |
| Il cache quelque chose **là-dessous**. | *He's hiding something under it.* |
| Il a mis cent mille euros **dans cette affaire**. | *He put one hundred thousand euros into this business.* |
| Il a mis cent mille euros **là-dedans**. | *He put one hundred thousand euros into it.* |

## Verbs followed by à + an animate noun

**aller bien à qqn**  *to look nice on someone*
**convenir à qqn**  *to suit someone, be good for someone*
**déplaire à qqn**  *to displease someone*
**désobéir à qqn**  *to disobey someone*
**en vouloir à qqn**  *to have a grudge against someone*
**obéir à qqn**  *to obey someone*
**plaire à qqn**  *to please someone*
**répondre à qqn**  *to answer someone*
**ressembler à qqn**  *to look like someone*
**succéder à qqn**  *to succeed someone*
**téléphoner à qqn**  *to phone someone*

The phrase **à qqn** in each case can be replaced by **lui** or **leur**.

However, in sentences with **penser à qqn** and **songer à qqn**, the disjunctive pronouns, rather than the indirect object pronouns, are usually used.

| | |
|---|---|
| Quand il était loin de ses enfants il pensait constamment **à eux**. | *When he was far from his children, he thought about them all the time.* |
| Marie veut abandonner ses études, mais je crois que ça ne **lui** convient pas du tout. | *Marie wants to quit school, but I think that that is not good for her (to do).* |
| S'ils m'écrivent, je **leur** répondrai. | *If they write to me, I will answer them.* |
| Quand son père est tombé malade, Élisabeth **lui** a succédé à la tête de leur usine. | *When her father became ill, Élisabeth succeeded him as the head of their factory.* |
| Ils ne m'ont jamais aidé et c'est pour ça que je **leur** en veux. | *They have never helped me, and that's why I resent them.* |

## Expressions with complements consisting of à + an inanimate noun that can be replaced by y

**assister à qqch**  *to attend something* (events, etc.)
**échapper à qqch**  *to escape/avoid something*
**échouer à qqch**  *to fail in something*
**jouer à qqch**  *to play something* (a game)
**participer à qqch**  *to participate in something*
**parvenir à qqch**  *to reach/attain something*
**penser à qqch**  *to think about something*
**réfléchir à qqch**  *to think about something, reflect on something*
**remédier à qqch**  *to rectify/fix something*
**renoncer à qqch**  *to give something up, quit something*
**réussir à qqch**  *to succeed in something*
**songer à qqch**  *to think about something, reflect on something, contemplate something*
**survivre à qqch**  *to survive something*
**toucher à qqch**  *to touch something, mess up something*
**veiller à qqch**  *to see to something*

| | |
|---|---|
| J'ai laissé toutes mes affaires dans le salon. N'y touche pas. | *I left all my stuff in the living room. Don't mess it up.* |

| | |
|---|---|
| Il y a beaucoup d'activités au lycée mais Luc n'**y** participe pas. | *There are many activities at the school, but Luc doesn't participate in any.* |
| Cette situation est frustrante, mais je ne sais pas **y** remédier. | *This situation is frustrating, but I don't know how to rectify it.* |
| Je n'ai pas encore pu faire un stage à l'étranger, mais j'**y** songe beaucoup. | *I still haven't been able to do an internship abroad, but I think about it a lot.* |

The pronoun **y** follows the same rules for position as other object pronouns.

It precedes the conjugated verb.

| | |
|---|---|
| Ils **y** renoncent. | *They're giving it up.* |

It precedes the infinitive in verb + infinitive constructions.

| | |
|---|---|
| Ils vont **y** renoncer. | *They're going to give it up.* |

It precedes the auxiliary verb in the passé composé. With verbs conjugated with **avoir**, **y** does not cause agreement of the past participle.

| | |
|---|---|
| Ils **y** ont renoncé. | *They gave it up.* |

In affirmative commands of **-er** verbs, the final **s** of the **tu** form is restored and pronounced as /z/ before **y**.

| | |
|---|---|
| Vas-y. | *Go there. / Come on.* |
| Retournes-y. | *Go back to it. / Go back there.* |

Note that the final **s** of all command forms is pronounced as /z/ before **y**, as is the final **z** of **vous** commands.

| | |
|---|---|
| Réfléchis-y. | *Think it over.* |
| Réponds-y. | *Answer it.* |
| Passons-y nos vacances. | *Let's spend our vacation there.* |
| Allez-y. | *Come on.* |

**J**  *Rewrite the following sentences, replacing each underlined complement with the correct object pronoun or replacement phrase.*

1. Elle pensait à son travail. _____

2. Les étudiants répondent à leur professeur.

   _____

3. Est-ce que vous répondez à tous vos courriels?

   _____

4. Pourquoi est-ce qu'il a renoncé à son travail?

   _____

5. Je songeais constamment à mon voyage en France.

   _____

6. Tu penses beaucoup à ta fiancée. _____

7. Nous ne pouvons pas remédier à cette situation.

   _____

8. Les habitants de ce village n'ont pas survécu à la guerre.

   _____

9. Vous songez beaucoup à vos parents?

   _____

10. Le criminel a échappé aux recherches de la police.

    _____

11. Notre chat dormait sur mon lit. _____

12. Les enfants jouaient au sous-sol. _____

13. Le chien obéit à son maître. _____

14. C'est un professeur qui plaît à ses étudiants.

    _____

15. J'ai assisté aux concerts cet été. _____

16. Il ne voulait pas échouer à l'examen.

    _____

17. Est-ce que vous participez toujours aux élections?

    _____

18. Les alpinistes sont parvenus au sommet de la montagne.

    _____

19. Vous n'allez pas toucher à mes cédés!

    _____

20. Il faut faire attention aux recommandations du médecin.

    _____

**K** *Complete the following conversational exchanges with* **lui**, **leur**, *or* **y**.

1. —Est-ce qu'il a téléphoné à Christine?

   —Oui, il _____ a déjà téléphoné.

2. —Ils jouent au bridge?

   —Non, ils ne savent pas _____ jouer.

3. —Ces parents n'ont pas la vie facile.

   —Oui, leurs enfants _____ désobéissent constamment.

4. —L'orage a fait beaucoup de victimes.

   —Oui, personne ne/n'_____ a survécu.

5. —Et tes examens?

   —Je/J'_____ ai réussi.

6. —Tu vas accepter cet offre d'emploi?

   —Je/J'_____ réfléchis encore.

7. —Il n'a pas veillé à nos intérêts.

   —C'est pour ça que nous _____ en voulons.

8. —Jacques est son père tout craché (*the spitting image of his father*).

   —Oui, il _____ ressemble beaucoup.

**L**  *Answer the following questions in the affirmative, replacing each underlined complement with the appropriate pronoun.*

MODÈLE     Est-ce que Lise a répondu <u>à votre courriel</u>?

   *Oui, elle y a répondu.*

1. Est-ce que tu vas participer <u>aux activités de l'université</u>?

   _____

2. Est-ce que cette famille a survécu <u>au tremblement de terre</u>?

   _____

3. Est-ce que le fils a succédé <u>à son père</u>?

   _____

4. Est-ce que les agents ont veillé <u>à vos intérêts</u>?

   _____

5. Est-ce que ces enfants ressemblent <u>à leurs parents</u>?

   _____

6. Est-ce que tu as téléphoné <u>à tes voisins</u>?

   _____

7. Est-ce qu'ils jouaient <u>au bridge</u>?

   _____

8. Est-ce que notre secrétaire comptait renoncer <u>à son poste</u>?

   _____

9. Est-ce que tu songeais souvent <u>à ta grand-mère</u>?

   _____

10. Est-ce que Christine ressemble <u>à sa mère</u>?

   _____

11. Est-ce que les étudiants ont assisté <u>à la conférence</u>?

   _____

12. Est-ce que Paul a déplu <u>à sa petite amie</u>?

   _____

13. Est-ce que ces jeunes gens réfléchissaient <u>à leur avenir</u>?

   _____

14. Est-ce que Maurice a échoué <u>à son examen</u>?

   _____

15. Est-ce que cet horaire convient <u>aux touristes</u>?

   _____

16. Est-ce que Rachelle en veut <u>à son frère</u>?

   _____

17. Est-ce que les enfants ont touché <u>à mes papiers</u>?

   _____

18. Est-ce que ce chien désobéissait <u>à son maître</u>?

   _____

## The Pronoun **en**

The basic function of the French pronoun **en** is to replace complements that consist of the preposition **de** + a noun. In most cases, but not all, **en** can replace complements consisting of **de** + either an animate or an inanimate noun.

The pronoun **en** can replace **de** + any noun when **de** + the article is a partitive article or a plural indefinite article. **En** is often translated as *some* or *any* in English, but in many cases it has no English equivalent.

| | |
|---|---|
| Vous avez **des clés USB**? | *Do you have (any) flash drives?* |
| Vous **en** avez? | *Do you have any?* |
| Tu veux **des frites**? | *Do you want any French fries?* |
| Tu **en** veux? | *Do you want any?* |
| Il boit **du vin**. | *He's drinking wine.* |
| Il **en** boit. | *He's drinking some.* |
| Je connais **des ingénieurs** en France. | *I know (some) engineers in France.* |
| J'**en** connais en France. | *I know some in France.* |
| Elle a **des cousins** en Californie. | *She has cousins in California.* |
| Elle **en** a en Californie. | *She has some in California.* |
| Cette usine ne cherche pas **d'ouvriers**. | *This factory is not looking for workers.* |
| Cette usine n'**en** cherche pas. | *This factory is not looking for any.* |

The pronoun **en** can replace both animate and inanimate nouns that follow a quantity word (most of which contain **de**) or a numeral.

| | |
|---|---|
| J'ai beaucoup **de travail**. | *I have a lot of work.* |
| J'**en** ai beaucoup. | *I have a lot.* |
| Elle fait tant **de voyages**. | *She takes so many trips.* |
| Elle **en** fait tant. | *She takes so many.* |
| Nous avons résolu la plupart **des problèmes**. | *We have solved most of the problems.* |
| Nous **en** avons résolu la plupart. | *We have solved most of them.* |
| L'immeuble a assez **de locataires**. | *The apartment building has enough tenants.* |
| L'immeuble **en** a assez. | *The apartment building has enough.* |
| Ce professeur enseigne cinq **cours**. | *This teacher teaches five courses.* |
| Ce professeur **en** enseigne cinq. | *This teacher teaches five.* |
| Nous avons acheté deux mille **livres**. | *We have bought two thousand books.* |
| Nous **en** avons acheté deux mille. | *We have bought two thousand.* |
| Cette ville a trois cent mille **habitants**. | *This city has three hundred thousand inhabitants.* |
| Cette ville **en** a trois cent mille. | *This city has three hundred thousand.* |
| Cette entreprise a embauché dix **employés**. | *This firm hired ten employees.* |
| Cette entreprise **en** a embauché dix. | *This firm hired ten.* |

The phrase with **de** in the quantity expression **bien du / de la / de l' / des** cannot be replaced by **en**.

| | |
|---|---|
| J'ai eu **bien du mal** à le contacter. | *I had a lot of difficulty getting in touch with him.* |
| Il connaît **bien des gens** en Italie. | *He knows a lot of people in Italy.* |

When a noun following **quelques** is replaced by **en**, **quelques** becomes **quelques-uns** or **quelques-unes**.

| | |
|---|---|
| Nous avons lu quelques **articles**. | *We read some articles.* |
| Nous **en** avons lu **quelques-uns**. | *We read some.* |
| Je peux te donner **quelques clés USB**. | *I can give you some flash drives.* |
| Je peux t'**en** donner **quelques-unes**. | *I can give you some.* |

With the colloquial expression **en avoir marre de** *to be fed up with*, both the pronoun **en** and the noun may appear.

| | |
|---|---|
| J'**en** ai marre **de ses bêtises**. | *I am fed up with his nonsense.* |

In idiomatic expressions where **de** is required before the complement, **en** usually replaces only inanimate nouns. When the complement is **de** + an animate noun, **de** remains and the noun is replaced by the corresponding stressed pronoun (usually **lui**, **elle**, **leur**, or **elles**), especially in spoken French. Formal written French allows animate nouns to be replaced by **en** in these cases.

| | |
|---|---|
| Tu te souviens **de cette rue**? | *Do you remember this street?* |
| Tu t'**en** souviens? | *Do you remember it?* |
| Tu te souviens **de cette chanteuse**? | *Do you remember this singer?* |
| Tu te souviens **d'elle**? | *Do you remember her?* |

**En** also replaces inanimate nouns when **de** means *from*.

| | |
|---|---|
| Elle est revenue **de la campagne**. | *She came back from the country.* |
| Elle **en** est revenue. | *She came back (from there).* |

### Verbs and expressions requiring **de** before a complement

**abuser de**  *to take advantage of, misuse*
**accabler de**  *to overwhelm with*
**avoir besoin de**  *to need*
**avoir peur de**  *to be afraid of*
**couvrir de**  *to cover with*
**dépendre de**  *to depend on*
**douter de (qqch)**  *to doubt (something)*
**encombrer de**  *to clutter with, litter with*
**entourer de**  *to surround with*
**hériter de**  *to inherit*
**jouer de**  *to play* (an instrument)
**jouir de**  *to enjoy, have at one's disposal*
**menacer de**  *to threaten with*
**munir de**  *to supply with*
**parler de**  *to talk about*
**planter de**  *to plant with*
**remplir de**  *to fill with*
**se servir de**  *to use*
**se souvenir de**  *to remember*
**trembler de**  *to tremble with*

| | |
|---|---|
| Vous abusez **de ma bonté**. | *You're taking advantage of my kindness.* |
| Vous **en** abusez. | *You're taking advantage of it.* |
| Nous sommes accablés **de travail**. | *We are swamped with work.* |
| Nous **en** sommes accablés. | *We are swamped (with it).* |
| Tout dépend **de la décision du patron**. | *Everything depends on the boss's decision.* |
| Tout **en** dépend. | *Everything depends on it.* |
| Cette région jouit **d'un bon climat**. | *This region enjoys a good climate.* |
| Cette région **en** jouit. | *This region enjoys one (that).* |
| Tout le monde parle **de ce film**. | *Everyone is talking about this movie.* |
| Tout le monde **en** parle. | *Everyone is talking about it.* |
| Tout le monde parle **de cette vedette**. | *Everyone is talking about this movie star.* |
| Tout le monde parle **d'elle**. | *Everyone is talking about her.* |
| Je ne me souviens pas **de tes cousins**. | *I don't remember your cousins.* |
| Je ne me souviens pas **d'eux**. | *I don't remember them.* |

## Verbs That Always Take **en**

Note that the pronoun **en** is an essential part of some verbs. The most common of these is **s'en aller** *to go away*. Study the present and passé composé of this verb. Note that **s'en aller** is a reflexive verb (see Chapter 7).

PRESENT TENSE

| | |
|---|---|
| je m'en vais | nous nous en allons |
| tu t'en vas | vous vous en allez |
| il/elle/on s'en va | ils/elles s'en vont |

PASSÉ COMPOSÉ

| | |
|---|---|
| je m'en suis allé(e) | nous nous en sommes allé(e)s |
| tu t'en es allé(e) | vous vous en êtes allé(e)(s) |
| il s'en est allé | ils s'en sont allés |
| elle s'en est allée | elles s'en sont allées |
| on s'en est allé(e)(s) | |

### Common verbs that always appear with **en**

**s'en prendre à qqn**  *to attack someone, pick a fight with someone*
**en revenir**  *to get over it*
**s'en tenir à**  *to stick to* (facts, etc.)
**en vouloir à qqn**  *to have a grudge against someone*

| | |
|---|---|
| Le prof **s'en prend** toujours à lui. | *The teacher always attacks him.* |
| Elle ne m'a pas invité. Je n'**en reviens** pas. | *She didn't invite me. I can't get over it.* |
| Il faut **s'en tenir aux faits**. | *One must stick to the facts.* |
| Pourquoi est-ce que **tu m'en veux**? | *Why do you have a grudge against me?* |

The pronoun **en** follows the same rules for position as other object pronouns.

It precedes the conjugated verb.

| | |
|---|---|
| Ils **en** retournent. | *They come back from there.* |

It precedes the infinitive in verb + infinitive constructions.

| | |
|---|---|
| Ils vont **en** acheter. | *They're going to buy some.* |

It precedes the auxiliary verb in the passé composé. With verbs conjugated with **avoir**, **en** does not cause agreement of the past participle.

| | |
|---|---|
| Ils **en** ont acheté. | *They bought some.* |

In affirmative commands of **-er** verbs, the final **s** of the **tu** form is restored and pronounced as /z/ before **en**.

| | |
|---|---|
| Parles-en. | *Talk about it.* |
| Achètes-en. | *Buy some.* |

Note that the final **s** of all command forms is pronounced as /z/ before **en**, as is the final **z** of **vous** commands.

| | |
|---|---|
| Choisis-en. | *Choose some.* |
| Prends-en. | *Take some.* |
| Cherchons-en. | *Let's look for some.* |
| Mangez-en. | *Eat some.* |

**M** *Rewrite each sentence, replacing the underlined phrases with* **en** *or* **de** + *a stressed pronoun, as required.*

1. Elle achète des chocolats. _____

2. Cet enfant ne mange pas de bananes. _____

3. On vend des livres d'occasion dans cette librairie.

   _____

4. Nous doutions de sa bonne foi. _____

5. Je me souviens de votre grand-père. _____

6. Elle abusait de ta gentillesse. _____

7. Nous avons planté le jardin de roses. _____

8. Tout dépend de sa bonne volonté. _____

9. Tu avais peur de ces gens-là? _____

10. Je reviens de la ville. _____

11. Cet étudiant suivait six cours. _____

12. Ils ont beaucoup d'amis. _____

13. On parlait beaucoup de ce joueur de foot. _____

14. Il a lu la plupart de ses courriels. _____

15. J'ai reçu dix cadeaux. _____

**N** *Rewrite each sentence, replacing the underlined complement with the correct pronoun:* **le, la, l', les, lui, leur, y,** *or* **en.** *Two of the sentences will require* **là-dessus** *instead of* **y.**

1. Il écoute le répondeur. _____

2. Il fait attention aux messages. _____

3. Il écoute trois messages. _____

4. Il téléphonait à sa fiancée. _____

5. Ils ont parlé de leurs projets pour le week-end. _____

6. Tu peux poser tes affaires sur la table de la cuisine.

   _____

7. Il mangeait toujours au bistrot du coin. _____

8. Il commandait toujours des frites. _____

9. Elle a besoin de ses amies. _____

10. Elle a besoin <u>de leurs conseils</u>. _____

11. Ils en veulent <u>à leurs voisins</u>. _____

12. Cet enfant ressemble beaucoup <u>à sa grand-mère</u>.

    _____

13. L'armée était munie <u>d'armes modernes</u>. _____

14. Nous attendions <u>nos amis</u>. _____

15. Les rues sont encombrées <u>de vieux pneus</u>. _____

16. Nous comptons <u>sur votre aide</u>. _____

17. Tu peux me prêter quelques <u>cédéroms</u>? _____

18. Notre chien a peur <u>des orages</u>. _____

19. La police l'a interrogé <u>sur ses activités</u>. _____

20. Il a mis les documents <u>dans un tiroir</u>. _____

**O** **_Translation._** _Express the following sentences in French._

1. _There's a meeting today, but I'm not attending it._

   _____

2. _He went there (to the Internet café)._ _____

3. _You (tu) were thinking about him._ _____

4. _This Web site? I remember it._ _____

5. _The new tablet? Everyone was talking about it._

   _____

6. _I was trying to stick to the rules._ _____

7. _She looks a lot like them._ _____

8. _Yes, in the drawer. They put the tickets there._

   _____

9. _You (vous) have a grudge against me, don't you?_

   _____

10. _The passwords? We needed them._ _____

# Reflexive Verbs

Reflexive verbs are called **verbes pronominaux** in French because these verbs always appear with a pronoun that refers to the same person or thing as the subject.

English reflexive verbs, a relatively small category, usually emphasize that the subject is doing something to himself or herself, for example, *I hurt myself, the little girl dresses herself.* French reflexive verbs are much more common, and they usually correspond to English intransitive verbs (verbs that do not take a direct object) rather than to English reflexive verbs. English translations of French pronominal verbs often include the phrase *to get* or *to be* + an adjective or past participle.

In the verb lists and vocabulary of this book, French reflexive verbs appear with the reflexive pronoun **se** (elided to **s'** before a vowel) before the main verb form.

> **se réveiller**  *to wake up*
> **s'amuser**  *to have a good time*
> **se détendre**  *to relax*
> **s'endormir**  *to fall asleep*

## Formation of Reflexive Verbs

Examine the French pronominal verb **se réveiller** *to wake up.* The reflexive pronouns are in boldface type. Note that the reflexive pronoun **se** changes to agree with the subject of the verb.

### se réveiller

| | |
|---|---|
| je **me** réveille | nous **nous** réveillons |
| tu **te** réveilles | vous **vous** réveillez |
| il/elle/on **se** réveille | ils/elles **se** réveillent |

## Reflexive and Nonreflexive Verb Pairs

French verbs are either transitive or intransitive. French transitive verbs must appear with a direct object, while French intransitive verbs cannot appear with a direct object.[1] Most French pronominal verbs have a transitive counterpart, a nonreflexive verb that must have a direct object.

---

[1] In English, verbs move easily between the categories of transitive and intransitive: *He cooks the meat. / The meat cooks. // I open the door. / The door opens. // I wake the children up. / I wake up.* The categories transitive and intransitive are therefore less significant in English grammar than in French.

Compare the following pairs of verbs.

| TRANSITIVE VERB | REFLEXIVE VERB |
|---|---|
| **amuser quelqu'un**  *to amuse someone* | **s'amuser**  *to have a good time* |
| **approcher la chaise**  *to move the chair closer* | **s'approcher**  *to approach, move closer* |
| **ennuyer les spectateurs**  *to bore the spectators* | **s'ennuyer**  *to get bored* |
| **habiller le bébé**  *to dress the baby* | **s'habiller**  *to get dressed* |
| **laver le parquet**  *to wash the floor* | **se laver**  *to wash up* |
| **offenser quelqu'un**  *to insult someone* | **s'offenser**  *to get insulted* |
| **promener le chien**  *to walk the dog* | **se promener**  *to take a walk* |
| **réveiller les enfants**  *to wake up the children* | **se réveiller**  *to wake up* |

Thus, the most useful way of understanding reflexive, or pronominal, verbs in French is to think of the reflexive pronoun as taking the place of the required direct object with transitive verbs when there is no direct object present.[1]

Reflexive verbs are common in the expression of one's daily routine. The verbs in the left column are transitive and express an action that one person does to another, as in the first example of each pair above. The verbs in the right column are reflexive and correspond to intransitive verbs in English.

| | |
|---|---|
| **coucher qqn**  *to put someone to bed* | **se coucher**  *to go to bed* |
| **débarbouiller qqn**  *to wash someone's face* | **se débarbouiller**  *to wash one's face* |
| **déshabiller qqn**  *to undress someone* | **se déshabiller**  *to get undressed* |
| **détendre qqn**  *to cause someone to relax* | **se détendre**  *to relax* |
| **endormir qqn**  *to put someone to sleep* | **s'endormir**  *to fall asleep* |
| **fatiguer qqn**  *to make someone tired* | **se fatiguer**  *to get tired* |
| **habiller qqn**  *to dress someone* | **s'habiller**  *to get dressed* |
| **laver qqn/qqch**  *to wash someone/something* | **se laver**  *to wash up* |
| **lever qqch**  *to raise/lift something* | **se lever**  *to get up* |
| **maquiller qqn**  *to put makeup on someone* | **se maquiller**  *to put on makeup* |
| **peigner qqn**  *to comb someone's hair* | **se peigner**  *to comb one's hair* |
| **raser qqn**  *to shave someone* | **se raser**  *to shave* |
| **reposer qqn**  *to give rest to someone* | **se reposer**  *to rest* |
| **réveiller qqn**  *to wake someone up* | **se réveiller**  *to wake up* |
| **soigner qqn**  *to take care of someone* | **se soigner**  *to take care of oneself* |

Other reflexive expressions related to our daily routine contain a reflexive verb followed by a direct object. In these expressions, the reflexive pronouns are *indirect objects*. This construction is most common with parts of the body.

**se brosser les cheveux**  *to brush one's hair*
**se brosser les dents**  *to brush one's teeth*
**se casser le bras**  *to break one's arm*
**se couper le doigt**  *to cut one's finger*
**se couper les cheveux**  *to cut one's hair*
**se couper/limer les ongles**  *to cut/file one's nails*
**se laver la tête**  *to wash one's hair*

---

[1]This analysis is valid only for those pronominal verbs that have a non-pronominal transitive counterpart.

**se laver les mains / la figure** *to wash one's hands / one's face*
**se sécher les cheveux** *to dry one's hair*

Nonreflexive verbs and expressions are also used to talk about one's daily routine.

**déjeuner** *to have lunch*
**dîner** *to have dinner*
**faire sa toilette** *to wash up, get ready to go out*
**mettre son costume / sa robe / ses chaussures** *to put on one's suit / one's dress / one's shoes*
**prendre le petit déjeuner** *to have breakfast*
**prendre une douche / un bain** *to take a shower / a bath*

**A** *Create sentences from the following strings of elements in order to tell at what time these people perform the tasks of their daily routine.*

MODÈLE    Maurice / se lever / 7h

*Maurice se lève à 7h.*

1. Émilie / se réveiller / 6h30 _____

2. les enfants / se brosser les dents / 7h10

   _____

3. je / se débarbouiller / 6h45 _____

4. Jacqueline / s'habiller / 7h20 _____

5. nous / se peigner / 7h35 _____

6. mes parents / faire leur toilette / 6h50

   _____

7. tout le monde / prendre le petit déjeuner / 7h30

   _____

8. Jacques / prendre une douche / 8h _____

9. ma sœur / se maquiller / 8h15 _____

10. nous / prendre le dîner / 7h30 _____

11. papa / se reposer dans son fauteuil / 8h30

    _____

12. les petits / se coucher / 8h45 _____

13. ils / s'endormir / vers 9h _____

14. Lise / se laver la tête / 9h45 _____

15. elle / se sécher les cheveux / 10h _____

16. nous / se laver les mains et le visage / 11h

    _____

17. nos grands-parents / se fatiguer / l'après-midi

_____

18. je / se soigner / le soir _____

**B** *Rewrite each sentence, changing the subject as indicated. Be careful to change the reflexive pronoun as well as the subject and the verb.*

MODÈLE   Nous nous lavons. (vous)

*Vous vous lavez.* _____

1. Elle s'offense. (tu) _____

2. Ils s'approchent de la ville. (je) _____

3. Vous vous limez les ongles. (nous) _____

4. Elles se débarbouillent. (tu) _____

5. Nous nous endormons. (je) _____

6. Vous vous séchez les cheveux. (elle) _____

7. Nous nous levons de bonne heure. (il) _____

8. Elles se promènent dans le parc. (nous) _____

9. Je me coupe les cheveux. (vous) _____

10. Elle s'habille. (nous) _____

11. Tu te maquilles. (elles) _____

12. Je me rase. (ils) _____

13. Vous vous reposez. (on) _____

14. Elle se fatigue. (tu) _____

15. Ils s'ennuient. (nous) _____

16. Tu t'amuses. (vous) _____

17. Nous nous soignons. (je) _____

18. Tu t'approches. (nous) _____

19. Elle se coupe le doigt. (vous) _____

20. Il se casse le pied. (tu) _____

Many verbs of motion follow the same pattern. They occur in pairs: nonreflexive verbs that express an action that one person does to another and reflexive verbs that correspond to intransitive verbs in English.

| | |
|---|---|
| **allonger qqn/qqch** *to stretch someone/ something out* | **s'allonger** *to stretch out, lie down* |
| **approcher qqch** *to bring/move something closer* | **s'approcher de** *to approach, move closer* |

| | |
|---|---|
| **arrêter**  *to stop, arrest* | **s'arrêter**  *to stop* |
| **asseoir qqn**  *to seat someone* | **s'asseoir**  *to sit down* |
| **dépêcher**  *to dispatch, send* | **se dépêcher**  *to hurry up* |
| **déplacer**  *to move, shift* | **se déplacer**  *to move, move about; to travel* |
| **diriger**  *to direct* | **se diriger vers**  *to head toward* |
| **éloigner qqch**  *to move something away* | **s'éloigner de**  *to move away from* |
| **installer qqch**  *to install/fix something, put something in* | **s'installer**  *to move in, settle in* |
| **mettre qqch debout**  *to stand something up* | **se mettre debout**  *to stand up* |
| **mettre qqch en route**  *to start something up* (machine) | **se mettre en route**  *to set out* |
| **promener**  *to take for a walk* | **se promener**  *to take a walk* |
| **réunir**  *to gather, collect* | **se réunir**  *to get together* |
| **trouver**  *to find* | **se trouver**  *to be located* |

The verb **s'asseoir** is irregular.

**s'asseoir**  *to sit down*

| | |
|---|---|
| je **m'assieds** | nous **nous asseyons** |
| tu **t'assieds** | vous **vous asseyez** |
| il/elle/on **s'assied** | ils/elles **s'asseyent** |

Reflexive verbs appear in all tenses. The imperfect of **se déplacer** follows.

**se déplacer**  *to move, move about; to travel*

| | |
|---|---|
| je me déplaçais | nous nous déplacions |
| tu te déplaçais | vous vous déplaciez |
| il/elle/on se déplaçait | ils/elles se déplaçaient |

The imperfect of the irregular verb **s'asseoir** is **je m'asseyais, tu t'asseyais, il/elle s'asseyait, nous nous asseyions, vous vous asseyiez, ils/elles s'asseyaient.**

**C**  *Using the elements given, create sentences in the imperfect to tell what was going on at Félice's apartment building when she got home today.*

1. le concierge / se mettre debout _____

2. les Forgeard / se mettre en route _____

3. la voisine / s'allonger sur le gazon dans la cour

   _____

4. un taxi / s'approcher de l'immeuble _____

5. moi / se trouver dans mon appartement

   _____

6. toi / se diriger vers la porte _____

7. personne / se reposer _____

8. les voitures / s'arrêter au feu rouge du coin

   _____

9. vous / se dépêcher _____

10. une vieille dame / s'asseoir sur une chaise

    _____

11. nous / se réunir dans la cour _____

12. une famille / s'installer au quatrième étage

    _____

## The Infinitive of Reflexive Verbs

In verb lists and vocabulary, reflexive verbs always appear with the reflexive pronoun **se**. However, when the infinitive of a reflexive verb is used with another verb that is conjugated—**aller**, **compter**, **devoir**, **pouvoir**, or **vouloir**, for example—the reflexive pronoun **se** changes to agree with the subject of the conjugated verb.

| | |
|---|---|
| Nous voulons **nous** mettre en route. | _We want to set out._ |
| Vous alliez **vous** amuser. | _You were going to have a good time._ |

Study the following chart to see the changes of the reflexive pronouns in all persons.

| **devoir** + **se reposer**  _should_ + _to rest_ | |
|---|---|
| Je dois **me** reposer. | Nous devons **nous** reposer. |
| Tu dois **te** reposer. | Vous devez **vous** reposer. |
| Il/Elle/On doit **se** reposer. | Ils/Elles doivent **se** reposer. |

The reflexive pronoun also changes when the subject is only implied, but not expressed in the sentence.

| | |
|---|---|
| Comment **me** reposer? Je suis tellement inquiet. | _How can I rest? I am so nervous._ |

**D**  _Complete each sentence with the missing reflexive pronoun._

1. Il ne voulait pas _____ asseoir.

2. Nous devons _____ détendre.

3. Les enfants vont _____ laver les mains.

4. Je ne veux pas _____ ennuyer.

5. Tu as besoin de _____ amuser un peu.

6. Vous devez _____ dépêcher.

7. Elle ne peut pas _____ déplacer.

8. Je veux _____ coucher maintenant.

9. Tu n'avais pas envie de _____ reposer?

10. Nous ne pouvons pas _____ mettre en route.

11. Vous voulez _____ promener en ville?

12. Je ne peux pas _____ endormir.

13. Qui peut _____ lever?

14. Tu dois _____ mettre debout.

15. Vous allez _____ couper le doigt.

**E**  *Rewrite each sentence, adding the correct form of the verb in parentheses. Retain the tense of the verb in the original sentence.*

MODÈLE   Elle se levait. (vouloir)

*Elle voulait se lever.* _____

1. Nous nous amusons. (avoir besoin de)

   _____

2. Je me reposais. (aller) _____

3. Nous nous réunissons avec nos amis. (compter)

   _____

4. Tu te couchais tôt. (devoir) _____

5. Je me lave les mains? (pouvoir) _____

6. Quand est-ce que vous vous mettiez en route? (aller)

   _____

7. Il se rase. (devoir) _____

8. Je m'allongeais. (avoir envie de) _____

9. Vous vous installez demain? (compter)

   _____

10. Tu te réveillais à huit heures? (préférer)

    _____

11. Nous nous arrêtions pour déjeuner. (vouloir)

    _____

12. Je m'assieds. (devoir) _____

13. Nous ne nous ennuyons pas. (vouloir)

    _____

14. Tu ne te peignais pas? (pouvoir) _____

15. Vous ne vous offensez pas. (devoir)

    _____

# The Passé Composé of Reflexive Verbs

All reflexive verbs are conjugated with **être** in the passé composé. The rules for agreement of the past participle are the same as those for **avoir** verbs.

In the passé composé of a reflexive verb, the past participle agrees with the reflexive pronoun—not the subject—if that pronoun is a direct object.

---

**s'amuser**  *to have a good time*

| | |
|---|---|
| je **me** suis amusé(e) | nous **nous** sommes amusé(e)s |
| tu **t'**es amusé(e) | vous **vous** êtes amusé(e)(s) |
| il **s'**est amusé | ils **se** sont amusés |
| elle **s'**est amusée | elles **se** sont amusées |
| on **s'**est amusé/amusés/amusées | |

---

However, when the reflexive pronoun is an indirect object, as it is in expressions such as **se sécher les cheveux** and **se laver les mains**, the past participle does *not* agree with the reflexive pronoun, because the direct object follows the verb.

---

**se laver les mains**  *to wash one's hands*

| | |
|---|---|
| je me suis lavé les mains | nous nous sommes lavé les mains |
| tu t'es lavé les mains | vous vous êtes lavé les mains |
| il s'est lavé les mains | ils se sont lavé les mains |
| elle s'est lavé les mains | elles se sont lavé les mains |
| on s'est lavé les mains | |

---

Remember that when **se laver** does not have a direct object, the reflexive pronoun is the direct object and the past participle agrees with it: **elle s'est lavée**, **elles se sont lavées**.

Verbs referring to feelings and emotions can also be either reflexive or nonreflexive (transitive). The verbs in the left column below are transitive and express an action that one person does to another. The verbs in the right column are reflexive and correspond to intransitive verbs in English. In these verbs of emotion and feeling, the English equivalents often include *to be* or *to get* + the past participle.

| | |
|---|---|
| **amuser qqn**  *to amuse someone* | **s'amuser**  *to have a good time* |
| **animer qqn**  *to rouse someone, cheer someone on* | **s'animer**  *to feel more lively* |
| **calmer qqn**  *to calm someone down* | **se calmer**  *to calm down* |
| **embêter qqn**  *to annoy someone* | **s'embêter**  *to be/get bored* |
| **énerver qqn**  *to irritate someone* | **s'énerver**  *to get nervous/upset* |
| **ennuyer qqn**  *to bore someone* | **s'ennuyer**  *to be/get bored* |
| **entendre qqn**  *to hear someone; to understand someone* | **s'entendre bien/mal avec quelqu'un**  *to get along/not get along with someone* |
| **enthousiasmer qqn**  *to fill someone with enthusiasm* | **s'enthousiasmer**  *to get enthusiastic/excited* |
| **fâcher qqn**  *to anger someone* | **se fâcher**  *to get angry* |
| **impatienter qqn**  *to annoy someone* | **s'impatienter**  *to get impatient* |
| **indigner qqn**  *to make someone indignant* | **s'indigner**  *to get indignant/annoyed* |

| | |
|---|---|
| **inquiéter qqn** *to worry someone* | **s'inquiéter** *to worry* |
| **mettre qqn de bonne / de mauvaise humeur** *to put someone in a good/bad mood* | **se mettre de bonne / de mauvaise humeur** *to get into a good/bad mood* |
| **mettre qqn en colère** *to make someone angry* | **se mettre en colère** *to get angry* |
| **offenser qqn** *to insult/offend someone* | **s'offenser** *to get insulted/offended* |
| **passionner qqn** *to fascinate someone* | **se passionner (pour)** *to get excited (about)* |
| **préoccuper qqn** *to worry someone* | **se préoccuper** *to worry* |
| **ranimer qqn** *to revive someone* | **se ranimer** *to regain consciousness, be revived* |
| **réjouir qqn** *to gladden someone* | **se réjouir (de)** *to be delighted/thrilled at* |
| **sentir** *to feel, smell* | **se sentir** *to feel* |

**F**   *Rewrite each sentence in the passé composé.*

1. Elle se fâche. _____

2. Ils se brossent les cheveux. _____

3. Elles se déplacent avec difficulté. _____

4. Tu te sèches les cheveux. _____

5. Les enfants se brossent les dents. _____

6. La secrétaire s'indigne. _____

7. Ma sœur se réveille. _____

8. Les étudiants s'embêtent. _____

9. Elle s'enthousiasme. _____

10. Nous nous limons les ongles. _____

11. Les spectateurs s'animent. _____

12. Elles se mettent de mauvaise humeur.

    _____

13. Ils se lavent les mains. _____

14. Vous vous calmez. _____

15. Ils s'inquiètent. _____

16. Nous nous entendons bien avec eux.

    _____

17. Elle se met en colère. _____

18. Ils s'en réjouissent. _____

19. Tu t'énerves. _____

20. Je me sens mal à l'aise. _____

**G** *Using the strings of elements given, create negative sentences in the passé composé to tell what has not yet happened. Use* **pas encore** *in each answer.*

MODÈLE    Paulette / se mettre en colère

   *Paulette ne s'est pas encore mise en colère.*

1. Robert / se laver _____

2. les étudiants / se coucher _____

3. les filles / se brosser les cheveux

   _____

4. elle / se laver la figure _____

5. ma femme / s'habiller _____

6. toi / se limer les ongles _____

7. le professeur / se mettre de mauvaise humeur

   _____

8. mon père / se réveiller _____

9. nos cousins / s'impatienter _____

10. le public / s'animer _____

11. Janine / se laver la tête _____

12. nos invités / se sentir chez eux

   _____

**H** *Complete each sentence with the correct form of the reflexive verb in parentheses for the tense indicated. Be sure the reflexive pronoun refers to the subject.*

***Present***

1. Je _____ chez moi.  (se sentir)

2. Elle _____ sur la plage.  (s'allonger)

3. L'avion _____ de Paris.  (s'approcher)

4. Tu _____ pour l'art moderne.  (se passionner)

5. Pourquoi est-ce que vous _____ toujours de mauvaise humeur? (se mettre)

6. Les membres de cette famille _____ bien.  (s'entendre)

7. Les enfants _____ ici.  (s'embêter)

8. Ils _____.  (s'asseoir)

9. Vous _____.  (s'inquiéter)

10. Tu _____ les cheveux.  (se sécher)

## Imperfect

11. Les touristes _____ parce qu'il faisait chaud.  (se fatiguer)

12. Nous _____ de bonne heure pour aller au travail.  (se lever)

13. Elle _____ avec ses enfants.  (s'impatienter)

14. Je _____ dans la classe de ce prof-là.  (s'ennuyer)

15. Vous _____ beaucoup.  (se soigner)

16. Tu _____.  (se calmer)

17. Je _____ en forme.  (se sentir)

18. Vous _____.  (se promener)

19. Le train _____ de la ville.  (s'éloigner)

20. Cette famille _____ beaucoup.  (se déplacer)

## Passé composé

21. Elles _____ debout.  (se mettre)

22. Je _____.  (s'énerver)

23. Tu _____.  (se fâcher)

24. Nous _____.  (s'endormir)

25. Ils _____.  (se ranimer)

26. Vous _____.  (s'enthousiasmer)

27. Elle _____ en colère.  (se mettre)

28. Les employés _____.  (s'installer)

29. Le patron _____.  (s'indigner)

30. La foule (*crowd*) _____ la place.  (se diriger)

**I** **Translation.** *Express the following sentences in French.*

1. *She's washing her face.* _____

2. *We had a great time.* _____

3. *They wanted to get together.* _____

4. *He was going to travel.* _____

5. *I got excited watching the video game.*

_____

6. *They [feminine] got angry.* _____

7. *They [masculine] got along well.* _____

8. *Do you (vous) intend to cut your hair?* _____

9. *You (tu) must put on your seat belt.* _____

10. *We brushed our teeth.* _____

# Reflexive Verbs with Reciprocal Meaning ("Each Other")

In the plural, reflexive verbs may convey a *reciprocal meaning* equivalent to English "each other."

| | |
|---|---|
| —Vous **vous contactez** souvent? | *"Do you contact each other often?"* |
| —Oui, nous **nous téléphonons** toutes les semaines. | *"Yes, we phone each other every week."* |
| —Le chef et les employés vont **se parler** aujourd'hui? | *"Are the boss and the employees going to talk to each other today?"* |
| —Oui, ils **se sont donné** rendez-vous pour trois heures. | *"Yes, they have made an appointment (to see each other) for three o'clock."* |

Note in the example above that in **ils se sont donné rendez-vous** there is no agreement of the past participle because the reflexive pronoun **se** is an indirect object. To determine whether or not the past participle agrees in the passé composé, determine if the non-reflexive verb takes a direct or an indirect object. In this case, **donner** takes an indirect object of the person (**donner quelque chose à quelqu'un**), so **se** is an indirect object. Compare the following.

voir quelqu'un          Ils se sont **vus**.

(**Quelqu'un** is a direct object; the past participle agrees with the preceding direct object **se**.)

écrire à quelqu'un          Ils se sont **écrit**.

(**Quelqu'un** is an indirect object; there is no agreement of the past participle because **se** is an indirect object.)

In the colloquial style where **on** replaces **nous**, **on se** may have a reciprocal ("each other") meaning.

| | |
|---|---|
| **On s'aime** beaucoup. | *We love each other very much.* |
| **On** ne **se ment** pas. | *We don't lie to each other.* |

Traditionally, **on** has been treated as singular for the purposes of past participle agreement. However, more and more writers today make the past participle agree with the referent of **on** when **se** is the direct object.

| | |
|---|---|
| On s'est **connus** au travail. | *We met each other at work.* |

### Some reciprocal verbs

*\*s'acheter des cadeaux  to buy gifts for each other*
**s'aider**  *to help each other*
**s'aimer**  *to love each other*
**se comprendre**  *to understand each other*
**se connaître**  *to know each other*
**se détester**  *to hate each other*
*\*se donner rendez-vous  to make an appointment to see each other*

---

*The reflexive pronoun is an *indirect* object.

*s'écrire* to write to each other
  *s'entraider* to help each other
*s'envoyer des courriels* to send each other e-mails
*se faire mal* to hurt each other
*se mentir* to lie to each other
*se parler* to speak to each other
*se poser des questions* to ask each other questions
  *se pousser* to push each other
  *se regarder* to look at each other
  *se rencontrer* to meet, run into each other
*se ressembler* to look alike
  *se retrouver* to meet (by appointment)
*se téléphoner* to phone each other
  *se voir* to see each other

**J**  *Using the elements given, create sentences in the present tense to convey reciprocal meaning. Use the verbs reflexively.*

1.  vous / se rencontrer en ville _____

2.  les jumeaux / se ressembler beaucoup

    _____

3.  les consultants / se poser des questions

    _____

4.  mon chien et moi, on / se regarder

    _____

5.  ces voisins / se détester _____

6.  toi et moi, nous / se comprendre _____

7.  cet homme et cette femme / ne jamais se mentir

    _____

8.  vous et ce monsieur / se connaître

    _____

9.  nous / se voir souvent _____

10. elles / se téléphoner _____

11. nous et les voisins, nous / s'entraider

    _____

12. toi et moi, on / se parler tous les jours

    _____

**K**   *Rewrite each of the following reciprocal meaning sentences in the passé composé.*

1. Ils s'écrivent en français. _____

2. Nous nous aidons. _____

3. Elles se mentent. _____

4. Toi et moi, on se pose des questions.

_____

5. Vous vous comprenez. _____

6. Ils se donnent rendez-vous. _____

7. Elles ne se voient pas. _____

8. Les deux enfants se regardent. _____

9. Toi et moi, nous nous achetons des cadeaux.

_____

10. Le patron et le représentant du syndicat se parlent.

_____

**L**   ***Translation.*** *Express the following sentences in French.*

1. *Did you talk to each other yesterday?*

_____

2. *No, but we wrote (= sent) each other e-mails.*

_____

3. *The engineers made an appointment to see each other.*

_____

4. *You and I (on) ran into each other at the mall.*

_____

5. *They used to love each other and now they hate each other.*

_____

6. *We didn't see each other.* _____

7. *Do you often buy gifts for each other?*

_____

8. *The women understood each other well.*

_____

9. *We never lie to each other.* _____

10. *They helped each other.* _____

# The Imperative of Reflexive Verbs

Reflexive pronouns follow the same rules in commands as direct and indirect object pronouns. To review the placement of object pronouns with the imperative, see Chapter 4.

In negative commands, reflexive pronouns appear in their usual position before the verb.

| | |
|---|---|
| Ne **t'**inquiète pas. | *Don't worry.* |
| Ne **nous** dépêchons pas. | *Let's not hurry.* |
| Ne **vous** fâchez pas. | *Don't get angry.* |

In affirmative commands, reflexive pronouns are placed after the verb and attached to it by a hyphen in writing. The pronoun **te** changes to **toi** when it follows the verb in an affirmative command.

| | |
|---|---|
| **Lève-toi** et **mets-toi** en route. | *Get up and start your trip.* |
| **Approchons-nous** de la place. | *Let's go over to the square.* |
| **Asseyez-vous** avec moi. | *Sit down with me.* |

### Additional reflexive verbs often used in the imperative

**s'organiser** *to get organized*
**se disputer** *to quarrel, argue*
**se faire mal** *to hurt each other*
**se préparer** *to get ready*
**se salir** *to get dirty*

**M** *Children, get ready!* For each of these verbs, give a command to one child, then to a group of children. Note that both affirmative and negative commands will be needed.

MODÈLE　　se peigner

　　　　*Peigne-toi.*　　*Peignez-vous.*

| VERB | TO ONE CHILD | TO A GROUP OF CHILDREN |
|---|---|---|
| 1. se réveiller | _____ | _____ |
| 2. se lever | _____ | _____ |
| 3. se débarbouiller | _____ | _____ |
| 4. se laver les mains | _____ | _____ |
| 5. s'habiller | _____ | _____ |
| 6. se dépêcher | _____ | _____ |
| 7. ne pas se faire mal | _____ | _____ |
| 8. ne pas se disputer | _____ | _____ |
| 9. ne pas se salir | _____ | _____ |
| 10. ne pas se diriger vers la porte | _____ | _____ |
| 11. s'organiser | _____ | _____ |

| VERB | TO ONE CHILD | TO A GROUP OF CHILDREN |
|---|---|---|
| 12. se préparer pour sortir | _____ | _____ |
| 13. ne pas s'énerver | _____ | _____ |
| 14. ne pas se fâcher | _____ | _____ |

**N**    Write both the affirmative and the negative **nous** commands for each of the following verbs.

MODÈLE    se laver

*Lavons-nous.*     *Ne nous lavons pas.*

| VERB | AFFIRMATIVE COMMAND | NEGATIVE COMMAND |
|---|---|---|
| 1. s'organiser | _____ | _____ |
| 2. se préparer pour partir | _____ | _____ |
| 3. se dépêcher | _____ | _____ |
| 4. se diriger vers la gare | _____ | _____ |
| 5. se réjouir | _____ | _____ |
| 6. se donner rendez-vous | _____ | _____ |
| 7. s'éloigner de la place | _____ | _____ |
| 8. s'approcher du fleuve | _____ | _____ |
| 9. se laver la tête | _____ | _____ |
| 10. s'asseoir | _____ | _____ |

## Reflexive Verbs: Special Cases

### Reflexive Verbs with **en** as Part of the Verb

Some reflexive verbs have **en** as part of the verb. **En** may be written either as a separate word, as in **s'en aller** *to go away,* or as a prefix, as in **s'envoler** *to fly away* and **s'enfuir** *to flee.* (See Chapter 6, p. 130, for the conjugation of **s'en aller**.)

### Tromper

The verb **tromper** means *to deceive, fool.* The corresponding reflexive verb **se tromper** means *to make a mistake.* **Se tromper de** + a noun means *to get to / go to the wrong (place), select the wrong (thing).*

| | |
|---|---|
| On est arrivés en retard parce qu'on **s'est trompés d'autobus.** | *We got there late because we took the wrong bus.* |
| —Qui a sonné? | *"Who was that at the door?"* |
| —Quelqu'un qui **s'est trompé de porte.** | *"Someone who came to the wrong door."* |

## Se servir de quelque chose

The expression **se servir de qqch** *to use something* is a synonym of **employer** and **utiliser**.

—Tu **te sers** de l'ordinateur pour rédiger?    *"Do you use the computer to write?"*
—Oui, et je **m'en sers** aussi pour tenir    *"Yes, and I also use it to do my household*
    les comptes du ménage.        *accounts."*

## Se rendre compte de quelque chose

In the common expression **se rendre compte de qqch** *to realize something*, the reflexive pronoun is an indirect object. Therefore, the past participle does not agree with it.

Elles ne **se sont** pas **rendu compte** de    *They didn't realize the difficulty.*
    la difficulté.

### Verbs that appear only as reflexives in French

**s'abstenir de qqch / de faire qqch**   *to refrain from (doing) something*
**s'efforcer de faire qqch**   *to strive to do something, try hard to do something*
**s'emparer de qqch**   *to get hold of something*
**s'évanouir**   *to faint*
**se fier à qqn/qqch**   *to trust someone/something*
**se méfier de qqn/qqch**   *to distrust someone/something, be wary of someone/something*
**se repentir de qqch**   *to regret something*
**se soucier de qqn/qqch**   *to worry about someone/something, be concerned about*
    *someone/something*
**se souvenir de qqn/qqch**   *to remember someone/something*
**se suicider**   *to commit suicide*

The reflexive construction in the third person can sometimes be the equivalent of the English passive.

Ça ne **se dit** pas.    *That's not **said**. (You don't say that.)*
C'est un ordinateur qui **se vend** beaucoup.    *It's a computer that **is sold** a lot.*
Cette rue **s'appelle** Avenue Kennedy.    *This street **is called** Kennedy Avenue.*

### Other useful reflexive verbs

**s'adonner à qqch**   *to dedicate oneself to something*
**s'adresser à qqn**   *to address / speak to / be aimed at someone*
**s'apercevoir de qqch**   *to notice something*
**s'attendre à qqch**   *to expect something*
**se cacher**   *to hide*
**se consacrer à qqch**   *to devote oneself to something*
**se débarrasser de qqn/qqch**   *to get rid of someone/something*
**se demander**   *to wonder*
**se donner la peine de faire qqch**   *to take the trouble to do something*
**se douter de**   *to suspect, imagine*
**s'échapper de**   *to run away from, escape from, slip away from*
**se faire à qqch**   *to get used to / accustomed to something*

**se fiancer avec qqn**  *to get engaged to someone*
**s'habituer à qqch**  *to get used to / accustomed to something*
**se marier avec qqn**  *to marry someone*
**se mêler à**  *to mingle with, join in*
**se mettre en panique**  *to fly into a panic*
**se moquer de qqn/qqch**  *to make fun of someone/something*
**se mouiller**  *to get wet*
**se noyer**  *to drown*
**se passer de qqch**  *to do without something*
**se perdre**  *to get lost*
**se plaindre de qqn/qqch**  *to complain about someone/something*
**se priver de qqch**  *to deprive oneself of something*
**se rappeler qqch**  *to recall/remember something*
**se tenir à qqch / à faire qqch**  *to insist on something*

**O**  *How many of the new verbs have you learned?* For each verb in Column A, find a synonym in Column B. Write the letter for that synonym on the blank line.

| COLUMN A | COLUMN B |
|---|---|
| 1. _____ se tenir à | a. mourir sous l'eau |
| 2. _____ se passer de qqch | b. s'habituer à |
| 3. _____ se consacrer à | c. comprendre |
| 4. _____ se faire à | d. aller près de |
| 5. _____ se préoccuper de | e. s'adonner à |
| 6. _____ se noyer | f. utiliser |
| 7. _____ se mettre en route | g. s'embêter |
| 8. _____ s'ennuyer | h. se soucier de |
| 9. _____ s'approcher de | i. se priver de qqch |
| 10. _____ s'efforcer de | j. partir |
| 11. _____ se servir de | k. insister sur |
| 12. _____ se rendre compte de | l. essayer |

**P**  *Translation.* Express the following sentences in French.

1. *She complains all the time.* _____

2. *The tourists got lost.* _____

3. *The children hid in the garden.* _____

4. *We were expecting good results.* [Use imperfect.]

   _____

5. *He dedicated himself to teaching* (l'enseignement). [Use passé composé.]

   _____

6. *To whom should I speak?* _____

7. *They got used to French life.* [Use passé composé.]

_____

8. *We didn't take the trouble to ask.* [Use passé composé.]

_____

9. *I am striving to understand him.* _____

10. *He regretted his words.* [Use passé composé.]

_____

11. *The other team got hold of the ball.* [Use passé composé.]

_____

12. *We used to refrain from answering.* [Use imperfect.]

_____

13. *I needed to slip away from the office.* [Use imperfect.]

_____

14. *She fainted because of the heat.* _____

15. *I don't remember them.* _____

16. *We didn't realize our mistake.* _____

---

**BUILDING SENTENCES** | **Sentences with double object pronouns**

## The Order and Placement of Double Object Pronouns in Statements

English doesn't allow a direct and an indirect object pronoun to occur together—the indirect object appears in a prepositional phrase beginning with *to* or *for* when a direct object is present.

*I gave **it to him**.*

In French, however, double object pronouns are very common.

When the indirect object pronoun is a first- or second-person pronoun, the indirect object pronoun precedes the direct object pronoun. Thus, **me, te, nous,** and **vous** precede **le, la, l',** and **les.**

—J'ai besoin du livre de biologie. Tu **me le** prêtes?
*"I need the biology book. Will you lend it to me?"*

—Je **te le** passe demain.
*"I'll give it to you tomorrow."*

—On dit que vous avez fait de belles photos pendant votre voyage. Vous pouvez **nous les** montrer?
*"They say you took some beautiful photos during your trip. Can you show them to us?"*

—Bien sûr. On va **vous les** envoyer par courrier électronique.
*"Of course. We'll send them to you by e-mail."*

When the indirect object is third-person singular or plural, it *follows* the direct object pronoun. Thus, **le**, **las**, and **les** precede **lui** and **leur**.

| | |
|---|---|
| Ils ne compreneaient pas la leçon, mais le prof **la leur** a expliquée. | *They didn't understand the lesson, but the teacher explained it to them.* |
| Elle voulait voir tes logiciels. Est-ce que tu **les lui** a envoyés? | *She wanted to see your software packages. Did you send them to her?* |

Here is a list of common verbs that frequently appear with double object pronouns. In the list below, **qqch** (**quelque chose** *something*) represents any direct object, and **qqn** (**quelqu'un** *someone*) represents any indirect object.

**annoncer qqch à qqn** *to announce something to someone*
**apporter qqch à qqn** *to bring something to someone*
**apprendre qqch à qqn** *to teach something to someone*
**communiquer qqch à qqn** *to communicate something to someone*
**demander qqch à qqn** *to ask someone for something*
**dire qqch à qqn** *to tell/say something to someone*
**donner qqch à qqn** *to give something to someone*
**enseigner qqch à qqn** *to teach something to someone*
**envoyer qqch à qqn** *to send something to someone*
**expliquer qqch à qqn** *to explain something to someone*
**laisser qqch à qqn** *to leave something for someone*
**montrer qqch à qqn** *to show something to someone*
**offrir qqch à qqn** *to give something (as a gift) to someone*
**passer qqch à qqn** *to pass something to someone*
**prêter qqch à qqn** *to lend something to someone*
**promettre qqch à qqn** *to promise something to someone*
**rendre qqch à qqn** *to give something back to someone*
**suggérer qqch à qqn** *to suggest something to someone*
**vendre qqch à qqn** *to sell something to someone*

With several French verbs, the indirect object is the equivalent of English *from*.

**acheter qqch à qqn** *to buy something from someone*
**arracher qqch à qqn** *to snatch something from someone*
**cacher qqch à qqn** *to hide something from someone*
**dérober qqch à qqn** *to steal something from someone*
**emprunter qqch à qqn** *to borrow something from someone*
**enlever qqch à qqn** *to take something away from someone*
**louer qqch à qqn** *to rent something from someone*
**prendre qqch à qqn** *to take something from someone*
**voler qqch à qqn** *to steal something from someone*

From the point of view of an English speaker, a French sentence such as **Je lui ai acheté la voiture** is ambiguous because it can mean either *I bought the car **from** him/her* or *I bought the car **for** him/her*. Context clarifies which is meant.

Double object pronouns follow the same rules of position as single object pronouns. They precede the conjugated verb unless there is also an infinitive, in which case they occur between the conjugated verb and the infinitive.

Direct object pronouns cause agreement of the past participle when they appear in double object pronoun constructions.

<table>
<tr><td>Les documents? Vous ne me **les** avez pas envoyé**s**.</td><td>*The documents? You didn't send them to me.*</td></tr>
</table>

**Q** *Rewrite the following sentences, replacing each underlined noun object with the corresponding object pronoun. All of your answers will have double object pronouns.*

MODÈLE  Il a donné l'enveloppe à son chef.

_Il la lui a donnée._

1. J'ai offert <u>cette cravate</u> à mon père. _____

2. Elle compte enseigner <u>le français</u> à ses enfants. _____

3. Il a volé <u>l'ordinateur</u> à son chef. _____

4. Je vous ai rendu <u>votre passeport</u>. _____

5. Elle ne nous a pas envoyé <u>les documents</u>. _____

6. Nous avons montré <u>le message</u> à nos collègues. _____

7. Le voleur a arraché <u>son sac</u> à la vieille dame. _____

8. Il expliquait <u>les textes</u> à ses enfants. _____

9. Nous avons loué <u>cet appartement</u> au propriétaire de l'immeuble.

   _____

10. Ils voulaient demander <u>le chemin</u> à un passant. _____

11. Je vais donner <u>ce message</u> au consultant. _____

12. Tu peux me passer <u>le sel</u>, s'il te plaît? _____

13. Le patron a promis <u>l'augmentation</u> à ses employés. _____

14. Je vais cacher <u>la vérité</u> à mes collègues. _____

The pronouns **y** and **en** also appear in double object pronoun constructions. The pronoun **y** usually appears with a direct object pronoun, and the direct object pronoun precedes the word **y**. Possible combinations are as follows.

| | |
|---|---|
| **m'y** | **nous y** |
| **t'y** | **vous y** |
| **l'y** | **les y** |

Note the elisions of **me**, **te**, **le**, and **la** before **y**.

| | |
|---|---|
| —J'étais à la bibliothèque aujourd'hui. | *"I was at the library today."* |
| —Je sais, Nicole. Je **t'y** ai vue. | *"I know, Nicole. I saw you there."* |
| —Les enfants aiment aller à la piscine. | *"The children like to go to the pool."* |
| —Je **les y** emmène souvent. | *"I often take them there."* |

The pronoun **en** usually appears with an indirect object pronoun, and the indirect object pronoun precedes the word **en**. Possible combinations are as follows.

| | |
|---|---|
| **m'en** | **nous en** |
| **t'en** | **vous en** |
| **lui en** | **leur en** |

Note the elisions of **me** and **te** before **en**. The pronouns **y** and **en** may also occur together. When they do, **y** precedes **en**.

—Tu trouve des occasions dans ce magasin?    *"Do you find bargains at that store?"*
—Oui, j'**y en** trouve toujours.    *"Yes, I always find some there."*

**R**   *Rewrite the following sentences, replacing each underlined noun object with the corresponding object pronoun. All of your answers will have double object pronouns, at least one of which will be **y** or **en**.*

MODÈLE   Il me donne de l'argent.

   *Il m'en donne.*

1. Ils posent des questions à leur professeur. _____

2. Elle m'envoie beaucoup de courriels. _____

3. Je prête des livres à mes amis. _____

4. Est-ce que vous retrouvez vos amis au cinéma?

   _____

5. Je vais laisser ma voiture dans le parking. _____

6. Il empruntait souvent de l'argent à son père. _____

7. Est-ce que tu as cherché tes clés au sous-sol? _____

8. Elle aime donner des conseils à son fils. _____

9. Nous avons acheté du poisson au port. _____

10. On peut trouver beaucoup de boutiques dans cette rue.

    _____

11. Je vais envoyer des photos à mes parents. _____

12. Il a jeté les vieilles lettres à la poubelle. _____

## Double Object Pronouns with Commands

In negative commands, the order of pronouns follows the rules given above. In affirmative commands, the order of the object pronouns is somewhat different. The object pronouns follow the verb and are attached to it with hyphens in writing. **Le**, **la**, and **les** precede the indirect object pronouns, and **me** changes to **moi**.

J'ai besoin de ce logiciel. Prête-**le-moi**.    *I need that software. Lend it to me.*

—Christine veut vendre sa voiture.    *"Christine wants to sell her car."*
—Achetons-**la-lui**.    *"Let's buy it from her."*

**Y** and **en** follow the other pronouns. **Moi** elides to **m'** before both **y** and **en**.

Tu as des bonbons? Donne-**m'en**!      *You have candies? Give me some!*
Tes copains sont au stade. Cherche-**les-y**.      *Your friends are at the stadium. Look for them there.*

**S**   *Rewrite the following commands, replacing each underlined noun object with the corresponding object pronoun. All of your answers will have double object pronouns.*

1. Apportez-moi des revues. _____

2. Demandez le numéro de téléphone à Paulette. _____

3. Envoyons des courriels à nos amis. _____

4. Rendez les cédéroms à Philippe et Joseph. _____

5. Offrons un appareil digital à Marguerite. _____

6. Achète les fleurs au marché. _____

7. Pose-moi des questions. _____

8. Lisez-moi le message. _____

9. Annonçons les résultats aux employés. _____

10. Suggère des projets de vacances à tes cousins. _____

**T**   *Translation. Express the following sentences in French.*

1. *Get organized.* (tu) _____

2. *Don't argue.* (vous) _____

3. *Let's get ready to go sightseeing.* _____

4. *He took the wrong train.* _____

5. *Let's not get wet.* _____

6. *The iPod? She gave it (as a gift) to them.* _____

7. *The car? I lent it to him.* _____

8. *As for the files, you didn't send them to us.* (vous)

_____

9. *And the software packages? Can you show them to her?* (tu)

_____

10. *The e-mail? Read it to me.* (tu) _____

11. *(My friends are at the ballpark.) I'm going to meet them there.*

_____

12. *(I need good advice.) Give me some.* (vous) _____

13. *Sit down on this chair and relax there.* (tu)

_____

14.   *The questions? We asked them of them.* _____

15.   *That's not done. (You don't do that).* _____

## Double Object Pronouns with Reflexive Verbs

When a reflexive pronoun is an indirect object and the verb also has a direct object, that direct object can be replaced by the corresponding direct object pronoun. The reflexive pronoun always comes first.

| | |
|---|---|
| Je me brosse **les dents**. | *I brush my teeth.* |
| Je me **les** brosse. | *I brush them.* |
| Il se lave **la tête**. | *He washes his hair.* |
| Il se **la** lave. | *He washes it.* |
| Elle se lime **les ongles**. | *She files her nails.* |
| Elle se **les** lime. | *She files them.* |

The pronouns **y** and **en** also appear with reflexive pronouns.

| | |
|---|---|
| Je me suis mêlé **à la conversation**. | *I joined in the conversation.* |
| Je **m'y** suis mêlé. | *I joined in.* |
| Ils se sont repentis **de leurs actes**. | *They regretted their actions.* |
| Ils **s'en** sont repentis. | *They regretted them.* |
| Nous nous sommes habitués **à cet appartement**. | *We got used to that apartment.* |
| Nous **nous y** sommes habitués. | *We got used to it.* |
| Vous vous doutiez **de son incompétence**. | *You suspected his incompetence.* |
| Vous **vous en** doutiez. | *You suspected it.* |
| Je me suis fait mal **au bras**. | *I hurt my arm.* |
| Je **m'y** suis fait mal. | *I hurt it.* |

Commands are formed with **y** and **en** as follows.

| | |
|---|---|
| Arrête-toi au feu rouge. | *Stop at the red light.* |
| Arrête-**t'y**. | *Stop there.* |

Note that **toi** elides to **t'** before **y**.[1]

| | |
|---|---|
| Va-t'en. OR Allez-vous-en. | *Go away.* |
| Allons-nous-en. | *Let's go away.* |

The direct object pronouns cause agreement of the past participle because they precede the verb.[2]

| | |
|---|---|
| Il s'est acheté **cette voiture**. | *He bought himself that car.* |
| Il se **l'**est achetée. | *He bought it for himself.* |
| Elle s'est cassé **la jambe**. | *She broke her leg.* |
| Elle se **l'**est cassée. | *She broke it.* |

---

[1]In colloquial speech, this is often pronounced **"Arrête-toi-z-y."**

[2]Note that this agreement also takes place if the direct object is the antecedent of a relative clause that precedes the past participle: **la voiture** qu'il s'est achetée.

**U**  *Rewrite the following sentences with reflexive verbs, replacing underlined phrases with the appropriate pronouns.*

1. Elle s'est fait mal aux pieds. _____

2. Ils se sont brossé les dents. _____

3. Je me suis offert des vacances. _____

4. Arrêtez-vous au coin de la rue. _____

5. Ne te coupe pas le doigt. _____

6. Tu te caches la vérité. _____

7. Ils s'achètent des cédés. _____

8. Je ne me fie pas à ses promesses. _____

9. L'enfant s'est sali les mains. _____

10. Il se passe de ces luxes. _____

# The Future
# and the Conditional

Conditional sentences: possible conditions,
 contrary-to-present-fact conditions
Cleft sentences: highlighting an element of a sentence

## The Future Tense

The future tense in French is formed by adding a specific set of endings to the infinitive of the verb. The endings are the same for all French verbs.

### -Er Verbs in the Future

**parler**  *to speak*

| | |
|---|---|
| je parler**ai** | nous parler**ons** |
| tu parler**as** | vous parler**ez** |
| il/elle/on parler**a** | ils/elles parler**ont** |

Verbs with spelling changes in the present before a mute **e** have the same change in all persons of the future tense where the **e** of the -**er** infinitive ending becomes mute.

| INFINITIVE | **je** FORM<br>PRESENT TENSE | **nous** FORM<br>PRESENT TENSE | FUTURE TENSE |
|---|---|---|---|
| acheter | j'achète | nous achetons | j'achèterai, nous achèterons |
| appeler | j'appelle | nous appelons | j'appellerai, nous appellerons |
| jeter | je jette | nous jetons | je jetterai, nous jetterons |
| nettoyer | je nettoie | nous nettoyons | je nettoierai, nous nettoierons |

However, verbs with **é** as the stem vowel of the infinitive keep **é** in the future tense.

| INFINITIVE | **je** FORM<br>PRESENT TENSE | **nous** FORM<br>PRESENT TENSE | FUTURE TENSE |
|---|---|---|---|
| compléter | je complète | nous complétons | je compléterai, nous compléterons |
| espérer | j'espère | nous espérons | j'espérerai, nous espérerons |
| préférer | je préfère | nous préférons | je préférerai, nous préférerons |

---

**LA LANGUE FRANÇAISE   French spelling**

---

In 1990, the French government attempted to regularize French orthography. According to the new spelling rules, verbs with **é** in the infinitive may follow the pattern of **acheter**, thus giving the following future forms: **je complète-rai, j'espèrerai, je préfèrerai**.

In France, language issues are taken very seriously, and the new spelling rules were discussed at length on evening news shows. Many other aspects of the spelling reform were controversial, and most publications adhere to the orthographic norms in effect before 1990.

## -Ir Verbs in the Future

**finir**  *to finish*

| | |
|---|---|
| je finir**ai** | nous finir**ons** |
| tu finir**as** | vous finir**ez** |
| il/elle/on finir**a** | ils/elles finir**ont** |

The verbs **cueillir** *to gather* and **accueillir** *to welcome, receive* (people) change **-ir** to **-er** in the future.

| | |
|---|---|
| cueillir | je cueill**erai** |
| accueillir | je accueill**erai** |

## -Re Verbs in the Future

Verbs ending in **-re** lose the final **e** of the infinitive when the endings of the future are added.

**vendre**  *to sell*

| | |
|---|---|
| je vendr**ai** | nous vendr**ons** |
| tu vendr**as** | vous vendr**ez** |
| il/elle/on vendr**a** | ils/elles vendr**ont** |

## Modified Infinitive Forms in the Future

Several verbs have modified infinitive forms in the future. These verbs have the same endings as the verbs in the charts above. The **je** form is given as a model for the entire conjugation except in the case of **pleuvoir**, which is used only in third-person form.

Verbs whose infinitive ends in **-oir** lose the **oi** in the future tense.

| | |
|---|---|
| rece**voir** | je rece**vrai** |
| déce**voir** | je déce**vrai** |
| de**voir** | je de**vrai** |
| pleu**voir** | il pleu**vra** |

However, **prévoir** *to foresee* and **pourvoir** *to supply* have the future forms **je prévoirai** and **je pourvoirai**. The future of **s'asseoir** is **je m'assiérai**.

**Avoir** and **savoir** lose the **oi** of the infinitive, and the final **v** of their stems changes to **u**.

| | |
|---|---|
| av**oir** | j'a**urai** |
| sav**oir** | je sa**urai** |

The future of **il y a** is **il y aura** *there will be.*

**Vouloir** loses the **oi** of the infinitive, and the final **l** of the stem changes to **d**.

| | |
|---|---|
| voul**oir** | je vou**drai** |

**Valoir** *to be worth* and **falloir** *must* also lose the **oi** of the infinitive and modify the stem.

| | |
|---|---|
| val**oir** | je va**udrai** |
| fall**oir** | il fa**udra** |

**Tenir** and **venir** change their stem vowels to **ie**, and the **i** of the infinitive changes to **d**.

| | |
|---|---|
| tenir | je **tiendrai** |
| venir | je **viendrai** |

Several verbs have **rr** in the future tense, sometimes with a modified stem.

| | |
|---|---|
| acquérir | j'**acquérr**ai |
| courir | je **courr**ai |
| envoyer | j'**enverr**ai |
| mourir | je **mourr**ai |
| pouvoir | je **pourr**ai |
| voir | je **verr**ai |

Three verbs have irregular stems in the future.

| | |
|---|---|
| aller | j'**irai** |
| être | je **serai** |
| faire | je **ferai** |

Most compounds of verbs that are irregular in the future show the same irregularities.

| | |
|---|---|
| **défaire** *to undo* | je **déferai** |
| **devenir** *to become* | je **deviendrai** |
| **revenir** *to come back* | je **reviendrai** |
| **soutenir** *to support* | je **soutiendrai** |

## Uses of the Future Tense

The future tense corresponds to English *will* or *shall* do something. It contrasts with the *futur proche*, which consists of **aller** + an infinitive. The *futur proche* implies the action will be completed soon, while the future tense is open-ended as to completion of the action. Thus, if you ask for a book at the library desk, the librarian's response would normally be in the *futur proche* as follows.

| | |
|---|---|
| Je **vais chercher** votre livre. | *I'll get your book.* |

Were the librarian to respond with the future tense, **Je *chercherai* votre livre**, you would be left wondering how long you might have to wait.

In English we often use the future tense to ask for instructions. French uses **devoir** + an infinitive rather than the future for this function.

Qu'est-ce que je **dois faire**? *What shall I do?*

French may use the present tense to express future time when another element of the sentence makes it clear that the future is referred to.

Je pars demain. *I'm leaving tomorrow.*

**A** *Rewrite each sentence in the future tense.*

1. Il se dépêche. _____

2. On parle anglais. _____

3. Ils font du chinois. _____

4. Elle pense à toi. _____

5. Je finis le projet. _____

6. Qui vient? _____

7. Qu'est-ce qu'elle veut voir? _____

8. Nous la connaissons. _____

9. L'avion est à l'heure. _____

10. Vous regardez le film. _____

11. J'attends en bas. _____

12. Tu ne cueilles pas de fleurs. _____

13. Vous appelez les pompiers (*firemen*). _____

14. Elles se lavent les mains. _____

15. Tu t'en souviens. _____

16. Les enfants s'ennuient. _____

17. Nous nous débarbouillons. _____

18. Je m'endors. _____

19. Tu te casses la jambe. _____

20. L'autocar s'éloigne. _____

21. Le professeur ne se fâche pas. _____

22. Vous vous amusez. _____

23. Tu ne t'énerves pas. _____

24. Elle ne se met pas en colère. _____

25. On se téléphone. _____

**B** *Complete each sentence with the future tense of the verb in parentheses.*

1. (aller) Tu _____ avec nous?

2. écouter) Il _____ sûrement ses messages.

3. (nettoyer) Je _____ l'écran de mon ordinateur.

4. (choisir) Nous _____ un beau cadeau pour elle.

5. (envoyer) On lui _____ des fleurs aussi.

6. (remercier) Elle nous _____.

7. (accueillir) Qui _____ les étudiants étrangers?

8. (revenir) Elles _____ mardi.

9. (recevoir) Il _____ notre colis (*package*) demain.

10. (lire) Quand est-ce que vous _____ les documents?

11. (dire) Je ne lui _____ jamais la vérité.

12. (appuyer) Tout le monde _____ ce candidat.

13. (emmener) Si vous voulez y aller, je vous _____.

14. (rejeter) Je suis sûr qu'ils _____ cette idée.

15. (commencer) Le concert _____ dans une demi-heure.

16. (rendre) Quand est-ce que tu me _____ mon livre?

17. (écrire) Tu sais quand il nous _____?

18. (manger) Nous _____ ensemble.

19. (faire) Je _____ le ménage après-demain.

20. (avoir) Elle _____ du mal à le faire.

21. (réussir) Vous _____ aux examens.

22. (sortir) Ils _____ ensemble.

23. (savoir) Quand _____-vous où il habite?

24. (rompre) Elle _____ avec lui.

25. (s'occuper) Ma grand-mère _____ des enfants.

**C** *Respond to each question by saying that you think these things will happen.*

MODÈLE   Elle va retourner ou elle ne va pas retourner?

_Je crois qu'elle retournera._

1. Il va être en retard ou il ne va pas être en retard?

_____

2. Ils vont m'inviter ou ils ne vont pas m'inviter?

   _____

3. Il va pleuvoir ou il ne va pas pleuvoir? _____

4. Il va faire froid ou il ne va pas faire froid? _____

5. Ce film va nous plaire ou il ne va pas nous plaire?

   _____

6. Tu vas sortir ou tu ne vas pas sortir? _____

7. Tu vas descendre ou tu ne vas pas descendre?

   _____

8. Ils vont se voir ou ils ne vont pas se voir? _____

9. Il va m'envoyer un courriel ou il ne va pas m'envoyer un courriel?

   _____

10. Ils vont s'entraider ou ils ne vont pas s'entraider?

    _____

11. Les enfants vont se salir ou ils ne vont pas se salir?

    _____

12. Nous allons nous disputer ou nous n'allons pas nous disputer?

    _____

13. Elle va se repentir de ses mots ou elle ne va pas se repentir de ses mots?

    _____

14. Tu vas participer aux activités ou tu ne vas pas participer aux activités?

    _____

15. Elles vont s'habituer à la vie universitaire ou elles ne vont pas s'habituer à la vie

    universitaire? _____

---

### LA LANGUE FRANÇAISE   the future

The endings of the future tense in French look very much like the forms of the auxiliary verb **avoir** for good reason. In late spoken Latin, the original Latin future was replaced by a verb + infinitive construction consisting of the auxiliary verb **habere** (ancestor of French **avoir**) + the infinitive. The meaning shifted from *I have to go* or *I am to go* to *I will go*. The forms of **habere** were usually placed after the infinitive in spoken Latin and eventually became fused with it, giving the forms of the future in modern French.

## Use of the Future After Conjunctions of Time

English uses the present tense in a subordinate clause when the main clause of the sentence is in the future or the imperative, even when the reference is to future time. In such cases French, however, uses the future tense in the subordinate clause if that clause begins with one of the following conjunctions.

**quand**  *when*
**lorsque**  *when* (literary)
**aussitôt que**  *as soon as*
**dès que**  *as soon as*
**après que**  *after*

| | |
|---|---|
| Envoie-moi un courriel **quand tu seras** prêt. | *Send me an e-mail when you are ready.* |
| **Aussitôt que je recevrai** ton message, je passerai te prendre. | *As soon as I get your message, I'll come by for you.* |
| **Quand tu entendras** mes trois coups de klaxon, descends. | *When you hear me honk three times, come downstairs.* |
| Je te ramènerai **dès que la réunion finira**. | *I'll take you back home as soon as the meeting is over.* |
| On parlera de la réunion **après qu'on sera** de retour. | *We'll talk about the meeting after we are back.* |

**D**  *Combine each pair of sentences into a single sentence containing two clauses, using the conjunction in parentheses.*

MODÈLE   Nous ferons nos valises. Le linge est sec. (dès que)

*Nous ferons nos valises dès que le linge sera sec.*

1. Danielle descendra. Elle voit ma voiture. (quand)

   _____

2. On rentrera. Il commence à pleuvoir. (aussitôt que)

   _____

3. Il sera d'accord avec nous. Il comprend le problème. (lorsque)

   _____

4. Je passerai te voir. On répare ma voiture. (dès que)

   _____

5. Nous nous assiérons. Nous trouvons une table libre. (aussitôt que)

   _____

6. Téléphonez-moi. Vous savez quelque chose. (lorsque)

   _____

7. Ils paieront leurs dettes. Ils ont de l'argent. (quand)

   _____

8. On se mettra en route. Tout le monde est prêt.  (dès que)

   _____

9. Fais-moi savoir (*let me know*). Tu reçois les billets.  (aussitôt que)

   _____

10. On le verra. Nous sortons.  (quand)

    _____

## The Conditional

The conditional tense in French is formed by adding the imperfect endings to the infinitive. All French verbs have the same endings in the conditional.

**parler** *to speak*

| | |
|---|---|
| je parler**ais** | nous parler**ions** |
| tu parler**ais** | vous parler**iez** |
| il/elle/on parler**ait** | ils/elles parler**aient** |

**finir** *to finish*

| | |
|---|---|
| je finir**ais** | nous finir**ions** |
| tu finir**ais** | vous finir**iez** |
| il/elle/on finir**ait** | ils/elles finir**aient** |

**vendre** *to sell*

| | |
|---|---|
| je vendr**ais** | nous vendr**ions** |
| tu vendr**ais** | vous vendr**iez** |
| il/elle/on vendr**ait** | ils/elles vendr**aient** |

Those verbs that have irregular stems or modified infinitive forms in the future also form the conditional from the same modified infinitives.

### -Er Verbs with Spelling Changes

| FUTURE | CONDITIONAL |
|---|---|
| j'achèterai, nous achèterons | j'achèterais, nous achèterions |
| j'appellerai, nous appellerons | j'appellerais, nous appellerions |
| je jetterai, nous jetterons | je jetterais, nous jetterions |
| je nettoierai, nous nettoierons | je nettoierais, nous nettoierions |
| je compléterai, nous compléterons | je compléterais, nous compléterions[1] |
| j'espérerai, nous espérerons | j'espérerais, nous espérerions[1] |
| je préférerai, nous préférerons | je préférerais, nous préférerions[1] |

---

[1]Other acceptable forms include **je complèterais / nous complèterions, j'espèrerais / nous espèrerions, je préfèrerais / nous préfèrerions**. See "La langue française: French spelling," p. 159.

## -Ir Verbs with Modified Infinitives

| INFINITIVE | FUTURE | CONDITIONAL |
|---|---|---|
| cueillir | je cueillerai | je cueillerais |
| accueillir | j'accueillerai | j'accueillerais |

## Verbs Ending in -oir

| INFINITIVE | FUTURE | CONDITIONAL |
|---|---|---|
| recevoir | je recevrai | je recevrais |
| décevoir | je décevrai | je décevrais |
| devoir | je devrai | je devrais |
| pleuvoir | il pleuvra | il pleuvrait |

*but*

| | | |
|---|---|---|
| prévoir | je prévoirai | je prévoirais |
| pourvoir | je pourvoirai | je pourvoirais |
| s'asseoir | je m'assiérai | je m'assiérais |

## Other Verbs with Modified Infinitives in the Future and Conditional

| INFINITIVE | FUTURE | CONDITIONAL |
|---|---|---|
| avoir | j'aurai | j'aurais |
| savoir | je saurai | je saurais |
| vouloir | je voudrai | je voudrais |
| valoir | je vaudrai | je vaudrais |
| falloir | il faudra | il faudrait |
| tenir | je tiendrai | je tiendrais |
| venir | je viendrai | je viendrais |
| aller | j'irai | j'irais |
| être | je serai | je serais |
| faire | je ferai | je ferais |

The conditional of **il y a** is **il y aurait** *there would be.*

## Verbs with rr in the Future and Conditional

| INFINITIVE | FUTURE | CONDITIONAL |
|---|---|---|
| acquérir | j'acquérrai | j'acquérrais |
| courir | je courrai | je courrais |
| envoyer | j'enverrai | j'enverrais |
| mourir | je mourrai | je mourrais |
| pouvoir | je pourrai | je pourrais |
| voir | je verrai | je verrais |

## Uses of the Conditional

As in English, the conditional in French is used in hypotheses, or statements about what *would* happen.

| | |
|---|---|
| Lui, il ne partirait pas avec eux. | *He wouldn't go on vacation with them.* |
| Dans ce cas-là, on vous aiderait. | *In that case, we would help you.* |
| Je ne dirais pas ça. | *I wouldn't say that.* |
| Personne ne pourrait comprendre. | *No one could understand.* |

The conditional appears frequently in subordinate (dependent) clauses after main verbs of communication (e.g., **dire**, **écrire**) and knowledge or belief (**savoir**, **croire**) when the main verb is in one of the past tenses. There is a correspondence of tenses in French and English in such situations: *main clause in present / subordinate clause in future; main clause in past / subordinate clause in conditional.*

| | |
|---|---|
| Le prof **dit** qu'il y **aura** un examen demain. | *The teacher says there will be a test tomorrow.* |
| Le prof **a dit** qu'il y **aurait** un examen demain. | *The teacher said there would be a test tomorrow.* |
| Charlotte **écrit** qu'elle **arrivera** demain. | *Charlotte writes that she will arrive tomorrow.* |
| Charlotte **a écrit** qu'elle **arriverait** demain. | *Charlotte wrote that she would arrive tomorrow.* |
| Je **crois** qu'ils **viendront**. | *I think that they will come.* |
| Je **croyais** qu'ils **viendraient**. | *I thought that they would come.* |

Note that English often uses the auxiliary verb *would* to express habitual or repeated action in the past. In this function, French uses the imperfect tense, not the conditional.

| | |
|---|---|
| Elle m'**envoyait** toujours des courriels. | *She would always send me e-mails.* |
| Le samedi on **allait** au cinéma. | *On Saturdays we would go to the movies.* |

The conditional of some verbs is used to express polite requests, suggestions, or refusals. The English conditional is often used in the same way.

| | |
|---|---|
| **Pourriez**-vous m'aider? | *Could you help me?* |
| **Voudriez**-vous sortir un peu? | *Would you like to go out for a while?* |
| Je regrette, mais je ne **saurais** pas vous le dire. | *I'm sorry but I don't know (the information you asked for).* |

In journalistic language, the conditional may be used to express an assertion that the writer sees as alleged but not yet verified, one deriving from sources rather than investigation. The English equivalent is usually the future tense or the present.

| | |
|---|---|
| Selon un porte-parole du gouvernement, les pourparlers **reprendraient** demain. | *According to a government spokesperson, talks will resume tomorrow.* |
| Michel Landry **serait** nommé PDG de l'entreprise. | *Michel Landry will be named (implication: it is rumored) CEO of the company.* |

**E** *Complete each sentence with the conditional of the verb in parentheses to tell what would happen in each case. The phrases in parentheses explain why these things would happen.*

MODÈLE    *(Ils mettent longtemps à arriver à l'aéroport.)* Ils _arriveraient_ en courant à la porte.  (arriver)

1. *(Tu n'as ni bu ni mangé.)* Tu _____ faim et soif.  (avoir)

2. *(On voit le nouveau-né.)* Nous le _____ dans nos bras.  (prendre)

3. *(On vient d'ouvrir un restaurant excellent.)* Je _____ essayer sa cuisine. (vouloir)

4. *(Personne ne sait à quelle heure il viendra.)* On _____ de la vérifier. (essayer)

5. *(Vous êtes inquiets et épuisés.)* Vous _____ un peu de musique pour vous détendre.  (écouter)

6. *(Elle a besoin de faire un peu d'exercice.)* Elle _____ une promenade. (faire)

7. *(La soupe est fade [tasteless].)* Ils _____ un peu de sel.  (ajouter)

8. *(On a beaucoup de choses à acheter.)* Vous _____ au grand magasin. (aller)

9. *(Sa petite amie est en colère.)* Il lui _____ acheter des fleurs.  (pouvoir)

10. *(Notre collègue ne sait pas ce qui se passe.)* Nous le _____ au courant. (mettre)

11. *(Vous ne connaissez pas la route.)* Vous _____ une carte routière. (acheter)

12. *(Il n'est pas content au travail.)* Il _____ un nouvel emploi.  (chercher)

**F** *Complete each sentence with the correct form of the verb in parentheses. Choose between the future and the conditional, depending on the tense of the verb in the main clause.*

MODÈLES    (écrire)   Il dit qu'il nous _écrira_ .

(écrire)   Il a dit qu'il nous _écrirait_ .

1. (venir)        J'ai promis que je _____.

2. (rentrer)      Il dit qu'il _____ à sept heures.

3. (être)         Tu crois que les enfants _____ contents?

4. (atterrir)     Nous ne savions pas à quelle heure l'avion _____.

5. (avoir)        Il m'a fait savoir qu'il n'y _____ pas de réunion aujourd'hui.

6. (pouvoir)      Elle écrit qu'elle _____ nous aider.

7. (vendre)       Ils nous ont expliqué qu'ils ne _____ pas leur maison.

8. (intéresser)   Je suis sûre que cet article vous _____.

9. (devoir)       Je ne sais pas si elle _____ rappeler ce client.

10. (vouloir)     Elle lui a dit qu'elle ne _____ sortir pas avec lui.

11. (s'en aller)    J'ai l'impression qu'il _____ .

12. (avoir)    Ils ont dit qu'ils _____ besoin de trois informaticiens
       cette année.

13. (faire)    À la radio on a dit qu'il _____ beau aujourd'hui.

14. (falloir)    Je vous préviens qu'il _____ être à l'heure.

15. (voir)    Il m'a dit qu'il ne _____ pas pareil film.

---

| BUILDING SENTENCES | **Conditional sentences: possible conditions, contrary-to-present-fact conditions** |
|---|---|

Conditional sentences have two clauses, an *if*-clause (a **si**-clause in French) and a main clause. Either clause may come first in the sentence. There are three main types of conditional sentences, two of which will be presented here.

## Possible Conditions

This type of conditional sentence expresses something that may well happen or that will happen if a condition is met. In these sentences, the **si**-clause is in the present tense and the main clause is in the future. English possible conditions are expressed with the same tenses: The *if*-clause is in the present tense and the main clause is in the future.

| | |
|---|---|
| Si tu sors, je sortirai avec toi. | *If you're going out, I'll go out with you.* |
| Il sera là-bas ce soir s'il prend le train. | *He'll be there this evening if he takes the train.* |
| Si je suis libre, je passerai te voir. | *If I'm free, I'll come by to see you.* |
| Ils seront fâchés s'ils s'en rendent compte. | *They'll be angry if they realize (it).* |

**G**  *Possible conditions. Complete each sentence with the correct form of the verb in parentheses for the **si**-clause and the main clause. Use the present indicative and the future tenses.*

MODÈLE    Si j'__*ai*__ le temps, j'__*irai*__ au cybercafé. (avoir, aller)

1. Si je _____ mes vacances en Aquitaine, je _____
   des randonnées en montagne.  (passer, faire)

2. S'il _____ son travail, il _____ sortir.  (finir, pouvoir)

3. Si j'_____ besoin d'aide, je te _____ signe.
   (avoir, faire)

4. Si vous m'_____ le problème, j'_____ de le résoudre.
   (expliquer, essayer)

5. Moi, je t'_____ si tu _____ les fleurs.  (aider, arroser)

6. Tout le monde _____ se baigner si tu _____ une
   maison avec piscine.  (venir, acheter)

7. Je t'_____ si tu _____ en ville maintenant.
   (emmener, aller)

8. Nous _____ trop d'argent si nous _____ au casino.
   (perdre, aller)

9. Ils _____ ce soir s'il ne _____ pas. (sortir, pleuvoir)

10. Si tu t'_____, le prof te _____. (excuser, pardonner)

**H**  *From the two sentences given, create a new sentence expressing possible conditions.*
  *Remember that the **si**-clause is in the present tense and the main clause is in the future.*

MODÈLE       CONDITION              ACTION

             Il a soif.        On lui offre une bière.

  *S'il a soif, on lui offrira une bière.* _____

| CONDITION | ACTION |
|-----------|--------|
| 1. Il pleut. | Nous restons à la maison. |
| 2. Le programme continue à être lent. | Il faut réamorcer (*reboot*). |
| 3. Ils veulent créer un site Web. | Ils doivent réserver un nom de domaine. |
| 4. Vous mettez un mot de passe. | Vous limitez l'accès à vos pages Web. |
| 5. Elle travaille toute la journée. | Elle finit le projet. |
| 6. Vous me donnez votre numéro. | Je vous téléphone la semaine prochaine. |
| 7. Il est au courant du problème. | Il peut vous renseigner. |
| 8. Vous arrivez à six heures et demie. | La banque est fermée. |
| 9. Vous avez un compte en banque en ligne. | Vous gérez (*manage*) vos finances sur l'ordinateur. |
| 10. Vous préparez votre retraite (*retirement*). | Vous vivez en toute tranquillité. |
| 11. Tu donnes le numéro de la carte de crédit. | Tu paies tes factures en ligne. |
| 12. La ville accepte ma soumission (*bid*). | Je gagne beaucoup d'argent. |

## Contrary-to-present-fact Conditions

Some sentences express a condition that is contrary to a fact or situation existing in *present* time. In such cases, French uses the imperfect in the **si**-clause and the conditional in the main clause. For instance, **Si tu sortais, je sortirais avec toi** expresses a condition that is *contrary to fact*. The fact is that **tu ne sors pas** and the result is that **je ne sors pas avec toi**. The meaning is **(Mais) si tu sortais** (*But if you were going out, which you're not*), **je sortirais avec toi** (*I'd go out with you*). Remember that either the **si**-clause or the main clause can appear first in the sentence.

Si tu **étais** libre, je **passerais** te voir.    *If you were free, I'd stop by to see you.*
Les prix **baisseraient** s'il y **avait** moins   *Prices would go down if there were less*
  de demande.                            *demand.*

**I**   *Contrary-to-fact conditions in present time. Complete each sentence with the correct form of the verb in parentheses for the si-clause and the main clause. Use the imperfect and the conditional tenses.*

> MODÈLE   Si ces enfants *obéissaient* à leurs parents, il y *aurait* moins
> de conflits dans leur famille. (obéir, avoir)

1. Si nous _____ ce logiciel, nous _____ plus
   rapidement. (avoir, travailler)

2. S'ils _____ une entreprise, ils _____ beaucoup
   d'argent. (monter, gagner)

3. Vous _____ leurs services si vous _____ leur site
   Web. (connaître, visiter)

4. Si tu _____ au Danemark, tu ne _____ pas y
   employer des euros. (partir, pouvoir)

5. On _____ acheter des devises étrangères (*foreign currency*) à la poste

   si on en _____ besoin. (pouvoir, avoir)

6. Vous _____ de perdre de l'argent si vous _____
   en bourse maintenant. (risquer, investir)

7. Le pays _____ plus prospère si on _____ moins
   d'impôts (*taxes*). (être, payer)

8. S'ils _____ parler avec un conseiller financier, ils

   _____ notre bureau. (vouloir, contacter)

9. S'il _____ ce logiciel, il _____ graver (*burn*) des CD.
   (télécharger, pouvoir)

10. Si vous _____ un tableur (*spreadsheet*), vous _____
    vos données. (acheter, organiser)

11. S'il _____ la situation économique, il _____
    des placements (*investments*) plus intelligents. (comprendre, faire)

12. Beaucoup d'employés _____ leur travail si cette entreprise

    _____ faillite (*bankruptcy*). (perdre, faire)

*Change each factual sentence into a contrary-to-fact conditional sentence.*

MODÈLE   Tu ne le verras pas parce qu'il n'est pas là.
                  *Tu le verrais s'il était là.*

1. Je ne peux pas le faire parce que je ne m'y connais pas.

   _____

2. Parce qu'il ne neige pas les enfants ne veulent pas sortir.

   _____

3. Je ne vais pas au cinéma parce que toi, tu n'y vas pas.

   _____

4. Ils ne maigrissent pas parce qu'ils ne sont pas au régime.

   _____

5. Tu ne t'endors pas parce que tu bois tant de café.

   _____

6. Vous n'avez pas beaucoup de débouchés (*career prospects*) parce que vous ne savez
   pas l'espagnol.

   _____

   _____

7. Parce que vous ne profitez pas des soldes vous n'économisez pas beaucoup d'argent.

   _____

   _____

8. Je n'en veux plus parce que je n'ai pas faim.

   _____

9. Elle souffre de la chaleur parce que son appartement n'est pas climatisé (*air conditioned*).

   _____

   _____

10. Il ne va pas chez le médecin parce qu'il se sent bien.

   _____

**K** **Translation.** *Express the following sentences in French.*

1. *You* (vous) *will be hungry if you only eat a croissant.*

   _____

2. *If I had time, I'd answer all my e-mails.*

   _____

3. *They'd want to go to the movies if the weather were bad.*

   _____

4. *If you* (tu) *feel like dancing salsa, we can go to the discotheque.*

   _____

5. *He'd finish the project more quickly if he used this software program.*

   _____

6. *If they stop worrying, they'll have a good time.*

   _____

7. *We thought that she would be in a good mood.*

   _____

8. *She says that we'll buy gifts for each other.*

   _____

9. *Could you* (vous) *accompany me?*

   _____

10. *Would you* (vous) *like to have a drink with them?*

   _____

| BUILDING SENTENCES | **Cleft sentences: highlighting an element of a sentence** |
| --- | --- |

French and English have very different ways of highlighting, or focusing on, a specific element of a sentence in speech. English speakers move the main stress of the sentence to the word they wish to focus on.

A neutral sentence would be the following: *I am walking to the store.*

Each of the sentences below highlights one specific element of the sentence. Read these sentences aloud, stressing the word in bold type.

> **I** am walking to the store. (*I, and not you or he, am walking.*)
> I **am** walking to the store. (*Why do you say I am not?*)
> I am **walking** to the store. (*I am walking, not driving.*)
> I am walking **to** the store. (*I am walking to, not from, the store.*)
> I am walking to **the** store. (*I am walking to the one store around here* [*among other possibilities*].)
> I am walking to the **store**. (*I am walking to the store, not to the office.*)

French, however, highlights an element in a sentence through a structural change in the sentence itself—the use of *cleft sentences,* which involves changes in word order and phrasing. The word "cleft" comes from the verb "cleave," which means to cut or divide something into two parts. By extension, a *cleft sentence* is a sentence whose single clause has been split into two clauses, and it is used to highlight an element in one of the clauses.

In the spoken language, English uses stress and intonation to highlight an element. In writing, however, where stress and intonation cannot be conveyed, English may use the cleft sentence or put the element of the sentence focused upon in italic or boldface type. The English cleft construction has the following pattern.

> *It* + verb *to be* + highlighted element + subordinate clause (introduced by *who* or *that*).

A neutral sentence can be transformed into multiple cleft sentences, depending on which element is to be highlighted. See the possible cleft sentences that can be formed from the neutral sentence *The consultant manages the software project in Dallas.*

> It is **the consultant** who manages the software project in Dallas.
> It is **the software project** that the consultant manages in Dallas.
> It is **in Dallas** that the consultant manages the software project.

French moves the element to be highlighted into a structure beginning with **c'est X qui**, thus converting the entire predicate into a relative clause.

| | |
|---|---|
| C'est Pierre qui va. | ***Pierre** is going.* |
| C'est le patron qui était en colère. | ***The boss** was angry.* |
| C'est le gouvernement qui doit y veiller. | ***The government** is supposed to see to it.* |
| C'est ce placement qui m'inquiète. | ***This investment** worries me.* |
| C'est ce logiciel qui nous intéresse. | ***This software** interests us.* |

**C'est** may also introduce a plural noun. In such cases, the verb following **qui** must be plural.

| | |
|---|---|
| C'est **les ouvriers** qui **sont** en colère. | *It's the workers who are angry.* |
| C'est **ces placements** qui m'inquiè**tent**. | *It's those investments that worry me.* |

In formal French, **c'est** is replaced by **ce sont** before a plural noun.

| | |
|---|---|
| **Ce sont les ouvriers** qui **sont** en colère. | *It's the workers who are angry.* |
| **Ce sont ces placements** qui m'inquiè**tent**. | *It's those investments that worry me.* |

A pronoun subject may also be highlighted in the **c'est X qui** construction by inserting the disjunctive pronoun after **c'est**. In this construction, the verb following **qui** agrees with the original subject.

| | |
|---|---|
| Je vais au stade.<br>C'est **moi qui vais** au stade. | *I'm going to the stadium.* |
| Tu es en retard.<br>C'est **toi qui es** en retard. | *You are late.* |
| Vous dites quelque chose d'important.<br>C'est **vous qui dites** quelque chose d'important. | *You are saying something important.* |
| Ils ne font aucun effort.<br>C'est **eux qui** ne **font** aucun effort. | *They are not putting forth any effort.* |

Elles ont envie de partir.
C'est **elles qui ont** envie de partir. } *They feel like going away (on vacation).*

Remember that **nous** is the disjunctive pronoun for **on** when **on** means *we*. The verb after **qui** is then in the **nous** form.

On est toujours à l'heure.
C'est **nous** qui sommes toujours à l'heure. } *We are always on time.*

In formal French, **c'est** is replaced by **ce sont** before **eux** and **elles**.

**Ce sont eux qui ne font** aucun effort.          *They are not putting forth any effort.*
**Ce sont elles qui ont** envie de partir.          *They feel like going away (on vacation).*

**L**  *Rewrite each sentence as a cleft sentence, highlighting the subject.*

1. Le conseiller arrive. _____

2. Ce logiciel ne sert à rien. _____

3. Les informaticiens ont réparé le réseau (*network*).

   _____

4. Le commerçant travaille tous les jours.

   _____

5. Les ouvriers protestent contre la nouvelle loi.

   _____

6. Le patronat (*the employers*) est content.

   _____

7. Le médecin m'a dit de faire ça. _____

8. Cette matière me passionne. _____

9. Le commerce l'attire. _____

10. La vieillesse lui fait peur. _____

11. Ils se détendent. _____

12. Elles aiment les jeux vidéo. _____

**M**  *Rewrite each sentence as a cleft sentence, highlighting the pronoun subject.*

1. Il connaît bien la ville. _____

2. Je m'occupe de tout. _____

3. Elles paient toujours les consommations (*drinks*) des autres.

   _____

4. Tu as refusé de le faire. _____

5. Vous nettoyez toujours la maison. _____

6. Ils ont tort. _____

7. Nous voulons faire le voyage. _____

8. Tu as téléchargé ce programme? _____

9. On comprend ce problème. _____

10. Je te le dis. _____

# Compound Tenses: The Pluperfect; The Future Perfect; The Conditional Perfect

**BUILDING SENTENCES**

*Conditional sentences: contrary-to-past-fact conditions*
*Cleft sentences: highlighting the direct object of the sentence*

The passé composé is not the only compound tense in French. As in English, French changes the tense of the auxiliary verb (**avoir** or **être**) to express completed actions in the past (pluperfect), the future (future perfect), and conditional situations (conditional perfect).

## The Pluperfect (**le plus-que-parfait**)

The pluperfect consists of the imperfect of the auxiliary verb **avoir** or **être** + the past participle. The past participle follows the same agreement rules as in the passé composé (see Chapter 5).

**avoir** VERBS IN THE PLUPERFECT

| | |
|---|---|
| j'avais parlé, fini, vendu | nous avions parlé, fini, vendu |
| tu avais parlé, fini, vendu | vous aviez parlé, fini, vendu |
| il/elle/on avait parlé, fini, vendu | ils/elles avaient parlé, fini, vendu |

**être** VERBS IN THE PLUPERFECT

| | |
|---|---|
| j'étais parti(e), rentré(e), allé(e) | nous étions parti(e)s, rentré(e)s, allé(e)s |
| tu étais parti(e), rentré(e), allé(e) | vous étiez parti(e)(s), rentré(e)(s), allé(e)(s) |
| il était parti, rentré, allé | ils étaient partis, rentrés, allés |
| elle était partie, rentrée, allée | elles étaient parties, rentrées, allées |
| on était parti(s/es), rentré(s/es), allé(s/es) | |

In both formation and function, the French pluperfect is very much like the English pluperfect (past perfect): *had done something*. The pluperfect labels a past event that was completed before another past event occurred.

| Quand moi, je suis arrivé, elle **était** déjà **partie**. | *When I arrived, she **had already left**.* |

Je suis passé te voir parce qu'on m'**avait dit** que tu n'allais pas bien.

*I've come by to see you because they **had told** me that you weren't feeling well.*

Formidable! Je ne savais pas que vous **aviez résolu** le problème.

*Terrific! I didn't know that you **had solved** the problem.*

Note that in the example sentences above, the boldfaced action of the verb in the pluperfect was completed before the action of the verb in the passé composé or imperfect.

The following example has only one verb, which is in the pluperfect. In this sentence it is the time expression **à cinq heures** that implies a point in past time before which the action of finishing their work took place.

À cinq heures tous les employés **avaient fini** leur travail.

*At five, all the employees **had finished** their work.*

The pluperfect of **il y a** is **il y avait eu** *there had been.*

**A** *Using the cues given, create sentences using verbs in the pluperfect tense to say that things happened before the past events asked about. Use **déjà** in your responses, and replace the underlined words with the appropriate object pronouns.*

MODÈLE    Vous êtes retournés <u>de la Côte</u> la semaine dernière?  (il y a trois semaines)

*Non, nous en étions déjà retournés il y a trois semaines.*

1. Tu as vu <u>le bébé</u> pour la première fois hier?  (mardi dernier)

   _____

2. Charles et Christine ont déménagé cette semaine?  (il y a un mois)

   _____

3. Marc a vendu <u>sa voiture</u> le mois dernier?  (il y a longtemps)

   _____

4. Chantal a dîné avec <u>son chef</u> avant-hier?  (lundi soir)

   _____

5. Tu as téléphoné <u>à Nicole</u> ce matin pour l'inviter?  (hier)

   _____

6. Ses parents ont offert <u>une voiture à Édouard</u> cette année?  (l'année dernière)

   _____

   _____

7. Les enfants ont rangé <u>leur chambre</u> aujourd'hui?  (hier)

   _____

8. Vous avez fait <u>le marché</u> cet après-midi, Madame?  (ce matin)

   _____

9.  Vous vous êtes vus après les vacances?  (avant les vacances)

_____

10. Ils ont mis en œuvre <u>ce réseau</u> (*network*) dans votre bureau cette année?
    (il y a deux ans)

_____

_____

**B**  *Create sentences from the following strings of elements, using the passé composé
in the* **quand** *clause and the pluperfect in the main clause. Use* **déjà** *in your responses.*

MODÈLE    Marie / rentrer du gymnase / ses amis / sortir

*Quand Marie est rentrée du gymnase, ses amis étaient déjà sortis.*

1.  toi, tu / téléphoner / nous / descendre

_____

2.  moi, je / arriver au cinéma / le film / commencer

_____

3.  lui, il / venir nous aider / nous, on / finir

_____

4.  l'administrateur / m'offrir ce logiciel / je / le télécharger

_____

5.  ils / frapper à notre porte / nous / servir le dessert

_____

6.  je / descendre à huit heures et quart / on / fermer la charcuterie

_____

7.  toi, tu / me dire de quoi il s'agissait / eux, ils / me mettre au courant

_____

_____

8.  nous / se rendre compte des fautes / le chef / lire notre compte rendu

_____

_____

9.  je / demander l'addition / vous / la payer

_____

10. elle / appeler / je / lire son courriel

_____

**C** *Create a new sentence from each pair of causes and effects. Use the pluperfect in a clause that begins with* **parce que** *to express the cause.*

| MODÈLE | EFFECT | CAUSE |
|---|---|---|

je / ne pas aller avec eux au cinéma  je / voir le film

*Je ne suis pas allé avec eux au cinéma parce que j'avais vu le film.*

EFFECT                                        CAUSE

1. nous / faire cet effort inutile            personne / nous avertir

   _____

2. je / ne pas prendre de barque              l'orage / commencer

   _____

3. elle / ne pas venir au restaurant avec nous   elle / manger

   _____

4. nous / prendre le train                    notre voiture / tomber en panne

   _____

5. il / grossir                               il / arrêter de faire du jogging

   _____

6. je / ne pas assister au concert            je / prendre un rhume

   _____

7. il / ne pas pouvoir faire ses devoirs      il / perdre son cahier

   _____

8. elle / ne pas rester au café avec nous     elle / prendre rendez-vous avec Jean-Claude

   _____

9. nous / venir                               Paulette / nous dire de venir

   _____

10. ces étudiants / ne pas réussir l'examen   ils / ne pas étudier

    _____

11. on / ne pas pouvoir se mettre en route    il / neige

    _____

12. il / ne pas vouloir aller au bistro       il / manger

    _____

# The Future Perfect

The future perfect tense in French consists of the future of the auxiliary verb **avoir** or **être** + the past participle. The past participle follows the same agreement rules as in the passé composé.

---

**avoir** VERBS IN THE FUTURE PERFECT

| | |
|---|---|
| j'aurai parlé, fini, vendu | nous aurons parlé, fini, vendu |
| tu auras parlé, fini, vendu | vous aurez parlé, fini, vendu |
| il/elle/on aura parlé, fini, vendu | ils/elles auront parlé, fini, vendu |

---

**être** VERBS IN THE FUTURE PERFECT

| | |
|---|---|
| je serai parti(e), rentré(e), allé(e) | nous serons parti(e)s, rentré(e)s, allé(e)s |
| tu seras parti(e), rentré(e), allé(e) | vous serez parti(e)(s), rentré(e)(s), allé(e)(s) |
| il sera parti, rentré, allé | ils seront partis, rentrés, allés |
| elle sera partie, rentrée, allée | elles seront parties, rentrées, allées |
| on sera parti(s/es), rentré(s/es), allé(s/es) | |

---

The future perfect expresses the idea *will have spoken, will have finished, will have sold.* In both French and English, the future perfect tense indicates an event that will be completed in the future before another event occurs, or an event that will be completed before some point of time in the future. The simple future tense does not necessarily express the completion of the action—just that it takes place in the future.

The future perfect may appear in main clauses to indicate a future action that will be completed by a certain time.

| | |
|---|---|
| Ils seront tous partis avant la tombée de la nuit. | *They all will have left before nightfall.* |

The future perfect may appear in subordinate clauses when they are introduced by a conjunction of time indicating that the action of a subordinate clause will be completed before the action of a main clause in the future tense. English uses the present perfect, not the future perfect, in these cases.

| | |
|---|---|
| On passera le voir quand **il se sera levé**. | *We'll go by to see him when he has gotten up.* |
| Je te dirai ce qui se passe dès que **j'aurai appris** quelque chose. | *I will tell you what's going on as soon as I have learned something.* |

**D**  *Using the following strings of elements, create sentences with verbs in the future perfect to tell what will have happened by some point of time in the future.*

MODÈLE   je / finir le compte rendu / avant de partir en vacances
   *J'aurai fini le compte rendu avant de partir en vacances.*

1. tu / recevoir son courriel / avant son arrivée

2. nous / finir les préparatifs / avant de partir en voyage

_____

3. ils / faire ce travail / pas plus tard que lundi

_____

4. est-ce que tu / finir ta toilette / avant cinq heures

_____

5. elle / faire sa valise / dans une minute

_____

6. je / résoudre le problème / avant la prochaine classe

_____

7. nous / se voir / avant l'arrivée de notre lettre

_____

8. elles / rentrer / peu avant le dîner

_____

**E**  *Complete each sentence with the correct forms of the verbs in parentheses, one of which will be in the future and the other in the future perfect.*

1. Nous _____ sortir quand on _____
   le ménage.  (pouvoir, faire)

2. Aussitôt qu'elle m'_____, j'_____ la voir.
   (téléphoner, aller)

3. Je _____ à préparer le dîner dès que tu

   _____ du marché.  (commencer, revenir)

4. Il _____ aussitôt qu'il _____ son ordinateur.
   (s'en aller, éteindre)

5. Nous _____ cette ville dès que nous _____
   le musée.  (quitter, voir)

6. Je vous _____ quand j'_____ la livraison.
   (avertir, recevoir)

7. On _____ la voir aussitôt qu'elle _____
   de sa maladie.  (aller, se remettre [*recover*])

8. Nous _____ servir le café quand les enfants

   _____.  (pouvoir, s'endormir)

9. Je _____ la porte dès que j'_____ ma clé.
   (fermer, trouver)

10. Elles _____ leur entreprise aussitôt qu'elles

    _____ un prêt (*loan*) de la banque.  (monter, obtenir)

## The Conditional Perfect

The conditional perfect tense in French consists of the conditional of the auxiliary verbs **avoir** or **être** + the past participle. The past participle follows the same agreement rules as in the passé composé.

| **avoir** VERBS IN THE CONDITIONAL PERFECT | |
|---|---|
| j'aurais parlé, fini, vendu | nous aurions parlé, fini, vendu |
| tu aurais parlé, fini, vendu | vous auriez parlé, fini, vendu |
| il/elle/on aurait parlé, fini, vendu | ils/elles auraient parlé, fini, vendu |

| **être** VERBS IN THE CONDITIONAL PERFECT | |
|---|---|
| je serais parti(e), rentré(e), allé(e) | nous serions parti(e)s, rentré(e)s, allé(e)s |
| tu serais parti(e), rentré(e), allé(e) | vous seriez parti(e)(s), rentré(e)(s), allé(e)(s) |
| il serait parti, rentré, allé | ils seraient partis, rentrés, allés |
| elle serait partie, rentrée, allée | elles seraient parties, rentrées, allées |
| on serait parti(s/es), rentré(s/es), allé(s/es) | |

The conditional perfect expresses the idea *would have spoken, would have finished, would have sold.* In other words, it labels actions that did not take place, but that would have or could have taken place if certain conditions had been met.

| Moi, je n'**aurais** pas **fait** ça. | *I wouldn't have done that.* |
|---|---|
| Personne ne l'**aurait compris**. | *Nobody would have understood him.* |
| Tu lui **aurais dit** la vérité, toi? | *Would you have told her the truth?* |

In journalistic language, the conditional perfect may be used to express an assertion that the writer sees as alleged but not yet verified, one deriving from sources rather than investigation. The English equivalent is usually the present perfect tense. Compare the use of the conditional in journalistic language (see Chapter 8, p. 167).

| L'entreprise aurait demandé un prêt considérable. | *The company has asked* (implication: *it is rumored*) *for a large loan.* |
|---|---|
| Selon des sources en générale bien informées, des officiels de l'ONU auraient été à la solde de régimes brutaux du Moyen-Orient. | *According to usually knowledgeable sources, UN officials have been on the payroll of brutal Middle Eastern regimes.* |

**F**   *Write sentences expressing that people (the subjects in parentheses) would have done things that the others did not do.*

MODÈLE   Martine n'a pas protesté. (toi)

     *Toi, tu aurais protesté.*           

1. Toi, tu ne l'a pas aidé. (moi) _____

2. Eux, ils n'ont pas fini le compte rendu. (nous)

_____

3. Paul n'est pas parti sous la pluie. (vous) _____

4. Renée n'a pas pris le métro. (toi) _____

5. Moi, je n'ai pas appelé la police. (Robert) _____

6. Nous, nous ne leur avons pas emprunté leur voiture. (Marc et Jean)

   _____

7. Moi, je ne lui ai pas prêté d'argent. (eux) _____

8. Elle, elle n'a pas joué aux cartes. (nous) _____

9. Vous, vous n'êtes pas sortis le soir. (moi) _____

10. Elle n'a pas fait attention. (toi) _____

11. Ils ne lui ont pas dit «bonjour». (on) _____

12. Je n'ai pas résolu le mystère. (toi) _____

**G** *Write sentences expressing that people (the subjects in parentheses) would not have done things that the others did do.*

MODÈLE    Martine a raconté des blagues (*jokes*). (vous)

   *Vous n'auriez pas raconté de blagues.*

1. Hélène a menti. (moi) _____

2. Je les ai invités à manger dans un restaurant très cher. (toi)

   _____

3. Christophe est tombé dans un piège (*trap*). (nous)

   _____

4. Tu as dit une bêtise. (eux) _____

5. Vous avez mangé des aliments vides (*junk food*). (moi)

   _____

6. Marthe et Françoise ont fait l'éloge de ce chanteur. (vous)

   _____

7. On a mangé des saucissons à l'ail. (Lise) _____

8. Vous avez regardé cette émission de télé-réalité. (mes amis)

   _____

9. J'ai offert un appareil photo numérique (*digital camera*) au jeune couple.
   (Gisèle et Jacques)

   _____

   _____

10. Martin a utilisé une antisèche (*cheat sheet*) à l'examen. (toi)

    _____

| BUILDING SENTENCES | **Conditional sentences: contrary-to-past-fact conditions** |
|---|---|

Chapter 8 introduced conditional sentences that express a condition contrary to present fact. The compound tenses can also be combined in sentences to express a condition that is contrary to a fact in the past.

French expresses a condition that is contrary to a fact or situation in *past* time by using the pluperfect in the **si**-clause and the conditional perfect in the main clause.

| **si**-CLAUSE | MAIN CLAUSE | MEANING |
|---|---|---|
| **Si j'avais reçu le courriel,** (pluperfect) | **je l'aurais lu.** (conditional perfect) | *If I had gotten the e-mail, I would have read it.* |
| **Si tu étais rentrée plus tôt,** (pluperfect) | **tu m'aurais vu.** (conditional perfect) | *If you had come back earlier, you would have seen me.* |

The order of the clauses may be reversed.

| MAIN CLAUSE | **si**-CLAUSE | MEANING |
|---|---|---|
| **Vous auriez réussi** (conditional perfect) | **si vous aviez étudié.** (pluperfect) | *You would have passed if you had studied.* |

**H**    *Contrary-to-fact conditions in past time.* *Complete each sentence with the correct forms of the verbs in parentheses, using the pluperfect and the conditional perfect forms. Choose the appropriate tense for the si-clause and the main clause.*

> MODÈLE    S'ils __*avaient fait*__ un voyage en Suisse, ils __*auraient fait*__ de l'alpinisme. (faire, faire)

1. Tu _____ un bon emploi si tu _____ de l'informatique. (trouver, faire)

2. S'ils _____ l'amour et l'appui de leur famille, ils

   _____ tant de succès dans la vie. (ne pas avoir, ne pas avoir)

3. Léon et Olga _____ s'ils _____ au bal. (ne pas se connaître, ne pas aller)

4. Cet élève _____ de bonnes notes s'il _____ attention en classe. (avoir, faire)

5. Si on _____ le message, on _____ au courant de l'affaire. (lire, être)

6. Ils _____ moins de chaleur s'ils _____ la climatisation. (avoir, allumer)

7. J'_____ si j'_____ un bogue dans le programme. (réamorcer [*to reboot*], trouver)

8. S'il _____ son régime, il _____. (suivre, mincir)

9. Si elle _____ tôt, elle _____ si fatiguée.
(se coucher, ne pas être)

10. Si j'_____ moins de café, je _____
sans difficulté.  (boire, s'endormir)

**I** *Write contrary-to-fact conditional sentences for each of these situations in the past. Choose the appropriate tense for the **si**-clause and the main clause.*

MODÈLE     Je ne savais pas que l'ordinateur était en panne. Je ne l'ai pas réparé.

   *Si j'avais su que l'ordinateur était en panne, je l'aurais réparé.*

1. Il n'y avait pas de bogues dans le programme. Je n'ai pas réamorcé.

   _____

   _____

2. Ils ne m'ont pas remboursé. Je me suis plaint auprès d'eux.

   _____

3. L'autobus n'est pas venu. On y est allés à pied.

   _____

4. Tu n'es pas allé avec nous. Tu t'es ennuyé.

   _____

5. Il y a eu une défaillance (*failure*). L'ordinateur n'a pas accompli la fonction.

   _____

   _____

6. Tu as oublié le mot de passe. Tu n'as pas accès à cette base de données.

   _____

   _____

7. Serge n'a pas déjeuné. Il avait faim.

   _____

8. Alice était crevée (*exhausted* [colloquial]). Elle a couru cinq kilomètres.

   _____

9. On n'était pas sur la plage. On n'a pas vu les feux d'artifice (*fireworks*).

   _____

10. Tu n'as pas mis l'arobase (@). Je n'ai pas reçu ton courriel.

   _____

**J** *Translation.* *Express the following sentences in French.*

1. *If we see him at the game, we'll say hello to him.*

   _____

2. *They would share the expenses if they could.*

   _____

3. *The company would have hired her if she had had five years of experience.*

   _____

   _____

4. *If it weren't raining, we'd take a walk.*

   _____

5. *If you (vous) had given me the contract, I would have signed it.*

   _____

6. *I'd wait for them if I didn't have to (il me faut) take the six o'clock train.*

   _____

7. *They'll go skiing this weekend if the weather is good.*

   _____

8. *If our colleagues were more hardworking, we wouldn't have so much to do.*

   _____

   _____

9. *If you (tú) wanted to take the car, we'd lend it to you.*

   _____

10. *If she had asked them for a digital camera, they would have given (as a gift) her one.*

   _____

   _____

---

**BUILDING SENTENCES** | **Cleft sentences: highlighting the direct object of the sentence**

The tense of the introductory **c'est** construction of a cleft sentence varies according to meaning.

| | |
|---|---|
| C'était lui qui le lui a dit. | *He was the one who told her.* |
| Ce sera moi qui le ferai. | *I'll be the one who will do that.* |

The present tense form **c'est** can be used in the following cases.

| | |
|---|---|
| C'est lui qui le leur a dit. | *He told them.* |
| C'est moi qui le ferai. | *I will do that.* |

The direct object (as well as the subject) of the verb may be highlighted in a cleft sentence construction by means of **c'est X que**. The direct object is placed after **c'est**, and the rest of the sentence is converted into a relative clause. In formal style, **c'est** is replaced by **ce sont** before a plural noun or a third-person plural pronoun.

| | |
|---|---|
| **C'est le CD** qu'il cherche, pas la clé USB. | *He's looking for **the CD**, not the flash drive.* |
| **C'est cette boutique** que tu dois visiter. | *You ought to visit **this store**.* |
| **C'est (Ce sont) nos placements** qu'il faut protéger. | *It's necessary to protect **our investments**.* |

When the clause following **c'est X que** is in the passé composé or another compound tense, the past participle agrees with the direct object noun preceding **que**, because the direct object now precedes the past participle.

| | |
|---|---|
| Nous avons acheté les billets.<br>C'est **les billets** que nous avons acheté**s**. | *We bought **the tickets**.* |
| Vous l'aviez appelée.<br>C'est **elle** que vous aviez appelé**e**. | *You had called **her**.* |
| Le prof a grondé ces filles.<br>C'est (Ce sont) **ces filles** que le prof a grondé**es**. | *The teacher scolded **these girls**.* |
| Le chef a licencié ces trois employés.<br>C'est (Ce sont) **ces trois employés** que le chef a licencié**s**. | *The boss fired **these three employees**.* |
| Je les aurais aidés.<br>C'est (Ce sont) **eux** que j'aurais aidé**s**. | *I would have helped **them**.* |

**K**  *Rewrite each sentence as a cleft sentence, highlighting the direct object. Remember to make necessary agreements of the past participle.*

MODÈLE   Il connaît le conseiller.

　　　　　*C'est le conseiller qu'il connaît.*

1. Il attend l'avion de Marseille. _____

2. Il a lu ces trois articles. _____

3. J'aurais appelé l'informaticien pour déboguer (*debug*) le nouveau programme.

　　_____

4. Elle a perdu son billet. _____

5. Il a téléchargé un nouveau programme de traitement de textes (*word processing*).

　　_____

6. Nous avons fini le compte rendu. _____

7. Vous avez ouvert les courriels? _____

8. J'ai étudié les finances. _____

9. Elle m'a offensé. _____

10. Vous avez transmis les nouvelles données.

_____

**L**    *Answer each question, highlighting the first choice given as the answer and negating the second choice with* **pas.**

MODÈLE     Quelle langue est-ce qu'il parle? L'espagnol ou l'italien?

     *C'est l'espagnol qu'il parle, pas l'italien.*

1. Qu'est-ce qu'on vous a montré? Le laboratoire ou le bureau?

_____

2. Qu'est-ce qu'ils nous ont passé? La commande ou le contrat?

_____

3. Qu'est-ce que vous admirez dans ce candidat? Sa formation ou son style?

_____

4. Qui est-ce que vous avez appelé? L'ingénieur ou l'informaticien?

_____

5. Qu'est-ce qu'ils ont lu? Les dépliants (*brochures*) ou les annonces?

_____

6. Qu'est-ce que tu as commandé? Le canard ou le saumon?

_____

7. Qu'est-ce que nous devons négocier? Les conditions de travail ou les prix?

_____

8. Qu'est-ce qu'on a livré (*delivered*) aujourd'hui? L'imprimante ou le moniteur?

_____

9. Qu'est-ce que le gouvernement craint le plus? L'inflation ou le chômage (*unemployment*)?

_____

10. Qu'est-ce qu'il a étudié? Les dossiers ou les rapports?

_____

11. Qui a-t-il licencié? La secrétaire ou la programmeuse?

_____

12. Qu'est-ce qu'elle a vendu? Sa bicyclette ou sa voiture?

_____

**M**  *Translation.  Express the following sentences in French. Write them as cleft sentences, highlighting the direct object.*

1. *He found the e-mails, not the data.*

   _____

2. *I would have finished the project.*

   _____

3. *We had learned the verbs, not the adjectives.*

   _____

4. *They will have modernized the kitchen, not the bathroom.*

   _____

5. *She erased the files.* _____

6. *We are going to see that film.* _____

7. *You (vous) were looking for the appointment book.*

   _____

8. *You (tu) had downloaded the last document.*

   _____

9. *I would have phoned them.* _____

10. *They had served the appetizers (snacks).*

   _____

# The Subjunctive (Part I): The Present Subjunctive

**BUILDING SENTENCES**

**Cleft sentences: highlighting the indirect object and other elements of the sentence**

The subjunctive is a mood used largely in subordinate clauses—clauses that do not stand alone but that are part of a larger sentence. The subjunctive is used after main clauses that express volition (the imposition of will to get someone else to do something), emotion (feelings, a personal reaction to an event or condition, or a subjective judgment), and doubt (uncertainty, denial, or negation of facts and opinions).

## Formation of the Present Subjunctive

All French verbs except **être** have the same endings in the present subjunctive. The stem of the present subjunctive for most verbs is the **nous** form of the present tense minus the -**ons** ending. Examples of subjunctive forms will be shown after **il faut que** *one must, it is necessary to/that.*

**parler** (1ST-PERSON PLURAL PRESENT **parlons**, STEM **parl-**) *to speak*

| | |
|---|---|
| Il faut que je parl**e**. | Il faut que nous parl**ions**. |
| Il faut que tu parl**es**. | Il faut que vous parl**iez**. |
| Il faut qu'il/elle/on parl**e**. | Il faut qu'ils/elles parl**ent**. |

**finir** (1ST-PERSON PLURAL PRESENT **finissons**, STEM **finiss-**) *to finish*

| | |
|---|---|
| Il faut que je finiss**e**. | Il faut que nous finiss**ions**. |
| Il faut que tu finiss**es**. | Il faut que vous finiss**iez**. |
| Il faut qu'il/elle/on finiss**e**. | Il faut qu'ils/elles finiss**ent**. |

**vendre** (1ST-PERSON PLURAL PRESENT **vendons**, STEM **vend-**) *to sell*

| | |
|---|---|
| Il faut que je vend**e**. | Il faut que nous vend**ions**. |
| Il faut que tu vend**es**. | Il faut que vous vend**iez**. |
| Il faut qu'il/elle/on vend**e**. | Il faut qu'ils/elles vend**ent**. |

**NOTES**

1 · For all regular verbs and most irregular verbs, the third-person plural of the present subjunctive is identical to the corresponding form of the present indicative.

2 · The present subjunctive forms of the singular of **-er** verbs are identical to those of the indicative.

3 · The **nous** and **vous** forms of the present subjunctive are identical to the corresponding forms of the imperfect.

4 · In the subjunctive of **-ir** and **-re** verbs, the final consonant of the stem is sounded in the singular as well as the plural. The presence of that final consonant is the signal of the subjunctive in speech:

> **je finis** vs. **je finisse**
> **je vends** vs. **je vende**

5 · Verbs ending in **-cer** and **-ger** such as **commencer** and **manger** do not have any spelling changes in the present subjunctive because none of the endings begin with **a** or **o**: **il faut que nous commencions, il faut que nous mangions**.

Verbs having accent mark changes or the change of **y** to **i** in some forms of the present tense have these same changes in the present subjunctive.

**acheter** (1ST-PERSON PLURAL PRESENT **achetons**, STEM **achet-**)  *to buy*

| | |
|---|---|
| Il faut que j'achète. | Il faut que nous achetions. |
| Il faut que tu achètes. | Il faut que vous achetiez. |
| Il faut qu'il/elle/on achète. | Il faut qu'ils/elles achètent. |

**gérer** (1ST-PERSON PLURAL PRESENT **gérons**, STEM **gér-**)  *to manage*

| | |
|---|---|
| Il faut que je gère. | Il faut que nous gérions. |
| Il faut que tu gères. | Il faut que vous gériez. |
| Il faut qu'il/elle/on gère. | Il faut qu'ils/elles gèrent. |

**nettoyer** (1ST-PERSON PLURAL PRESENT **nettoyons**, STEM **nettoy-**)  *to clean*

| | |
|---|---|
| Il faut que je nettoie. | Il faut que nous nettoyions. |
| Il faut que tu nettoies. | Il faut que vous nettoyiez. |
| Il faut qu'il/elle/on nettoie. | Il faut qu'ils/elles nettoient. |

Most irregular verbs follow the patterns of regular verbs in the subjunctive. The final consonant of the stem is pronounced in the singular as well as the plural. Study the present subjunctive of **lire**, **écrire**, and **craindre**.

**lire** (1ST-PERSON PLURAL PRESENT **lisons**, STEM **lis-**)  *to read*

| | |
|---|---|
| Il faut que je lis**e**. | Il faut que nous lis**ions**. |
| Il faut que tu lis**es**. | Il faut que vous lis**iez**. |
| Il faut qu'il/elle/on lis**e**. | Il faut qu'ils/elles lis**ent**. |

**écrire** (1ST-PERSON PLURAL PRESENT **écrivons**, STEM **écriv-**)  *to write*

| | |
|---|---|
| Il faut que j'écriv**e**. | Il faut que nous écriv**ions**. |
| Il faut que tu écriv**es**. | Il faut que vous écriv**iez**. |
| Il faut qu'il/elle/on écriv**e**. | Il faut qu'ils/elles écriv**ent**. |

**craindre** (1ST-PERSON PLURAL PRESENT **craignons**, STEM **craign-**) *to fear*

| | |
|---|---|
| Il faut que je craigne. | Il faut que nous craignions. |
| Il faut que tu craignes. | Il faut que vous craigniez. |
| Il faut qu'il/elle/on craigne. | Il faut qu'ils/elles craignent. |

Verbs that have vowel changes in their stems in the present indicative have similar changes in the present subjunctive. Study the present subjunctive of **boire**, **venir**, and **prendre**.

**boire** (1ST-PERSON PLURAL PRESENT **buvons**, STEM **buv-**;
3RD-PERSON PLURAL PRESENT **boivent**, STEM **boiv-**) *to drink*

| | |
|---|---|
| Il faut que je **boiv**e. | Il faut que nous **buv**ions. |
| Il faut que tu **boiv**es. | Il faut que vous **buv**iez. |
| Il faut qu'il/elle/on **boiv**e. | Il faut qu'ils/elles **boiv**ent. |

**venir** (1ST-PERSON PLURAL PRESENT **venons**, STEM **ven-**;
3RD-PERSON PLURAL PRESENT **viennent**, STEM **vienn-**) *to come*

| | |
|---|---|
| Il faut que je **vienn**e. | Il faut que nous **ven**ions. |
| Il faut que tu **vienn**es. | Il faut que vous **ven**iez. |
| Il faut qu'il/elle/on **vienn**e. | Il faut qu'ils/elles **vienn**ent. |

**prendre** (1ST-PERSON PLURAL PRESENT **prenons**, STEM **pren-**;
3RD-PERSON PLURAL PRESENT **prennent**, STEM **prenn-**) *to take*

| | |
|---|---|
| Il faut que je **prenn**e. | Il faut que nous **pren**ions. |
| Il faut que tu **prenn**es. | Il faut que vous **pren**iez. |
| Il faut qu'il/elle/on **prenn**e. | Il faut qu'ils/elles **prenn**ent. |

The following verbs have irregular stems in the present subjunctive.

**faire** *to do, make*

| | |
|---|---|
| Il faut que je **fass**e. | Il faut que nous **fass**ions. |
| Il faut que tu **fass**es. | Il faut que vous **fass**iez. |
| Il faut qu'il/elle/on **fass**e. | Il faut qu'ils/elles **fass**ent. |

**savoir** *to know*

| | |
|---|---|
| Il faut que je **sach**e. | Il faut que nous **sach**ions. |
| Il faut que tu **sach**es. | Il faut que vous **sach**iez. |
| Il faut qu'il/elle/on **sach**e. | Il faut qu'ils/elles **sach**ent. |

**pouvoir** *can, to be able to*

| | |
|---|---|
| Il faut que je **puiss**e. | Il faut que nous **puiss**ions. |
| Il faut que tu **puiss**es. | Il faut que vous **puiss**iez. |
| Il faut qu'il/elle/on **puiss**e. | Il faut qu'ils/elles **puiss**ent. |

The verbs **aller**, **avoir**, **valoir**, and **vouloir** have two stems in the present subjunctive.

**aller**  *to go*

| | |
|---|---|
| Il faut que j'**aille**. | Il faut que nous **allions**. |
| Il faut que tu **ailles**. | Il faut que vous **alliez**. |
| Il faut qu'il/elle/on **aille**. | Il faut qu'ils/elles **aillent**. |

**avoir**  *to have*

| | |
|---|---|
| Il faut que j'**aie**. | Il faut que nous **ayons**. |
| Il faut que tu **aies**. | Il faut que vous **ayez**. |
| Il faut qu'il/elle/on **ait**. | Il faut qu'ils/elles **aient**. |

**valoir**  *to earn, win*

| | |
|---|---|
| Il faut que je **vaille**. | Il faut que nous **valions**. |
| Il faut que tu **vailles**. | Il faut que vous **valiez**. |
| Il faut qu'il/elle/on **vaille**. | Il faut qu'ils/elles **vaillent**. |

**vouloir**  *to want*

| | |
|---|---|
| Il faut que je **veuille**. | Il faut que nous **voulions**. |
| Il faut que tu **veuilles**. | Il faut que vous **vouliez**. |
| Il faut qu'il/elle/on **veuille**. | Il faut qu'ils/elles **veuillent**. |

**NOTE**

A form **veuillez** also exists. It is used before an infinitive to form a polite request.

> **Veuillez** nous avertir.                              *Please inform us.*

The subjunctive of **être** is irregular in both stem and ending.

**être**

| | |
|---|---|
| Il faut que je **sois**. | Il faut que nous **soyons**. |
| Il faut que tu **sois**. | Il faut que vous **soyez**. |
| Il faut qu'il/elle/on **soit**. | Il faut qu'ils/elles **soient**. |

## The Subjunctive in Noun Clauses

A *noun clause* is a subordinate clause that functions as a noun, that is, it can serve as either the subject or the object of a verb. Noun clauses are introduced in French by the conjunction **que**.

All the French tenses studied so far belong to the *indicative mood*. Verbs in the *indicative mood* express events or states that are considered factual, definite, or part of the speaker's experience or of reality as perceived by the speaker. The following examples have dependent noun clauses in the indicative. They show events perceived as part of reality because they are the objects of verbs such as **savoir**, **penser**, **entendre (dire)**, and **voir**.

| | |
|---|---|
| **Je sais** que Jean **habite** ce quartier. | *I know that Jean lives in this neighborhood.* |
| **Je pense** que la réunion **est** en haut. | *I think that the meeting is upstairs.* |
| **On a entendu dire** que l'entreprise **a** des problèmes. | *We have heard that the firm has problems.* |
| **Je vois** que les résultats **sont** bons. | *I see that the results are good.* |

Note that in the above sentences, the subordinate clauses beginning with **que** are the direct objects of the verbs. They all answer the question **Qu'est-ce que?**

**Qu'est-ce que** tu sais?
Je sais **que Jean habite ce quartier**.

**Qu'est-ce que** tu penses?
Je pense **que la réunion est en haut**.

**Qu'est-ce que** vous avez entendu dire?
On a entendu dire **que l'entreprise a des problèmes**.

**Qu'est-ce que** tu vois?
Je vois **que les résultats sont bons**.

**A** *Complete each sentence with the correct present subjunctive form of the verb in parentheses.*

1. (avoir)      Il faut que tu _____ de la chance.

2. (rejoindre)      Il faut que l'enfant _____ ses parents.

3. (vouloir)      Il faut que tu _____ le faire.

4. (devenir)      Il faut qu'elle _____ médecin.

5. (apprendre)      Il faut que j'_____ ce vocabulaire.

6. (recevoir)      Il faut qu'il _____ une bourse d'études.

7. (écrire)      Il faut que j'_____ un courriel.

8. (télécharger)      Il faut que vous _____ ce programme.

9. (voir)      Il faut que tu _____ ce film.

10. (suivre)      Il faut que tu me _____.

11. (éteindre)      Il faut que j'_____ le poste.

12. (rompre)      Il faut qu'elle _____ avec lui.

13. (s'en aller)      Il faut qu'ils _____.

14. (être)      Il ne faut pas qu'il _____ en retard.

15. (reprendre)      Il faut que les conversations _____.

16. (offrir)      Il faut que nous lui _____ un cadeau.

17. (accueillir)      Il faut que j'_____ ces étudiants étrangers.

18. (battre)      Il faut que tu _____ les cartes.

19. (courir)      Il faut que tu _____ vite.

20. (traduire)      Il faut que je _____ ce paragraphe.

21. (croire)        Il faut que tu me _____.

22. (vaincre)       Il faut que notre équipe _____.

23. (savoir)        Il faut que la police _____ où il habite.

24. (connaître)     Il faut que tu _____ la Belgique.

25. (commencer)     Il faut que vous _____.

26. (gérer)         Il faut qu'elle _____ l'entreprise.

## Uses of the Subjunctive

### Volition (Imposition of Will)

The present subjunctive is used in subordinate clauses appearing after main clauses that imply that someone wants someone to do something or that someone wants something to happen that is not yet part of reality or that person's experience.

Verbs of wanting or ordering someone to do something include **vouloir**, **désirer**, **souhaiter** *to wish*, **vouloir bien** *to be willing*, **commander** *to order*, **ordonner** *to order*, and **exiger** *to demand*. The present subjunctive can follow a verb in any tense in the main clause.

| | |
|---|---|
| Elle ne veut pas qu'il **revienne**. | *She doesn't want him to come back.* |
| Nous souhaitons que vous **trouviez** un poste. | *We hope that you will find a job.* |
| Je veux bien que tu **fasses** sa connaissance. | *I'd like for you to meet him.* |
| J'ai ordonné que vous **restiez**. | *I ordered you to remain.* |
| Le prof a exigé que nous **sachions** tout. | *The teacher demanded that we know everything.* |

Verbs of permitting, forbidding, and preventing include **permettre** *to allow, permit*, **autoriser** *to authorize*, **défendre**, **interdire** *to prohibit, forbid*, and **éviter**, **empêcher** *to avoid, prevent*.

| | |
|---|---|
| Je ne permettrai pas que vous me **parliez** comme ça. | *I won't allow you to talk to me like that.* |
| Personne n'a autorisé que vous **sortiez**. | *No one has authorized you to go out.* |
| Je défends que tu me **répondes** sur ce ton. | *I forbid you to answer me like that.* |
| Il empêche que nous **fassions** notre travail. | *He's keeping us from doing our work.* |

Verbs of asking and suggesting include **dire**, **demander**, **suggérer**, **proposer**, and **recommander**.

| | |
|---|---|
| Je dis qu'il **vienne**. | *I'm telling him to come.* |
| Il a demandé que tout le monde **soit** présent. | *He asked that everyone be present.* |
| Je suggère qu'ils y **aillent**. | *I suggest that they go there.* |
| Il propose que nous **travaillions** ensemble. | *He suggests that we work together.* |
| Vous recommandez que je **prenne** l'avion? | *Do you recommend that I take the plane?* |

Verbs that try to get someone to do something by expressing likes, preferences, or waiting include **aimer** *to want,* **aimer mieux** *to prefer,* **préférer**, *to prefer,* **accepter** *to agree,* **admettre** *to allow,* and **attendre** *to wait for.*

| | |
|---|---|
| J'aimerais que vous m'**aidiez**. | *I'd like for you to help me.* |
| J'aimerais mieux qu'elle **s'en aille**. | *I'd prefer for her to go away.* |
| Personne n'acceptera que tu **partes**. | *No one will agree to your leaving.* |
| Sa mère n'admettra pas qu'elle **mette** cette robe. | *Her mother won't allow her to wear that dress.* |
| Nous attendons que vous **soyez** prêt. | *We're waiting for you to be ready.* |

In the examples above, the subjunctive clause beginning with **que** is a noun clause functioning as the direct object of the verb of the main clause.

Some verbs with meanings similar to the above verbs are always followed by prepositions.

| | |
|---|---|
| **s'attendre à** *to expect* | **s'opposer à** *to be against* |
| **consentir à** *to agree to* | **tenir à** *to insist on* |
| **insister pour** *to insist on* | **veiller à** *to see to, make sure that* |

The prepositions following these verbs are retained before a **que** clause. After **à**, you add **ce que** before a clause.

| | |
|---|---|
| Je ne m'attendais pas **à ce qu'il puisse** venir. | *I didn't expect him to be able to come.* |
| Vous consentez **à ce qu'elle vous dise** des mensonges? | *You allow her to tell you lies?* |
| Le chef insiste **pour que nous le lisions**. | *The boss insists that we read it.* |
| Je m'oppose **à ce qu'il nous fasse** des excuses. | *I am against his making excuses to us.* |
| Ils tiennent **à ce que nous achetions** cette maison. | *They insist that we buy that house.* |
| Elle veillera **à ce que les enfants ne fassent pas** trop de bruit. | *She'll make sure that the children don't make too much noise.* |

Verbs such as **savoir, croire,**[1] **penser,**[1] **affirmer, espérer, assurer, promettre,** and **jurer** are not followed by subjunctive clauses in French.

| | |
|---|---|
| Je sais qu'ils **font** du français. | *I know that they are studying French.* |
| Elle croit qu'elle **réussira** l'examen. | *She believes that she will pass the test.* |
| Je pense qu'il **a** un iPod. | *I think he has an iPod.* |
| Vous affirmez que ça **présente** un problème. | *You affirm that that presents a problem.* |
| Elle m'assure qu'elle nous **aidera**. | *She assures me that she will help us.* |
| Nous avions promis que tout **serait** prêt. | *We had promised that everything would be ready.* |
| Il a juré qu'il **est** innocent. | *He swore that he is innocent.* |

---

[1]**Croire** and **penser** are usually followed by the subjunctive when negative or interrogative. See p. 204 for further explanation.

**Dire** is followed by the subjunctive when the subordinate clause expresses an order, but by the indicative when the subordinate clause is a statement.

| | |
|---|---|
| J'ai dit **qu'il y soit**. | *I said for him to be there.* |
| J'ai dit **qu'il y était**. | *I said that he was there.* |

When the verbs of both clauses have the same subject, the infinitive is used instead of a subordinate clause.

| | |
|---|---|
| Il propose **travailler** ensemble. | *He suggests working together.* |
| Je ne m'attendais pas à **pouvoir** venir. | *I didn't expect to be able to come.* |
| Ils tiennent à **acheter** cette maison. | *They insist on buying that house.* |

**B** *Complete each sentence with the correct form of the verb in parentheses. Choose between the present indicative and the present subjunctive. Remember that the present subjunctive can follow any tense of the verb in the main clause.*

1.  (parler)        Je défends que vous me _____ comme ça.

2.  (être)          Je vous assure que tout le monde _____ d'accord.

3.  (éteindre)      Il demande qu'on _____ le poste.

4.  (venir)         Ils ont autorisé qu'elle _____.

5.  (sortir)        Sa mère ne permet pas qu'elle _____ avec ce garçon.

6.  (travailler)    Il jure qu'il _____ sérieusement.

7.  (s'en aller)    Nous jurons que nous _____.

8.  (savoir)        Je veux que vous le _____.

9.  (vouloir)       Pour réussir, il faut que tu _____ le faire.

10. (avoir)         J'aimerais mieux qu'il _____ envie de nous accompagner.

11. (faire)         Le professeur affirme que cette étudiante _____ trop de fautes d'orthographe.

12. (surprendre)    Empêchons qu'elle _____ notre conversation.

13. (battre)        Il faut que tu _____ les cartes.

14. (boire)         Il m'assure qu'il ne _____ pas trop.

15. (réduire)       Le patron exige que nous _____ les frais.

**C** *Combine each pair of clauses into a single sentence by incorporating the first sentence as a dependent clause of the second. Object pronouns in the second sentence of each pair will be eliminated. Choose between the present indicative and the present subjunctive.*

MODÈLE    Il fait le ménage. Je l'exige.

*J'exige qu'il fasse le ménage.*

1.  On abat ces arbres. Nous le défendons.

_____

2. Elle comprend la leçon. Tu le veux.

   _____

3. Vous gardez les enfants. Ils y tiennent.

   _____

4. Tu me reconduis. J'insiste. _____

5. Elle revient aujourd'hui. Je ne m'y attendais pas.

   _____

6. On produit de l'acier dans cette région. Je le pense.

   _____

7. Nous fuyons devant le danger. L'honneur l'empêche.

   _____

8. Il peut venir. Je le souhaite. _____

9. Elle est l'animatrice (*leader*) du groupe. J'y consens.

   _____

10. Son fils va au lycée habillé comme ça. Sa mère ne l'accepte pas.

    _____

11. Je connais sa ville. Il le veut. _____

12. Les étudiants sont malades. Le directeur le confirme.

    _____

## Emotions, Feelings, and Subjective Judgments

The subjunctive is used in subordinate clauses dependent on main clauses that express feelings or emotions about the action of the subordinate clause, or that express a subjective judgment about it. The main clause may consist of a conjugated verb or an impersonal expression beginning with **il est**: **il est étonnant/surprenant que**, **il est possible que**, etc.

### Verbs of feeling

**accepter**  *to agree*
**approuver/désapprouver**  *to approve/disapprove*
**avoir honte**  *to be ashamed*
**avoir peur**  *to be afraid*
**craindre**  *to fear*
**s'étonner**  *to be astonished*
**se plaindre**  *to complain*
**regretter**  *to regret*
**se réjouir**  *to rejoice*

### Expressions of feeling

**il est acceptable/inacceptable que**  *it's acceptable/unacceptable that*
**il est étonnant/surprenant que**  *it's astonishing/surprising that*
**il est peu probable que**  *it's improbable that*
**il est possible/impossible que**  *it's possible/impossible that*

Note that the categories of verbs requiring the subjunctive in the subordinate clause are not airtight. **Aimer**, **aimer mieux**, and **préférer**, as well as **accepter**, listed above, can be considered either verbs of volition or verbs of emotion.

| | |
|---|---|
| Le chef approuve que nous **travaillions** ensemble. | *The boss approves of our working together.* |
| J'ai honte que mes enfants ne **veuillent** pas nous aider. | *I'm ashamed that my children don't want to help us.* |
| J'ai peur qu'il **se perde**. | *I'm afraid he'll get lost.* |
| Vous ne craignez pas qu'il **se fasse** mal? | *Aren't you afraid he'll get hurt?* |
| Elle se plaint que nous n'**ayons** pas envie de collaborer au projet. | *She complains that we don't feel like collaborating on the project.* |
| Je regrette qu'elle **soit** en retard. | *I'm sorry she's late.* |
| Je me réjouis que vous **puissiez** venir. | *I'm so happy that you can come.* |
| Il est surprenant qu'ils ne le **sachent** pas. | *It's surprising that they don't know that.* |
| Il est possible qu'elle s'en **rende** compte. | *It's possible that she'll realize.* |
| Il est peu probable que je **revienne** demain. | *It's improbable that I'll be back tomorrow.* |

After **avoir peur** and **craindre**, formal French often places **ne** before the verb of the subordinate clause. This **ne** does not impart a negative meaning to the verb.

| | |
|---|---|
| J'ai peur qu'il **ne se perde**. | *I'm afraid he'll get lost.* |
| Vous ne craignez pas qu'il **ne se fasse** mal? | *Aren't you afraid he'll get hurt?* |

Many adjectives of emotion and feeling appear in expressions that take subordinate clauses with a verb in the subjunctive.

**être déçu que**  *to be disappointed that*
**être désolé/triste que**  *to be sad that*
**être étonné/surpris que**  *to be surprised that*
**être fâché/furieux/en colère que**  *to be angry that*
**être fier/ravi/satisfait que**  *to be proud/delighted/satisfied that*
**être heureux/content que**  *to be happy that*
**être malheureux/mécontent que**  *to be unhappy that*

Impersonal expressions that express subjective evaluation are followed by a subordinate clause with a verb in the subjunctive.

**il convient que**  *it is suitable/advisable that*
**il importe que**  *it matters that, it is important that*
**peu importe que**  *it matters little that*
**il suffit que**  *it is enough that*
**il vaut mieux que**  *it is better that*
**il est bizarre/curieux/extraordinaire que**  *it's strange/strange/extraordinary that*
**il est ennuyeux/agaçant/énervant que**  *it's annoying/irritating/irritating that*
**il est logique/normal/naturel/juste que**  *it's logical/normal/natural/fair that*

**il est rare que**  *it isn't often that*
**il est utile/inutile que**  *it's useful/useless that*
**il n'y a aucune chance que**  *there's no chance that*
**il n'y a pas de danger que**  *there's no danger that*
**il se peut que**  *it's possible that*

Expressions involving *luck* are also followed by the subjunctive.

Vous avez de la chance qu'il **soit** là.          *You are lucky that he is here.*
C'est une chance que tu la **connaisses**.          *It's lucky that you know her.*

Expressions of need are followed by the subjunctive.

**avoir besoin que**  *to need that*
**il est nécessaire/essentiel/indispensable que**  *it is necessary/essential/indispensable that*
**il faut que**  *it is necessary that, one has to*

In colloquial speech, the phrases beginning with **il est** often change to **c'est**.

**C'est inutile** que vous fassiez cet effort.          *It's useless for you to make such an effort.*
**C'est curieux** qu'il ne soit pas venu.          *It's strange that he hasn't come.*

Several expressions beginning with **cela (ça)** or **ce**, related in meaning to expressions of emotion or of subjective evaluation, also take the subjunctive.

**Cela (Ça) m'étonne que**  *It amazes me that*
**Cela (Ça) m'ennuie/m'agace/m'énerve/m'embête que**  *It annoys/irritates me that*
**Ce n'est pas la peine que**  *It's not worth it that, It's pointless that*

Ce n'est pas la peine que j'**aille** en ville.          *It's not worth it for me to go to town.*
Cela m'étonne que vous ne le **sachiez** pas.          *It amazes me that you don't know.*
Ça m'agace qu'il ne nous **écrive** pas.          *It irritates me that he doesn't write to us.*

**D**  *Complete each sentence with the correct form of the verb in parentheses. Choose between the present indicative and the present subjunctive.*

1. (avoir)          Il est important que vous _____ un ordinateur portatif.

2. (déménager)     Je sais qu'elle _____ demain.

3. (connaître)     Nous avons peur qu'elle ne _____ personne dans cette ville.

4. (se servir)     Il ne permet pas que je _____ de son téléphone mobile.

5. (être)          Il est triste qu'elle _____ malade.

6. (vouloir)       Je me rends compte qu'ils _____ partir.

7. (ranger)        J'aimerais que vous _____ vos affaires.

8. (chercher)      Il est inutile que vous _____ votre iPod ici.

9. (dire)          Ce n'est pas la peine que vous le lui _____.

10. (faire)        Je comprends que vous _____ de grands efforts.

11. (aller)        Mes parents défendent que j'y _____.

12. (savoir)       Il est impossible qu'ils le _____.

**E**  *Combine each pair of clauses into a single sentence by incorporating the first sentence as a dependent clause of the second. Object pronouns in the second sentence of each pair will be eliminated.*

MODÈLE    Il fait de l'informatique. Ça m'étonne.

   *Ça m'étonne qu'il fasse de l'informatique.*

1. Vous lui rendez visite. Il convient.

   _____

2. Cet enfant se bat avec son frère. Sa mère est furieuse.

   _____

3. Les étudiants sont en retard. Le professeur s'en plaint.

   _____

4. Tu ne comprends pas le texte. C'est rare.

   _____

5. Elle met le collier que je lui ai offert. J'en suis ravi.

   _____

6. Le port de la cravate deviendra obligatoire à l'école. Les étudiants s'y opposent.

   _____

   _____

7. Les employés du chemin de fer font grève demain. Je désapprouve.

   _____

8. Elle sait piloter un avion. C'est extraordinaire.

   _____

9. Tu ne t'aperçois pas du problème. J'ai peur.

   _____

10. Nous téléchargeons beaucoup de programmes. Il est normal.

    _____

11. Nous avons tant de documents à lire. Ça m'ennuie.

    _____

12. Tu reçois les billets électroniques aujourd'hui. Il est indispensable.

    _____

13. Il peut assister à la conférence. Il est peu probable.

    _____

14. Je prends l'autoroute. Vous proposez.

    _____

15. Nous parlons de ce sujet. Vous désirez.

    _____

## Doubt, Uncertainty, and Negation of Facts and Opinions

The subjunctive is used in subordinate clauses that are dependent on main clauses expressing doubt or uncertainty about the action of the subordinate clause, or that deny its existence. Here are some expressions that negate, deny, or doubt the existence of the action of the subordinate clause.

**nier que**  *to deny that*
**douter que**  *to doubt that*
**il est douteux que**  *it's doubtful that*

| | |
|---|---|
| Je nie qu'il **sache** plus que moi. | *I deny that he knows more than I do.* |
| Tu doutes que j'**aie** raison. | *You doubt that I am right.* |
| Il est douteux qu'ils **puissent** venir. | *It's doubtful that they can come.* |

However, the negative of the above verbs and expressions does *not* negate or deny the existence of the action of the subordinate clause, and therefore it is followed by a subordinate clause in the indicative.

| | |
|---|---|
| Je ne nie pas qu'il **sait** plus que moi. | *I don't deny that he knows more than I do.* |
| Tu ne doutes pas que j'**ai** raison. | *You don't doubt that I am right.* |
| Il n'est pas douteux qu'ils **peuvent** venir. | *It's not doubtful that they can come.* |

The following negative expressions are followed by a subordinate clause in the subjunctive.

**il n'est pas certain que**  *it's not certain that*
**il n'est pas clair que**  *it's not clear that*
**il n'est pas évident que**  *it's not evident that*
**il n'est pas exact que**  *it's not correct/accurate that*
**il n'est pas sûr que**  *it's not sure that*
**il n'est pas vrai que**  *it's not true that*
**il ne paraît pas que**  *it doesn't seem that*
**je ne dis pas que**  *I'm not saying that*
**je ne suis pas sûr(e)/certain(e) que**  *I'm not sure/certain that*
**ça ne veut pas dire que**  *it doesn't mean that*
**ce n'est pas que**  *it's not that, the fact isn't that*

| | |
|---|---|
| Il n'est pas certain qu'elle **suive** ce que tu dis. | *It's not certain that she is following what you are saying.* |
| Il n'est pas exact qu'il **sache** faire ce travail. | *It's not correct that he knows how to do this work.* |
| Il n'est pas vrai qu'il **s'en aille**. | *It's not true that he's leaving.* |
| Il ne paraît pas qu'il **s'en rende** compte. | *It doesn't seem that he realizes.* |
| Ce n'est pas qu'elle **comprenne**. | *It's not that she understands.* |

When the above expressions are affirmative, they are followed by the indicative.

| | |
|---|---|
| Il est certain qu'elle **suit** ce que tu dis. | *It is certain that she is following what you are saying.* |
| Il est exact qu'il **sait** faire ce travail. | *It is accurate that he knows how to do this work.* |
| Il est vrai qu'il **s'en va**. | *It's true that he's leaving.* |

| Il paraît qu'il **s'en rend** compte. | *It seems that he realizes.* |
| C'est qu'elle **comprend**. | *The fact is that she understands.* |

The verbs **penser** and **croire** function like the above expressions. When negative, they are followed by a subordinate clause in the subjunctive; when affirmative, they are followed by a subordinate clause in the indicative.

| Je pense qu'il **reviendra**. | *I think he'll come back.* |
| Je ne pense pas qu'il **revienne**. | *I don't think he'll come back.* |
| Elle croit qu'il **veut** nous inviter. | *She thinks he wants to invite us.* |
| Elle ne croit pas qu'il **veuille** nous inviter. | *She doesn't think he wants to invite us.* |

The subjunctive may be used after the interrogative forms of these verbs, especially when there is inversion.

| Pensez-vous que nous **devions** vous raccompagner? | *Do you think that we ought to see you home?* |
| Croyez-vous qu'il les **connaisse**? | *Do you think that he knows them?* |

In formal language, the indicative is also possible after the negative of **penser** and **croire**. This conveys that the speaker is really sure about the action of the subordinate clause.

| Je ne pense pas qu'il **reviendra**. | *I don't think he'll come back. (I am sure he won't.)* |
| Elle ne croit pas qu'il **veut** nous inviter. | *She doesn't think he wants to invite us. (She's pretty sure that he doesn't.)* |

If the implied subject of both clauses is the same, an infinitive is used instead of a subordinate clause. An infinitive is also used after impersonal expressions when making a general statement.

| Je suis content **de vous voir**. | *I'm happy to see you.* |
| Il ne croit pas nous **connaître**. | *He doesn't think he knows us.* |
| Il faut **faire** un effort. | *One must make an effort.* |

**F** *Complete each sentence with the present indicative or present subjunctive, as required.*

1. (savoir)        Il est vrai que cet étudiant _____ toutes les réponses.

2. (mentir)        Je ne crois pas qu'il _____.

3. (écrire)        Ce n'est pas que je lui _____.

4. (devoir)        Penses-tu que je _____ aller le voir?

5. (comprendre)    Il est peu probable que Françoise _____ ces étrangers.

6. (descendre)     Il ne paraît pas que tu _____ faire les courses aujourd'hui.

7. (rendre)        Ça ne veut pas dire qu'il s'en _____ compte.

8. (compter)       Il ne sait pas si nous _____ acheter ces logiciels.

9. (être)          Il n'est pas certain que sa voiture _____ en panne.

10. (pouvoir)      Il ne pense pas que nous _____ comprendre ce texte.

11. (boire)      Ce n'est pas qu'il _____ trop.

12. (aller)      Il est douteux que vous _____ avec eux.

13. (avoir)      Nous ne nions pas que vous _____ besoin de notre aide.

14. (être)      Il paraît qu'ils _____ en retard.

15. (craindre)      Je doute qu'elle _____ l'inconnu.

16. (admettre)      Je ne dis pas qu'elle l'_____.

17. (produire)      Il n'est pas exact que cette région _____ du vin.

18. (réussir)      Nous ne croyons pas qu'il _____.

19. (vendre)      Il est peu probable que je _____ ma maison.

20. (servir)      Je ne suis pas sûr qu'elle _____ une bonne bière avec le repas.

**G**   *Combine each conversational exchange into a single sentence by incorporating the first sentence as a dependent clause of the second. Any object pronouns such as **le** or **en** or the pronoun **ça** will be eliminated in your response, and **ce** will be replaced by **il**.*

MODÈLE     —Janine ne lit pas ses courriels.
              —Ce n'est pas vrai.

           *Il n'est pas vrai que Janine ne lise pas ses courriels.*

1. —Paul reçoit trop de pourriel (*spam*).
    —Ce n'est pas exact.

    _____

2. —Marianne en a marre de son boulot (*job* [colloquial]).
    —Il ne paraît pas.

    _____

3. —Nos collègues de travail peuvent venir à la réunion.
    —Je ne crois pas.

    _____

4. —Christophe et Philippe veulent une augmentation de salaire.
    —Je n'en suis pas sûr.

    _____

5. —Le chef part en voyage d'affaires.
    —Je ne dis pas ça.

    _____

6. —Cette entreprise fait faillite (*to go bankrupt*).
    —Je le doute.

    _____

7. —On met les employés à la porte (*to fire*).
   —C'est douteux.

   _____

8. —Le conseiller relit le contrat.
   —Ce n'est pas évident.

   _____

**H** *Rewrite each sentence, changing the main clause from affirmative to negative or from negative to affirmative as needed. Be sure to make all necessary changes.*

MODÈLE    Il n'est pas vrai que les enfants aient sommeil.

           *Il est vrai que les enfants ont sommeil.*

1. Je suis sûr qu'elles viendront nous voir.

   _____

2. Ça ne veut pas dire qu'il comprenne.

   _____

3. Elle ne doute pas que tu finiras le projet.

   _____

4. Il est évident qu'elle sait la leçon. _____

5. Je pense qu'il dit la vérité. _____

6. C'est qu'il a honte. _____

7. Nous nions que cet homme soit notre collègue.

   _____

8. Il est clair que cette propriété ne vaut rien.

   _____

9. Il paraît qu'ils peuvent nous aider.

   _____

10. Je crois qu'elle fait des progrès en mathématiques.

    _____

**I** *Translation. Express the following sentences in French.*

1. *I prefer that we go to see a film this evening.*

   _____

2. *We want you (*vous*) to know the news.*

   _____

3. *They expect that she'll be able to download the file.*

   _____

4. *He recommended that you (tu) buy a tablet.*

   _____

5. *It's strange that he doesn't answer my e-mail.*

   _____

6. *Their parents hope that they will be successful in life.*

   _____

7. *It's not certain that we're renting a car this weekend.*

   _____

8. *She told us to be on time.*

   _____

9. *I doubt that they feel like jogging today.*

   _____

10. *It's necessary that you (vous) tell him what you're thinking.*

    _____

11. *I'm delighted that you (tu) are coming with us.*

    _____

12. *It's not worth it that they recycle paper.*

    _____

---

**BUILDING SENTENCES** | **Cleft sentences: highlighting the indirect object and other elements of the sentence**

Cleft sentences in French can be used to highlight elements of the sentence other than the subject and the direct object. For example, the indirect object can be placed after **c'est**, and the rest of the sentence is converted into a relative clause.

J'ai donné les clés USB **à mon collègue.**
C'est **à mon collègue** que j'ai donné les clés USB. } *I gave **my co-worker** the flash drives.*

Il a demandé un prêt **à ses parents.**
C'est **à ses parents** qu'il a demandé un prêt. } *He asked **his parents** for a loan.*

Indirect object pronouns can also be highlighted as **à** + a disjunctive pronoun and placed after **c'est** in a **c'est X que** construction.

Je **lui** ai envoyé un courriel.
C'est à **lui** que j'ai envoyé un courriel.
OR C'est à **elle** que j'ai envoyé un courriel. } *I sent **him** an e-mail.*
*I sent **her** an e-mail.*

Il **leur** a téléphoné hier.
C'est à **eux** qu'il a téléphoné hier.
OR C'est à **elles** qu'il a téléphoné hier. } *He called **them** yesterday.*
*He called **them** yesterday.*

Prepositional phrases can be highlighted by placing them after **c'est** in a **c'est X que** construction.

Nous avons acheté le cadeau **pour Monique**.
C'est **pour Monique** que nous avons acheté le cadeau. } *We bought the gift **for Monique**.*

Il a travaillé **avec Robert et Nicole**.
C'est **avec Robert et Nicole** qu'il a travaillé. } *He worked **with Robert and Nicole**.*

Ils ont joué au foot **dans le parc**.
C'est **dans le parc** qu'ils ont joué au foot. } *They played soccer **in the park**.*

**J**   *Rewrite each sentence as a cleft sentence, highlighting the underlined material.*

1. Elle a montré sa dissertation <u>au professeur</u>.

_____

2. Ils ont vendu leur appartement <u>à leurs voisins</u>.

_____

3. J'ai donné le message <u>au patron</u>.

_____

4. Il va retrouver ses amis <u>au cinéma</u>.

_____

5. Elle a accepté l'invitation <u>avec joie</u>.

_____

6. Nous avons emprunté les dix mille euros <u>à la banque</u>.

_____

7. On a volé la serviette (*briefcase*) <u>à mon père</u>.

_____

8. J'ai promis des vacances en France <u>à ma femme</u>.

_____

9. Je travaille mieux <u>dans mon bureau</u>.

_____

10. On compte lui parler <u>avant la réunion</u>.

_____

**K** *Answer the following sentences, highlighting the first choice given as the answer and negating the second with* **pas.**

MODÈLE   Où est-ce qu'il travaille? Au bureau ou chez lui?

   *C'est au bureau qu'il travaille, pas chez lui.*

1. Où est-ce qu'ils vont se voir? Chez eux ou en ville?

   _____

2. Où est-ce que tu les as vus? À la fac ou au café?

   _____

3. À qui est-ce qu'il a offert le bijou? À Lise ou à Marthe?

   _____

4. À qui est-ce qu'il a dit ça? Au patron ou à l'employé?

   _____

5. À qui est-ce qu'il ressemble? À sa mère ou à son père?

   _____

6. À qui est-ce que tu as apporté les documents? Au chef ou à la secrétaire?

   _____

   _____

7. À qui est-ce que le douanier a enlevé la bouteille de vin? Aux garçons ou à leurs parents?

   _____

   _____

8. Pour qui as-tu acheté ce cadeau? Pour Philippe ou pour Hubert?

   _____

9. Où est-ce qu'il a trouvé son passeport? Dans le tiroir ou dans sa serviette?

   _____

   _____

10. À qui est-ce qu'elle a répondu? Aux clients ou aux vendeurs?

   _____

11. Pour qui a-t-il commandé des livres sur Internet? Pour Émilie ou pour Laurent?

   _____

   _____

12. Où est-ce qu'elle a mis le ragoût (*stew*)? Sur le fourneau (*stove*) ou sur la table?

   _____

   _____

French uses **ce n'est pas... qui/que** to highlight the negative as it pertains to the element selected.

## Subject + Negative

| | |
|---|---|
| **Ce n'est pas nous qui** le disons. | *We're not the ones saying it.* |
| **Ce n'est pas lui qui** doit décider. | *He's not the one who has to decide.* |
| **Ce n'est pas moi qui** l'ai fait. | *I'm not the one who did it.* |
| **Ce n'est pas le gouvernement qui** va nous aider. | *The government is not going to help us.* |
| **Ce n'est pas l'argent qui** le pousse à le faire. | *It's not money that is motivating him to do it.* |
| **Ce ne sont pas les voisins qui** ont appelé la police. | *The neighbors aren't the ones who called the police.* |

## Direct Object + Negative

| | |
|---|---|
| **Ce n'est pas toi qu'**il cherche. | *He isn't looking for you.* |
| **Ce n'est pas le courriel qu'**il a lu. | *The e-mail wasn't what he read.* |
| **Ce ne sont pas ces ministres qu'**il a critiqués. | *It wasn't those government ministers that he criticized.* |

## Indirect Object or Prepositional Phrase + Negative

| | |
|---|---|
| **Ce n'est pas à tes ennemis que** tu as nui. | *Your enemies aren't the ones you hurt.* |
| **Ce n'est pas à nous qu'**ils ont téléphoné. | *They didn't call us.* |
| **Ce n'est pas avec eux que** je vais parler. | *They are not the ones I am going to talk to.* |
| **Ce n'est pas en France que** tu vas travailler. | *France is not where you are going to work.* |
| **Ce n'est pas dans le jardin qu'**on reçoit. | *The garden is not the place where we have company.* |

**L**  *Rewrite each sentence, highlighting the underlined element and moving the negative to the highlighting phrase.*

MODÈLE   Nous n'allons pas <u>au cinéma</u>.

_Ce n'est pas au cinéma que nous allons._

1.  Les enfants ne jouent pas <u>dans le salon</u>.

    _____

2.  <u>Cette méthode</u> ne convient pas à ce groupe d'étudiants.

    _____

3.  Il ne cache pas <u>la vérité</u> à ses parents.

    _____

4.  Cet enfant ne ressemble pas <u>à sa mère</u>.

    _____

5. Il n'a pas emprunté l'ordinateur à Claudette.

_____

6. Elle n'enseigne pas la chimie.

_____

7. Je n'ai pas fait tout ça pour eux.

_____

8. Il a promis son cœur à Françoise.

_____

9. Le professeur n'a pas expliqué les problèmes aux étudiants.

_____

10. On ne met pas ses pieds sur la table.

_____

**M**   *Translation. Express the following sentences in French. Write them as cleft sentences, highlighting the indirect object or the prepositional phrase.*

1. *I sent the programmer the flash drive.* _____

2. *He wrote me the e-mail.* _____

3. *She is not the one they must work with.*

_____

4. *We went to the concert after dinner.*

_____

5. *You* (vous) *bought the silk tie for him.*

_____

6. *He brought them a bottle of wine.* _____

7. *The owners want to show their condominium to their friends.*

_____

8. *We're going to have drinks and hors d'oeuvres in the garden.*

_____

# The Subjunctive (Part II): The Subjunctive in Adjective Clauses; The Past Subjunctive; The Subjunctive in Adverb Clauses

**BUILDING SENTENCES**

**Compound and complex sentences**

## Uses of the Subjunctive in Adjective Clauses

An adjective clause is a subordinate clause that describes a noun much as an adjective does. Adjective clauses are also called *relative clauses*.

Most adjective clauses appear in the indicative.

| | |
|---|---|
| Il a un travail **qui lui plaît**. | *He has a job that he likes.* |
| Nous avons un bureau **qui est confortable**. | *We have an office that's comfortable.* |
| Je me sers d'un ordinateur **qui a beaucoup de mémoire**. | *I use a computer that has a lot of memory.* |
| Il y a des entreprises ici **qui font du commerce avec le Mexique**. | *There are firms here that trade with Mexico.* |

However, if the noun of the main clause is not identified or is negated, then the verb of the adjective clause appears in the subjunctive.

| | |
|---|---|
| Il veut un travail **qui lui plaise**. | *He wants a job that he will like.* |
| On a besoin d'un bureau **qui soit confortable**. | *We need an office that's comfortable.* |
| Je cherche un ordinateur **qui ait beaucoup de mémoire**. | *I'm looking for a computer that has a lot of memory.* |
| Il n'y a pas d'entreprises ici **qui fassent du commerce avec le Mexique**. | *There are no firms here that trade with Mexico.* |

The subjunctive is therefore used after **il n'y a rien qui/que**, **il n'y a personne qui/que**, and **il n'y a aucun/aucune X qui/que**.

| | |
|---|---|
| **Il n'y a rien qui** me **plaise**. | *There's nothing that appeals to me.* |
| **Il n'y a personne** ici **qui sache** programmer. | *There's no one here who knows how to program.* |
| **Il n'y a aucune banque qui soit** ouverte. | *There's no bank that's open.* |

212

*but the indicative is used when there is no negative:*

**Il y a quelque chose qui** me **plaît.**          *There's something that appeals to me.*
**Il y a quelqu'un** ici **qui sait** programmer.   *There's someone here who knows how to program.*

**Il y a une banque qui est** ouverte.              *There's a bank that's open.*

**A**  *Complete each sentence with the correct form of the verb in parentheses. Choose either the present indicative or the present subjunctive for the adjective clause.*

1.  (plaire)      Robert a un travail qui lui _____.

2.  (faire)       Je ne connais personne qui _____ tant de bruit.

3.  (savoir)      Il n'y a personne qui _____ réparer l'ordinateur.

4.  (avoir)       Nous avons besoin d'employés qui _____ de l'expérience.

5.  (être)        Il veut des amis qui _____ sincères.

6.  (trouver)     Il y a un musée près d'ici que nous _____ très intéressant.

7.  (conduire)    Il n'y a aucun chemin qui _____ directement au village.

8.  (traduire)    J'ai besoin d'un programme qui _____ automatiquement en anglais.

9.  (apprendre)   Je cherche un prof qui m'_____ à prononcer mieux.

10. (faire)       Nous cherchons un film qui nous _____ rire.

11. (être)        Je cherche un appartement qui _____ près de la faculté.

12. (connaître)   L'entreprise cherche un conseiller qui _____ l'Europe.

**B**  *Rewrite each sentence, changing the main clause from affirmative to negative or from negative to affirmative as needed. Be sure to make all necessary changes. Remember that verbs in adjective clauses will be in either the present indicative or the present subjunctive.*

MODÈLE    Il y a quelqu'un qui attend.

   *Il n'y a personne qui attende.* _____

1.  Il y a quelque chose qui me plaît. _____

2.  Il y a un bus qui va au marché. _____

3.  Il y a quelqu'un qui réussis. _____

4.  Il y a un étudiant qui suit bien dans ce cours.

   _____

5.  Nous avons un employé qui peut faire l'interprète.

   _____

6.  Il dit quelque chose qui me fait changer d'avis.

   _____

7.  Je connais quelqu'un qui lit le chinois.

    _____

8.  Il n'y a personne qui me comprenne.

    _____

9.  Il n'y a aucun parfum qui sente bon.

    _____

10. Il n'y a personne ici qui s'exprime bien en anglais.

    _____

## The Past Subjunctive

The past subjunctive in French is the subjunctive of the passé composé. It consists of the subjunctive of the auxiliary verb (**avoir** or **être**) plus the past participle. The same rules of agreement apply as in the passé composé (see Chapter 5).

**parler, finir, vendre**

| | |
|---|---|
| que j'**aie parlé, fini, vendu** | que nous **ayons parlé, fini, vendu** |
| que tu **aies parlé, fini, vendu** | que vous **ayez parlé, fini, vendu** |
| qu'il/elle/on **ait parlé, fini, vendu** | qu'ils/elles **aient parlé, fini, vendu** |

**aller**

| | |
|---|---|
| que je **sois allé(e)** | que nous **soyons allé(e)s** |
| que tu **sois allé(e)** | que vous **soyez allé(e)(s)** |
| qu'il **soit allé** | qu'ils **soient allés** |
| qu'elle **soit allée** | qu'elles **soient allées** |
| qu'on **soit allé(s/es)** | |

The past subjunctive is used in the same types of subordinate clauses as the present subjunctive. It is used to indicate that the action of the subordinate clause happened before the action of the main clause. Study the following contrasting pairs of sentences.

| | |
|---|---|
| J'ai peur qu'il **parte**. | *I'm afraid he'll leave.* |
| J'ai peur qu'il soit **parti**. | *I'm afraid he left.* |
| Il est triste que tu **ne puisses pas** aller. | *It's sad that you can't go.* |
| Il est triste que tu **n'aies pas pu** aller. | *It's sad that you couldn't go.* |
| Je ne crois pas qu'ils **viennent**. | *I don't think they'll come.* |
| Je ne crois pas qu'ils **soient venus**. | *I don't think they came.* |
| Nous doutons que l'équipe **perde**. | *We doubt that the team will lose.* |
| Nous doutons que l'équipe **ait perdu**. | *We doubt that the team has lost.* |
| Elle est contente que tu **comprennes**. | *She's happy that you understand.* |
| Elle est contente que tu **aies compris**. | *She's happy that you understood.* |

Note that while the present subjunctive is translated as a present or future tense, the past subjunctive can be translated by a variety of past tenses. The subjunctive in French does not have the range of tense distinctions of the indicative.

**C**  *Using the cue in parentheses, rewrite each sentence to create a new sentence where the verb in the dependent clause is in the past subjunctive.*

MODÈLE     Il a imprimé les documents. (Je ne crois pas)

*Je ne crois pas qu'il ait imprimé les documents.*

1. Ils se sont amusés. (Il est peu probable)

_____

2. Maurice et Valérie étaient fiancés. (Je doute)

_____

3. Vous le leur avez expliqué. (Je me réjouis)

_____

4. Il a menti. (Nous sommes furieux)

_____

5. Ils n'avaient pas de vie privée. (Je regrette)

_____

6. Tu ne l'as pas vu. (Il est étonnant)

_____

7. L'avion a décollé. (Il est possible)

_____

8. Les médecins sont arrivés. (On est contents)

_____

9. Ils m'ont dit cela. (Je nie)

_____

10. Mon ordinateur a eu une panne soudaine. (Ce n'est pas bien)

_____

11. Ils sont rentrés un peu soûls (*drunk* [slang]). (Il n'est pas vrai)

_____

12. Leur chat est mort. (Ils sont désolés)

_____

13. Ils ont fait quelque chose d'intéressant. (Il ne semble pas)

_____

14. Elle n'a pas fait de charité. (Je n'approuve pas)

_____

15. Ses amis sont sortis sans elle. (Elle est déçue)

_____

**D** *Translation.* *Express the following sentences in French.*

1. *I doubt that Nicole found her necklace.*

   _____

2. *It's good that you (vous) solved your problem.*

   _____

3. *It's bad that they dropped by without calling (= warning prévenir).*

   _____

4. *It's useful that you (tu) downloaded the files.*

   _____

5. *Are you (vous) surprised that they didn't offer Charles a raise?*

   _____

6. *I'm glad it turned out well (finir bien) for you (tu).*

   _____

7. *It's not true that Isabelle quit her job.*

   _____

8. *He's furious that the dog tore the rug.*

   _____

9. *They're sorry that everything went from bad to worse.*

   _____

10. *It's improbable that he already returned the umbrella to her.*

    _____

The only time distinction that is made in the subjunctive in everyday French is simultaneity vs. anteriority. A present subjunctive indicates that the action of the subordinate clause happens at the same time or after the action of the main clause. A past subjunctive indicates that the action of the subordinate clause happened prior to the action of the main clause.

| | |
|---|---|
| Je regrette que notre équipe **perde**. | *I'm sorry our team will lose.* |
| Je regrette que notre équipe **ait perdu**. | *I'm sorry our team lost.* |
| Je regrettais que notre équipe **perde**. | *I was sorry our team was losing.* |
| Je regrettais que notre équipe **ait perdu**. | *I was sorry our team had lost.* |

## Uses of the Subjunctive in Adverb Clauses

An adverb clause is a subordinate clause that modifies a verb much as an adverb does. Adverbial clauses are introduced by adverbial conjunctions that express time, cause, means, purpose, or consequence such as *when, how, because, in order that, provided that, while,* etc.

Certain French adverbial conjunctions are always followed by the subjunctive.

**à condition que**  *on the condition that, provided that*
**à moins que**  *unless*
**afin que**  *so that, in order that* (formal)
**avant que**  *before*
**bien que / quoique**  *although, even though*
**de crainte que**  *for fear that*
**de peur que**  *for fear that*
**en attendant que**  *until*
**encore que**  *although* (literary)
**jusqu'à ce que**  *until*
**malgré que**  *in spite of the fact that, although*
**pour que**  *so that, in order that*
**pourvu que**  *provided that, as long as*
**sans que**  *without*

| | |
|---|---|
| Ce n'est pas la peine de nous réunir **à moins que tout le monde lise** les articles du journal électronique. | *It doesn't pay for us to have a meeting unless everyone reads the articles in the e-zine.* |
| Discutons le projet **avant que le conseiller revienne**. | *Let's discuss the project before the consultant returns.* |
| Je vais télécharger ce logiciel **bien qu'il soit** un peu vieux. | *I'm going to download this software even though it's a bit old.* |
| **Pour que vous puissiez** me contacter je vous donnerai l'adresse de mon compte e-mail. | *So that you can contact me, I'll give you my e-mail address.* |
| Je vais allumer mon ordinateur **pour que vous consultiez** le tableur. | *I'm going to turn on my computer in order for you to consult the spreadsheet.* |
| Je te dirai tout ce qui m'est arrivé **pourvu que tu ne racontes** ça à personne. | *I'll tell you what happened to me as long as you don't tell (it to) anyone.* |
| Ton ordinateur ne va pas fonctionner **sans que vous** y **installiez** ce nouveau système d'exploitation. | *Your computer won't work without your installing this new operating system (on it).* |

In formal style, **ne** may precede the subjunctive in a subordinate clause following **avant que**, **de peur que**, **de crainte que**, or **à moins que**. This **ne** does not make the meaning negative.

| | |
|---|---|
| Partez **avant qu'elle ne** s'en rende compte. | *Leave before she realizes.* |
| J'ai pris mon manteau **de peur qu'il ne** fasse froid. | *I took my coat with me for fear that it might get cold.* |
| Ils viendront **à moins qu'ils ne** soient pris. | *They will come unless they're busy.* |

If the subjects of both clauses are the same, the subordinate clause is usually replaced by an infinitive.

| | |
|---|---|
| Je ne peux pas commencer mon travail **sans déboguer** ce programme. | *I can't begin my work without debugging this program.* |
| Qu'est-ce que je dois faire **pour télécharger** la base de données? | *What do I have to do to download the database?* |

Ne quittez pas votre ordinateur **avant d'effacer** tous ces fichiers.

Tu ne pourras pas devenir consultant **à moins d'avoir** un bon portable.

*Don't leave your computer without deleting all those files.*

*You won't be able to become a consultant unless you have a good laptop computer.*

**E**  Complete each sentence with the correct form of the verb in parentheses. Some of the verbs are in the past subjunctive.

1. (jeter)      Je vais vous donner mon mot de passe pour que vous _____ un coup d'œil sur mon courrier électronique.

2. (prendre)    Je vais acheter le livre avant que tu le _____ à la bibliothèque.

3. (avoir)      Il ne te donnera plus de détails jusqu'à ce que vous en _____ besoin.

4. (choisir)    Il s'assied à la table d'un café en attendant que sa femme _____ une robe au magasin.

5. (avoir)      Ils iront faire du ski à moins qu'il n'y _____ pas de neige.

6. (être)       Nous allons servir le repas bien que tout le monde ne _____ pas encore arrivé.

7. (avoir)      Je ne suis pas sorti jusqu'à ce qu'il _____ commencé à s'éclaircir (*to clear up*).

8. (rendre)     Je te prêterai mon appareil photo pourvu que tu me le _____ avant samedi.

9. (finir)      Tu pourras sortir pourvu que tu _____ tes devoirs.

10. (dire)      Ne faites rien sans que je vous le _____.

**F**  Combine the following pairs of sentences to create a new sentence, using the second sentence for the main clause. Introduce the subordinate clause with **jusqu'à ce que**.

MODÈLE   Il viendra. J'attendrai.

   *J'attendrai jusqu'à ce qu'il vienne.* _____

1. Monique revient du marché. Nous serons là.

   _____

2. Elle s'en ira. Nous attendrons. _____

3. On finira le projet. Il nous aidera. _____

4. Vous pouvez vérifier la date. J'attendrai.

   _____

5. Je vous ferai signe. Soyez patients. _____

**G**  *Combine the following pairs of sentences to create a new sentence, using the second sentence for the main clause. Introduce the subordinate clause with* **à moins que**.

MODÈLE    Tu as déjà fini. Je t'aiderai.

   *Je t'aiderai à moins que tu (n')aies déjà fini.*

1.  Elle est occupée. Nous sortirons avec elle.

   _____

2.  Il pleut. Nous ferons une randonnée.

   _____

3.  Vous avez des choses à faire. On passera vous voir.

   _____

4.  Il fait mauvais. Nous pourrons passer la journée dehors.

   _____

5.  Elle peut nous rejoindre au bord de la mer. Nous n'allons pas voir Aude.

   _____

6.  On a fermé le supermarché. Descendons acheter à manger.

   _____


**H**  *Combine the following pairs of sentences to create a new sentence, using the second sentence for the main clause. Introduce the subordinate clause with* **pourvu que**.

MODÈLE    Tu finiras ton travail. Tu peux sortir.

   *Tu peux sortir pourvu que tu finisses ton travail.*

1.  Vous rentrez avant minuit. Vous pouvez sortir.

   _____

2.  L'avion part à l'heure. On partira.

   _____

3.  Tu fais les courses avant. Tu peux aller jouer au foot.

   _____

4.  Tout le monde est prêt. Nous pourrons parler du projet.

   _____

5.  Il y a une baisse à la bourse. J'achèterai des actions.

   _____

6.  Il sait les faits. Le consultant en gestion (*management consultant*) écrira le rapport.

   _____

**I** *Create a conversational exchange by responding with a clause that begins with* **Pour que** *and the cue in parentheses.*

MODÈLE —Pourquoi est-ce qu'on doit rester ici? (Il peut nous retrouver.)

— *Pour qu'il puisse nous retrouver.*

1. —Pourquoi est-ce que tu as baissé le poste? (L'enfant s'endort.)

—

2. —Pourquoi est-ce que tu lui as donné tant de couvertures? (Il n'a pas froid.)

—

3. —Pourquoi est-ce que tu nous a invité à cette soirée? (Vous faites la connaissance de mes amis.)

—

4. —Pourquoi est-ce que tu m'as acheté cette carte routière? (Tu ne te perds pas.)

—

5. —Pourquoi est-ce que tu lui a demandé de venir? (Elle me dit ce qui s'est passé.)

—

6. —Pourquoi est-ce que tu as préparé de la limonade? (Tout le monde prend quelque chose de froid.)

—

7. —Pourquoi est-ce que tu lui as prêté 300 dollars? (Elle achète des cadeaux de Noël.)

—

**J** *Combine the following pairs of sentences to create a new sentence, using the second sentence for the main clause. Introduce the subordinate clause with* **pour que**.

MODÈLE On l'appelle. Il est trop tôt.

*Il est trop tôt pour qu'on l'appelle.*

1. Je prends mon déjeuner dehors. Il fait trop mauvais.

2. On peut lui en parler. Il est trop inquiet.

3. Je le préviens. Il est trop tard.

4. Tu sors seule. Les rues sont trop désertes.

5. On le suit. Il marche trop vite.

6. Nous nous voyons fréquemment. Ils habitent trop loin.

**K** *These things will be done in spite of everything!* Combine the following pairs of sentences to create a new sentence, using the second sentence for the main clause. Introduce the subordinate clause with **bien que**.

MODÈLE    Il pleut. Nous sortirons.

_Nous sortirons bien qu'il pleuve._

1. Je ne me sens pas bien. Je vais au bureau.

   _____

2. Il fait froid. Je compte sortir. _____

3. Cette matière est très difficile. Ils vont réussir.

   _____

4. L'ordinateur est tombé en panne. Il faut travailler.

   _____

5. Le match a déjà commencé. Allons au stade.

   _____

## Indicative vs. Subjunctive in Adverb Clauses

French has several conjunctions that express English *so that*. They are followed by the subjunctive when they express a goal, intent, or purpose, but they are followed by the indicative when they introduce an actual result.

**de façon que**
**de manière que**
**de sorte que**
**de telle sorte que**
**en sorte que** (literary)

Compare the following sentences.

| | |
|---|---|
| Il parle **de façon qu'on lui fasse** attention. | *He talks in such a way that people will pay attention to him.* |
| Il parle **de façon qu'on lui fait** attention. | *He talks in such a way that people pay attention to him.* |
| Ils amènent souvent leur enfant au musée **de sorte qu'il prenne** goût aux beaux arts. | *They often take their child to the museum so that he may acquire a taste for fine arts.* |
| Ils amènent souvent leur enfant au musée **de sorte qu'il prend** goût aux beaux arts. | *They often take their child to the museum so that he is acquiring a taste for fine arts.* |
| Elle fait des économies **de manière qu'elle et son mari puissent acheter** une maison. | *She is thrifty so that she and her husband can buy a house.* |
| Elle a fait des économies **de manière qu'elle et son mari ont pu acheter** une maison. | *She was thrifty so that she and her husband were able to buy a house.* |

**L** **Translation.** *Express the following sentences in French.*

1. a. *You* (tu) *speak slowly so that she will understand.* (de sorte que)

   _____

   b. *You* (tu) *spoke slowly so that she understood.* (de sorte que)

   _____

2. a. *I'll warn him so that he realizes the danger.* (de façon que)

   _____

   b. *I warned him so that he realized the danger.* (de façon que)

   _____

3. a. *We're giving her our credit card so that she can buy the software.* (de sorte que)

   _____

   _____

   b. *We gave her our credit card so that she could buy (and did buy) the software.*
      (de sorte que)

   _____

   _____

---

### LA LANGUE FRANÇAISE   the circumflex accent

The circumflex accent has two functions in written French.

- It indicates that a letter (usually **s**) has dropped from the word, leaving a long vowel.

| MODERN FRENCH | OLD FRENCH (~1000–~1300 A.D.) |
|---|---|
| coût | cost |
| êtes | estes |
| fête | feste |
| mêler | mesler |
| maître | maistre |
| tête | teste |
| tôt | tost |

In modern French, the vowel lengthening originally indicated by the circumflex has merged with the corresponding short vowels, so that in most cases the circumflex has no phonetic value.

- It serves to differentiate homonyms in writing.

  **du** contraction of **de** + **le** vs. **dû** past participle of **devoir**
  **cru** past participle of **croire** vs. **crû** past participle of **croître** (*to grow*)

The 1990 spelling reform eliminated the circumflex accent from the letters **i** and **u** (so that **maître** and **coût** would be written **maitre** and **cout**) except in verb forms, but many publications continue to follow the old rules and preserve the circumflex. (See "La langue française: French spelling," p. 159.)

---

| BUILDING SENTENCES | **Compound and complex sentences** |

There are two types of conjunctions that join sentences together.

*Coordinating conjunctions* create compound sentences, sentences in which neither clause is subordinate to the other. Typical coordinating conjunctions are **et**, **mais**, and **ou**.

| | |
|---|---|
| Je suis allé à son bureau **et** j'ai demandé une interview. | *I went to his office and asked for an interview.* |
| Nous, on est sortis, **mais** elle, elle est restée à la maison. | *We went out, but she stayed home.* |
| Laissez-moi travailler **ou** je m'en vais. | *Let me work, or I'll leave.* |

The French equivalent of *not only . . . but also* is **non seulement... mais aussi**.

| | |
|---|---|
| **Non seulement** il fait froid, **mais** il neige **aussi**. | *It's not only cold, but it's also snowing.* |

The conjunction **ou** may be expanded to **ou alors**.

| | |
|---|---|
| Laissez-moi travailler **ou alors** je m'en vais. | *Let me work, or else I'll leave.* |

**Ou bien** adds a note of emphatic exclusion of one of the alternatives. It may appear at the head of both conjoined sentences.

| | |
|---|---|
| **Ou bien c'est** lui qui ment **ou bien c'est** elle. | *Either he's lying or she is.* |
| **Ou bien je reste** locataire **ou bien je deviens** propriétaire. | *Either I continue being a tenant or I become an owner.* |

**Soit... soit** also conjoins two sentences with the meaning *either . . . or*.

| | |
|---|---|
| **Soit** ils le savaient déjà, **soit** ils ont reçu un courriel à cet égard. | *Either they knew it already or they got an e-mail about it.* |

*Subordinating conjunctions* embed a sentence within a larger sentence, and that embedded sentence is then dependent on or subordinate to the main clause. This is called a complex sentence. The most common subordinating conjunction in French is **que**.

**Que** is followed by the indicative after verbs that emphasize the truth value of the subordinate clause, like **savoir**, **affirmer**, **confirmer**, **déclarer**, and **jurer**.

| | |
|---|---|
| **Nous savons qu'**ils aiment la France. | *We know they like France.* |
| **Il affirme qu'**il n'y est pour rien. | *He affirms that he is not at all to blame.* |
| **Je confirme que** j'ai vendu ma maison. | *I am confirming that I sold my house.* |
| **Elle a déclaré qu'**elle était l'auteur du message. | *She declared that she was the author of the message.* |
| **Je jure que** je le lui ai rendu. | *I swear that I returned it to him.* |

Subordinating conjunctions that express cause and result also introduce clauses in the indicative. One of the most common is **parce que** *because*.

| | |
|---|---|
| On ne peut pas sortir **parce qu'**il pleut. | *We can't go out because it's raining.* |

Je ne peux pas aller avec vous **parce que**       *I can't go with you because I have too*
j'ai trop à faire.                                  *much to do.*

There are many conjunctions of time that are always followed by the indicative.

**après que**  *after*
**aussitôt que / dès que**  *as soon as*
**chaque fois que**  *each time that*
**depuis que**  *since, from the time that*
**lorsque**  *when* (literary)
**maintenant que**  *now that*
**pendant que**  *while*
**quand**  *when*

**Après que tu installeras** ce logiciel, tu       *After you install this software, you will be*
pourras travailler avec plus d'efficacité.          *able to work more efficiently.*
**Chaque fois que je reçois** un de ses             *Each time I receive one of his e-mails,*
courriels, je le lis avec beaucoup                  *I read it with a great deal of interest.*
d'intérêt.
Je suis un peu effrayé **depuis que j'ai**          *I'm a bit frightened since I received his*
**reçu** son message.                               *message.*

Remember that **aussitôt que**, **dès que**, **lorsque**, and **quand** are followed by the future
when the main clause is in the future or the imperative (see Chapter 8, p. 164). In colloquial speech, there is a tendency to use the subjunctive after **après que**.

Je vous ai téléphoné **aussitôt qu'**il est         *I phoned you as soon as he left.*
parti.
Je vous téléphonerai **aussitôt qu'**il             *I'll phone you as soon as he leaves.*
partira.

Other conjunctions followed by the indicative are the following.

**à mesure que / au fur et à mesure que**  *as, in proportion*
**comme**  *as, since* (= *because*)
**étant donné que**  *given that*
**excepté que / sauf que / sinon que**  *except that*
**puisque**  *since* (= *because*)
**selon que / suivant que**  *depending (on) whether*
**tandis que**  *while* (= *whereas*)
**vu que**  *seeing that*

 *Combine the pairs of sentences with a conjunction to create a new sentence,*
*choosing one of the coordinating or subordinating conjunctions that appear*
*in parentheses.*

MODÈLE    Ils m'ont téléphoné. Je suis allé leur rendre visite.  (sans que | et)

*Ils m'ont téléphoné et je suis allé leur rendre visite.*

1.  Je l'ai invitée au concert. Elle n'a pas pu venir.  (mais | que)

2. Il ne peut pas s'inscrire au cours de sciences politiques. Il suit un cours d'histoire à la même heure. (et | parce que)

_____

_____

3. Tu arrives à l'heure. Ils te défendent d'entrer. (sauf que | ou)

_____

4. Elle a envoyé son courriel. Elle a éteint l'ordinateur. (et | parce que)

_____

5. On a du mal a le contacter. Il n'a pas de téléphone mobile. (tandis que | étant donné que)

_____

_____

6. Je suis parti. Il n'était pas là. (puisque | au fur et à mesure que)

_____

7. Je te jure. Ils sont dignes de notre confiance. (comme | que)

_____

8. La voiture roulait très vite. Nous n'avons pas pu l'atteindre. (parce que | de sorte que)

_____

_____

9. Il a fait suivre tous les messages. Il les recevait. (au fur et à mesure que | de façon que)

_____

10. Ma mère est brune. Moi, je suis roux. (quand | tandis que)

_____

**N** *Translation.* *Express the following sentences in French.*

1. *She doesn't only sing, but she dances also.*

_____

2. *Either we will phone them today or we will talk to them when we see them.*

_____

_____

3. *Please* (Veuillez) *confirm that you've received the e-tickets.*

_____

4. *I swear that I am not guilty.*

_____

5. *He's going to spend his vacation in San Francisco because his parents live there.*

   _____

   _____

6. *Turn on (tu) the computer so that I can see your website.*

   _____

7. *Everything was in order except that there was no water.*

   _____

8. *They went to the movies, but we decided to rent a film.*

   _____

9. *Since they had a housewarming party* (pendre la crémaillère), *we had to buy them a gift.*

   _____

10. *She logged on* (établir une connexion) *and went to (sur) her own website first.*

   _____

# The Present Participle and the Infinitive

**BUILDING SENTENCES**

Preposition + infinitive phrases as verbal complements
Verbs of perception and **laisser** + infinitive
The causative (**faire** + infinitive)

Both English and French have present participles and infinitives, but there is no direct correspondence in the role of these forms in the two languages.

## The Present Participle

The French present participle ends in **-ant**, which is added to the stem of the verb (the first-person plural of the present tense minus the **-ons** ending). Sometimes the present participle is called the *gerund*.

| INFINITIVE | **nous** FORM | PRESENT PARTICIPLE |
|---|---|---|
| parler | nous parlons | **parlant** |
| finir | nous finissons | **finissant** |
| rendre | nous rendons | **rendant** |
| lire | nous lisons | **lisant** |
| prendre | nous prenons | **prenant** |
| écrire | nous écrivons | **écrivant** |

Three common verbs have irregular present participles.

| | |
|---|---|
| avoir | **ayant** |
| être | **étant** |
| savoir | **sachant** |

Many present participles in French are used as adjectives, and as such they agree in gender and number with the nouns they modify.

| | | |
|---|---|---|
| charmer | un sourire **charmant** | *a **charming** smile* |
| courir | de l'eau **courante** | ***running** water* |
| étinceler | des étoiles **étincelantes** | ***twinkling** stars* |
| galoper | l'inflation **galopante** | ***galloping** inflation* |
| passer | une rue **passante** | *a **busy** street* |
| passionner | une histoire **passionnante** | *an **exciting** story* |
| payer | des spectacles **payants** | *shows **that charge admission*** |
| perdre | les chevaux **perdants** | *the **losing** horses* |

| reconnaître | une nation **reconnaissante** | *a **grateful** nation* |
| toucher | une rencontre **touchante** | *a **touching** encounter* |

Like other adjectives, some of these present participles can also function as nouns.

| **commander** *to command* | le **commandant** *commander* |
| **commercer** *to trade with* | le **commerçant** *storekeeper* |
| **détailler** *to sell at retail* | le **détaillant** *retailer* |
| **gagner** *to win* | le **gagnant** *winner* |
| **passer** *to pass by* | le **passant** *passerby* |
| **ressortir** *to come under the jurisdiction of* | le **ressortissant** *national, citizen* |

Some of these nouns have feminine forms ending in **-ante**, such as **la commandante** and **la commerçante**.

There are several verbal uses of the present participle. The present participle may be used instead of a relative clause. In this case it is invariable. This construction is typical of formal speech and writing.

| les trains **qui partent** pour le Midi<br>les trains **partant** pour le Midi | } | *trains leaving for southern France* |
| des guides **qui parlent** français<br>des guides **parlant** français | } | *French-speaking guides* |
| des bateaux **qui descendent** le fleuve<br>des bateaux **descendant** le fleuve | } | *boats going down the river* |

Present participles that substitute for clauses often stand at the beginning of a sentence, but they may also appear in the middle or at the end. The present participle functions almost as an adverb in such cases, specifying the time when something happened or the conditions under which it happened.

| **Voyant** la foule, j'ai pris une autre rue.<br>(**voyant** = **quand j'ai vu**) | *Seeing the crowd, I took a different street.* |
| Le temps **se mettant au chaud**, on pourra se baigner.<br>(**Le temps se mettant au chaud** = **si le temps se met au chaud**) | *If it gets warm, we can go swimming.* |
| Le train, **s'approchant de la gare**, a ralenti.<br>(**s'approchant** = **quand il s'approchait**) | *The train slowed down as it approached the station.* |

French has a construction consisting of **en** + the present participle called *le gérondif*. The subject of the main clause is understood as the subject of the *gérondif*. The *gérondif* has several functions.

- It conveys the idea of *while, as, at the time when.*

| J'écoute de la musique **en lisant**. | *I listen to music while reading.* |
| Il m'a salué **en sortant**. | *He said hello to me as he went out.* |

- It expresses cause.

| **En entendant** la pluie j'ai demandé qu'on ferme les fenêtres. | *When I heard the rain, I asked that they close the windows.* |
| **En voyant** le voleur j'ai appelé la police. | *When I saw the thief, I called the police.* |

- It expresses a condition.

**En fermant** le vendredi, vous perdrez beaucoup de clients.

*By closing on Fridays, you will lose a lot of customers.*

- It expresses the means or manner.

**En travaillant** comme ça vous ne finirez jamais le projet.

*Working like that, you'll never finish the project.*

**En lisant** les courriels reçus, vous vous mettrez au courant de tout.

*By reading the e-mails you have gotten, you will bring yourself up to speed.*

The word **tout** can be added before the *gérondif* to emphasize the simultaneity of the actions of the *gérondif* and the main clause or to express a contradiction between the two actions.

**Tout en parlant** avec son petit ami, elle faisait des clins d'œil à Robert.

*All the while she was talking with her boyfriend, she was winking at Robert.*

**Tout en affirmant** son appui, il a tout fait pour la faire congédier.

*Even as he affirmed his support, he did everything to get her fired.*

French uses a compound present participle to emphasize that the action of the present participle happened before the action of the main clause. The compound present participle is composed of the present participle of the auxiliary verb **ayant** (for **avoir** verbs) or **étant** (for **être** verbs) plus the past participle.

**En ayant offensé** son chef, il s'est fait renvoyer.

*By offending (= by having offended) his boss, he got himself fired.*

**Ayant payé** l'addition, elle a laissé un pourboire et est sortie du restaurant.

*Once she paid the check, she left a tip and left the restaurant.*

**Ayant posé** notre question, nous avons attendu sa réponse.

*Having asked our question, we waited for his answer.*

**Étant sorties** du cinéma, elles ont appelé un taxi.

*After leaving the movie theater, they called a cab.*

**A** *Rewrite each sentence, replacing the subordinate clause with the* ***gérondif***.

MODÈLE    J'arrive à connaître les gens parce que je les écoute attentivement.

*J'arrive à connaître les gens en les écoutant attentivement.*

1. J'évite les crises au bureau parce que j'organise bien le travail.

   _____

   _____

2. Si tu regardes les émissions en espagnol à la télé, tu te perfectionneras dans cette langue.

   _____

   _____

3. Nous arriverons à l'avance si nous prenons un taxi.

   _____

4. Si on apprend le vocabulaire spécialisé, on pourra utiliser le français dans sa profession.

_____

_____

5. On s'enrichit si on fait des placements intelligents.

_____

6. Vous réussirez dans votre nouvelle entreprise si vous étudiez le marché.

_____

_____

7. Elle a maigri parce qu'elle a mangé beaucoup de fruits et de légumes tous les jours.

_____

8. Si vous buvez moins de café, vous serez moins nerveux.

_____

9. Si tu sors un peu moins, tu finiras ta thèse.

_____

10. Ils ont gagné beaucoup d'argent quand ils ont vendu leur appartement.

_____

_____

**B** _Rewrite each sentence, replacing the relative clause with a present participle to imitate the language of official announcements._

MODÈLE    Les patients qui ont un rendez-vous peuvent passer à la salle d'attente.

_Les patients ayant un rendez-vous peuvent passer à la salle_
_d'attente._

1. Les visiteurs qui désirent visiter la cathédrale sont priés de prendre un billet.

_____

_____

2. Les passagers qui voyagent en TGV sont priés de passer au quai numéro huit.

_____

_____

3. Mesdames et Messieurs, nous annonçons l'arrivée de l'avion qui provient du Sénégal.

_____

_____

4. C'est un site Web qui contient toutes les informations nécessaires.

   _____

   _____

5. Voici une carte qui montre l'emplacement des centrales nucléaires françaises.

   _____

   _____

6. C'est un hôpital pour les malades qui souffrent des problèmes pulmonaires.

   _____

   _____

7. Les candidats qui ont une interview seront reçus cet après-midi.

   _____

   _____

8. Les candidats qui parlent plus d'une langue ont une bonne chance d'être embauchés.

   _____

   _____

9. Nous avons reçu un message qui demande de rassembler toute l'information sur ces actions.

   _____

   _____

10. C'est un métier qui offre de bonnes possibilités d'emploi.

    _____

## The Infinitive

The French infinitive parallels many of the uses of the English present participle, which ends in *-ing*.

In French, the infinitive can be a verbal noun that functions as the subject of a sentence.

| | |
|---|---|
| **Trouver** un bon travail n'est pas facile. | *Finding a good job is not easy.* |
| Mon but, c'est de **travailler** à Paris. | *Working in Paris is my goal.* |
| **Voir**, c'est **croire**. | *Seeing is believing.* |

The infinitive in French is used after prepositions.

| | |
|---|---|
| avant de **sortir** | *before going out* |

The French infinitive is often used for impersonal instructions.

| | |
|---|---|
| **Ralentir.** | *Slow.* (on road signs) |
| **Agiter** avant emploi. | *Shake before using.* |

When an infinitive follows another verb, it may or may not be preceded by a preposition, depending on which verb it follows.

In the lists below, **qqn** stands for **quelqu'un** *someone* and designates an animate subject or object, and **qqch** stands for **quelque chose** *something* and designates an inanimate subject or object. **Faire** *to do* stands for any infinitive.

## Verbs Followed Directly by an Infinitive

A list of some of the verbs that are followed directly by an infinitive, with no intervening preposition, follows.

**adorer faire qqch**  *to love to do something*
**affirmer faire qqch**  *to affirm that*
**aimer faire qqch**  *to like to do something*
**aimer mieux faire qqch**  *to prefer to do something*
**aller faire qqch**  *to be going to* (future meaning) *do something*
**avoir beau faire qqch**  *to do something in vain*
**compter faire qqch**  *to intend to do something*
**daigner faire qqch**  *to deign to do something*
**désirer faire qqch**  *to want to do something*
**détester faire qqch**  *to hate to do something*
**devoir faire qqch**  *should do something, must / ought to do something*
**espérer faire qqch**  *to hope to do something*
**oser faire qqch**  *to dare to do something*
**penser faire qqch**  *to intend to do something, be thinking of doing something*
**pouvoir faire qqch**  *to be able to do something*
**préférer faire qqch**  *to prefer to do something*
**reconnaître faire qqch**  *to admit to doing something*
**savoir faire qqch**  *to know how to do something*
**souhaiter faire qqch**  *to wish to do something*
**vouloir faire qqch**  *to want to do something*

The impersonal expressions **il faut** *one must, you have to* and **il vaut mieux** *it's better to* are also followed directly by an infinitive. These expressions are not conjugated for person, because impersonal **il** is the only possible subject. However, they are conjugated for tense.

| | |
|---|---|
| IMPERFECT | il fallait, il valait mieux |
| PASSÉ COMPOSÉ | il a fallu, il a mieux valu |
| FUTURE | il faudra, il vaudra mieux |
| CONDITIONAL | il faudrait, il vaudrait mieux |

—Quand est-ce que tu **veux partir** en vacances?    *"When do you want to go on vacation?"*

—J'**aime prendre** mes vacances en hiver. Toi?    *"I like to take my vacation in the winter. How about you?"*

—Moi, je **préfère les prendre** au printemps.    *"I like to take it in the spring."*

—Je **déteste voyager** quand il fait froid.    *"I hate to travel when it's cold."*

| | |
|---|---|
| —Tu **comptes avertir** Paul? | *"Do you intend to alert Paul?"* |
| —Oui, mais j'**ai beau l'appeler**. Il ne fait pas attention. | *"Yes, but it's no use calling him. He pays no attention."* |
| —Il **affirme pouvoir nous aider**. | *"He affirms that he can help us."* |
| —Nous **devons accepter** son offre. | *"We must accept his offer."* |
| —**Il faut lui téléphoner**, alors. | *"Then we must phone him."* |
| —**Il vaut mieux lui envoyer** un courriel. | *"It's better to send him an e-mail."* |

Verbs of motion are followed directly by an infinitive in French.

**aller faire qqch** *to be going to do something*
**descendre faire qqch** *to go down to do something*
**s'en aller faire qqch** *to go off to do something*
**entrer faire qqch** *to go inside to do something*
**monter faire qqch** *to go up to do something*
**rentrer faire qqch** *to go home to do something*
**revenir faire qqch** *to come back to do something*
**sortir faire qqch** *to go out to do something*
**venir faire qqch** *to come to do something*

The following expressions are related to verbs of motion.

**amener qqn faire qqch** *to bring someone to do something*
**emmener qqn faire qqch** *to take someone to do something*

| | |
|---|---|
| —Tu **descends faire** les courses? | *"Are you going downstairs to do the shopping?"* |
| —Oui, et je **rentrerai préparer** le dîner. | *"Yes, and I'll come back home to prepare dinner."* |
| —Qu'est-ce qu'il **vient faire** ici? | *"What's he coming to do here?"* |
| —Il **vient nous rendre** visite. | *"He's coming to visit us."* |

**C** *Expand each of the following sentences to incorporate the verb in parentheses.*

MODÈLE (aller) Il fait beau aujourd'hui.

     *Il va faire beau aujourd'hui.*

1. (compter) J'invite toute la famille ce week-end.

    _____

2. (aller) Nous célébrons les fiançailles de mon neveu.

    _____

    _____

3. (vouloir) Tout le monde fait la connaissance de sa fiancée.

    _____

    _____

4.  (il faut)        J'appelle le traiteur (*caterer*).

   _____

5.  (pouvoir)       Je ne prépare pas un repas pour tant de personnes.

   _____

   _____

6.  (aimer)         Toute ma famille mange.

   _____

7.  (aimer mieux)   Ils dégustent des plats exquis.

   _____

8.  (venir)         Ils nous rendent visite samedi.

   _____

9.  (devoir)        Tout est prêt à trois heures de l'après-midi.

   _____

10. (désirer)       Nous passons tout le week-end ensemble.

   _____


**D**  *Expand each sentence to incorporate the verb in parentheses. Retain the tense of the original sentence.*

   MODÈLE    (descendre)   Il fera les courses.

   *Il descendra faire les courses.*
   _____

1.  (aller)         Ils prennent leurs vacances à la Martinique.

   _____

2.  (adorer)        Ils faisaient du ski nautique.

   _____

3.  (aller)         Elle a peur de la mer.

   _____

4.  (savoir)        Tu ne nages pas.

   _____

5.  (oser)          Il ne se baignera pas.

   _____

6.  (espérer)       Vous ne voyez pas de requins (*sharks*).

   _____

7.  (compter)       Je mangeais bien à la Martinique.

   _____

8.  (il faut)  Il réserve un hôtel sur Internet.

    _____

9.  (aimer mieux)  Ils descendraient (*stay*) dans un hôtel près de la plage.

    _____

    _____

10. (adorer)  Nous passons une semaine aux tropiques.

    _____

---

**BUILDING SENTENCES** | **Preposition + infinitive phrases as verbal complements**

## Phrases with à

Not all French verbs can take an infinitive as a complement. Most require a preposition to connect the conjugated verb to a following infinitive. The most common prepositions are **à** and **de**.

Verbs that express beginnings or starting points of actions often require **à** before a following infinitive.

**apprendre à**  *to learn how to*
**s'apprêter à**  *to get ready to*
**s'attendre à**  *to expect to*
**avoir à**  *to have to*
**commencer à**  *to begin to*
**consentir à**  *to consent to*
**se décider à**  *to make up one's mind to*
**s'habituer à**  *to get used to*
**hésiter à**  *to hesitate to*
**s'intéresser à**  *to be interested in*
**se mettre à**  *to begin to*
**penser à**  *to be thinking of (doing something)*
**se préparer à**  *to get ready to*
**se résoudre à**  *to resolve to*
**songer à**  *to be thinking of (doing something)*
**tenir à**  *to insist on*

Many verbs that express effort or involvement require **à** before a following infinitive.

**s'acharner à**  *to try desperately to*
**s'adonner à**  *to devote oneself to*
**s'amuser à**  *to enjoy oneself (by doing)*
**s'appliquer à**  *to apply oneself to*
**s'apprêter à**  *to prepare oneself to*
**se borner à**  *to limit oneself to*
**chercher à**  *to try to*
**se complaire à**  *to take pleasure in*

**se consacrer à**  *to devote oneself to*
**s'énerver à**  *to get annoyed (doing something)*
**s'ennuyer à**  *to get/be bored (doing something)*
**s'entraîner à**  *to train to, practice*
**s'éreinter à**  *to tire oneself by*
**s'essouffler à**  *to get out of breath (doing something)*
**s'exercer à**  *to practice*
**se fatiguer à**  *to tire oneself by*
**s'irriter à**  *to get annoyed (doing something)*
**s'obstiner à**  *to persist stubbornly in*
**passer son temps à**  *to spend one's time (doing something)*
**perdre son temps à**  *to waste one's time (doing something)*
**persister à**  *to persist in (doing something)*
**se plaire à**  *to take pleasure in*
**prendre plaisir à**  *to take pleasure in*
**se résigner à**  *to resign oneself to*

Several verbs that express the achievement or failure of an action require **à** before a following infinitive.

**arriver à**  *to manage to*
**s'attarder à**  *to linger (doing something)*
**continuer à**  *to continue to*
**parvenir à**  *to manage to, succeed in*
**renoncer à**  *to give up (doing something)*
**réussir à**  *to succeed in*

—**Marc n'hésite pas à causer** avec tous les passagers japonais.
"*Marc doesn't hesitate to chat with all the Japanese passengers.*"

—De cette façon, **il s'exerce à parler** japonais.
"*That's the way he practices speaking Japanese.*"

—**Il parviendra à chasser** tous les passagers de nos avions.
"*He'll wind up driving all the passengers away from our planes.*"

—Tu exagères. **Les touristes prennent plaisir à converser** avec lui.
"*You're exaggerating. The tourists are delighted to converse with him.*"

In the examples above, the implied subject of the infinitive is the same as the subject of the conjugated verb. Thus, in **il s'exerce à parler**, the implied subject of **parler** is **il** (*Marc*).

Verbs that convey the idea of getting someone to do something have two subjects. Examine the following expressions, in which **quelqu'un** *someone* is both the direct object of the first verb and the subject of the infinitive.

**accoutumer qqn à faire qqch**  *to get someone used to doing something*
**aider qqn à faire qqch**  *to help someone do something*
**autoriser qqn à faire qqch**  *to authorize someone to do something*
**condamner qqn à faire qqch**  *to condemn someone to do something*
**contraindre qqn à faire qqch**  *to compel someone to do something*
**décider qqn à faire qqch**  *to help someone decide to do something*
**encourager qqn à faire qqch**  *to encourage someone to do something*

**engager qqn à faire qqch** *to urge someone to do something*
**forcer qqn à faire qqch** *to force someone to do something*
**inciter qqn à faire qqch** *to incite someone to do something*
**inviter qqn à faire qqch** *to invite someone to do something*
**obliger qqn à faire qqch** *to oblige someone to do something*
**pousser qqn à faire qqch** *to talk someone into doing something*
**préparer qqn à faire qqch** *to prepare someone to do / for doing something*

When it means *to teach*, **apprendre** patterns like **enseigner**, and it takes the indirect object of the person, as follows.

**apprendre/enseigner à qqn à faire qqch** *to teach someone to do something*

—Qui **vous a poussé à accepter** ce poste?    *"Who talked you into taking that job?"*
—Mes parents **m'ont encouragé à l'accepter.**    *"My parents encouraged me to accept it."*

—Il faut **accoutumer les enfants à regarder** un peu moins la télé.    *"We have to get the children used to watching TV a bit less."*
—D'accord. Je vais **les obliger à sortir** un peu plus.    *"I agree. I'm going to make them go out a little more."*

**E**   *Complete each sentence with **à**, if necessary. If no **à** is necessary, mark the blank with an X.*

1. Elle a contraint les enfants _____ l'aider avec le ménage.

2. Je vais _____ lui dire ce que je pense.

3. Qui vous a autorisé _____ envoyer ce message?

4. Ils incitent le peuple _____ se soulever.

5. Elles passent leur temps _____ se plaindre.

6. Tu ne montes pas _____ t'habiller?

7. Qu'est-ce qui t'a décidé _____ changer d'emploi?

8. Elle réussit _____ se faire comprendre en japonais.

9. Je me borne _____ vous prévenir que le chef est au courant.

10. Nous souhaitons _____ vous y revoir.

11. Il reconnaît _____ avoir besoin d'un cours de formation professionnelle.

12. Je ne peux pas m'habituer _____ travailler dans un bureau si bruyant.

**F**   *Expand each sentence to incorporate the material in parentheses. Retain the tense of the original sentence.*

MODÈLE   Je travaille le soir aussi. (mon travail / m'obliger)

     *Mon travail m'oblige à travailler le soir aussi.*

1. Il lit. (passer son temps) _____

2. J'ai travaillé dans le jardin. (s'éreinter)

3. Elle perd de l'argent.  (se résigner)

_____

4. Elle sortait une fois par semaine.  (se borner)

_____

5. Nous suivions des cours.  (nos parents / encourager)

_____

6. Elle a mangé au restaurant.  (je / inviter)

_____

7. Il joue aux échecs.  (s'exercer) _____

8. Je la reçois demain.  (préférer) _____

9. Il taquine (_tease_) sa petite sœur.  (prendre plaisir)

_____

10. Elle fait le ménage.  (ses enfants / aider)

_____

**G**  _Translation._  _Express the following sentences in French._

1. _Who authorized him to smoke here?_

_____

2. _I urge you_ (vous) _to help them._ _____

3. _He taught his daughter to ride a bicycle._

_____

4. _She got us used to exercising every day._

_____

5. _We talked him into inviting her to the party._

_____

6. _I get annoyed reading so many e-mails._

_____

7. _I insist on seeing him._ _____

8. _She tires herself by walking the dog._

_____

9. _We continue to study Italian._ _____

10. _He's trying desperately to fix his keyboard._

_____

## Phrases with **de**

Many verbs and verbal expressions require **de** before an infinitive complement. Among them are verbs signifying an interruption of the action expressed by the infinitive.

**s'abstenir de**  *to refrain from*
**achever de**  *to finish*
**s'arrêter de**  *to stop*
**cesser de**  *to stop*
**s'empêcher de**  *to refrain from, keep oneself from*
**éviter de**  *to avoid*
**finir de**  *to finish*
**se garder de**  *to be wary of, be careful not to*
**manquer de**  *to fail to*
**négliger de**  *to neglect to*
**omettre de**  *to omit, neglect to*
**oublier de**  *to forget to*
**refuser de**  *to refuse to*

| | |
|---|---|
| Elle **a refusé de nous montrer** le compte rendu. | *She refused to show us the report.* |
| Il **a évité d'être** vu. | *He avoided being seen.* |
| J'avais **oublié de vous le dire**. | *I had forgotten to tell you.* |
| **Gardez-vous de lui en parler**. | *Be careful not to talk to him about it.* |

Verbs that convey an attitude toward the action expressed by the infinitive often use the preposition **de** before the infinitive complement.

**accepter de**  *to agree to*
**affecter de**  *to pretend to*
**s'applaudir de**  *to be pleased with oneself for (having done something)*
**s'aviser de**  *to dare to, take it into one's head to*
**avoir peur de**  *to be afraid of*
**avoir raison de**  *to be right to*
**avoir regret de**  *to regret*
**avoir tort de**  *to be wrong to*
**brûler de**  *to be burning/dying to*
**craindre de**  *to fear*
**se dépêcher de**  *to hurry to*
**s'empresser de**  *to hurry/rush to*
**entreprendre de**  *to undertake to*
**s'étonner de**  *to marvel at*
**s'excuser de**  *to apologize for*
**faire semblant de**  *to pretend to*
**se flatter de**  *to claim to (be able to)*
**se hâter de**  *to hasten to*
**s'inquiéter de**  *to worry about (doing something)*
**mériter de**  *to deserve to*
**parler de**  *to talk about*
**se presser de**  *to hurry/rush to*
**redouter de**  *to dread*

**regretter de**  *to regret*
**se réjouir de**  *to be delighted to*
**se repentir de**  *to regret*
**rougir de**  *to be ashamed of*
**se soucier de**  *to care about*
**se vanter de**  *to boast of*

| | |
|---|---|
| —Elle **parle de lancer** une entreprise. | *"She talks about starting a business."* |
| —Elle **a tort de ne pas s'associer** à quelqu'un. | *"She's wrong not to get someone to be her partner."* |
| —Je **redoute de le revoir.** | *"I dread seeing him again."* |
| —Je **me repens de l'avoir invité.** | *"I regret having invited him."* |

Verbs that express an effort or plan to perform the action expressed by the infinitive use the preposition **de** before the infinitive complement.

**avoir l'intention de**  *to intend to*
**se charger de**  *to make sure to; to see to it that (something is done)*
**choisir de**  *to choose to*
**décider de**  *to decide to*
**essayer de**  *to try to*
**être forcé/obligé de**  *to be forced/obliged to*
**jurer de**  *to swear to*
**menacer de**  *to threaten to*
**promettre de**  *to promise to*
**se proposer de**  *to set out to, mean/intend to*
**résoudre de**  *to resolve to*
**risquer de**  *to risk, run the risk of*
**tâcher de**  *to try to*
**tenter de**  *to try to*

| | |
|---|---|
| —Il **a décidé de ne pas aller** avec nous. | *"He has decided not to go with us."* |
| —Mais il **avait promis de nous accompagner.** | *"But he had promised to accompany us."* |
| —Qui **se chargera de la contacter?** | *"Who will make sure to get in touch with her?"* |
| —Moi, j'**essaierai de l'appeler** aujourd'hui. | *"I'll try to call her today."* |

## Special Cases with **de**

- **S'indigner de** is usually translated as *it makes (someone) indignant that.*

| | |
|---|---|
| Le prof **s'indigne de voir** que nous ne travaillons pas. | *It makes the teacher indignant to see that we are not studying.* |

- **Se souvenir de** is most often followed by the infinitive of the auxiliary + the past participle (the perfect infinitive).

| | |
|---|---|
| Je ne **me souviens** pas **de l'avoir vu.** | *I don't remember having seen him.* |
| Elle ne **se souvient** pas **d'être sortie** avec lui. | *She doesn't remember going out with him.* |

In French, **n'oubliez pas de** is used to tell someone to remember to do something.

**N'oubliez pas de rédiger** le rapport.        *Remember to write up the report.*

■ **Bien faire de** means *to be right in (doing something), to do the wise thing by (doing something).*

Tu **as bien fait de nous prévenir.**        *You were wise to let us know.*

■ **Venir de** means *to have just (done something).*

Il n'est plus là. Il **vient de quitter** le bureau.        *He's not here anymore. He has just left the office.*

## Phrases with **par** and **pour**

**Par** and **pour** can be used to introduce an infinitive complement.

**commencer par faire qqch**  *to begin by doing something*
**finir par faire qqch**  *to wind up doing something*
**suffire pour faire qqch**  *to be enough to / adequate for doing something*

Nous **commencerons par dessiner** les grandes lignes du projet.        *We'll start by outlining the project.*

Elle **a fini par aliéner** tous ses amis.        *She wound up alienating all her friends.*

Un mot **suffit pour la faire pleurer.**        *A (mere) word is enough to make her cry.*

**H**  *Complete each sentence with* **à** *or* **de**, *if necessary. If neither preposition is necessary, mark the blank with an X.*

1.  Il a menacé _____ renoncer à son poste.

2.  Je crains _____ le recevoir dans mon bureau.

3.  Le juge l'a condamné _____ rester en prison.

4.  Il vaut mieux _____ partir demain matin.

5.  Qui tentera _____ résoudre le problème?

6.  Cet étudiant fait semblant _____ comprendre.

7.  J'accepte _____ les embaucher.

8.  Elle daigne _____ recevoir.

9.  Je me mets _____ travailler sérieusement.

10. Vous tenez _____ visiter l'usine?

11. Nous nous proposons _____ ouvrir une succursale à Marseille.

12. Je me dépêche _____ vous répondre.

13. Nous sommes obligés _____ considérer son offre.

14. Il m'a obligé _____ l'écouter.

15. Je me souviens _____ l'avoir rencontré.

16. Il nous engage _____ répondre.

**I**   *Expand each sentence to incorporate the material in parentheses. Retain the tense of the original sentence.*

MODÈLE   Il a loué un appartement dans notre quartier. (tenter)

*Il a tenté de louer un appartement dans notre quartier.*

1. J'ai acheté des titres (*stocks*). (choisir)

2. Il sait le faire. (jurer) _____

3. Je vous rends votre document. (s'empresser)

4. Il est renvoyé. (mériter) _____

5. Il nous offensait. (risquer) _____

6. Il m'a remboursé. (manquer) _____

7. Elle part seule. (avoir peur) _____

8. J'arrive sans prévenir. (s'excuser) _____

9. Il nous embête. (ne pas s'arrêter) _____

10. Tu as pleuré? (finir) _____

**J**   **Translation.** *Express the following sentences in French.*

1. *I refrained from sneezing.* _____

2. *They neglected to call us.* _____

3. *I was careful not to reveal our plans.*

4. *The child pretends not to understand.*

5. *I wound up asking him for a loan.* _____

6. *We have resolved to hire new employees.*

7. *He took it into his head to tell it to the boss.*

8. *I regret having said it.* _____

9. *He cares about pleasing his parents.*

10. *Remember (vous) to buy some flash drives.*

11. *She's pleased with herself for having gotten a good grade.*

   _____

12. *You* (tu) *were wise to sell those stocks.* _____

13. *I'm dying to read that article.* _____

14. *She started by introducing herself.* _____

In French, many verbs that take **de** before a following infinitive take a direct object as well. Examine the following expressions in which **quelqu'un** is both the direct object of the first verb and the subject of the infinitive.

> **accuser qqn de faire qqch**  *to accuse someone of doing something*
> **avertir qqn de (ne pas) faire qqch**  *to warn someone (not) to do something*
> **contraindre qqn de faire qqch**  *to compel someone to do something*
> **convaincre qqn de faire qqch**  *to convince someone to do something*
> **décourager qqn de faire qqch**  *to discourage someone from doing something*
> **défier qqn de faire qqch**  *to challenge someone to do something*
> **dissuader qqn de faire qqch**  *to dissuade someone from doing something*
> **empêcher qqn de faire qqch**  *to prevent someone from doing something*
> **excuser qqn de faire qqch**  *to excuse/forgive someone for doing something*
> **féliciter qqn d'avoir fait qqch**  *to congratulate someone for having done something*
> **louer qqn d'avoir fait qqch**  *to praise someone for having done something*
> **menacer qqn de faire qqch**  *to threaten someone with doing something*
> **persuader qqn de faire qqch**  *to persuade someone to do something*
> **presser qqn de faire qqch**  *to pressure someone to do something*
> **prier qqn de faire qqch**  *to beg someone to do something*
> **remercier qqn de faire qqch**  *to thank someone for doing something*
> **soupçonner qqn de faire qqch**  *to suspect someone of doing something*
> **supplier qqn de faire qqch**  *to beg someone to do something*

Some French verbs that take **de** before a following infinitive also take an indirect object. Examine the following expressions in which **à quelqu'un** is both the indirect object of the first verb and the subject of the infinitive.

> **commander à qqn de faire qqch**  *to order someone to do something*
> **conseiller à qqn de faire qqch**  *to advise someone to do something*
> **déconseiller à qqn de faire qqch**  *to advise someone not to do something*
> **défendre à qqn de faire qqch**  *to forbid someone to do something*
> **demander à qqn de faire qqch**  *to ask someone to do something*
> **dire à qqn de faire qqch**  *to tell someone to do something*
> **écrire à qqn de faire qqch**  *to write someone to do something*
> **faire signe à qqn de faire qqch**  *to signal someone to do something*
> **interdire à qqn de faire qqch**  *to forbid someone to do something*
> **ordonner à qqn de faire qqch**  *to order someone to do something*
> **pardonner à qqn de faire qqch**  *to forgive someone for doing something*
> **permettre à qqn de faire qqch**  *to allow someone to do something*
> **proposer à qqn de faire qqch**  *to suggest to someone to do something*
> **reprocher à qqn de faire qqch**  *to reproach someone for doing something*
> **suggérer à qqn de faire qqch**  *to suggest to someone to do something*

**K**  *Complete each sentence with **à** or **de**, if necessary. If neither preposition is necessary, mark the blank with an X.*

1. Il m'a demandé _____ l'aider.

2. Nous souhaitons _____ les revoir l'été prochain.

3. Je vous reproche _____ ne pas vous intéresser à ma situation.

4. Qu'est-ce tu me conseilles _____ faire?

5. Il s'obstine _____ passer son temps avec des gens comme ça.

6. Quand j'ai vu les flammes, j'ai couru _____ téléphoner aux pompiers.

7. On m'a convaincu _____ suivre ce cours.

8. Qui t'a suggéré _____ voyager en première classe?

9. Ils persistent _____ nous demander de l'argent.

10. On le loue _____ avoir dénoncé ces criminels.

11. Il m'a fait signe _____ m'asseoir.

12. Je me suis attardé _____ discuter avec eux.

13. On l'a accusé _____ être associé à une cellule terroriste.

14. Je te félicite _____ avoir reçu ce prix.

15. Il faudra _____ veiller au bon fonctionnement de la moteur.

16. Je me suis tenu _____ corriger les fautes d'orthographe.

17. Qu'est-ce qui t'empêche _____ sortir?

18. J'ai emmené mon petit frère _____ voir un film.

19. Vous vous mettez _____ créer le site Web.

**L**  *Complete each sentence with **le**, **la**, **l'**, **les**, **lui**, or **leur**, as required.*

1. Laure? Je _____ ai priée de venir.

2. Les voisins? Nous _____ avons conseillé de vendre leur appartement.

3. Christine? J'ai essayé de _____ convaincre de venir nous voir.

4. Les étudiants? Rien ne _____ empêche d'étudier un peu plus.

5. Philippe? Je _____ ai défendu de m'appeler.

6. Les invités? Qui _____ a fait signe d'entrer?

7. Cet homme-là? On _____ soupçonne d'avoir volé une voiture.

8. Les soldats? Le sergent _____ a commandé de tirer (*shoot*).

9. Les manifestants? On _____ a menacé d'une amende (*fine*).

10. Les passagers? On _____ a permis de monter.

11. Cet employé? Le patron _____ demande de travailler demain.

**M**   *Translation.*  *Express the following sentences in French.*

1.  *He reproaches his friends for not inviting him.*

    _____

2.  *The guide proposed to the tourists to visit the ruins.*

    _____

3.  *The teacher challenged the students to learn the poem by heart.*

    _____

4.  *He persuaded his family to move.*  _____

5.  *I thanked her for having called.*  _____

6.  *Her parents have forbidden her to go out.*

    _____

7.  *The police accused them of helping the terrorists.*

    _____

8.  *We warned those women not to believe him.*

    _____

9.  *They discouraged him from playing cards.*

    _____

10.  *His father forgave him for not finishing his studies.*

    _____

---

**BUILDING SENTENCES**   **Verbs of perception and laisser + infinitive**

Verbs of perception, such as **voir, regarder, entendre,** and **écouter,** and the verb **laisser** *to leave, let* are followed directly by the infinitive. The direct object of these verbs is the subject of the infinitive. If it is a noun, it can be placed either before or after the infinitive.

| | |
|---|---|
| Nous voyons **les enfants** jouer. <br> Nous voyons jouer **les enfants**. } | *We see the children play.* |
| On va entendre **les trains** siffler. <br> On va entendre siffler **les trains**. } | *We'll hear the trains whistle.* |
| Elle a laissé **les étudiants** entrer. <br> Elle a laissé entrer **les étudiants**. } | *She let the students come in.* |

When a direct object noun is replaced by a direct object pronoun in sentences with verbs of perception or **laisser**, it must stand before the verb of perception or **laisser**.

| | |
|---|---|
| Nous **les** voyons jouer. | *We see them play.* |
| On va **les** entendre siffler. | *We'll hear them whistle.* |
| Elle **les** a laissé entrer. | *She let them come in.* |

Verbs of perception and **laisser** may appear in sentences with two direct objects—a direct object of the verb of perception together with a direct object of the infinitive.

| | |
|---|---|
| J'ai regardé **les ouvriers** construire **le pont**. | *I saw the workers building the bridge.* |
| Nous écoutons **les musiciens** jouer **le morceau**. | *We are listening to the musicians play the piece.* |
| J'ai laissé **ma fille** manger **ce dessert**. | *I let my daughter eat that dessert.* |

In general, the past participles of verbs of perception and **laisser** agree with a preceding direct object pronoun.

| | |
|---|---|
| Je **les** ai vus construire le pont. | *I saw them build the bridge.* |
| Je **l'**ai laissée manger ce dessert. | *I let her eat that dessert.* |

**N**  *Using the present tense, create sentences from the following strings of elements. Then rewrite each sentence in the passé composé, replacing the underlined noun with a pronoun.*

MODÈLE    je / entendre / les choristes / chanter / ma chanson préférée

_J'entends les choristes chanter ma chanson préférée._

_Je les ai entendus chanter ma chanson préférée._

1. nous / entendre / les chats / miauler (*to meow*)

_____

_____

2. ils / voir / les bateaux / arriver

_____

_____

3. nous / ne pas laisser / les enfants / jouer dans la rue

_____

_____

4. je / regarder / les soldats / défiler

_____

_____

5. nous / voir / la serveuse / débarrasser / la table

_____

_____

6. tu / regarder / l'artiste / peindre / le portrait

_____

_____

7. le chef / laisser / ses employés / partir à quatre heures

_____

_____

8. elle / écouter / les cloches / sonner

_____

_____

**BUILDING SENTENCES**   **The causative (faire + infinitive)**

French has a special construction to express the idea that one person causes another person to do something. This construction, called *the causative,* consists of the verb **faire** followed by an infinitive.

| | |
|---|---|
| —Mon ordinateur ne marche pas bien. | *"My computer isn't working well."* |
| —Il faut **le faire réparer**, alors. | *"Then you've got to have it fixed."* |
| —Notre bureau n'est pas propre. | *"Our office isn't clean."* |
| —Il faut **le faire nettoyer**. | *"We have to have it cleaned."* |
| —Je ne peux pas **faire démarrer la voiture**. | *"I can't get the car to start."* |
| —Je crois qu'il faut **faire charger la batterie**. | *"I think you have to have the battery charged."* |

A sentence in the causative may include the person whom you cause to do the work or perform the action. That person usually appears at the end of the sentence if there is no other object present.

| | |
|---|---|
| Il a fait attendre **ses clients**. | *He kept his customers waiting.* |
| J'ai fait entrer **les invités**. | *I had the guests come in.* |

However, if there is another object present, the person who is caused to do something may appear in an agent phrase beginning with **par**, as in the passive voice (see Chapter 5, p. 104), or as an indirect object introduced by the preposition **à**.

J'ai fait réparer ma voiture **par le mécanicien**.
J'ai fait réparer ma voiture **au mécanicien**. } *I had the mechanic repair my car.*

Elle a fait raccourcir ses robes **par son tailleur**.
Elle a fait raccourcir ses robes **à son tailleur**. } *She had her tailor shorten her dresses.*

One or both of the objects in the examples above can be replaced by object pronouns. The object pronouns always precede **faire** in the causative.

J'ai fait réparer ma voiture **au mécanicien**.
Je la **lui** ai fait réparer.

Elle a fait raccourcir ses robes **à son tailleur**.
Elle les **lui** a fait raccourcir.

Note that **fait**, the past participle of **faire**, does not agree with a preceding direct object in the causative.

**O**   *Using the verb in parentheses, create sentences to tell what has to be done to correct these situations. Write one sentence with the underlined noun, then write a second sentence replacing the noun with a direct object pronoun.*

MODÈLE   Le document a beaucoup de fautes.  (corriger)

   *Il faut faire corriger le document.*

   *Il faut le faire corriger.*

1. La bicyclette est en panne.  (réparer)

   _____

   _____

2. Les pneus sont crevés.  (changer)

   _____

   _____

3. Ces meubles doivent être dans l'autre appartement.  (transporter)

   _____

   _____

4. Cet appartement est vraiment sale.  (nettoyer)

   _____

   _____

5. Ce pantalon est trop court.  (rallonger *to lengthen*)

   _____

   _____

6. La jupe est trop étroite.  (élargir *to let out* [*garment*])

   _____

   _____

7. Cette chaise est usée.  (retapisser *to reupholster*)

   _____

   _____

8. Les murs n'ont presque plus de couleur.  (repeindre *to repaint*)

   _____

   _____

9. Cette porte est cassée.  (enlever *to remove*)

   _____

   _____

10. <u>Ces fenêtres</u> ne s'ouvrent plus. (remplacer)

_____

_____

## Faire + Infinitive: Idiomatic Uses

English translations of phrases consisting of the **faire** + infinitive construction vary greatly.

**faire attendre qqn**  *to keep someone waiting*
**faire boire un enfant**  *to give a child something to drink*
**faire entrer/sortir qqn**  *to show someone in/out*
**faire faire les devoirs aux enfants**  *to help the children with their homework*
**faire manger un malade**  *to feed a sick person*
**faire monter qqn**  *to invite someone up*
**faire pousser les fleurs / l'herbe**  *to make the flowers/grass grow, to grow flowers/grass*
**faire remarquer**  *to point out*
**faire savoir**  *to inform, let know*
**faire traverser la rue à un vieillard**  *to help an old man across the street*
**faire venir le médecin / la secrétaire**  *to send for the doctor / the secretary*
**faire visiter la ville à qqn**  *to show someone around the city*
**faire voir**  *to show*

Some of the expressions with **faire** + the infinitive are very idiomatic.

**faire chanter qqn**  *to blackmail someone*
**faire écouter un cédé à qqn**  *to play a CD for someone*
**faire faire le tour du propriétaire à qqn**  *to show someone around one's house*
**faire suivre le courrier**  *to forward the mail*
**Il ne se l'est pas fait dire deux fois.**  *You didn't have to tell him twice.*
**Je ne vous le fais pas dire.**  *I'm not putting words into your mouth.*
**On se fait embêter chez eux.**  *We really get bored at their house.*
**Tu me fais suer!**  *You're a real pain in the neck!*

Many verbs referring to cooking are intransitive and are used with **faire** to express their transitive meanings in English.

| | |
|---|---|
| La viande **cuit**. | *The meat is cooking.* |
| Nous **faisons cuire** la viande. | *We're cooking the meat.* |
| L'eau **bout**. | *The water is boiling.* |
| Je vais **faire bouillir** de l'eau. | *I'm going to boil water.* |
| Le poulet **rôtit** dans le four. | *The chicken is roasting in the oven.* |
| Ma femme **fait rôtir** un poulet pour ce soir. | *My wife is roasting a chicken for this evening.* |
| La soupe **mijote**. | *The soup is simmering.* |
| Tu **fais mijoter** la soupe. | *You're letting the soup simmer.* |

Note also the expression **faire sauter des tranches d'oignon** *to sauté onion slices.*

The French expression **se faire faire qqch** means *to have something done to or for oneself.* Its English translation often has the verb *to get.*

**se faire accompagner de qqn**  *to get someone to go with you*
**se faire avoir**  *to be fooled / taken in*
**se faire comprendre**  *to make oneself understood*
**se faire couper les cheveux**  *to get one's hair cut*
**se faire écraser**  *to get run over*
**se faire engueuler**  *to get scolded / yelled at* (slang)
**se faire entendre**  *to be heard*
**se faire faire une robe**  *to have a dress made*
**se faire gronder**  *to get scolded / yelled at*
**se faire mettre à la porte**  *to get fired*
**se faire nettoyer les dents par le dentiste**  *to get one's teeth cleaned by the dentist*
**se faire opérer**  *to get operated on*
**se faire ouvrir par**  *to be let in by*
**se faire payer**  *to get paid*
**se faire prendre**  *to get caught* (of a criminal, etc.)
**se faire prier**  *to be begged/coaxed*
**se faire remarquer**  *to get noticed; to call attention to oneself*
**se faire rembourser**  *to get paid back*
**se faire remettre le rapport**  *to have the report handed over to one*
**se faire renverser par une voiture**  *to get run over by a car*
**se faire renvoyer**  *to get fired*
**se faire rouler**  *to get cheated*
**se faire soigner**  *to see a doctor, get medical treatment*
**se faire tuer**  *to get oneself killed*

Note that **se faire** in **se faire** + infinitive constructions is conjugated with **être** in the passé composé, like all reflexive verbs (see Chapter 7, p. 140). There is no agreement of the past participle in the passé composé of **se faire** + infinitive constructions.

| | |
|---|---|
| Il **ne s'est pas fait** prier. | *He didn't require coaxing.* |
| Elle **s'est fait** gronder par le prof. | *She got scolded by the teacher.* |
| Nous **nous sommes fait** rembourser. | *We got our money refunded.* |

**P**  *Translation. Express the following sentences in French.*

1. *Pay attention when you* (tu) *cross the street. You don't want to get run over by a truck.*

   _____

   _____

2. *He complained a lot and he got himself fired.*

   _____

3. *She likes to be coaxed.* _____

4. *I got my hair cut yesterday.* _____

5. *He had a suit made.* _____

6. *We got cheated at the restaurant.* _____

7. *I got let in by the concierge.* _____

8. *I have been letting the soup simmer for an hour.*

_____

9. *They will show us around their house.*

_____

10. *He blackmailed his neighbor.* _____

11. *Those students are a real pain in the neck!*

_____

12. *They always get scolded.* _____

13. *She helped an old man across the street.*

_____

14. *Please send* (vous) *for the doctor.* _____

15. *You* (tu) *need medical treatment.* _____

16. *Don't* (tu) *put words in my mouth.* _____

17. *You don't have to tell him twice.* _____

18. *I'll boil some water to make tea.* _____

19. *He showed me his new ring* (la bague).

_____

20. *We showed our friends around the city.*

_____

# Literary Tenses: The Passé Simple; The Imperfect Subjunctive; The Pluperfect Subjunctive

---

**LA LANGUE FRANÇAISE** literary tenses

An important characteristic of French is the preservation of certain tenses in writing that have disappeared in the spoken language. These tenses are the *passé simple,* the imperfect subjunctive, and the pluperfect subjunctive. The loss of these tenses is one of the major features distinguishing spoken French from the other Romance languages. Although they are not used in the spoken language, these tenses are necessary for reading French texts from earlier periods, and many of their forms are used for stylistic effect even in today's literary and journalistic writing.

## The Passé Simple

The *passé simple* is perhaps the most common of the three literary tenses. The passé simple covers only part of the meaning of the passé composé. **Nous réfléchîmes** means *we thought, we reflected* but not *we have thought, we have reflected.*

Study the passé simple of first conjugation (**-er**) verbs.

**parler**

| | |
|---|---|
| je parl**ai** | nous parl**âmes** |
| tu parl**as** | vous parl**âtes** |
| il/elle parl**a** | ils/elles parl**èrent** |

Verbs ending in **-cer** and **-ger** show the same spelling change in the passé simple (in all forms except the **ils** form) that they show in the first-person singular of the present and in the imperfect.

**commencer**

| | |
|---|---|
| je commen**çai** | nous commen**çâmes** |
| tu commen**ças** | vous commen**çâtes** |
| il/elle commen**ça** | ils/elles commen**cèrent** |

**ranger**

| | |
|---|---|
| je rang**eai** | nous rang**eâmes** |
| tu rang**eas** | vous rang**eâtes** |
| il/elle rang**ea** | ils/elles rang**èrent** |

The second and third conjugations (-**ir** verbs and -**re** verbs) share the same set of endings in the passé simple.

| réfléchir | | vendre | |
| --- | --- | --- | --- |
| je réfléch**is** | nous réfléch**îmes** | je vend**is** | nous vend**îmes** |
| tu réfléch**is** | vous réfléch**îtes** | tu vend**is** | vous vend**îtes** |
| il/elle réfléch**it** | ils/elles réfléch**irent** | il/elle vend**it** | ils/elles vend**irent** |

Irregular -**ir** verbs such as **dormir, partir, ouvrir**, and **cueillir** form the passé simple regularly, like **réfléchir**: **je dormis, je partis, j'ouvris, je cueillis**.

The irregular -**re** verbs **battre, suivre, écrire, vaincre**, and **naître** form the passé simple like **vendre**: **je battis, je suivis, j'écrivis, je vainquis, je naquis**.

Many other irregular -**ir** and -**re** verbs form the passé simple in -**is**.

| voir | je **vis** |
| --- | --- |
| s'asseoir | je **m'assis** |
| faire | je **fis** |
| prendre | je **pris** |

Verbs ending in -**evoir** have the vowel **u** in the passé simple.

| recevoir | | devoir | |
| --- | --- | --- | --- |
| je re**çus** | nous re**çûmes** | je d**us** | nous d**ûmes** |
| tu re**çus** | vous re**çûtes** | tu d**us** | vous d**ûtes** |
| il/elle re**çut** | ils/elles re**çurent** | il/elle d**ut** | ils/elles d**urent** |

Most other irregular verbs with infinitives ending in -**oir** and -**oire** also have **u** as the vowel of the passé simple. (But see **voir** and **s'asseoir**, above.) These verbs also have a past participle ending in **u**.

| pouvoir | | avoir | |
| --- | --- | --- | --- |
| je p**us** | nous p**ûmes** | j'**eus** | nous e**ûmes** |
| tu p**us** | vous p**ûtes** | tu e**us** | vous e**ûtes** |
| il/elle p**ut** | ils/elles p**urent** | il/elle e**ut** | ils/elles e**urent** |

Other verbs that form the passé simple like **pouvoir** and **avoir** are the following.

| boire | je **bus** |
| --- | --- |
| croire | je **crus** |
| savoir | je **sus** |
| vouloir | je **voulus** |
| lire | je **lus** |
| vivre | je **vécus** |
| courir | je **courus** |

**Être** has an irregular stem: **f-**.

**être**

| je **fus** | nous **fûmes** |
|---|---|
| tu **fus** | vous **fûtes** |
| il/elle **fut** | ils/elles **furent** |

Verbs ending in **-indre** (like **craindre**) and verbs ending in **-uire** (like **produire**) form the passé simple with the vowel **i** added to their stem from the plural forms of the present tense. The stem for **craindre** ends in -**gn**-: **nous craignons, vous craignez, ils/elles craignent**. The stem for **produire** ends in -**uis**-: **nous produisons, vous produisez, ils/elles produisent**.

**craindre**

| je craig**nis** | nous craig**nîmes** |
|---|---|
| tu craig**nis** | vous craig**nîtes** |
| il/elle craig**nit** | ils/elles craig**nirent** |

**produire**

| je produi**sis** | nous produi**sîmes** |
|---|---|
| tu produi**sis** | vous produi**sîtes** |
| il/elle produi**sit** | ils/elles produi**sirent** |

The verbs **venir** and **tenir** are irregular in the passé simple.

**venir**

| je **vins** | nous **vînmes** |
|---|---|
| tu **vins** | vous **vîntes** |
| il/elle **vint** | ils/elles **vinrent** |

**tenir**

| je **tins** | nous **tînmes** |
|---|---|
| tu **tins** | vous **tîntes** |
| il/elle **tint** | ils/elles **tinrent** |

The third-person singular of the passé simple is used even in contemporary writing to indicate quoted speech. In this function, the subject and verb are inverted.

Bonjour, dit-elle.
Il faut que je parte maintenant, fit-il.
Au voleur, au voleur, s'écria-t-il.

Note, in the second example, the use of **faire** to mean *to say* in this context.

**A**  *Translate the passé simple form. Then write the corresponding passé composé form.*

1. vous craignîtes  _____  _____

2. il crut  _____  _____

3. je fus  _____  _____

4. elle fit  _____  _____

5. vous vîtes  _____  _____

6. elles sortirent  _____  _____

7. tu descendis  _____  _____

8. vous tîntes  _____  _____

9. nous mangeâmes  _____  _____

10. il lança     _____     _____

11. je pus     _____     _____

12. il écrivit     _____     _____

13. elles durent     _____     _____

14. vous reçûtes     _____     _____

15. ils vinrent     _____     _____

16. nous fûmes     _____     _____

## The Imperfect Subjunctive

The imperfect subjunctive is a literary form used in formal writing and in older texts. For **-er** verbs, it is formed by adding the following endings to the stem of the first-person form of the passé simple.

| SINGULAR | | PLURAL | |
|---|---|---|---|
| je | **-asse** | nous | **-assions** |
| tu | **-asses** | vous | **-assiez** |
| il/elle | **-ât** | ils/elles | **-assent** |

Study the imperfect subjunctive of **parler** (*that I might speak*).

| que **je parlasse** | que **nous parlassions** |
|---|---|
| que **tu parlasses** | que **vous parlassiez** |
| qu'**il/elle parlât** | qu'**ils/elles parlassent** |

**NOTE**

Verbs such as **commencer** and **manger** show spelling changes in all persons of the imperfect subjunctive, since all the endings begin with **a**: **que je commençasse**, **que je mangeasse**.

For **-ir** and **-re** verbs and for irregular verbs, the endings of the imperfect subjunctive are added to the passé simple form, minus the consonants of the ending. The circumflexes of the **nous** and **vous** forms are dropped.

| SINGULAR | | PLURAL | |
|---|---|---|---|
| je | **-sse** | nous | **-ssions** |
| tu | **-sses** | vous | **-ssiez** |
| il/elle | **-^t** | ils/elles | **-ssent** |

Study these sample conjugations.

| **finir** | | **vendre** | |
|---|---|---|---|
| que **je finisse** | que **nous finissions** | que **je vendisse** | que **nous vendissions** |
| que **tu finisses** | que **vous finissiez** | que **tu vendisses** | que **vous vendissiez** |
| qu'**il/elle finît** | qu'**ils/elles finissent** | qu'**il/elle vendît** | qu'**ils/elles vendissent** |

The imperfect subjunctive of irregular verbs is also based on the passé simple. Study the imperfect subjunctive forms of **avoir**, **être**, **faire**, and **venir**.

| avoir | |
|---|---|
| que **j'eusse** | que **nous eussions** |
| que **tu eusses** | que **vous eussiez** |
| qu'**il/elle eût** | qu'**ils/elles eussent** |

| être | |
|---|---|
| que **je fusse** | que **nous fussions** |
| que **tu fusses** | que **vous fussiez** |
| qu'**il/elle fût** | qu'**ils/elles fussent** |

| faire | |
|---|---|
| que **je fisse** | que **nous fissions** |
| que **tu fisses** | que **vous fissiez** |
| qu'**il/elle fît** | qu'**ils/elles fissent** |

| venir | |
|---|---|
| que **je vinsse** | que **nous vinssions** |
| que **tu vinsses** | que **vous vinssiez** |
| qu'**il/elle vînt** | qu'**ils/elles vinssent** |

In formal written French, the imperfect subjunctive is used in a subordinate clause in sentences where the main verb is in a past tense and the subjunctive is required in the subordinate clause.

| EVERYDAY FRENCH | FORMAL FRENCH | ENGLISH |
|---|---|---|
| Je veux **qu'il vienne**. | Je veux **qu'il vienne**. | *I want him to come.* |
| Je voulais **qu'il vienne**. | Je voulais **qu'il vînt**. | *I wanted him to come.* |
| Je suis content **qu'il le fasse**. | Je suis content **qu'il le fasse**. | *I'm happy he's doing it.* |
| J'étais content **qu'il le fasse**. | J'étais content **qu'il le fît**. | *I was happy he did it.* |
| Il faut **qu'il attende**. | Il faut **qu'il attende**. | *It's necessary for him to wait.* |
| Il a fallu **qu'il attende**. | Il a fallu **qu'il attendît**. | *It was necessary for him to wait.* |

An inverted third-person singular imperfect subjunctive (especially of **être**) often means *even if*. This construction is commonly used for stylistic effect in newspaper writing.

| | |
|---|---|
| Il ne pourrait pas prendre cette décision, **fût-il** le PDG de l'entreprise. | *He wouldn't be able to make this decision even if he were the CEO of the firm.* |
| Il faudrait que le patron s'adresse aux employés, ne **fût-ce** que pour cinq minutes. | *It would be necessary for the boss to speak to the employees, even if it were only for five minutes.* |

In everyday French, the above sentences would be expressed as follows.

| | |
|---|---|
| Il ne pourrait pas prendre cette décision, **même s'il était** le PDG de l'entreprise. | *He wouldn't be able to make this decision even if he were the CEO of the firm.* |
| Il faudrait que le patron s'adresse aux employés, **même si ce n'était que** pour cinq minutes. | *It would be necessary for the boss to speak to the employees, even if it were only for five minutes.* |

**B**  *Rewrite each sentence in everyday French.*

MODÈLE    Je n'ai pas voulu qu'il vous parlât.

_Je n'ai pas voulu qu'il vous parle._

1. Nous insistions pour qu'il fît son travail. _____

2. Je ne croyais pas qu'elle pût le comprendre.

_____

3. Je craignais que le vieillard ne tombât. _____

4. Il valait mieux que l'étudiant relût son propre thème.

_____

5. Il fallait travailler tous les jours, fût-ce un jour de fête.

_____

## The Pluperfect Subjunctive

The pluperfect subjunctive consists of the imperfect subjunctive of the auxiliary verb (**avoir** or **être**) plus the past participle.

VERBS CONJUGATED WITH **avoir**

| | |
|---|---|
| que **j'eusse parlé, réfléchi, rendu** | que **nous eussions parlé, réfléchi, rendu** |
| que **tu eusses parlé, réfléchi, rendu** | que **vous eussiez parlé, réfléchi, rendu** |
| qu'il/elle **eût parlé, réfléchi, rendu** | qu'ils/elles **eussent parlé, réfléchi, rendu** |

VERBS CONJUGATED WITH **être**

| | |
|---|---|
| que **je fusse descendu(e)** | que **nous fussions descendu(e)s** |
| que **tu fusses descendu(e)** | que **vous fussiez descendu(e)(s)** |
| qu'il **fût descendu** | qu'ils **fussent descendus** |
| qu'elle **fût descendue** | qu'elles **fussent descendues** |

The pluperfect subjunctive is used to indicate that the action of the subordinate clause happened before the action of the main clause in sentences where the verb of the main clause is in the past. Compare the following pairs of sentences in formal and everyday French.

| EVERYDAY FRENCH | FORMAL FRENCH | ENGLISH |
|---|---|---|
| Je n'étais pas sûr **qu'il vienne.** | Je n'étais pas sûr **qu'il vînt.** | *I wasn't sure he was coming.* |
| Je n'étais pas sûr **qu'il soit venu.** | Je n'étais pas sûr **qu'il fût venu.** | *I wasn't sure he had come.* |
| J'étais content **qu'il le fasse.** | J'étais content **qu'il le fît.** | *I was happy he did it.* |
| J'étais content **qu'il l'ait fait.** | J'étais content **qu'il l'eût fait.** | *I was happy he had done it.* |

The pluperfect subjunctive can also replace the pluperfect and the conditional perfect in both parts of a conditional sentence.

EVERYDAY FRENCH

**S'il me l'avait dit, j'aurais compris.**
**S'il était venu, nous aurions parlé.**

FORMAL FRENCH

**S'il me l'eût dit, j'eusse compris.**
**S'il fût venu, nous eussions parlé.**

French language learners rarely need to use the forms of the imperfect subjunctive or the pluperfect subjunctive. It is enough to recognize them in reading and in their occasional occurrences in very formal speech.

**C** Rewrite each formal French sentence in everyday French.

MODÈLES   Il ne croyait pas qu'elle fût partie.

_Il ne croyait pas qu'elle soit partie._

S'ils eurent vécu au Japon, ils eurent compris cette société.

_S'ils avaient vécu au Japon, ils auraient compris cette société._

1. Si la France n'eût pas construit des centrales nucléaires, elle n'eût pas pu réduire ses importations de pétrole.

2. Si ce médecin ne fût pas mort si jeune, il eût gagné le prix Nobel.

3. Si les employés n'eussent pas fait grève, ils n'eussent pas été renvoyés.

4. Nous nous sommes réjouis qu'elle eût voulu passer l'été avec nous.

5. Je ne pensais pas que vous eussiez tellement souffert.

**D** **Translation.** Express the following sentences in English.

1. Ils virent le roi. _____

2. Je naquis à Baton Rouge. _____

3. Vous vîntes en avance. _____

4. Je pus m'exprimer dans leur langue. _____

5. Il ne croyait pas que tu allasses. _____

6. Elle doutait que nous eussions reçu la lettre.

_____

7. Il faudrait parler avec eux, ne fût-ce que pour une demi-heure.

_____

8. Je ne regrette rien, fit-elle. _____

9. Tu eus de la chance. _____

10. Nous sûmes la nouvelle. _____

11. Ils craignaient qu'elle fût partie. _____

12. Si vous fussiez allés à la fête, vous vous fussiez bien amusés.

_____

# Oral Exercises

Go to www.audiostudyplayer.com to access the recordings for the following oral exercises, which correspond to the 12 chapters in this book. Most exercises contain eight items.

## Chapter 1
### The Present Tense of Regular Verbs

 *Restate each of the following sentences, changing the subject from **nous** to **je**. Make sure not to pronounce the final consonant of the stem in the **je** form.*

MODÈLE    Nous interrompons le professeur.  →  J'interromps le professeur.

 *Restate each of the following sentences about using the computer. Change the subject from **tu** to **vous**.*

MODÈLE    Tu cliques sur le bouton.  →  Vous cliquez sur le bouton.

 ***What is Caroline doing today?*** *Use the elements given to construct sentences with a verb and a direct object noun.*

MODÈLE    aménager / sa cuisine  →  Caroline aménage sa cuisine.

 *Restate each of the following sentences, changing the subject from **je** to **nous**.*

MODÈLE    J'achète un appartement.  →  Nous achetons un appartement.

 *Create questions from the elements given to ask how long these people have been doing things. Use **Depuis combien de temps est-ce que…?** and the present tense of the verb.*

MODÈLE    Pierre / habiter ce quartier
          →  Depuis combien de temps est-ce que Pierre habite ce quartier?

 *Restate each of the following sentences in the plural. The only difference in pronunciation of the verb will be the addition of the final consonant of the verb stem, unless the verb begins with a vowel. In those cases, there will be liaison between the final **s** of the subject pronoun and the vowel.*

MODÈLE    Il réfléchit avant de parler.  →  Ils réfléchissent avant de parler.

# Chapter 2
## Irregular Verbs (Part I)

**A** *Restate each of the following sentences, changing the subject from* **nous** *to* **je**.

MODÈLE   Nous allons en France.  →  Je vais en France.

**B** *Restate each of the following sentences, changing the subject from the third-person plural* (**ils**) *to the third-person singular* (**il**). *The final consonant of the verb stem will not be pronounced in the singular.*

MODÈLE   Ils partent jeudi.  →  Il part jeudi.

**C** *Restate each of the following questions in the* **tu** *form. Make sure not to pronounce the final consonant of the verb stem.*

MODÈLE   Vous permettez?  →  Tu permets?

**D** *Restate each of the following sentences in the negative, using* **ne... pas**. *Note that the indefinite article and the partitive article change to* **de** *after a negative.*

MODÈLE   Il offre des cadeaux.  →  Il n'offre pas de cadeaux.

**E** *Create sentences from the elements given to tell what these people are doing.*

MODÈLE   mes amis / comprendre / la plaisanterie
                →  Mes amis comprennent la plaisanterie.

**F** *Say that these people never do the things they are said to do.*

MODÈLE   Barbara est toujours en retard.  →  Mais non! Elle n'est jamais en retard.

# Chapter 3
## Irregular Verbs (Part II)

**A** *Restate each of the following yes/no questions in the* **tu** *form. The final consonant of the verb stem will not be pronounced in the singular unless that consonant is* **r**.

MODÈLE   Vous voyez beaucoup de films?  →  Tu vois beaucoup de films?

**B** *Create sentences from the elements given to find out what the people in the neighborhood are doing. Pay special attention to pronunciation of the verb forms. Remember that the final consonant of the verb stem of* **-ir**, **-re**, *and most irregular verbs is not pronounced in the singular.*

MODÈLE   ma voisine / voir beaucoup de films  →  Ma voisine voit beaucoup de films.

**C** *Create sentences to say that these people should do the things they are not doing. Add* **devoir** *to each sentence, and change the original verb to the infinitive.*

MODÈLE   Le professeur n'instruit pas ses étudiants.
                →  Le professeur doit instruire ses étudiants.

**D** *Restate each of the following sentences in the plural. Be sure to pronounce the final consonant of the verb stem in your answer.*

MODÈLE    Il dit la vérité. → Ils disent la vérité.

**E** *Respond to each of the following questions, saying that you think these people want to do the things asked about. Add the correct form of the verb* **vouloir** *in your response.*

MODÈLE    Il boit un verre? → Je ne sais pas, mais je crois qu'il veut boire un verre.

**F** *Expand each of the following sentences with the verb in the cue to create a sentence with a verb + infinitive construction.*

MODÈLES    Je passe mes vacances en France./adorer
                    → J'adore passer mes vacances en France.

                    Nous ne finissons pas le projet aujourd'hui./pouvoir
                    → Nous ne pouvons pas finir le projet aujourd'hui.

# Chapter 4
## The Imperative

**A** *Give a new colleague advice on how to conduct himself in his job. Restate each of the following sentences as a* **vous** *command.*

MODÈLE    Vous devez arriver au bureau à neuf heures.
                    → Arrivez au bureau à neuf heures.

**B** *Restate each of the following sentences, replacing the indirect object noun with the corresponding indirect object pronoun.*

MODÈLE    Elle donne des cadeaux aux enfants pauvres. → Elle leur donne des cadeaux.

**C** *Answer each of the following questions in the negative, replacing the direct object noun with the corresponding object pronoun.*

MODÈLE    Est-ce que tu ranges tes affaires? → Non, je ne les range pas.

**D** *Answer each of the following questions in the affirmative, replacing object nouns with the corresponding object pronouns. Each response will have double object pronouns.*

MODÈLE    Est-ce que le directeur donne le message aux employés?
                    → Oui, il le leur donne.

**E** *Answer each of the following questions with an affirmative* **vous** *command. Replace the direct or indirect object noun with the correct pronoun.*

MODÈLE    Est-ce que je dois lire ces documents? → Oui, lisez-les.

**F** *Respond to each of the following statements with a negative* **nous** *command. Use the verb in the cue and a direct or indirect object pronoun in your answer.*

MODÈLE    Ces documents ne sont pas très importants./lire → Alors, ne les lisons pas.

# Chapter 5
## The Passé Composé

**A**  *Restate each of the following sentences, changing the verb from present tense to the passé composé. Note that some of the verbs form the passé compose with the auxiliary **être**.*

MODÈLE    Nous jouons aux cartes.  →  Nous avons joué aux cartes.

**B**  *Restate each of the following sentences in the passé composé. All the past participles are irregular. Note that some of the verbs form the passé compose with the auxiliary **être**.*

MODÈLE    Tu écris un courriel.  →  Tu as écrit un courriel.

**C**  *Your friend gives you some very vague information, so you ask for more detail. Create questions with **est-ce que** that begin with a question word.*

MODÈLE    Elle a apporté quelque chose.  →  Qu'est-ce qu'elle a apporté?

**D**  *Restate each of the following sentences, adding the adverb in the cue.*

MODÈLE    Elle est parti./vite  →  Elle est vite parti.

**E**  *Answer each of the following questions in the affirmative. Replace the direct object noun with the corresponding direct object pronoun in your response. Make the past participle agree with the object pronoun by pronouncing the final consonant.*

MODÈLE    Est-ce que ce journaliste a couvert la campagne présidentielle?
               →  Oui, il l'a couverte.

**F**  *Restate each of the following sentences, changing from active to passive voice. Use the passé composé in each case.*

MODÈLE    Paul a réparé les ordinateurs.  →  Les ordinateurs ont été réparés par Paul.

# Chapter 6
## The Imperfect; The Imperfect vs. the Passé Composé

**A**  *Restate each of the following sentences in the imperfect tense to tell what Hélène's life was like as a child in the country.*

MODÈLE    J'habite à la campagne.  →  J'habitais à la campagne.

**B**  *Create sentences from the elements given to tell what time it was when these events occurred. Use the imperfect tense for the expression of time in the first clause and the passé composé for the event in the second clause.*

MODÈLE    trois heures et demi/Sylvie/finir son travail
               →  Il était trois heures et demi quand Sylvie a fini son travail.

**C**  *How was the weather?  Restate each of the following sentences, replacing the weather expression in the first clause with the weather expression in the cue. Keep verbs in the first clause in the imperfect.*

MODÈLE    Il faisait soleil quand je suis sorti./faire froid
               →  Il faisait froid quand je suis sorti.

**D** *Create questions from the elements given to ask how long these people had been doing things. Use* **Depuis combien de temps est-ce que...?** *and the imperfect of the verb.*

MODÈLE    tu / travailler à Québec
        → Depuis combien de temps est-ce que tu travaillais à Québec?

**E** *Answer the following questions in the negative, replacing the noun complements with* **y** *or* **en.**

MODÈLE    Est-ce qu'il avait besoin de nos conseils? → Non, il n'en avait pas besoin.

**F** *Answer each of the following questions in the affirmative, replacing the noun complement with the correct object pronoun.*

MODÈLE    Est-ce que vous avez vu les voisins? → Oui, nous les avons vus.

# Chapter 7
## Reflexive Verbs

 *Create a series of sentences from the verb phrases given to describe Philippe's day.*

MODÈLE    se réveiller à sept heures → Il se réveille à sept heures.

 *This mother takes care of her children; afterward, she takes care of herself. Create sentences using the corresponding reflexive verb to tell what the mother does.*

MODÈLE    D'abord, elle débarbouille les enfants. → Ensuite, elle se débarbouille.

 *Answer each of the following questions, saying that people already did the things asked about. Use the passé composé of the reflexive verb in your response.*

MODÈLE    Est-ce qu'il va se fâcher? → Il s'est déjà fâché.

 *Your friend has come down with a cold. Create informal commands from the reflexive verbs given to suggest what your friend should or should not do.*

MODÈLES   se calmer → Calme-toi.
               ne pas s'impatienter → Ne t'impatiente pas.

 *Answer each of the following questions in the affirmative, replacing the direct object noun with the corresponding direct object pronoun. Each response will have double object pronouns.*

MODÈLE    Est-ce qu'il vous a donné les documents? → Oui, il me les a donnés.

**F** *Restate each of the following sentences, replacing object nouns with the corresponding pronouns. Replace other complements with* **lui, leur, y,** *or* **en,** *as required. Each response will have double object pronouns.*

MODÈLE    Il donne les clés à son collègue. → Il les lui donne.

# Chapter 8
## The Future and the Conditional

 **A** *Restate each of the following sentences, changing the verb from the present tense to the future.*

MODÈLE    Il pense à tout.  →  Il pensera à tout.

**B** *Create sentences from the elements given to tell what these people would do on a trip to France. Use the conditional in your response.*

MODÈLE    moi, je / parler français avec tout le monde
            → Moi, je parlerais français avec tout le monde.

**C** *Restate each of the following sentences. Change the first verb from the present to the imperfect, and change the second verb from the future to the conditional.*

MODÈLE    Je sais qu'il viendra.  →  Je savais qu'il viendrait.

**D** *Tell what these people would do to set up a successful business. Create sentences from the elements given, using the conditional tense.*

MODÈLE    Paulette / monter une affaire  →  Paulette monterait une affaire.

**E** *Combine each pair of sentences into a single sentence to express the condition under which an event will occur. The first sentence of each pair will become a **si**-clause in the present. The second sentence will become a clause with the verb in the future.*

MODÈLE    Il ne pleut pas. Nous pouvons partir.
            → S'il ne pleut pas, nous pourrons partir.

**F** *Tell how these people need to change their lifestyle in order to get in shape. Create contrary-to-fact statements to express what they should or should not do. Each sentence will have a **si**-clause in the imperfect and a main clause in the conditional.*

MODÈLE    Monique ne fait pas d'exercice. Elle grossit.
            → Si Monique faisait de l'exercice, elle ne grossirait pas.

# Chapter 9
## Compound Tenses: The Pluperfect; The Future Perfect; The Conditional Perfect

 **A** *All of these things had already happened by the time you returned from work. Create sentences from the elements given to express this. Use the pluperfect tense, and include the word **déjà** in your response.*

MODÈLE    ma belle-mère / préparer le dîner
            → Ma belle-mère avait déjà préparé le dîner.

**B** *Three friends are opening a new store together, and tomorrow is opening day. Create sentences from the elements given to tell what will have been done before the opening. Use the future perfect tense in your response.*

MODÈLE    on / choisir le nom du magasin  →  On aura choisi le nom du magasin.

**C** *Create sentences to say that the people mentioned would not have done these things. Use the conditional perfect, and replace object nouns with the corresponding object pronouns in your response.*

MODÈLE    Caroline a acheté cette maison. / moi, je   →   Moi, je ne l'aurais pas achetée.

**D** *Combine each pair of sentences into a single sentence to express a contrary-to-fact past condition. Each sentence will have a **si**-clause in the pluperfect and a main clause in the conditional perfect.*

MODÈLE    Il n'a pas travaillé assez. Il n'a pas fini le compte rendu.
               →   S'il avait travaillé assez, il aurait finit le compte rendu.

**E** *Create a cleft sentence using a **c'est...** + relative clause construction to highlight the subject of each sentence.*

MODÈLE    Le directeur arrive.   →   C'est le directeur qui arrive.

**F** *Create a cleft sentence using a **c'est...** + relative clause construction to highlight the direct object of the verb in each sentence.*

MODÈLE    Tu dois visiter ce musée.   →   C'est ce musée que tu dois visiter.

# Chapter 10
## The Subjunctive (Part I): The Present Subjunctive

**A** *Say that these people must do the things that they don't want to do. Use the **il faut que** + present subjunctive construction, and replace object nouns with the corresponding pronouns.*

MODÈLE    Les enfants ne veulent pas manger leurs légumes.
               →   Mais il faut qu'ils les mangent.

**B** *Combine each of the following pairs of sentences into a single sentence to express Luc's reaction to each of these situations.*

MODÈLE    Elle est malade. Je regrette.   →   Je regrette qu'elle soit malade.

**C** *Combine each of the following pairs of sentences into a single sentence. Some subordinate clauses will be in the subjunctive; others will be in the indicative.*

MODÈLE    Elle s'en souvient. Je doute.   →   Je doute qu'elle s'en souvienne.

**D** *Combine each pair of sentences into a single sentence, using the subjunctive in the subordinate clause. Use a preposition before the subordinate clause if the verb in the main clause requires it, and eliminate the pronoun of the second sentence.*

MODÈLE    Il part. Je le préfère.   →   Je préfère qu'il parte.

**E** *Restate each of the following sentences as a cleft sentence that highlights the indirect object.*

MODÈLE    J'ai prêté le logiciel à Jean.   →   C'est à Jean que j'ai prêté le logiciel.

**F**  *Answer each of the following questions in the affirmative, using a cleft sentence that highlights the prepositional phrase.*

MODÈLE    Ils sont arrivés en taxi?  →  Oui, c'est en taxi qu'ils sont arrivés.

# Chapter 11
The Subjunctive (Part II): The Subjunctive in Adjective Clauses; The Past Subjunctive; The Subjunctive in Adverb Clauses

**A**  *Restate each of the following sentences in the negative. Change affirmative words to negative words, and change the verb of the subordinate clause from indicative to subjunctive.*

MODÈLE    Je connais quelqu'un qui peut faire ce travail.
              →  Je ne connais personne qui puisse faire ce travail.

**B**  *Restate each of the following sentences, using the verb phrase in the cue to modify the main clause. Because this change causes the noun to be unidentified, you will also change the verb in the subordinate clause to the subjunctive.*

MODÈLE    Nous avons un appartement qui est confortable. / nous cherchons
              →  Nous cherchons un appartement qui soit confortable.

**C**  *Combine each pair of sentences into a single sentence, using the past subjunctive in the subordinate clause.*

MODÈLE    On a appelé la police. / Je ne crois pas.
              →  Je ne crois pas qu'on ait appelé la police.

**D**  *Combine each pair of sentences into a single sentence, using the conjunction given in the cue. The subordinate clause will be in the present subjunctive.*

MODÈLE    Nous allons lui parler. Nous ne le connaissons pas. / bien que
              →  Nous allons lui parler bien que nous ne le connaissions pas.

**E**  *Restate each of the conditions for Roger to be hired, using a clause beginning with* **à condition que.** *The verb will be in the subjunctive.*

MODÈLE    On va l'embaucher. Mais seulement s'il peut s'installer à Paris.
              →  À condition qu'il puisse s'installer à Paris.

**F**  *Say that we will call a meeting unless the following things happen. Change each of the following si-clauses to a clause beginning with* **à moins que.** *The verb will be in the present subjunctive or the past subjunctive.*

MODÈLE    Nous convoquerons une réunion aujourd'hui. Mais s'il n'est pas libre...
              →  À moins qu'il ne soit pas libre.

# Chapter 12
## The Present Participle and the Infinitive

 *Restate each of the following sentences, replacing the subordinate clause with the* **en** + *present participle construction.*

MODÈLE    Il écoute de la musique pendant qu'il lit.  →  Il écoute de la musique en lisant.

 *Restate each of the following sentences, adding the correct form of the verb in the cue to create a verb + infinitive construction.*

MODÈLE    Elle travaille à la maison. / aimer  →  Elle aime travailler à la maison.

 *Expand each of the following sentences with the verb of motion in the cue. Create a verb + infinitive construction, and keep verbs in the same tense as the original sentence.*

MODÈLE    Elle cherchait un nouvel emploi. / aller
                →  Elle allait chercher un nouvel emploi.

 *Expand each of the following sentences with the verb in the cue. Connect the verbs with the preposition* **à**, *and keep verbs in the same tense as the original sentence.*

MODÈLE    Il mange la cuisine africaine. / s'habituer
                →  Il s'habitue à manger la cuisine africaine.

 *Restate each of the following sentences, adding the verb in the cue. Connect the verbs with the preposition* **de**, *and keep the same meaning. Keep verbs in the same tense as the original sentence.*

MODÈLE    Il ne nous l'a pas dit. / oublier  →  Il a oublié de nous le dire.

**F** *Expand each of the following sentences with the verb in the cue to create a verb + infinitive construction. The verb may be connected to the infinitive by* **à** *or* **de**, *or it may require no preposition.*

MODÈLE    Je vous apporte les documents. / s'empresser
                →  Je m'empresse de vous apporter les documents.

# Answer Key

## Chapter 1
### The Present Tense of Regular Verbs

**A**
1. retrouve
2. étudie
3. retournent
4. passons
5. aidez
6. aimes
7. sauvegardent
8. rentre
9. téléphone
10. saluez
11. roule
12. volent
13. marchez
14. donne
15. dépenses
16. fermons
17. jouent
18. dessines
19. gagnent
20. oublie

**B**
1. a. Moi, j'accepte l'invitation.
   b. Eux, ils acceptent le paquet.
   c. Nous, nous acceptons le cadeau.
2. a. Les étudiants remercient leur professeur.
   b. L'enfant remercie ses parents.
   c. Toi, tu remercies ton ami.
3. a. Vous, vous travaillez en ville.
   b. Lui, il travaille au bureau.
   c. Les voisines travaillent à la maison.
4. a. Elle, elle invite son fiancé.
   b. Vous autres, vous invitez toute la famille.
   c. Eux, ils invitent les voisins.
5. a. Moi, j'organise un dîner d'affaires.
   b. Toi, tu organises une réunion.
   c. Mon chef organise une réception.

**C**
1. interrompez
2. descend
3. réussissent
4. mord
5. entends
6. obéissons
7. réfléchis
8. agit
9. attendons
10. vendent
11. choisissez
12. rendons
13. confonds
14. perds
15. remplis
16. réponds
17. guérissent
18. rougissez
19. applaudissons
20. bâtit

**D**  1. Oui, nous aménageons la cuisine.
2. Oui, nous renonçons à ce voyage.
3. Oui, nous tutoyons les amis.
4. Oui, nous plaçons cet argent.
5. Oui, nous nageons tous les jours.
6. Oui, nous balayons la maison.
7. Oui, nous partageons ces opinions.
8. Oui, nous changeons de route.
9. Oui, nous lançons un projet.
10. Oui, nous appuyons ce candidat.
11. Oui, nous remplaçons cet employé.
12. Oui, nous mangeons en ville.
13. Oui, nous téléchargeons des chansons.
14. Oui, nous payons la facture.
15. Oui, nous rédigeons des lettres.

**E**  1. On balaie/balaye le parquet.
2. On nettoie les tables.
3. On appuie les chaises contre le mur.
4. On essuie les verres.
5. On broie le poivre.
6. On emploie des ingrédients de qualité.
7. On essaie/essaye la viande.
8. On paie/paye les serveurs.
9. On tutoie nos amis.
10. On raie/raye les fautes.

**F**  1. tu parles
2. je réussis
3. vous vendez
4. nous voyageons
5. elle monte
6. ils descendent
7. nous remplaçons
8. on retourne
9. vous fermez
10. nous aménageons
11. tu fournis
12. il ennuie
13. vous mincissez
14. tu réponds
15. ils choisissent
16. elles paient/payent
17. je perds
18. ils jouent
19. vous étudiez
20. tu nettoies
21. nous partageons
22. il demande
23. nous lançons
24. on tutoie
25. j'envoie
26. nous téléchargeons

**G**  1. on complète
2. on renouvelle
3. on ramène
4. on achète
5. on révèle
6. on promène
7. on jette
8. on préfère
9. on répète
10. on lève
11. on rappelle
12. on pèle
13. on pénètre
14. on enlève
15. on sème
16. on célèbre
17. on amène
18. on projette

**H**  1. Quand est-que tu préfères prendre tes vacances?
2. Qu'est-ce que tu espères faire cet été?
3. Combien est-ce que tu pèses?
4. Comment est-ce que tu épelles ton nom?
5. Est-ce que tu rejettes les idées extrémistes?
6. Où est-ce que tu achètes tes vêtements?
7. Quand est-ce que tu nous ramènes?
8. Est-ce que tu répètes les nouveaux mots?
9. Comment est-ce que tu célèbres ton anniversaire?
10. Comment est-ce que tu relèves ton entreprise?
11. Quelle revue feuillettes-tu là?
12. Où est-ce que tu promènes ton chien?

**I**  1. Depuis combien de temps est-ce que Raoul travaille à la banque?
Il travaille à la banque depuis trois ans.

2. Depuis combien de temps est-ce que vous discutez de politique?
Je discute de politique depuis une heure.

3. Depuis combien de temps est-ce qu'ils téléchargent des programmes?
Ils téléchargent des programmes depuis trois heures.

4. Depuis combien de temps est-ce que les vieilles dames bavardent?
Elles bavardent depuis deux heures.

5. Depuis combien de temps est-ce que vous et votre mari cherchez un appartement?
Nous cherchons un appartement depuis trois mois.

6. Depuis combien de temps est-ce que tu regardes cette émission?
Je regarde cette émission depuis dix minutes.

7. Depuis combien de temps est-ce que vous autres les professeurs enseignent dans ce lycée?
Nous enseignons dans ce lycée depuis deux ans.

8. Depuis combien de temps est-ce que cet enfant agit comme ça?
Il agit comme ça depuis trois semaines.

9. Depuis combien de temps est-ce que les fermiers sèment du maïs?
Ils sèment du maïs depuis des siècles.

10. Depuis combien de temps est-ce que toi et ton frère, vous nettoyez la maison?
Nous nettoyons la maison depuis une heure et demie.

11. Depuis combien de temps est-ce que vous autres, vous rédigez le compte rendu?
Nous rédigeons le compte rendu depuis une semaine.

12. Depuis combien de temps est-ce qu'ils photocopient des documents?
Ils photocopient des documents depuis vingt minutes.

**J**  1. Il y a dix ans que nos voisins habitent à côté.

2. Ça fait deux heures que vous attendez l'avion.

3. Voilà cinq ans qu'ils étudient l'anglais.

4. Ça fait combien de temps qu'ils rédigent le compte rendu?

5. Il y a une demi-heure qu'elle promène son chien.

6. Voilà quarante minutes qu'il feuillette le magazine.

7. Il y a combien de temps que vous logez des étudiants étrangers?

8. Ça fait deux minutes déjà que le public applaudit.

**K**  1. Depuis quand est-ce que Suzanne étudie en Allemagne?
Elle étudie en Allemagne depuis 2005.

2. Depuis quand est-ce que cette famille habite en France?
Cette famille habite en France depuis le début de l'été.

3. Depuis quand est-ce que tu achètes tes légumes chez ce marchand?
J'achète mes légumes chez ce marchand depuis l'année dernière.

4. Depuis quand est-ce que vous rangez la chambre?
Je range / Nous rangeons la chambre depuis hier.

5. Depuis quand est-ce que les élèves répondent en français?
Ils répondent en français depuis la semaine dernière.

6. Depuis quand est-ce qu'ils passent leurs vacances en Bretagne?
Ils passent leurs vacances en Bretagne depuis 1999.

7. Depuis quand est-ce que vous voyagez pour affaires?
Je voyage / Nous voyageons pour affaires depuis 2003.

8. Depuis quand est-ce que tu tutoies le chef?
Je tutoie le chef depuis l'été.

9. Depuis quand est-ce que ton ami fume?
   Il fume depuis janvier.
10. Depuis quand est-ce que ce conseiller organise des réunions?
   Il organise des réunions depuis le mois d'août.

**L** 1. intransitive
2. transitive
3. transitive
4. transitive
5. transitive
6. transitive
7. transitive
8. intransitive
9. intransitive
10. intransitive
11. intransitive
12. intransitive
13. transitive
14. transitive
15. intransitive

**M** 1. Marc ferme la porte.
2. Tu attends le train.
3. Nous finissons notre projet.
4. Vous vendez votre maison.
5. J'étudie la leçon.
6. Elle choisit une université.
7. Il entend un bruit.
8. Ils trouvent un appartement.
9. Christine cherche un travail.
10. Nous plaçons notre argent.
11. Les enfants regardent un film.
12. Les piétons traversent la rue.
13. Vous nettoyez les tables.
14. Tu écoutes la radio.
15. Nous rangeons nos livres.
16. Les étudiants vouvoient le professeur.

**N** 1. Nous nageons bien.
2. Tu montes vite.
3. Elle retourne demain.
4. Je descends bientôt.
5. Vous travaillez tous les jours.
6. Elles réussissent toujours.
7. Ils jouent constamment.
8. Je marche dans la neige.
9. La voiture roule lentement.
10. Vous dansez très bien.
11. Nous voyageons en été.
12. Il réfléchit beaucoup.

**O** 1. Toi, tu descends, mais moi, je reste ici.
2. Lui, il retrouve ses amis et nous, on rentre.
3. Vous, vous quittez le restaurant tandis qu'elle, elle reste à table.
4. Eux, ils finissent leur travail tandis que vous, vous commencez votre projet.
5. Moi, je monte, mais elles, elles continuent leur promenade.
6. Nous, on range nos livres et elle, elle nettoie les meubles.
7. Eux, ils écoutent des cédés tandis que toi, tu regardes la télé.
8. Vous, vous cherchez un restaurant et moi, je visite les monuments.
9. Nous autres, nous téléchargeons des programmes tandis que toi, tu sauvegardes tes fichiers.
10. Eux, ils rédigent un contrat et nous, nous corrigeons leur prose.

**P** 1. Je descends, moi.
2. Il rougit, lui.
3. Ils effacent leurs fautes, eux.
4. On répond aux lettres, nous.
5. Tu commences ton nouveau travail, toi.
6. Elle quitte le bureau, elle.
7. Vous mangez au restaurant, vous.
8. Nous attendons l'autobus, nous.
9. Il escalade la montagne, lui.
10. Elles perdent leurs papiers, elles.

**Q** 1. Il attend l'autobus.
2. Elle quitte la maison.
3. J'écoute la chanson.
4. Vous abusez de ma bonté.
5. Nous cherchons un hôtel.
6. Je réponds à la lettre.
7. Tu joues du piano.
8. Ils jouent au football.
9. Je paie/paye l'appartement.
10. Ils discutent de la politique.
11. Elle ressemble à sa mère.
12. Il demande de l'argent.

# Chapter 2
## Irregular Verbs (Part I)

**A**  1. Je vais à Paris.
 2. Tu vas au Mexique.
 3. Mes parents vont au bord de la mer.
 4. Vous allez à la montagne.
 5. Nous allons à Moscou.
 6. Christine et Paulette vont au Portugal.
 7. Samuel va à la campagne.
 8. Albert et Joseph vont à Jérusalem.

**B**  1. a
 2. ai
 3. ont
 4. as
 5. avons
 6. avez
 7. a
 8. a

**C**  1. sommes
 2. êtes
 3. sont
 4. suis
 5. es
 6. est
 7. est
 8. êtes
 9. sont
 10. sommes

**D**  1. a
 2. ai
 3. sont
 4. avons
 5. as
 6. est
 7. a
 8. sont
 9. est
 10. avez
 11. sommes
 12. suis
 13. as
 14. avez
 15. êtes

**E**  1. Nous faisons de la varappe.
 2. Claude fait de l'alto.
 3. Vous faites une randonnée.
 4. Les enfants font du foot.
 5. Tu fais un voyage.
 6. Je fais une promenade.
 7. On fait de la bicyclette.
 8. Vous faites un petit tour.
 9. Mes amis font la grasse matinée.

**F**  1. Tu fais la grasse matinée.
 2. Elles font une randonnée.
 3. Je fais des fautes d'orthographe.
 4. Nous faisons attention au professeur.
 5. Vous faites acte de présence.
 6. Ma mère fait la lessive / le linge.
 7. Mon frère et ma sœur font les carreaux.

**G**  1. Je prends un thé.
 2. Les enfants prennent une glace.
 3. Ma mère prend un citron pressé.
 4. Mon père prend une bière.
 5. Tu prends de l'eau minérale.
 6. Nous prenons du vin.
 7. Vous prenez un dessert.
 8. On prend un jus de pomme.

**H**  1. entreprenons
 2. prennent
 3. apprends
 4. reprend
 5. prends
 6. reprenez
 7. surprend
 8. comprends
 9. prenez
 10. entreprennent
 11. prend

**I**  1. souffre
   2. ouvrons
   3. offre
   4. couvrez
   5. rouvre
   6. découvrent
   7. souffrent
   8. ouvres
   9. découvrons
   10. cueille
   11. offres
   12. accueillez
   13. couvre
   14. ouvrez
   15. cueillent

**J**  1. sors
   2. part
   3. sentons
   4. dorment
   5. servez
   6. ment
   7. repars
   8. sert
   9. dors
   10. sentez
   11. sortent
   12. partons
   13. repars
   14. mens
   15. sortez
   16. sers
   17. dormons
   18. ment

**K**  1. finis
   2. souffrent
   3. sentez
   4. partons
   5. choisissons
   6. ouvrent
   7. applaudissent
   8. réfléchis
   9. dors
   10. découvres
   11. avertit
   12. sert
   13. offre
   14. grossis
   15. sors
   16. repartez
   17. réussissez
   18. rougit
   19. atterrissent
   20. mincissent
   21. désobéit

**L**  1. teint
   2. rejoignent
   3. peins
   4. craignons
   5. éteins
   6. atteignez
   7. plaint
   8. contraignons
   9. feint
   10. étreignent

**M**  1. Elles ne battent pas le chat.
   2. Nous mettons la table.
   3. Vous mettez la télé?
   4. Ils abattent un arbre.
   5. Vous permettez ça?
   6. Nous remettons le compte rendu.
   7. Les soldats combattent.
   8. Elles mettent de l'argent à côté.

**N**  1. Le médecin combat les maladies.
   2. L'enfant bat des mains.
   3. Je mets la famille avant tout.
   4. Il met les employés à la porte.
   5. Tu mets un imperméable.
   6. Je bats des œufs.
   7. Il débat la question.
   8. Tu bats les cartes.

**O**  1. ouvrons
   2. part
   3. éteignons
   4. combattent
   5. mets
   6. fait
   7. vais
   8. as
   9. prend
   10. suis
   11. fait
   12. craignent
   13. es
   14. font

**P**  1. Philippe met une veste. Philippe ne met pas de veste.
2. Ils abattent des arbres. Ils n'abattent pas d'arbres.
3. Ma sœur fait son déjeuner. Ma sœur ne fait pas son déjeuner.
4. Nous prenons le raccourci. Nous ne prenons pas le raccourci.
5. Tu apprends le nouveau vocabulaire. Tu n'apprends pas le nouveau vocabulaire.
6. Les étudiants font des langues. Les étudiants ne font pas de langues.
7. Notre équipe bat son rival. Notre équipe ne bat pas son rival.
8. J'entreprends un projet. Je n'entreprends pas de projet.
9. Les enfants cueillent des fleurs. Les enfants ne cueillent pas de fleurs.
10. Elle reprend son travail. Elle ne reprend pas son travail.
11. Nous découvrons des quartiers intéressants. Nous ne découvrons pas de quartiers intéressants.
12. Ils finissent leur travail. Ils ne finissent pas leur travail.
13. Tu ouvres les fenêtres. Tu n'ouvres pas les fenêtres.
14. Vous accueillez des étudiants étrangers. Vous n'accueillez pas d'étudiants étrangers.
15. Il offre des cadeaux. Il n'offre pas de cadeaux.
16. Je surprends des conversations. Je ne surprends pas de conversations.

**Q**  1. Marie-Claire n'invite pas ses amis.
2. Moi, je n'appelle pas le traiteur.
3. Christine ne prépare pas d'hors-d'œuvre.
4. Luc n'achète pas de café.
5. Nos amis ne font pas de pizza.
6. Nous ne cherchons pas de CD.
7. Vous n'apportez pas de pain.
8. Moi, je ne lave pas la nappe.
9. Toi, tu ne laves pas les verres.
10. Albertine n'ouvre pas de bouteille de vin.
11. Nous, on ne sert pas de bonbons.
12. Toi, tu ne sors pas les gobelets en papier.

**R**  1. Non, je ne vais jamais au théâtre.
2. Non, je ne vais nulle part cet été.
3. Non, ils n'ont pas de voiture.
4. Non, elle ne va pas à la banque.
5. Non, je ne travaille pas aujourd'hui.
6. Non, je n'ai pas d'argent sur moi.
7. Non, Valérie ne sort pas avec Vincent (OR avec lui).
8. Non, je ne cherche personne.
9. Non, je ne fais rien.
10. Non, il n'y a plus de vin.

**S**  1. Ils ont besoin d'un appartement.
2. Il n'est pas en vacances.
3. Elle ne sert pas de gâteau.
4. Il n'éteint jamais la lumière.
5. Ils rejoignent leurs familles.
6. Personne ne nettoie la maison.
7. Il ne prend pas de raccourci.
8. Personne ne comprend le professeur.
9. Elle bat des œufs pour le gâteau.
10. Je n'ai plus soif.
11. Ils battent les cartes.
12. Elle surprend leur conversation.

# Chapter 3
## Irregular Verbs (Part II)

**A**    1. suivez
       2. écrivent
       3. boit
       4. écris
       5. vit
       6. buvons
       7. vivent
       8. boivent
       9. suit
      10. écrivez

**B**    1. Ils lisent.
       2. Je cours.
       3. Elles meurent.
       4. Vous dites.
       5. Tu lis.
       6. Je meurs.
       7. Tu cours.
       8. Ils disent.

**C**    1. courent
       2. meurs
       3. lisons
       4. dis
       5. mourons
       6. disons
       7. court
       8. lis

**D**    1. reconduisent
       2. détruit
       3. instruisons
       4. traduis
       5. introduit
       6. déduis
       7. nuisez
       8. construisent

**E**    1. Elles croient.
       2. Tu vois.
       3. Je reçois.
       4. Vous fuyez.
       5. Elle convainc.
       6. Il aperçoit.
       7. Nous vainquons.
       8. Ils conçoivent.
       9. Il voit.
      10. Tu convaincs.
      11. Vous recevez.
      12. Je vois.

**F**    1. reçoivent
       2. crois
       3. déçoit
       4. fuyez
       5. vois
       6. vainquent
       7. conçoivent
       8. convainquent
       9. croyons
      10. aperçoit

**G**    1. déçoit
       2. fuyez
       3. conduis
       4. voyons
       5. boit
       6. écris
       7. lisent
       8. séduit
       9. traduis
      10. croyez
      11. convainquons
      12. reçois
      13. produit
      14. suivent
      15. meurent
      16. buvez
      17. écrivent
      18. réduit
      19. fuis
      20. dites
      21. lis
      22. meurs
      23. fuit
      24. voient
      25. convainc
      26. bois
      27. écrivez
      28. disent
      29. vainc
      30. suit

**H**  1. connaissez
   2. sais
   3. connais
   4. sait
   5. savons
   6. connais
   7. connaît
   8. savent
   9. connaissent
   10. savez
   11. connaît
   12. sais

**I**  1. produit
   2. boivent
   3. conduit
   4. suivons
   5. vit
   6. bois
   7. reçoivent
   8. fuient
   9. voyez
   10. reçoit
   11. instruit
   12. connaissent
   13. suivent

**J**  1. Je dois cent euros.
   2. Vous devez dix dollars.
   3. Nous devons mille francs suisses.
   4. On doit beaucoup d'argent.
   5. Tu dois trois cents dollars.
   6. Marc doit mille euros.
   7. Les voisins doivent trois mille francs suisses.
   8. Christine doit deux cents dollars canadiens.

**K**  1. veulent
   2. veux
   3. voulons
   4. veut
   5. voulez
   6. veux
   7. veut
   8. veulent

**L**  1. Je n'en peux plus.
   2. Nous n'en pouvons plus.
   3. Les touristes n'en peuvent plus.
   4. Ma sœur n'en peut plus.
   5. On n'en peut plus.
   6. Tu n'en peux plus.
   7. Vous n'en pouvez plus.
   8. Mes amis n'en peuvent plus.

**M**  1. tiens
   2. venons
   3. tenir
   4. tienne
   5. venir
   6. tiennent
   7. vient
   8. viens

**N**  1. Mon fils souhaite réussir à ses examens.
   2. Je ne peux plus venir.
   3. Il aime sortir le samedi soir.
   4. J'aime mieux sortir le vendredi.
   5. Les étudiants n'osent pas dire la vérité.
   6. Nous espérons finir notre travail avant cinq heures.
   7. Vous préférez rentrer en autobus.
   8. Tu sais rédiger des lettres en allemand.
   9. Robert ne semble pas comprendre.
   10. Je ne compte voir personne.
   11. Maryse semble être contente.
   12. Elle adore faire du camping.
   13. Cette région peut produire des fruits et des légumes.
   14. Il ne doit pas fuir devant ses responsabilités.

15. J'espère convaincre les autres.
16. Elles veulent voir ce film.
17. Je compte écrire ma thèse cet été.
18. Ils aiment boire un verre avec nous.

**O**
1. Non, je ne peux jamais jouer au football.
2. Non, il ne veut voir personne.
3. Non, nous ne devons / je ne dois rien acheter.
4. Non, nous n'aimons / je n'aime pas faire de la varappe.
5. Non, les enfants ne veulent rien boire.
6. Non, Paul ne sait pas piloter un avion.
7. Non, Marc n'ose pas inviter Christine à sortir.
8. Non, je ne souhaite pas trouver un nouveau travail.
9. Non, Jeanne ne compte pas faire de l'informatique.
10. Non, je ne veux plus attendre nos amis.

**P**
1. Arrive-t-il à l'heure?
2. Allons-nous en France?
3. Comprenez-vous ce texte?
4. Voient-ils leurs collègues?
5. Neige-t-il aujourd'hui?
6. Va-t-elle en avion?
7. Sais-tu nager?
8. Va-t-on en Amérique?
9. A-t-elle un bon travail?
10. Rédigeons-nous la lettre?
11. Mange-t-il au restaurant?
12. Réduisent-ils leurs frais?
13. Sauvegarde-t-on les archives?
14. Retourne-t-il en Afrique?
15. Reçoit-on un message?
16. Répondent-elles en français?
17. Télécharge-t-on des documents?
18. Renvoie-t-il ses employés?
19. Voyage-t-elle en Asie?
20. Prononce-t-il correctement?

**Q**
1. Encourageons-nous les étudiants?
2. Ce pays a-t-il besoin de notre aide?
3. Le PDG renonce-t-il à son poste?
4. Est-ce que je travaille dans une entreprise internationale?
5. Arrive-t-on en avance?
6. Fait-elle de la flûte?
7. Les touristes prennent-ils un raccourci?
8. Mes amis appuient-ils ce candidat?
9. L'autocar roule-t-il vite?
10. Est-ce que je présente les résultats?
11. La bonne fait-elle les carreaux?
12. Les ouvriers quittent-ils l'usine à cinq heures?
13. Ces agences dépensent-elles trop?
14. La compagnie emprunte-t-elle trop d'argent?
15. Discutons-nous constamment?
16. Habitez-vous à la campagne?
17. Est-ce que je téléphone à nos fournisseurs?
18. Le public va-t-il applaudir?
19. La direction annonce-t-elle la fusion des entreprises?
20. Cette famille loge-t-elle des étudiants étrangers?

**R**   1. Ils boivent du vin à table.
   2. Nous buvons à votre réussite.
   3. Tu lis les documents? / Est-ce que tu lis les documents?
   4. Elle vit près du centre commercial.
   5. Il court très vite.
   6. Je crois que oui. Et toi?
   7. Je crois que non.
   8. Vous voyez le café Internet?
   9. Tu reçois beaucoup de courriels?
  10. Nous connaissons New York.
  11. Je ne sais pas quand ils arrivent.
  12. Vous savez l'heure?
  13. Nous ne voulons plus espérer.
  14. Elle peut m'accompagner.
  15. Il compte entreprendre le projet.
  16. Va-t-elle en Angleterre?
  17. A-t-on faim?
  18. J'aime chanter mais je préfère danser.

# Chapter 4
## The Imperative

**A**   1. Ramasse tes vêtements.
   2. Ne crie pas si fort.
   3. Finis tes devoirs.
   4. Téléphone à ta tante.
   5. Ne laisse pas tes livres par terre.
   6. Mets tes crayons dans le tiroir.
   7. Mange tout ce qu'il y a sur ton assiette.
   8. Ne joue pas dans le salon.
   9. N'invite pas tes amis aujourd'hui.
  10. Viens au supermarché avec moi.
  11. Ne va pas chez les voisins.
  12. N'allume pas la télé.
  13. Ferme le lecteur de cédés.
  14. Lace tes chaussures.
  15. Ne salis pas la nappe.
  16. Aie un peu de patience.
  17. N'embête pas le chat.
  18. Sois gentil avec tout le monde.

**B**   1. Arrivez au bureau à neuf heures.
   2. Allumez votre ordinateur.
   3. Choisissez un mot de passe.
   4. Lisez vos courriels.
   5. Répondez à tous les messages.
   6. Ne prenez pas de rendez-vous.
   7. N'ennuyez pas le chef.
   8. Ne faites pas de coups de téléphone personnels.
   9. Ne commandez pas de repas.
  10. Ne mettez pas votre bureau en désordre.
  11. Rangez toujours vos affaires.
  12. Soyez patient avec vos collègues.
  13. N'ayez pas peur de demander de conseils.
  14. Aidez les nouveaux employés.
  15. Sachez où se trouvent nos clients.
  16. Réfléchissez avant d'agir.
  17. Finissez tout votre travail avant de partir.
  18. Ne sortez pas du bureau avant six heures.

**C**
1. Faisons quelque chose ensemble.
2. Ne restons pas à la maison.
3. Allons à la campagne.
4. Prenons nos bicyclettes.
5. Nageons dans le lac.
6. Jouons au foot.
7. N'ayons pas peur de faire du ski nautique.
8. Mangeons au bord de l'eau.
9. Rentrons vers six heures du soir.
10. Changeons de vêtements.
11. Dînons au restaurant.
12. Achetons un journal.
13. Cherchons une boîte de nuit.
14. Réservons une table.
15. Soyons ponctuels.
16. Voyons le spectacle.
17. Retournons à pied.
18. Réfléchissons à nos activités pour demain.

**D**
1. a. leurs cédés
   b. X
   c. écouter qqch
2. a. mes voitures
   b. ce concessionnaire
   c. acheter qqch à qqn
3. a. vos courriels
   b. X
   c. recevoir qqch
4. a. X
   b. leur mère
   c. obéir à qqn
5. a. sa voiture
   b. son fils
   c. prêter qqch à qqn
6. a. le projet
   b. ses collègues
   c. présenter qqch à qqn
7. a. l'autobus
   b. X
   c. attendre qqch
8. a. la situation
   b. tes enfants
   c. expliquer qqch à qqn
9. a. un iPod
   b. ma fille
   c. offrir qqch à qqn
10. a. X
    b. le chef
    c. déplaire à qqn
11. a. X
    b. sa mère
    c. ressembler à qqn
12. a. la vérité
    b. leurs parents
    c. dire qqch à qqn

**E**
1. Les Durand vendent leur appartement aux Dupont.
2. Le chien apporte le journal à son maître.
3. Lucille demande l'argent à ses parents.
4. Je rends les livres à Jean-Claude.
5. Il laisse sa maison à sa fille.
6. Tu prêtes ta bicyclette à ton amie.
7. Ils envoient les courriels à leurs assistants.
8. Vous présentez le compte rendu au PDG.
9. Le voleur arrache le sac à la dame.
10. Elle offre les cédés à ses neveux.
11. Le professeur dit la réponse aux étudiants.
12. Je donne l'addition aux clients.
13. Nous promettons la voiture à notre fils.
14. Tu passes le sel aux invités.

**F**  1. Oui, il le reçoit.
    2. Oui, ils les apprennent.
    3. Oui, je les appelle.
    4. Oui, elle l'invite (au bal).
    5. Oui, ils le commandent.
    6. Oui, je la nettoie.

    7. Oui, ils la mettent.
    8. Oui, elle l'achète.
    9. Oui, il les a.
  10. Oui, elle les range.
  11. Oui, nous le finissons. / Oui, on le finit.
  12. Oui, il la raccompagne.

**G**  1. Non, ils ne la bâtissent pas.
    2. Non, nous ne l'écoutons pas. / Non, on ne l'écoute pas.
    3. Non, ils ne les aiment pas.
    4. Non, je ne les photocopie pas.
    5. Non, nous ne les téléchargeons pas. / Non, on ne les télécharge pas.
    6. Non, je ne la paie pas.
    7. Non, elle ne le promène pas.
    8. Non, je ne la perds pas souvent.
    9. Non, il ne le fait pas.
  10. Non, ils ne les mettent pas.
  11. Non, je ne les avertis pas.
  12. Non, je ne l'interromps pas. / Non, nous ne l'interrompons pas.

**H**  1. Oui, elle va les photocopier.
    2. Non, il ne va pas le préparer.
    3. Oui, il va les casser.
    4. Non, il ne peut pas les recevoir.
    5. Oui, tu dois la mettre. / Oui, vouz devez la mettre.
    6. Non, elle ne veut pas les sauvegarder.
    7. Oui, ils savent le programmer.
    8. Non, nous ne comptons pas le prendre avec vous. /
        Non, je ne compte pas le prendre avec vous.
    9. Oui, il peut l'accepter.
  10. Non, je n'aime pas le faire.
  11. Oui, ils vont les arroser.
  12. Non, je ne veux pas l'ouvrir.
  13. Oui, j'aime les lire.
  14. Non, vous ne devez pas les fermer.
  15. Oui, elle compte le remercier.
  16. Non, je ne vais pas l'imprimer.
  17. Oui, il veut les télécharger.
  18. Non, nous ne souhaitons pas la quitter. / Non, je ne souhaite pas la quitter.
  19. Oui, elle préfère les enseigner.
  20. Non, il n'espère pas les convaincre.

**I**  1. Il lui envoie un courriel.
    2. La secrétaire leur téléphone.
    3. Je veux leur louer un appartement.
    4. Elle va lui demander ce produit.
    5. Cette pièce de théâtre ne va pas lui plaire.
    6. Ils lui cachent la vérité.
    7. Nous lui apportons les documents.
    8. Ils lui écrivent un message.
    9. Je ne vais pas lui dire ce secret.
  10. Vous ne pouvez pas leur expliquer ces résultats.

11. Elle leur donne des cadeaux.
12. Ce professeur ne sait pas leur expliquer les problèmes difficiles.
13. Il ne veut pas lui prêter sa voiture.
14. Elle leur vend ses peintures.
15. Nous comptons leur rendre l'argent.
16. Je lui enseigne des chansons.

**J**  1. Je lui explique le projet.
2. Je vais leur demander un lecteur de cédés.
3. Elle va m'offrir une montre.
4. Il leur vend sa maison.
5. Il va leur dire la solution.
6. Tu dois / Vous devez lui envoyer un formulaire.
7. Je vais vous prêter mille dollars.
8. Il lui a pris son sac à main.
9. Je compte / Nous comptons / On compte leur apporter un gâteau.
10. Ils leur promettent un mois en Suisse.

**K**  1. Oui, mange-la.
2. Oui, bois-le.
3. Oui, jette-les à la corbeille.
4. Oui, lis-les.
5. Oui, sauvegarde-le.
6. Oui, attends-moi.
7. Oui, cherche-les.
8. Oui, imprime-les.
9. Oui, utilise-le.
10. Oui, remercie-la.
11. Oui, montre-moi ta photo.
12. Oui, dépose-moi en ville.
13. Oui, finis-le.
14. Oui, enlève-la.
15. Oui, répète-les.

**L**  1. Non, ne la mange pas.
2. Non, ne le bois pas.
3. Non, ne les jette pas à la corbeille.
4. Non, ne les lis pas.
5. Non, ne le sauvegarde pas.
6. Non, ne m'attends pas.
7. Non, ne les cherche pas.
8. Non, ne les imprime pas.
9. Non, ne l'utilise pas.
10. Non, ne la remercie pas.
11. Non, ne me montre pas ta photo.
12. Non, ne me dépose pas en ville.
13. Non, ne le finis pas.
14. Non, ne l'enlève pas.
15. Non, ne les répète pas.

**M**  1. Oui, raccompagnez-nous.
2. Oui, prenez-la.
3. Oui, dépensez-le.
4. Oui, lavez-les.
5. Oui, oubliez-le.
6. Oui, photocopiez-le.
7. Oui, traversez-le.
8. Oui, obéissez-lui.
9. Oui, répondez-leur.
10. Oui, écoutez-le.
11. Oui, annoncez-la.
12. Oui, corrigez-la.
13. Oui, rejetez-les.
14. Oui, feuilletez-la.
15. Oui, faites-les.
16. Oui, écrivez-leur.

**N**  1. Non, ne nous raccompagnez pas.
2. Non, ne la prenez pas.
3. Non, ne le dépensez pas.
4. Non, ne les lavez pas.
5. Non, ne l'oubliez pas.
6. Non, ne le photocopiez pas.
7. Non, ne le traversez pas.
8. Non, ne lui obéissez pas.
9. Non, ne leur répondez pas.
10. Non, ne l'écoutez pas.
11. Non, ne l'annoncez pas.
12. Non, ne la corrigez pas.
13. Non, ne les rejetez pas.
14. Non, ne la feuilletez pas.
15. Non, ne les faites pas.
16. Non, ne leur écrivez pas.

**O**　1. Répondons-leur.
　　2. Téléchargeons-le.
　　3. Écoutons-les.
　　4. Commandons-les.
　　5. Écrivons-lui un courriel.
　　6. Emmenons-les.
　　7. Ouvrons-la.
　　8. Servons-les.
　　9. Mettons-le à la porte.
　10. Téléphonons-lui.
　11. Remplaçons-la.
　12. Mangeons-le.

**P**　1. Ne les ouvrons pas.
　　2. Ne l'invitons pas.
　　3. Ne les remplaçons pas.
　　4. Ne les lavons pas.
　　5. Ne la mangeons pas.
　　6. Ne lui téléphonons pas.
　　7. Ne le nettoyons pas.
　　8. Ne le promenons pas.
　　9. Ne le décourageons pas.
　10. Ne les attendons pas.

**Q**　1. Ne parlez pas trop bas.
　　2. Parlez plus haut (fort).
　　3. Viens manger cette pizza aux champignons.
　　4. Les champignons? Je les déteste, moi. Mange-la toi-même.
　　5. Tu vas voir le film?
　　6. Non, je ne veux pas le voir.
　　7. Prenons le train pour aller à Paris mais ne le prenons pas pour aller en Normandie.
　　8. Ne soyons pas en retard.
　　9. D'accord, partons tout de suite.
　10. Je compte leur envoyer les fichiers aujourd'hui.
　11. Sauvegardez-les. Ensuite, envoyez-leur les fichiers la semaine prochaine.
　12. Tu peux me prêter ton appareil digital?
　13. Je ne l'ai pas. Juliette va me rendre l'appareil digital demain.
　14. Attends-moi à Starbucks.
　15. Écris-lui un courriel.
　16. Faites attention.

# Chapter 5
## The Passé Composé

**A**　1. surpris
　　2. plaint
　　3. attendu
　　4. atteint
　　5. introduit
　　6. déçu
　　7. recouvert
　　8. promis
　　9. déduit
　10. apparu
　11. relu
　12. craint
　13. admis
　14. maintenu
　15. revenu
　16. défait
　17. aperçu
　18. décrit
　19. revu
　20. disparu

**B**
1. Elles ont fait trois kilomètres à pied.
2. Elles ont marché avec leurs copines.
3. Elles ont mis des baskets.
4. J'ai été très content.
5. J'ai reçu un courriel de ma sœur.
6. Elle a décidé de venir me voir.
7. Elle a pris son billet d'avion.
8. Vous avez lu beaucoup d'articles.
9. Nous avons préparé le petit déjeuner.
10. Nous avons acheté des croissants.
11. Tu as réfléchi à ton avenir.
12. Il a attendu ses amis.
13. Nous avons compris le professeur.
14. Ils ont rejoint leurs amis.
15. Ils ont produit du fromage.
16. Nous avons téléchargé un programme.
17. Il a recommandé un logiciel.
18. Tu as entendu un bruit.
19. Elle a fini son travail.
20. La police a suivi le taxi.

**C**
1. Ma sœur a joué au basket-ball au parc.
2. Les étudiants ont étudié toute la journée.
3. Le public a applaudi après le spectacle.
4. J'ai vendu ma vieille voiture.
5. Nous avons mis la table pour dîner.
6. Elle a appris les théorèmes.
7. Ils ont bu un café.
8. Vous avez vécu en France.
9. Tu as écrit un courriel.
10. Le consultant a rédigé un document.
11. Nous avons aperçu un changement d'attitude.
12. J'ai couru cinq kilomètres.
13. Les soldats ont détruit la base de l'ennemi.
14. Les citoyens ont fui devant l'assaut.
15. Nous avons vu un très bon film.
16. J'ai voulu sortir.
17. Le chef a pu comprendre ce problème.
18. Elles ont eu besoin de notre aide.
19. Tout le monde a été en retard.
20. J'ai fait la grasse matinée.

**D**
1. Je n'ai pas compris.
2. Nous n'avons vu personne.
3. Ils n'ont rien acheté.
4. Tu n'as jamais interrompu.
5. Elle n'a jamais fait la grasse matinée.
6. Vous n'avez pas suivi la route.
7. Cette idée n'a intéressé personne.
8. Elles n'ont rien lu.
9. Tu n'as jamais téléchargé de programmes.
10. Elle n'a rien mangé.
11. Je n'ai pas fini.
12. Ce pays n'a rien produit.
13. Je n'ai attendu personne.
14. Ils n'ont rien promis.
15. Vous n'avez jamais conduit.

**E**
1. Jean est arrivé à huit heures.
2. Michèle n'est pas partie aujourd'hui.
3. Mes amis sont venus me voir.
4. Qui est sorti?
5. Nous ne sommes jamais allé(e)s en ville.
6. Les autres sont rentré(e)s.
7. Ma cousine est devenue programmeuse.
8. Le train n'est pas passé.
9. Mes tantes sont descendues faire le marché.
10. Mon chien est mort.

11. Mes copines sont entrées dans le restaurant.
12. Quand est-ce qu'elle est revenue?
13. Pourquoi est-ce qu'elles ne sont pas restées?
14. La petite fille est tombée.
15. Vous n'êtes pas ressorti(e)s, vous autres.

**F**  1. Mon frère a joué du violon au concert.
2. Nos cousins sont arrivés du Canada.
3. Le train est entré en gare.
4. Les voyageurs ont attendu sur le quai.
5. Les passagers sont montés dans le train.
6. Chacun a cherché sa place.
7. Le train est parti avec un quart d'heure de retard.
8. Ma tante est venue me voir.
9. Elle m'a apporté des livres.
10. Nous avons mangé ensemble.
11. Je suis resté(e) à la maison.
12. J'ai lu un livre.
13. Quelques amis m'ont téléphoné.
14. Ils m'ont invité à sortir avec eux.
15. Je n'ai pas pu les accompagner.
16. Je n'ai pas quitté mon appartement.
17. J'ai fini mon travail.
18. Christine a perdu sa montre.
19. Elle est retournée au bureau pour la chercher.
20. Elle est revenue avec sa montre.

**G**  1. J'ai trouvé un billet de cent euros.
2. J'ai mis le billet dans ma poche.
3. Je suis allé(e) au magasin d'informatique.
4. Je suis entré(e) dans le magasin.
5. Je suis monté(e) au troisième étage.
6. J'ai décidé d'acheter des logiciels.
7. Le vendeur est venu.
8. Il m'a montré des logiciels.
9. J'ai regardé tous les logiciels.
10. J'en ai choisi trois.
11. Ces logiciels ont coûté 98 euros.
12. Avec les deux euros restants j'ai pris un café.

**H**  1. ouvertes          9. achetées
2. mise              10. répondu
3. connu             11. envoyé
4. descendus         12. faites
5. écrits            13. entré
6. choisis           14. marché
7. gagné             15. découverts
8. donné             16. reçus

**I**   1. Il a vendu ses actions. A-t-il vendu ses actions?

2. Paulette a loué un appartement. Paulette a-t-elle loué un appartement?

3. Les Chardin ont monté une entreprise. Les Chardin ont-ils monté une entreprise?

4. L'entreprise a exporté des logiciels. L'entreprise a-t-elle exporté des logiciels?

5. Ils ont vendu leurs produits dans plusieurs pays. Ont-ils vendu leurs produits dans plusieurs pays?

6. La compagnie n'a pas perdu d'argent. La compagnie n'a-t-elle pas perdu d'argent?

7. Les Chardin ont embauché beaucoup d'employés. Les Chardin ont-ils embauché beaucoup d'employés?

8. Les employés ont reçu des primes. Les employés ont-ils reçu des primes?

9. J'ai répondu à toutes vos questions. Ai-je répondu à toutes vos questions?

10. Les ouvriers ont fait grève. Les ouvriers ont-ils fait grève?

11. Notre pays a adopté l'euro. Notre pays a-t-il adopté l'euro?

12. La Pologne est devenue membre de l'Union Européenne. La Pologne est-elle devenue membre de l'Union Européenne?

13. Le Sénat a approuvé une nouvelle loi. Le Sénat a-t-il approuvé une nouvelle loi?

14. Ces trois pays ont signé le traité. Ces trois pays ont-ils signé le traité?

15. Les autres pays ne l'ont pas signé. Les autres pays ne l'ont-ils pas signé?

**J**   1. Quel avion est-ce qu'Élisabeth a pris?

2. Qui est dans la salle d'attente? (Qui est-ce qui *is also possible, but less common.*)

3. Qu'est-ce qu'il a apporté?

4. Pourquoi est-ce qu'il est ici?

5. Comment est-ce qu'elle travaille?

6. Quand / À quelle heure est-ce que les employés sont partis?

7. Où est-ce que tu fais tes études? / Où est-ce que vous faites vos études?

8. Qu'est-ce qui l'intéresse beaucoup?

9. Quand est-ce qu'il y a une séance du film?

10. Combien de courriels est-ce qu'elle reçoit?

11. Pourquoi est-ce qu'il est en retard?

12. Comment est-ce que les étudiants répondent?

**K**   1. J'ai reçu mon billet électronique d'avion par courriel hier.

2. Nous n'avons pas pu les contacter par téléphone mobile.

3. Il est allé au café Internet à cinq heures et elle est arrivée à cinq heures et demie.

4. Tu as vu le site Web, n'est-ce pas?

5. Elle est née à Chicago.

6. Avez-vous su le numéro de vol?

7. Voilà toutes les données que j'ai entrées.

8. Nous avons voulu jouer au tennis.

9. Les logiciels? Je les ai achetés en solde.

10. Ont-ils créé une nouvelle base de données?

11. Elles sont venues nous voir au bureau.

12. Est-ce que tu as fini le projet?

**L**   1. À quelle heure leur autocar arrive-t-il à la gare routière? Il arrive à la gare routière à quelle heure, leur autocar?

2. Dans quel immeuble sa famille habite-t-elle? Elle habite dans quel immeuble, sa famille?

3. Où Mme Ducros fait-elle ses achats? Elle fait ses achats où, Mme Ducros?

4. Combien d'heures par jour le petit Pierre passe-t-il devant son ordinateur?
   Il passe combien d'heures par jour devant son ordinateur, le petit Pierre?
5. Que fais-tu pour t'amuser? Tu fais quoi pour t'amuser, toi?
6. Quelle sorte d'emploi Jean-Luc cherche-t-il? Il cherche quelle sorte d'emploi, Jean-Luc?
7. Comment ce mot se prononce-t-il? Il se prononce comment, ce mot?
8. Quel clavier ce programmeur préfère-t-il? Il préfère quel clavier, ce programmeur?
9. Avec qui Marie-Claire est-elle sortie? Elle est sortie avec qui, Marie-Claire?
10. Sur qui notre chef compte-t-il? Il compte sur qui, notre chef?

**M**  1. Les cousins ont mangé ensemble.
2. J'ai trop acheté.
3. Nous avons passé récemment nos vacances dans le Midi.
4. Les voisins ont certainement déménagé.
5. Les enfants l'ont fait exprès.
6. Vous avez très bien expliqué notre difficulté.
7. Ils sont vite partis.
8. Elle a peut-être perdu sa clé.
9. J'ai préparé le goûter n'importe comment.
10. Il a sûrement refusé de nous aider.
11. Tu as tout de suite répondu. / Tu a répondu tout de suite.
12. Nous avons dîné dehors.
13. Je ne l'ai pas vu ici.
14. Elles sont restées là-bas.
15. J'ai assez travaillé.
16. Nous avons beaucoup vu.
17. Ils sont déjà arrivés.
18. Elle a sans doute compris.
19. Il a souvent entré les données.

**N**  1. Le bureau a été ouvert par la secrétaire.
2. Cette entreprise a été sauvegardée par le propriétaire.
3. Les marchandises sont étalées par les commerçants.
4. Ces parfums sont achetés par les touristes.
5. Le marché a été étudié par les consultants.
6. Des chaussures sont fabriquées par cette usine.
7. Les actions ont été vendues par Marianne.
8. La note a été réglée par le client.
9. Un chèque postal a été envoyé par l'employée.
10. Un compte de chèques va être ouvert par les Poirier.
11. Ce fromage est apprécié par les étrangers.
12. Ce fromage est exporté dans le monde entier par les entreprises.
13. Une nouvelle ligne de chemin de fer a été construite par le gouvernement.
14. Les transports routiers sont utilisés par les entreprises.
15. Une déclaration pour la douane doit être remplie par l'expéditeur.
16. Un prêt a été accordé à cette entreprise par la banque.
17. Cet ouvrier va être embauché par le patron.
18. Une enquête a été menée auprès du public par les spécialistes en marketing.
19. Cette facture va être acquittée par le débiteur.
20. Des marchés étrangers pour nos produits ont été trouvés par nos agents.

**O**  1. On lit ces journaux.
    2. On estime les journalistes.
    3. On discute leurs articles.
    4. On a reçu votre courriel.
    5. On a imprimé votre courriel.
    6. On a réparti votre courriel à tout le monde.
    7. On a remplacé nos ordinateurs.
    8. On a installé de nouveaux programmes.
    9. On a acheté de nouveaux logiciels.
  10. On a organisé un cours de formation.
  11. On a ouvert une succursale.
  12. On cherche un informaticien.
  13. On a consulté des spécialistes en bureautique.
  14. On a acheté des meubles.
  15. On a annoncé l'ouverture du bureau.

**P**  1. La société a été transformée par la technologie.
    2. Les fichiers sont ouverts par le programmeur.
    3. Le gratte-ciel va être dessiné par un architecte célèbre.
    4. Ces tableaux ont été peints par Manet.
    5. Des hors-d'œuvre ont été servis à huit heures.
    6. On a retiré l'argent du GAB.
    7. Les romans d'espionnage ont été traduits en anglais par l'auteur lui-même.
    8. L'utilisation des téléphones mobiles est interdite.
    9. Notre décision doit être prise demain.
  10. Le rapport a été écrit par la consultante en marketing.

## Chapter 6
### The Imperfect; The Imperfect vs. the Passé Composé

**A**  1. elle mangeait
    2. je choisissais
    3. il recevait
    4. nous vendions
    5. vous sauvegardiez
    6. tu commençais
    7. elle payait
    8. ils nettoyaient
    9. je programmais
  10. on finissait
  11. tu buvais
  12. elles prenaient
  13. vous étiez
  14. j'avais
  15. il savait
  16. nous étions
  17. elles avaient
  18. nous étudiions
  19. ils faisaient
  20. elle allait
  21. tu convainquais
  22. il croyait
  23. tu voulais
  24. ils pouvaient
  25. elle venait

**B**
1. lisais
2. était
3. jouiez
4. montaient
5. travaillaient
6. rangeais
7. remplaçait
8. buvais
9. prenaient
10. avais
11. devait
12. neigeait
13. voyais
14. apprenions
15. allais
16. ouvraient
17. tournait
18. disions
19. étiez
20. nageais
21. tenais
22. faisait
23. savais
24. attendions
25. éteignait
26. réussissait
27. offraient
28. établissait
29. produisait
30. fuyait

**C**
1. Je voulais vous accompagner.
2. Qu'est-ce que vous disiez?
3. Il faisait chaud au mois de septembre.
4. Ils buvaient du jus de pomme.
5. Quelque chose sentait mauvais.
6. Il craignait le rhume.
7. Tu achetais des logiciels.
8. J'écrivais des courriels.
9. Elle ne pouvait pas trouver un travail.
10. Nous allions en avion.
11. Tu comprenais les poèmes.
12. Ils avaient peur.
13. Il devait partir.
14. Tu songeais à tes vacances.
15. Elle plaçait ses affaires sur le sofa.
16. Cet enfant suivait bien à l'école.
17. Tu conduisais beaucoup.
18. Vous étiez pressé.
19. Nous commencions nos études.
20. Je dormais bien.

**D**
1. Il était midi quand je suis arrivé(e).
2. Il faisait soleil quand on est partis au pique-nique.
3. Quand ils sont venus, il était déjà tard.
4. Il neigeait quand je suis sorti(e) de chez moi.
5. Il faisait noir quand l'avion a décollé.
6. Il y avait des éclairs quand l'avion a atterri.
7. Il pleuvait à verse quand la mariée est arrivée à l'église.
8. Le temps était couvert quand on s'est mis en route.
9. Il faisait du vent quand on a quitté le parc.
10. Il était tard quand elle m'a téléphoné.
11. Il était deux heures quand la séance a commencé.
12. Le temps était à l'orage quand la voiture est tombée en panne.
13. Quand on est sortis du théâtre, les rues étaient mouillées.
14. Il était neuf heures et quart quand le train est entré en gare.

**E**
1. Nous avions une maison à la campagne.
2. C'était une maison à trois étages.
3. Moi, je dormais dans la mansarde.
4. Il y avait un jardin autour de la maison.
5. Ma mère y cultivait des légumes.
6. Mes grand-parents habitaient avec nous.
7. La maison était entourée d'une clôture.
8. Nous gardions notre voiture dans le garage.

9. Mon père travaillait dans le village.
10. Ma mère restait à la maison avec les enfants.
11. Nous mangions dans la salle à manger.
12. La salle à manger était au rez-de-chaussée.
13. On utilisait le salon seulement pour recevoir.
14. Ma sœur et moi nous faisions nos devoirs dans nos chambres.
15. Nous aimions beaucoup notre maison.

**F**   1. J'apportais toujours des bonbons à mes grand-parents.
2. Tous les collègues prenaient un verre en sortant du bureau.
3. Daniel et Françoise sortaient le samedi.
4. Frédéric prêtait souvent sa voiture à son frère.
5. Tu nageais tous les jours en été.
6. Notre classe commençait toujours ponctuellement.
7. Il craignait l'obscurité quand il était petit.
8. Elle nettoyait son appartement toutes les semaines.
9. Avant, j'achetais ma viande au supermarché.
10. Ils étaient absents une fois par semaine.

**G**   1. Robert m'a écrit qu'il cherchait du travail.
2. Monique a mentionné qu'elle partait en vacances.
3. Claude et Philippe ont affirmé qu'ils pouvaient le faire.
4. J'ai dit que je ne pouvais pas le faire.
5. Il m'a assuré qu'il allait venir.
6. Elle a promis que tout était prêt.
7. L'accusé a juré qu'il était innocent.
8. Elle a demandé s'il rejoignait ses amis.
9. Il nous a répondu qu'il comptait nous aider.
10. On a annoncé que l'avion arrivait en retard.

**H**   1. était, sont arrivés
2. a reçu, avait
3. a accouché, était
4. ai demandé, finissaient
5. enseignait, a offert
6. s'est échappé, dormiez
7. étaient, ai pu
8. marchait, a entendu
9. suis né(e), était
10. sont entrés, étaient

**I**   1. Depuis quand est-ce que vous habitiez à New York quand vous avez acheté un appartement?
2. Nous y habitions depuis deux ans.
3. Depuis combien de temps est-ce que tu étudiais le français à Paris quand tu as décidé de retourner à ton université américaine?
4. J'étais là depuis six semaines. / Ça faisait six semaines que j'étais là.
5. Depuis combien de temps est-ce que Julie se servait de son ordinateur (OR utilisait son ordinateur) quand elle a changé de marque?
6. Elle l'avait depuis trois ans. / Ça faisait / Il y avait trois ans qu'elle l'avait.
7. Depuis quand est-ce que Paul travaillait comme consultant?
8. Depuis l'année dernière quand il a reçu son diplôme.

**J**   1. Elle y pensait.
2. Les étudiants lui répondent.
3. Est-ce que vous y répondez?
4. Pourquoi est-ce qu'il y a renoncé?

5. J'y songeais constamment.
6. Tu penses beaucoup à elle.
7. Nous ne pouvons pas y remédier.
8. Les habitants de ce village n'y ont pas survécu.
9. Vous songez beaucoup à eux?
10. Le criminel y a échappé.
11. Notre chat y dormait.
12. Les enfants y jouaient.
13. Le chien lui obéit.
14. C'est un professeur qui leur plaît.
15. J'y ai assisté cet été.
16. Il ne voulait pas y échouer.
17. Est-ce que vous y participez toujours?
18. Les alpinistes y sont parvenus.
19. Vous n'allez pas y toucher!
20. Il faut y faire attention.

**K**
1. lui
2. y
3. leur
4. y
5. y
6. y
7. lui
8. lui

**L**
1. Oui, je vais y participer.
2. Oui, elle y a survécu.
3. Oui, il lui a succédé.
4. Oui, ils y ont veillé.
5. Oui, ils leur ressemblent.
6. Oui, je leur ai téléphoné.
7. Oui, ils y jouaient.
8. Oui, elle comptait y renoncer.
9. Oui, je songeais souvent à elle.
10. Oui, elle lui ressemble.
11. Oui, ils y ont assisté.
12. Oui, il lui a déplu.
13. Oui, ils y réfléchissaient.
14. Oui, il y a échoué.
15. Oui, il leur convient.
16. Oui, elle lui en veut.
17. Oui, ils y ont touché.
18. Oui, il lui désobéissait.

**M**
1. Elle en achète.
2. Cet enfant n'en mange pas.
3. On en vend dans cette librairie.
4. Nous en doutions.
5. Je me souviens de lui.
6. Elle en abusait.
7. Nous en avons planté le jardin.
8. Tout en dépend.
9. Tu avais peur d'eux?
10. J'en reviens.
11. Cet étudiant en suivait six.
12. Ils en ont beaucoup.
13. On parlait beaucoup de lui.
14. Il en a lu la plupart.
15. J'en ai reçu dix.

**N**
1. Il l'écoute.
2. Il y fait attention.
3. Il en écoute trois.
4. Il lui téléphonait.
5. Ils en ont parlé.
6. Tu peux y poser tes affaires.
7. Il y mangeait toujours.
8. Il en commandait toujours.
9. Elle a besoin d'elles.
10. Elle en a besoin.
11. Ils leur en veulent.
12. Cet enfant lui ressemble beaucoup.
13. L'armée en était munie.
14. Nous les attendions.
15. Les rues en sont encombrées.
16. Nous comptons là-dessus.
17. Tu peux m'en prêter quelques-uns?
18. Notre chien en a peur.
19. La police l'a interrogé là-dessus.
20. Il y a mis les documents.

**O** 1. Il y a une réunion aujourd'hui mais je n'y assiste pas.
 2. Il y est allé.
 3. Tu pensais à lui.
 4. Ce site Web? Je m'en souviens.
 5. La nouvelle tablette? Tout le monde en parlait.
 6. J'essayais de m'en tenir aux règles.
 7. Elle leur ressemble beaucoup.
 8. Mais oui, dans le tiroir. Ils y ont mis les billets.
 9. Vous m'en voulez, n'est-ce pas?
 10. Les mots de passe? Nous en avions besoin.

## Chapter 7
### Reflexive Verbs

**A** 1. Émilie se réveille à 6h30.
 2. Les enfants se brossent les dents à 7h10.
 3. Je me débarbouille à 6h45.
 4. Jacqueline s'habille à 7h20.
 5. Nous nous peignons à 7h35.
 6. Mes parents font leur toilette à 6h50.
 7. Tout le monde prend le petit déjeuner à 7h30.
 8. Jacques prend une douche à 8h.
 9. Ma sœur se maquille à 8h15.
 10. Nous prenons le dîner à 7h30.
 11. Papa se repose dans son fauteuil à 8h30.
 12. Les petits se couchent à 8h45.
 13. Ils s'endorment vers 9h.
 14. Lise se lave la tête à 9h45.
 15. Elle se sèche les cheveux à 10h.
 16. Nous nous lavons les mains et le visage à 11h.
 17. Nos grands-parents se fatiguent l'après-midi.
 18. Je me soigne le soir.

**B** 1. Tu t'offenses.
 2. Je m'approche de la ville.
 3. Nous nous limons les ongles.
 4. Tu te débarbouilles.
 5. Je m'endors.
 6. Elle se sèche les cheveux.
 7. Il se lève de bonne heure.
 8. Nous nous promenons dans le parc.
 9. Vous vous coupez les cheveux.
 10. Nous nous habillons.
 11. Elles se maquillent.
 12. Ils se rasent.
 13. On se repose.
 14. Tu te fatigues.
 15. Nous nous ennuyons.
 16. Vous vous amusez.
 17. Je me soigne.
 18. Nous nous approchons.
 19. Vous vous coupez le doigt.
 20. Tu te casses le pied.

**C** 1. Le concierge se mettait debout.
 2. Les Forgeard se mettaient en route.
 3. La voisine s'allongeait sur le gazon dans la cour.
 4. Un taxi s'approchait de l'immeuble.
 5. Moi, je me trouvais dans mon appartement.
 6. Toi, tu te dirigeais vers la porte.
 7. Personne ne se reposait.

8. Les voitures s'arrêtaient au feu rouge du coin.
9. Vous vous dépêchiez.
10. Une vieille dame s'asseyait sur une chaise.
11. Nous nous réunissions dans la cour.
12. Une famille s'installait au quatrième étage.

**D**
| | |
|---|---|
| 1. s' | 9. te |
| 2. nous | 10. nous |
| 3. se | 11. vous |
| 4. m' | 12. m' |
| 5. t' | 13. se |
| 6. vous | 14. te |
| 7. se | 15. vous |
| 8. me | |

**E**
1. Nous avons besoin de nous amuser.
2. J'allais me reposer.
3. Nous comptons nous réunir avec nos amis.
4. Tu devais te coucher tôt.
5. Je peux me laver les mains?
6. Quand est-ce que vous alliez vous mettre en route?
7. Il doit se raser.
8. J'avais envie de m'allonger.
9. Vous comptez vous installer demain?
10. Tu préférais te réveiller à huit heures?
11. Nous voulions nous arrêter pour déjeuner.
12. Je dois m'asseoir.
13. Nous ne voulons pas nous ennuyer.
14. Tu ne pouvais pas te peigner?
15. Vous ne devez pas vous offenser.

**F**
1. Elle s'est fâchée.
2. Ils se sont brossé les cheveux.
3. Elles se sont déplacées avec difficulté.
4. Tu t'es séché les cheveux.
5. Les enfants se sont brossé les dents.
6. La secrétaire s'est indignée.
7. Ma sœur s'est réveillée.
8. Les étudiants se sont embêtés.
9. Elle s'est enthousiasmée.
10. Nous nous sommes limé les ongles.
11. Les spectateurs se sont animés.
12. Elles se sont mises de mauvaise humeur.
13. Ils se sont lavé les mains.
14. Vous vous êtes calmé(e)(s).
15. Ils se sont inquiétés.
16. Nous nous sommes bien entendus avec eux.
17. Elle s'est mise en colère.
18. Ils s'en sont réjouis.
19. Tu t'es énervé(e).
20. Je me suis senti(e) mal à l'aise.

**G**   1. Robert ne s'est pas encore lavé.

    2. Les étudiants ne se sont pas encore couchés.

    3. Les filles ne se sont pas encore brossé les cheveux.

    4. Elle ne s'est pas encore lavé la figure.

    5. Ma femme ne s'est pas encore habillée.

    6. Toi, tu ne t'es pas encore limé les ongles.

    7. Le professeur ne s'est pas encore mis de mauvaise humeur.

    8. Mon père ne s'est pas encore réveillé.

    9. Nos cousins ne se sont pas encore impatientés.

  10. Le public ne s'est pas encore animé.

  11. Janine ne s'est pas encore lavé la tête.

  12. Nos invités ne se sont pas encore sentis chez eux.

**H**  PRESENT

    1. me sens

    2. s'allonge

    3. s'approche

    4. te passionnes

    5. vous mettez

    6. s'entendent

    7. s'embêtent

    8. s'asseyent

    9. vous inquiétez

  10. te sèches

IMPERFECT

  11. se fatiguaient

  12. nous levions

  13. s'impatientait

  14. m'ennuyais

  15. vous soigniez

  16. te calmais

  17. me sentais

  18. vous promeniez

  19. s'éloignait

  20. se déplaçait

PASSÉ COMPOSÉ

  21. se sont mises

  22. me suis énervé(e)

  23. t'es fâché(e)

  24. nous sommes endormi(e)s

  25. se sont ranimés

  26. vous êtes enthousiasmé(e)(s)

  27. s'est mise

  28. se sont installés

  29. s'est indigné

  30. s'est dirigée

**I**   1. Elle se lave la figure.

    2. Nous nous sommes très bien amusé(e)s.

    3. Ils voulaient se réunir.

    4. Il allait se déplacer.

    5. Je me suis enthousiasmé(e) en regardant le jeu vidéo.

    6. Elles se sont mises en colère. / Elles se sont fâchées.

    7. Ils se sont bien entendus.

    8. Vous comptez vous couper les cheveux?

    9. Tu dois te mettre la ceinture de sécurité.

  10. Nous nous sommes brossé les dents.

**J**  1. Vous vous rencontrez en ville.
2. Les jumeaux se ressemblent beaucoup.
3. Les consultants se posent des questions.
4. Mon chien et moi, on se regarde.
5. Ces voisins se détestent.
6. Toi et moi, nous nous comprenons.
7. Cet homme et cette femme ne se mentent jamais.
8. Vous et ce monsieur se connaissent.
9. Nous nous voyons souvent.
10. Elles se téléphonent.
11. Nous et les voisins, nous nous entraidons.
12. Toi et moi, on se parle tous les jours.

**K**  1. Ils se sont écrit en français.
2. Nous nous sommes aidé(e)s.
3. Elles se sont menti.
4. Toi et moi, on s'est posé des questions.
5. Vous vous êtes compris(e)(s).
6. Ils se sont donné rendez-vous.
7. Elles ne se sont pas vues.
8. Les deux enfants se sont regardés.
9. Toi et moi, nous nous sommes acheté des cadeaux.
10. Le patron et le représentant du syndicat se sont parlé.

**L**  1. Vous vous êtes parlé hier?
2. Non, mais nous nous sommes écrit (envoyé) des e-mails.
3. Les ingénieurs se sont donné rendez-vous.
4. Toi et moi, on s'est rencontrés au centre commercial.
5. Ils s'aimaient et maintenant ils se détestent.
6. Nous ne nous sommes pas vu(e)s.
7. Vous vous achetez souvent des cadeaux?
8. Les femmes se sont bien comprises.
9. Nous ne nous mentons jamais. / On ne se ment jamais.
10. Ils se sont aidés (OR entraidés).

**M**  1. Réveille-toi. Réveillez-vous.
2. Lève-toi. Levez-vous.
3. Débarbouille-toi. Débarbouillez-vous.
4. Lave-toi les mains. Lavez-vous les mains.
5. Habille-toi. Habillez-vous.
6. Dépêche-toi. Dépêchez-vous.
7. Ne te fais pas mal. Ne vous faites pas mal.
8. Ne te dispute pas. Ne vous disputez pas.
9. Ne te salis pas. Ne vous salissez pas.
10. Ne te dirige pas vers la porte. Ne vous dirigez pas vers la porte.
11. Organise-toi. Organisez-vous.
12. Prépare-toi pour sortir. Préparez-vous pour sortir.
13. Ne t'énerve pas. Ne vous énervez pas.
14. Ne te fâche pas. Ne vous fâchez pas.

**N**   1. Organisons-nous. Ne nous organisons pas.
2. Préparons-nous pour partir. Ne nous préparons pas pour partir.
3. Dépêchons-nous. Ne nous dépêchons pas.
4. Dirigeons-nous vers la gare. Ne nous dirigeons pas vers la gare.
5. Réjouissons-nous. Ne nous réjouissons pas.
6. Donnons-nous rendez-vous. Ne nous donnons pas rendez-vous.
7. Éloignons-nous de la place. Ne nous éloignons pas de la place.
8. Approchons-nous du fleuve. Ne nous approchons pas du fleuve.
9. Lavons-nous la tête. Ne nous lavons pas la tête.
10. Asseyons-nous. Ne nous asseyons pas.

**O**   1. k                                7. j
2. i                                8. g
3. e                                9. d
4. b                               10. l
5. h                               11. f
6. a                               12. c

**P**   1. Elle se plaint tout le temps.
2. Les touristes se sont perdus.
3. Les enfants se sont cachés dans le jardin.
4. Nous nous attendions à de bons résultats.
5. Il s'est consacré/adonné à l'enseignement.
6. À qui est-ce que je dois m'adresser?
7. Ils se sont habitués/faits à la vie française.
8. Nous ne nous sommes pas donné la peine de demander.
9. Je m'efforce de le comprendre.
10. Il s'est repenti de ses mots.
11. L'autre équipe s'est emparée du ballon.
12. Nous nous abstenions de répondre.
13. J'avais besoin de m'échapper du bureau.
14. Elle s'est évanouie à cause de la chaleur.
15. Je ne me souviens pas d'eux.
16. Nous ne nous sommes pas rendu compte de notre faute.

**Q**   1. Je la lui ai offerte.                    8. Il les leur expliquait.
2. Elle compte le leur enseigner.          9. Nous le lui avons loué.
3. Il le lui a volé.                      10. Ils voulaient le lui demander.
4. Je vous l'ai rendu.                    11. Je vais le lui donner.
5. Elle ne nous les a pas envoyés.        12. Tu peux me le passer, s'il te plaît?
6. Nous le leur avons montré.             13. Le patron la leur a promise.
7. Le voleur le lui a arraché.            14. Je vais la leur cacher.

**R**   1. Ils lui en posent.                      7. Est-ce que tu les y as cherchées?
2. Elle m'en envoie beaucoup.              8. Elle aime lui en donner.
3. Je leur en prête.                       9. Nous y en avons acheté.
4. Est-ce que vous les y retrouvez?       10. On peut y en trouver beaucoup.
5. Je vais l'y laisser.                    11. Je vais leur en envoyer.
6. Il lui en empruntait souvent.          12. Il les y a jetées.

**S**
1. Apportez-m'en.
2. Demandez-le-lui.
3. Envoyons-leur-en.
4. Rendez-les-leur.
5. Offrons-lui-en un.
6. Achète-les-y.
7. Pose-m'en.
8. Lisez-le-moi.
9. Annonçons-les-leur.
10. Suggère-leur-en.

**T**
1. Organise-toi.
2. Ne vous disputez pas.
3. Préparons-nous pour faire du tourisme.
4. Il s'est trompé de train.
5. Ne nous mouillons pas.
6. Le iPod? / L'iPod? Elle le leur a offert.
7. La voiture? Je la lui ai prêtée.
8. Quant aux fichiers, vous ne nous les avez pas envoyés.
9. Et les logiciels? Tu peux les lui montrer?
10. Le courriel? Lis-le-moi.
11. Je vais les y retrouver.
12. Donnez-m'en.
13. Assieds-toi sur cette chaise et détends-t'y.
14. Les questions? Nous les leur avons posés.
15. Ça ne se fait pas.

**U**
1. Elle s'y est fait mal.
2. Ils se les sont brossées.
3. Je m'en suis offert.
4. Arrêtez-vous-y.
5. Ne te le coupe pas.
6. Tu te la caches.
7. Ils s'en achètent.
8. Je ne m'y fie pas.
9. L'enfant se les est salies.
10. Il s'en passe.

# Chapter 8
## The Future and the Conditional

**A**
1. Il se dépêchera.
2. On parlera anglais.
3. Ils feront du chinois.
4. Elle pensera à toi.
5. Je finirai le projet.
6. Qui viendra?
7. Qu'est-ce qu'elle voudra voir?
8. Nous la connaîtrons.
9. L'avion sera à l'heure.
10. Vous regarderez le film.
11. J'attendrai en bas.
12. Tu ne cueilleras pas de fleurs.
13. Vous appellerez les pompiers.
14. Elles se laveront les mains.
15. Tu t'en souviendras.
16. Les enfants s'ennuieront.
17. Nous nous débarbouillerons.
18. Je m'endormirai.
19. Tu te casseras la jambe.
20. L'autocar s'éloignera.
21. Le professeur ne se fâchera pas.
22. Vous vous amuserez.
23. Tu ne t'énerveras pas.
24. Elle ne se mettra pas en colère.
25. On se téléphonera.

**B**
1. iras
2. écoutera
3. nettoierai
4. choisirons
5. enverra
6. remerciera
7. accueillera
8. reviendront
9. recevra
10. lirez
11. dirai
12. appuiera
13. emmènerai
14. rejetteront
15. commencera
16. rendras
17. écrira
18. mangerons
19. ferai
20. aura
21. réussirez
22. sortiront
23. saurez
24. rompra
25. s'occupera

**C**
1. Je crois qu'il sera en retard.
2. Je crois qu'ils t'inviteront / vous inviteront.
3. Je crois qu'il pleuvra.
4. Je crois qu'il fera froid.
5. Je crois qu'il nous/vous plaira.
6. Je crois que je sortirai.
7. Je crois que je descendrai.
8. Je crois qu'ils se verront.
9. Je crois qu'il t'enverra / vous enverra un courriel.
10. Je crois qu'ils s'entraideront.
11. Je crois qu'ils se saliront.
12. Je crois que nous nous disputerons / vous vous disputerez.
13. Je crois qu'elle se repentira de ses mots.
14. Je crois que je participerai aux activités.
15. Je crois qu'elles s'habitueront à la vie universitaire.

**D**
1. Danielle descendra quand elle verra ma voiture.
2. On rentrera aussitôt qu'il commencera à pleuvoir.
3. Il sera d'accord avec nous lorsqu'il comprendra le problème.
4. Je passerai te voir dès qu'on réparera ma voiture.
5. Nous nous assiérons aussitôt que nous trouverons une table libre.
6. Téléphonez-moi lorsque vous saurez quelque chose.
7. Ils paieront leurs dettes quand ils auront de l'argent.
8. On se mettra en route dès que tout le monde sera prêt.
9. Fais-moi savoir aussitôt que tu recevras les billets.
10. On le verra quand nous sortirons.

**E**
1. aurais
2. prendrions
3. voudrais
4. essaierait
5. écouteriez
6. ferait
7. ajouteraient
8. iriez
9. pourrait
10. mettrions
11. achèteriez
12. chercherait

**F**  1. viendrais
2. rentrera
3. seront
4. atterrirait
5. aurait
6. pourra
7. vendraient
8. intéressera
9. devra
10. voudrait
11. s'en ira
12. auraient
13. ferait
14. faudra
15. verrait

**G**  1. passe, ferai
2. finit, pourra
3. ai, ferai
4. expliquez, essaierai
5. aiderai, arroses
6. viendra, achètes
7. emmènerai, vas
8. perdrons, allons
9. sortiront, pleut
10. excuses, pardonnera

**H**  1. S'il pleut, nous resterons à la maison.
2. Si le programme continue à être lent, il faudra réamorcer.
3. S'ils veulent créer un site Web, ils devront réserver un nom de domaine.
4. Si vous mettez un mot de passe, vous limiterez l'accès à vos pages Web.
5. Si elle travaille toute la journée, elle finira le projet.
6. Si vous me donnez votre numéro, je vous téléphonerai la semaine prochaine.
7. S'il est au courant du problème, il pourra vous renseigner.
8. Si vous arrivez à six heures et demie, la banque sera fermée.
9. Si vous avez un compte en banque en ligne, vous gérerez vos finances sur l'ordinateur.
10. Si vous préparez votre retraite, vous vivrez en toute tranquillité.
11. Si tu donnes le numéro de la carte de crédit, tu paieras tes factures en ligne.
12. Si la ville accepte ma soumission, je gagnerai beaucoup d'argent.

**I**  1. avions, travaillerions
2. montaient, gagneraient
3. connaîtriez, visitiez
4. partais, pourrais
5. pourrait, avait
6. risqueriez, investissiez
7. serait, payait
8. voulaient, contacteraient
9. téléchargeait, pourrait
10. achetiez, organiseriez
11. comprenait, ferait
12. perdraient, faisait

**J**  1. Je pourrais le faire si je m'y connaissais.
2. S'il neigeait, les enfants voudraient sortir.
3. J'irais au cinéma si toi, tu y allais.
4. Ils maigriraient s'ils étaient au régime.
5. Tu t'endormirais si tu ne buvais pas tant de café.
6. Vous auriez beaucoup de débouchés si vous saviez l'espagnol.
7. Si vous profitiez des soldes, vous économiseriez beaucoup d'argent.
8. J'en voudrais plus si j'avais faim.
9. Elle ne souffrirait pas de la chaleur si son appartement était climatisé.
10. Il irait chez le médecin s'il ne se sentait pas bien.

**K**    1. Vous aurez faim si vous ne mangez qu'un croissant.
2. Si j'avais le temps, je répondrais à tous mes courriels.
3. Ils voudraient aller au cinéma s'il faisait mauvais.
4. Si tu as envie de danser (la) salsa, nous pourrons aller à la discothèque.
5. Il finirait le projet plus rapidement s'il utilisait ce logiciel.
6. S'ils arrêtent de se préoccuper (OR s'inquiéter), ils s'amuseront.
7. Nous croyions qu'elle se mettrait de bonne humeur.
8. Elle dit que nous nous achèterons des cadeaux.
9. Pourriez-vous m'accompagner?
10. Voudriez-vous boire un verre avec eux?

**L**    1. C'est le conseiller qui arrive.
2. C'est ce logiciel qui ne sert à rien.
3. C'est / Ce sont les informaticiens qui ont réparé le réseau.
4. C'est le commerçant qui travaille tous les jours.
5. C'est / Ce sont les ouvriers qui protestent contre la nouvelle loi.
6. C'est le patronat qui est content.
7. C'est le médecin qui m'a dit de faire ça.
8. C'est cette matière qui me passionne.
9. C'est le commerce qui l'attire.
10. C'est la vieillesse qui lui fait peur.
11. C'est / Ce sont eux qui se détendent.
12. C'est / Ce sont elles qui aiment les jeux vidéo.

**M**    1. C'est lui qui connaît bien la ville.
2. C'est moi qui m'occupe de tout.
3. C'est / Ce sont elles qui paient toujours les consommations des autres.
4. C'est toi qui as refusé de le faire.
5. C'est vous qui nettoyez toujours la maison.
6. C'est / Ce sont eux qui ont tort.
7. C'est nous qui voulons faire le voyage.
8. C'est toi qui as téléchargé ce programme?
9. C'est nous qui comprenons ce problème.
10. C'est moi qui te le dis.

# Chapter 9

## Compound Tenses: The Pluperfect; The Future Perfect; The Conditional Perfect

**A**    1. Non, je l'avais déjà vu mardi dernier.
2. Non, ils avaient déjà déménagé il y a un mois.
3. Non, il l'avait déjà vendue il y a longtemps.
4. Non, elle avait déjà dîné avec lui lundi soir.
5. Non, je lui avais déjà téléphoné hier pour l'inviter.
6. Non, ils lui en avaient déjà offert une l'année dernière.
7. Non, ils l'avaient déjà rangée hier.
8. Non, je l'avais déjà fait ce matin.
9. Non, nous nous étions déjà vus avant les vacances.
10. Non, ils l'avaient déjà mis en œuvre il y a deux ans.

**B** 1. Quand toi, tu as téléphoné, nous étions déjà descendus.
   2. Quand moi, je suis arrivé au cinéma, le film avait déjà commencé.
   3. Quand lui, il est venu nous aider, nous, on avait déjà fini.
   4. Quand l'administrateur m'a offert ce logiciel, je l'avais déjà téléchargé.
   5. Quand ils ont frappé à notre porte, nous avions déjà servi le dessert.
   6. Quand je suis descendu à huit heures et quart, on avait déjà fermé la charcuterie.
   7. Quand toi, tu m'a dit de quoi il s'agissait, eux, ils m'avaient déjà mis(e) au courant.
   8. Quand nous nous sommes rendus compte des fautes, le chef avait déjà lu notre compte rendu.
   9. Quand j'ai demandé l'addition, vous l'aviez déjà payée.
   10. Quand elle a appelé, j'avais déjà lu son courriel.

**C** 1. Nous avons fait cet effort inutile parce que personne ne nous avait averti.
   2. Je n'ai pas pris de barque parce que l'orage avait commencé.
   3. Elle n'est pas venue au restaurant avec nous parce qu'elle avait mangé.
   4. Nous avons pris le train parce que notre voiture était tombée en panne.
   5. Il a grossi parce qu'il avait arrêté de faire du jogging.
   6. Je n'ai pas assisté au concert parce que j'avais pris un rhume.
   7. Il n'a pas pu faire ses devoirs parce qu'il avait perdu son cahier.
   8. Elle n'est pas restée au café avec nous parce qu'elle avait pris rendez-vous avec Jean-Claude.
   9. Nous sommes venus parce que Paulette nous avait dit de venir.
   10. Ces étudiants n'ont pas réussi l'examen parce qu'ils n'avaient pas étudié.
   11. On n'a pas pu se mettre en route parce qu'il avait neigé.
   12. Il n'a pas voulu aller au bistro parce qu'il avait mangé.

**D** 1. Tu auras reçu son courriel avant son arrivée.
   2. Nous aurons fini les préparatifs avant de partir en voyage.
   3. Ils auront fait ce travail pas plus tard que lundi.
   4. Est-ce que tu auras fini ta toilette avant cinq heures?
   5. Elle aura fait sa valise dans une minute.
   6. J'aurai résolu le problème avant la prochaine classe.
   7. Nous nous serons vus avant l'arrivée de notre lettre.
   8. Elles seront rentrées peu avant le dîner.

**E** 1. pourrons, aura fait
   2. aura téléphoné, irai
   3. commencerai, seras revenu(e)
   4. s'en ira, aura éteint
   5. quitterons, aurons vu
   6. avertirai, aurai reçu
   7. ira, se sera remise
   8. pourrons, se seront endormis
   9. fermerai, aurai trouvé
   10. monteront, auront obtenu

**F** 1. Moi, je l'aurais aidé.
   2. Nous, nous aurions fini le compte rendu.
   3. Vous, vous seriez parti(e)(s) sous la pluie.
   4. Toi, tu aurais pris le métro.
   5. Robert aurait appelé la police.
   6. Marc et Jean leur auraient emprunté leur voiture.
   7. Eux, ils lui auraient prêté de l'argent.
   8. Nous, nous aurions joué aux cartes.
   9. Moi, je serais sorti le soir.
   10. Toi, tu aurais fait attention.
   11. Nous, on lui aurait dit «bonjour».
   12. Toi, tu aurais résolu le mystère.

**G**   1.  Moi, je n'aurais pas menti.

2.  Toi, tu ne les aurais pas invités à manger dans un restaurant très cher.

3.  Nous, nous ne serions pas tombé(e)s dans un piège.

4.  Eux, ils n'auraient pas dit de bêtise.

5.  Moi, je n'aurais pas mangé d'aliments vides.

6.  Vous, vous n'auriez pas fait l'éloge de ce chanteur.

7.  Lise n'aurait pas mangé de saucissons à l'ail.

8.  Mes amis n'auraient pas regardé cette émission de télé-réalité.

9.  Gisèle et Jacques n'auraient pas offert d'appareil photo numérique au jeune couple.

10.  Toi, tu n'aurais pas utilisé d'antisèche à l'examen.

**H**   1.  aurais trouvé, avais fait

2.  n'avaient pas eu, n'auraient pas eu

3.  ne se auraient pas connus, n'étaient pas allés

4.  aurait eu, avait fait

5.  avait lu, aurait été

6.  auraient eu, avaient allumé

7.  aurais réamorcé, avais trouvé

8.  avait suivi, aurait minci

9.  s'était couchée, n'aurait pas été

10.  avais bu, me serais endormi(e)

**I**   1.  S'il y avait eu de bogues dans le programme, j'aurais réamorcé.

2.  S'ils m'avaient remboursé, je ne me serais pas plaint auprès d'eux.

3.  Si l'autobus était venu, on n'y serait pas allés à pied.

4.  Si tu étais allé avec nous, tu ne te serais pas ennuyé.

5.  S'il n'y avait pas eu de défaillance, l'ordinateur aurait accompli la fonction.

6.  Si tu n'avais pas oublié le mot de passe, tu aurais eu accès à cette base de données.

7.  Si Serge avait déjeuné, il n'aurait pas eu faim.

8.  Alice n'aurait pas été crevée si elle n'avait pas couru cinq kilomètres.

9.  Si on avait été sur la plage, on aurait vu les feux d'artifice.

10.  Si tu avais mis l'arobase, j'aurai reçu ton courriel.

**J**   1.  Si on le voit au match, on lui dira «bonjour».

2.  Ils partageraient les frais s'ils pouvaient.

3.  La compagnie (or L'entreprise) l'aurait embauchée si elle avait eu cinq ans d'expérience.

4.  Si il ne pleuvait pas, on ferait / nous ferions une promenade.

5.  Si vous m'aviez donné le contrat, je l'aurais signé.

6.  Je les attendrais s'il ne me fallait pas prendre le train de six heures.

7.  Ils iront faire du ski ce week-end s'il fait beau.

8.  Si nos collègues étaient plus travailleurs, nous n'aurions pas / on n'aurait pas tant à faire.

9.  Si tu voulais prendre la voiture, on te la prêterait / nous te la prêterions.

10.  Si elle leur avait demandé un appareil photo numérique, ils lui en auraient offert un.

**K**   1.  C'est l'avion de Marseille qu'il attend.

2.  C'est / Ce sont ces trois articles qu'il a lus.

3.  C'est l'informaticien que j'aurais appelé pour déboguer le nouveau programme.

4.  C'est son billet qu'elle a perdu.

5.  C'est un nouveau programme de traitement de textes qu'il a téléchargé.

6. C'est le compte rendu que nous avons fini.
7. C'est / Ce sont les courriels que vous avez ouverts?
8. C'est / Ce sont les finances que j'ai étudiées.
9. C'est moi qu'elle a offensé.
10. C'est / Ce sont les nouvelles données que vous avez transmises.

**L** 1. C'est le laboratoire qu'on m'a / nous a montré, pas le bureau.
2. C'est la commande qu'ils nous ont passée, pas le contrat.
3. C'est sa formation que j'admire, pas son style.
4. C'est l'ingénieur qu'on a appelé, pas l'informaticien.
5. C'est / Ce sont les dépliants qu'ils ont lus, pas les annonces.
6. C'est le canard que j'ai commandé, pas le saumon.
7. C'est / Ce sont les conditions de travail que vous devez / nous devons négocier, pas les prix.
8. C'est l'imprimante qu'on a livrée aujourd'hui, pas le moniteur.
9. C'est l'inflation que le gouvernement craint le plus, pas le chômage.
10. C'est / Ce sont les dossiers qu'il a étudiés, pas les rapports.
11. C'est la secrétaire qu'il a licenciée, pas la programmeuse.
12. C'est sa bicyclette qu'elle a vendue, pas sa voiture.

**M** 1. C'est / Ce sont les courriels qu'il a trouvés, pas les données.
2. C'est le projet que j'aurais fini.
3. C'est / Ce sont les verbes que nous avions appris, pas les adjectifs.
4. C'est la cuisine qu'ils auront modernisée, pas la salle de bain.
5. C'est / Ce sont les fichiers qu'elle a effacés.
6. C'est ce film que nous allons voir.
7. C'est l'agenda que vous cherchiez.
8. C'est le dernier document que tu avais téléchargé.
9. C'est / Ce sont eux que j'aurais appelés.
10. C'est / Ce sont les amuse-gueules qu'ils avaient servis.

# Chapter 10
## The Subjunctive (Part I): The Present Subjunctive

**A** 1. aies
2. rejoigne
3. veuilles
4. devienne
5. apprenne
6. reçoive
7. écrive
8. téléchargiez
9. voies
10. suives
11. éteigne
12. rompe
13. s'en aillent
14. soit
15. reprennent
16. offrions
17. accueille
18. battes
19. coures
20. traduise
21. croies
22. vainque
23. sache
24. connaisses
25. commenciez
26. gère

**B**    1. parliez
2. est
3. éteigne
4. vienne
5. sorte
6. travaille
7. nous en allons
8. sachiez
9. veuilles
10. ait
11. fait
12. surprenne
13. battes
14. boit
15. réduisions

**C**    1. Nous défendons qu'on abatte ces arbres.
2. Tu veux qu'elle comprenne la leçon.
3. Ils tiennent à ce que vous gardiez les enfants.
4. J'insiste pour que tu me reconduises.
5. Je ne m'attendais pas à ce qu'elle revienne aujourd'hui.
6. Je pense qu'on produit de l'acier dans cette région.
7. L'honneur empêche que nous fuyions devant le danger.
8. Je souhaite qu'il puisse venir.
9. Je consens à ce qu'elle soit l'animatrice du groupe.
10. Sa mère n'accepte pas que son fils aille au lycée habillé comme ça.
11. Il veut que je connaisse sa ville.
12. Le directeur confirme que les étudiants sont malades.

**D**    1. ayez
2. déménage
3. connaisse
4. me serve
5. soit
6. veulent
7. rangiez
8. cherchiez
9. disiez
10. faites
11. aille
12. sachent

**E**    1. Il convient que vous lui rendiez visite.
2. Sa mère est furieuse que cet enfant se batte avec son frère.
3. Le professeur se plaint que les étudiants soient en retard.
4. C'est rare que tu ne comprennes pas le texte.
5. Je suis ravi qu'elle mette le collier que je lui ai offert.
6. Les étudiants s'opposent à ce que le port de la cravate devienne obligatoire à l'école.
7. Je désapprouve que les employés du chemin de fer fassent grève demain.
8. C'est extraordinaire qu'elle sache piloter un avion.
9. J'ai peur que tu ne t'aperçoives pas du problème.
10. Il est normal que nous téléchargions beaucoup de programmes.
11. Ça m'ennuie que nous ayons tant de documents à lire.
12. Il est indispensable que tu reçoives les billets électroniques aujourd'hui.
13. Il est peu probable qu'il puisse assister à la conférence.
14. Vous proposez que je prenne l'autoroute.
15. Vous désirez que nous parlions de ce sujet.

**F**  1. sait
2. mente
3. écrive
4. doive
5. comprenne
6. descendes
7. rende
8. comptons
9. soit
10. puissions
11. boive
12. alliez
13. avez
14. sont
15. craigne
16. admette
17. produise
18. réussisse
19. vende
20. serve

**G**  1. Ce n'est pas exact que Paul reçoive trop de pourriel.
2. Il ne paraît pas que Marianne en ait marre de son boulot.
3. Je ne crois pas que nos collègues de travail puissent venir à la réunion.
4. Je ne suis pas sûr que Christophe et Philippe veuillent une augmentation de salaire.
5. Je ne dis pas que le chef parte en voyage d'affaires.
6. Je doute que cette entreprise fasse faillite.
7. Il est douteux qu'on mette les employés à la porte.
8. Il n'est pas évident que le conseiller relise le contrat.

**H**  1. Je ne suis pas sûr qu'elles viennent nous voir.
2. Ça veut dire qu'il comprend.
3. Elle doute que tu finisses le projet.
4. Il n'est pas évident qu'elle sache la leçon.
5. Je ne pense pas qu'il dise la vérité.
6. Ce n'est pas qu'il ait honte.
7. Nous ne nions pas que cet homme est notre collègue.
8. Il n'est pas clair que cette propriété ne vaille rien.
9. Il ne paraît pas qu'ils puissent nous aider.
10. Je ne crois pas qu'elle fasse des progrès en mathématiques.

**I**  1. Je préfère / J'aime mieux que nous allions voir un film ce soir.
2. Nous voulons que vous sachiez la nouvelle.
3. Ils s'attendent à ce qu'elle puisse télécharger le fichier.
4. Il a recommandé que tu achètes une tablette.
5. Il est bizarre/curieux qu'il ne réponde pas à mon courriel.
6. Ses parents espèrent qu'ils réussiront dans la vie.
7. Il n'est pas certain que nous louions une voiture ce week-end.
8. Elle a dit que nous soyons à l'heure.
9. Je doute qu'elles/qu'ils aient envie de faire du jogging aujourd'hui.
10. Il faut que / Il est nécessaire que vous lui disiez ce que vous pensez.
11. Je me réjouis que tu viennes avec nous.
12. Ce n'est pas la peine qu'ils recyclent le papier.

**J**  1. C'est au professeur qu'elle a montré sa dissertation.
2. C'est à leurs voisins qu'ils ont vendu leur appartement.
3. C'est au patron que j'ai donné le message.
4. C'est au cinéma qu'il va retrouver ses amis.
5. C'est avec joie qu'elle a accepté l'invitation.
6. C'est à la banque que nous avons emprunté les dix mille euros.
7. C'est à mon père qu'on a volé la serviette.

8. C'est à ma femme que j'ai promis des vacances en France.
9. C'est dans mon bureau que je travaille mieux.
10. C'est avant la réunion qu'on compte lui parler.

**K** 1. C'est chez eux qu'ils vont se voir, pas en ville.
2. C'est à la fac que je les ai vus, pas au café.
3. C'est à Lise qu'il a offert le bijou, pas à Marthe.
4. C'est au patron qu'il a dit ça, pas à l'employé.
5. C'est à sa mère qu'il ressemble, pas à son père.
6. C'est au chef que j'ai apporté les documents, pas à la secrétaire.
7. C'est aux garçons que le douanier a enlevé la bouteille de vin, pas à leurs parents.
8. C'est pour Philippe que j'ai acheté ce cadeau, pas pour Hubert.
9. C'est dans le tiroir qu'il a trouvé son passeport, pas dans sa serviette.
10. C'est aux clients qu'elle a répondu, pas aux vendeurs.
11. C'est pour Émilie qu'il a commandé des livres sur Internet, pas pour Laurent.
12. C'est sur le fourneau qu'elle a mis le ragoût, pas sur la table.

**L** 1. Ce n'est pas dans le salon que les enfants jouent.
2. Ce n'est pas cette méthode qui convient à ce groupe d'étudiants.
3. Ce n'est pas la vérité qu'il cache à ses parents.
4. Ce n'est pas à sa mère que cet enfant ressemble.
5. Ce n'est pas l'ordinateur qu'il a emprunté à Claudette.
6. Ce n'est pas la chimie qu'elle enseigne.
7. Ce n'est pas pour eux que j'ai fait tout ça.
8. Ce n'est pas à Françoise qu'il a promis son cœur.
9. Ce n'est pas le professeur qui a expliqué les problèmes aux étudiants.
10. Ce n'est pas sur la table qu'on met ses pieds.

**M** 1. C'est au programmeur que j'ai envoyé la clé USB.
2. C'est à moi qu'il a écrit le courriel.
3. Ce n'est pas elle avec qu'ils doivent travailler.
4. C'est après le dîner que nous avons assisté au concert.
5. C'est pour lui que vous avez acheté la cravate en soie.
6. C'est à eux qu'il a apporté une bouteille de vin.
7. C'est à leurs amis que les propriétaires veulent montrer leur condominium.
8. C'est dans le jardin que nous allons prendre un verre et des amuse-gueules.

# Chapter 11
## The Subjunctive (Part II): The Subjunctive in Adjective Clauses; The Past Subjunctive; The Subjunctive in Adverb Clauses

**A** 1. plaît
2. fasse
3. sache
4. aient
5. soient
6. trouvons
7. conduise
8. traduise
9. apprenne
10. fasse
11. soit
12. connaisse

**B** 1. Il n'y a rien qui me plaise.
2. Il n'y a pas de bus qui aille au marché.
3. Il n'y a personne qui réussisse.
4. Il n'y a pas d'étudiant (OR Il n'y a aucun étudiant) qui suive bien dans ce cours.

5. Nous n'avons pas d'employé qui puisse faire l'interprète.
6. Il ne dit rien qui me fasse changer d'avis.
7. Je ne connais personne qui lise le chinois.
8. Il y a quelqu'un qui me comprend.
9. Il y a un parfum qui sent bon.
10. Il y a quelqu'un ici qui s'exprime bien en anglais.

**C**   1. Il est peu probable qu'ils se soient amusés.
2. Je doute que Maurice et Valérie aient été fiancés.
3. Je me réjouis que vous le leur ayez expliqué.
4. Nous sommes furieux qu'il ait menti.
5. Je regrette qu'ils n'aient pas eu de vie privée.
6. Il est étonnant que tu ne l'aies pas vu.
7. Il est possible que l'avion ait décollé.
8. On est contents que les médecins soient arrivés.
9. Je nie qu'ils m'aient dit cela.
10. Ce n'est pas bien que mon ordinateur ait eu une panne soudaine.
11. Il n'est pas vrai qu'ils soient rentrés un peu soûls.
12. Ils sont désolés que leur chat soit mort.
13. Il ne semble pas qu'ils aient fait quelque chose d'intéressant.
14. Je n'approuve pas qu'elle n'ait pas fait de charité.
15. Elle est déçue que ses amis soient sortis sans elle.

**D**   1. Je doute que Nicole ait trouvé son collier.
2. Il est bon que vous ayez résolu votre problème.
3. Il est mauvais qu'ils soient passés (nous voir) sans prévenir.
4. Il est utile que tu aies téléchargé les fichiers.
5. Cela vous étonne qu'ils n'aient pas offert d'augmentation de salaire à Charles?
6. Je suis content que cela ait bien fini pour toi.
7. Il n'est pas vrai qu'Isabelle ait renoncé à son travail.
8. Il est furieux que le chien ait déchiré le tapis.
9. Ils regrettent que tout soit allé de mal en pis.
10. Il est peu probable qu'il lui ait déjà rendu le parapluie.

**E**   1. jetiez      6. soit
2. prennes    7. ait
3. ayez       8. rendes
4. choisisse   9. finisses
5. ait        10. dise

**F**   1. Nous serons là jusqu'à ce que Monique revienne du marché.
2. Nous attendrons jusqu'à ce qu'elle s'en aille.
3. Il nous aidera jusqu'à ce qu'on finisse le projet.
4. J'attendrai jusqu'à ce que vous puissiez vérifier la date.
5. Soyez patients jusqu'à ce que je vous fasse signe.

**G**   1. Nous sortirons avec elle à moins qu'elle (ne) soit occupée.
2. Nous ferons une randonnée à moins qu'il (ne) pleuve.
3. On passera vous voir à moins que vous (n')ayez des choses à faire.
4. Nous pourrons passer la journée dehors à moins qu'il (ne) fasse mauvais.
5. Nous n'allons pas voir Aude à moins qu'elle (ne) puisse nous rejoindre au bord de la mer.
6. Descendons acheter à manger à moins qu'on ait fermé le supermarché.

**H**　1. Vous pouvez sortir pourvu que vous rentriez avant minuit.
　　2. On partira pourvu que l'avion parte à l'heure.
　　3. Tu peux aller jouer au foot pourvu que tu fasses les courses avant.
　　4. Nous pourrons parler du projet pourvu que tout le monde soit prêt.
　　5. J'achèterai des actions pourvu qu'il y ait une baisse à la bourse.
　　6. Le consultant en gestion écrira le rapport pourvu qu'il sache les faits.

**I**　1. Pour que l'enfant s'endorme.
　　2. Pour qu'il n'ait pas froid.
　　3. Pour que vous fassiez la connaissance de mes amis.
　　4. Pour que tu ne te perdes pas.
　　5. Pour qu'elle me dise ce qui s'est passé.
　　6. Pour que tout le monde prenne quelque chose de froid.
　　7. Pour qu'elle achète des cadeaux de Noël.

**J**　1. Il fait trop mauvais pour que je prenne mon déjeuner dehors.
　　2. Il est trop inquiet pour qu'on puisse lui en parler.
　　3. Il est trop tard pour que je le prévienne.
　　4. Les rues sont trop désertes pour que tu sortes seule.
　　5. Il marche trop vite pour qu'on le suive.
　　6. Ils habitent trop loin pour que nous nous voyions fréquemment.

**K**　1. Je vais au bureau bien que je ne me sente pas bien.
　　2. Je compte sortir bien qu'il fasse froid.
　　3. Ils vont réussir bien que cette matière soit très difficile.
　　4. Il faut travailler bien que l'ordinateur soit tombé en panne.
　　5. Allons au stade bien que le match ait déjà commencé.

**L**　1. a. Tu parles lentement de sorte qu'elle comprenne.
　　　 b. Tu as parlé lentement de sorte qu'elle a compris.
　　2. a. Je le préviendrai de façon qu'il se rende compte du danger.
　　　 b. Je l'ai prévenu de façon qu'il s'est rendu compte du danger.
　　3. a. On lui donne notre carte de crédit de sorte qu'elle puisse acheter le logiciel.
　　　 b. On lui a donné notre carte de crédit de sorte qu'elle peut acheter le logiciel.

**M**　1. Je l'ai invitée au concert, mais elle n'a pas pu venir.
　　2. Il ne peut pas s'inscrire au cours de sciences politiques parce qu'il suit un cours d'histoire à la même heure.
　　3. Tu arrives à l'heure ou ils te défendent d'entrer.
　　4. Elle a envoyé son courriel et elle a éteint l'ordinateur.
　　5. On a du mal a le contacter étant donné qu'il n'a pas de téléphone mobile.
　　6. Je suis parti puisqu'il n'était pas là.
　　7. Je te jure qu'ils sont dignes de notre confiance.
　　8. La voiture roulait très vite de sorte que nous n'avons pas pu l'atteindre.
　　9. Il a fait suivre tous les messages au fur et à mesure qu'il les recevait.
　　10. Ma mère est brune tandis que moi, je suis roux.

**N**　1. Non seulement elle chante, mais elle danse aussi.
　　2. Ou bien on leur téléphonera aujourd'hui, ou bien on leur parlera quand on les verra.
　　3. Veuillez confirmer que vous avez reçu les billets électroniques.
　　4. Je jure que je ne suis pas coupable.
　　5. Il va passer ses vacances à San Francisco parce que ses parents habitent là.
　　6. Allume l'ordinateur de façon que je peux voir votre site Web.

7. Tout était en règle sauf qu'il (OR excepté qu'il) n'y avait pas d'eau.
8. Eux, ils sont allés au cinéma, mais nous, on a décidé de louer un film.
9. Puisqu'ils ont pendu la crémaillère, nous avons dû leur acheter un cadeau.
10. Elle a établi une connexion et elle est allée d'abord sur son propre site Web.

# Chapter 12
## The Present Participle and the Infinitive

**A**  1. J'évite les crises au bureau en organisant bien le travail.
2. En regardant les émissions en espagnol à la télé, tu te perfectionneras dans cette langue.
3. Nous arriverons à l'avance en prenant un taxi.
4. En apprenant le vocabulaire spécialisé, on pourra utiliser le français dans sa profession.
5. On s'enrichit en faisant des placements intelligents.
6. Vous réussirez dans votre nouvelle entreprise en étudiant le marché.
7. Elle a maigri en mangeant beaucoup de fruits et de légumes tous les jours.
8. En buvant moins de café, vous serez moins nerveux.
9. En sortant un peu moins, tu finiras ta thèse.
10. Ils ont gagné beaucoup d'argent en vendant leur appartement.

**B**  1. Les visiteurs désirant visiter la cathédrale sont priés de prendre un billet.
2. Les passagers voyageant en TGV sont priés de passer au quai numéro huit.
3. Mesdames et Messieurs, nous annonçons l'arrivée de l'avion provenant du Sénégal.
4. C'est un site Web contenant toutes les informations nécessaires.
5. Voici une carte montrant l'emplacement des centrales nucléaires françaises.
6. C'est un hôpital pour les malades souffrant des problèmes pulmonaires.
7. Les candidats ayant une interview seront reçus cet après-midi.
8. Les candidats parlant plus d'une langue ont une bonne chance d'être embauchés.
9. Nous avons reçu un message demandant de rassembler toute l'information sur ces actions.
10. C'est un métier offrant de bonnes possibilités d'emploi.

**C**  1. Je compte inviter toute la famille ce week-end.
2. Nous allons célébrer les fiançailles de mon neveu.
3. Tout le monde veut faire la connaissance de sa fiancée.
4. Il faut appeler le traiteur.
5. Je ne peux pas préparer un repas pour tant de personnes.
6. Toute ma famille aime manger.
7. Ils aiment mieux déguster des plats exquis.
8. Ils viennent nous rendre visite samedi.
9. Tout doit être prêt à trois heures de l'après-midi.
10. Nous désirons passer tout le week-end ensemble.

**D**  1. Ils vont prendre leurs vacances à la Martinique.
2. Ils adoraient faire du ski nautique.
3. Elle va avoir peur de la mer.
4. Tu ne sais pas nager.
5. Il n'osera pas se baigner.
6. Vous espérez ne pas voir de requins.
7. Je comptais manger bien à la Martinique.
8. Il faut réserver un hôtel sur Internet.
9. Ils aimeraient mieux descendre dans un hôtel près de la plage.
10. Nous adorons passer une semaine aux tropiques.

**E**  1. à  
2. X  
3. à  
4. à  
5. à  
6. X  
7. à  
8. à  
9. à  
10. X  
11. X  
12. à  

**F**  1. Il passe son temps à lire.  
2. Je me suis éreinté(e) à travailler dans le jardin.  
3. Elle se résigne à perdre de l'argent.  
4. Elle se bornait à sortir une fois par semaine.  
5. Nos parents nous encourageaient à suivre des cours.  
6. Je l'ai invitée à manger au restaurant.  
7. Il s'exerce à jouer aux échecs.  
8. Je préfère la recevoir demain.  
9. Il prend plaisir à taquiner sa petite sœur.  
10. Ses enfants l'aident à faire le ménage.  

**G**  1. Qui l'autorisé à fumer ici?  
2. Je vous engage à les aider.  
3. Il a enseigné/appris à sa fille à monter à bicyclette.  
4. Elle nous a accoutumé(e)s à faire de l'exercice tous les jours.  
5. On l'a / Nous l'avons poussé à l'inviter à la soirée.  
6. Je m'irrite à lire tant de courriels.  
7. Je tiens à le voir.  
8. Elle se fatigue à promener le chien.  
9. Nous continuons / On continue à faire de l'italien.  
10. Il s'acharne à réparer son clavier.  

**H**  1. de  
2. de  
3. à  
4. X  
5. de  
6. de  
7. de  
8. X  
9. à  
10. à  
11. d'  
12. de  
13. de  
14. à  
15. de  
16. à  

**I**  1. J'ai choisi d'acheter des titres.  
2. Il jure de savoir le faire.  
3. Je m'empresse de vous rendre votre document.  
4. Il mérite d'être renvoyé.  
5. Il risquait de nous offenser.  
6. Il a manqué de me rembourser.  
7. Elle a peur de partir seule.  
8. Je m'excuse d'arriver sans prévenir.  
9. Il ne s'arrête pas de nous embêter.  
10. Tu as fini de pleurer?  

**J**  1. Je me suis empêché d'éternuer.  
2. Ils ont négligé de nous appeler.  
3. Je me suis gardé de révéler nos projets.

4. L'enfant fait semblant de (OR affecte de) ne pas comprendre.
5. J'ai fini par lui demander un prêt.
6. Nous avons résolu d'embaucher de nouveaux employés.
7. Il s'est avisé de le dire au chef.
8. Je regrette/repens de l'avoir dit.
9. Il se soucie de plaire à ses parents.
10. N'oubliez pas d'acheter des clés USB.
11. Elle s'applaudit d'avoir reçu une bonne note.
12. Tu as bien fait de vendre ces titres.
13. Je brûle de lire cet article.
14. Elle a commencé par se présenter.

**K**
| | | |
|---|---|---|
| 1. de | 11. de |
| 2. X | 12. à |
| 3. de | 13. d' |
| 4. de | 14. d' |
| 5. à | 15. X |
| 6. X | 16. à |
| 7. de | 17. de |
| 8. de | 18. X |
| 9. à | 19. à |
| 10. d' | |

**L**
| | | |
|---|---|---|
| 1. l' | 7. le |
| 2. leur | 8. leur |
| 3. la | 9. les |
| 4. les | 10. leur |
| 5. lui | 11. lui |
| 6. leur | |

**M**
1. Il reproche à ses amis de ne pas l'inviter.
2. Le guide a proposé aux touristes de visiter les ruines.
3. Le professeur a défié aux étudiants d'apprendre le poème par cœur.
4. Il a persuadé sa famille de déménager.
5. Je l'ai remerciée d'avoir téléphoné.
6. Ses parents lui ont défendu/interdit de sortir.
7. La police les a accusés d'aider les terroristes.
8. Nous avons averti ces femmes de ne pas le croire.
9. Ils l'ont découragé de jouer aux cartes.
10. Son père lui a pardonné de ne pas avoir fini ses études.

**N**
1. Nous entendons les chats miauler. Nous les avons entendus miauler.
2. Ils voient les bateaux arriver. Ils les ont vus arriver.
3. Nous ne laissons pas les enfants jouer dans la rue. Nous ne les avons pas laissés jouer dans la rue.
4. Je regarde les soldats défiler. Je les ai regardés défiler.
5. Nous voyons la serveuse débarrasser la table. Nous l'avons vue débarrasser la table.
6. Tu regardes l'artiste peindre le portrait. Tu l'a regardé(e) peindre le portrait.
7. Le chef laisse ses employés partir à quatre heures. Le chef les a laissés partir à quatre heures.
8. Elle écoute les cloches sonner. Elle les a écoutées sonner.

**O**  1. Il faut faire réparer la bicyclette. Il faut la faire réparer.
  2. Il faut faire changer les pneus. Il faut les faire changer.
  3. Il faut faire transporter ces meubles dans l'autre appartement. Il faut les faire transporter dans l'autre appartement.
  4. Il faut faire nettoyer cet appartement. Il faut le faire nettoyer.
  5. Il faut faire rallonger ce pantalon. Il faut le faire rallonger.
  6. Il faut faire élargir la jupe. Il faut la faire élargir.
  7. Il faut faire retapisser cette chaise. Il faut la faire retapisser.
  8. Il faut faire repeindre les murs. Il faut les faire repeindre.
  9. Il faut faire enlever cette porte. Il faut la faire enlever.
  10. Il faut faire remplacer ces fenêtres. Il faut les faire remplacer.

**P**  1. Fais attention quand tu traverseras la rue. Tu ne veux pas te faire écraser par un camion.
  2. Il s'est plaint beaucoup et il s'est fait renvoyer.
  3. Elle aime se faire prier.
  4. Je me suis fait couper les cheveux hier.
  5. Il s'est fait faire un costume.
  6. Nous nous sommes / On s'est fait rouler au restaurant.
  7. Je me suis fait ouvrir par la/le concierge.
  8. Ça fait une heure que je fais mijoter la soupe.
  9. Ils nous feront faire le tour du propriétaire.
  10. Il a fait chanter son voisin.
  11. Ces étudiants me font suer.
  12. Ils se font toujours gronder/engueuler.
  13. Elle a fait traverser la rue à un vieillard.
  14. S'il vous plaît, faites venir le médecin.
  15. Il faut que tu te fasses soigner.
  16. Ne me le fais pas dire.
  17. Il ne se le fait pas dire deux fois.
  18. Je vais faire bouillir de l'eau pour faire du thé.
  19. Il m'a fait voir sa nouvelle bague.
  20. Nous avons / On a fait visiter la ville à nos amis.

# Appendix
## Literary Tenses: The Passé Simple; The Imperfect Subjunctive; The Pluperfect Subjunctive

**A**  1. you feared, vous avez craint
  2. he believed, il a cru
  3. I was, j'ai été
  4. she did, elle a fait
  5. you saw, vous avez vu
  6. they left, elles sont sorties
  7. you went down, tu es descendu(e)
  8. you held, vous avez tenu
  9. we ate, nous avons mangé
  10. he threw, il a lancé
  11. I was able, j'ai pu
  12. he wrote, il a écrit
  13. they had to, elles ont dû
  14. you received, vous avez reçu
  15. they came, ils sont venus
  16. we were, nous avons été

**B**  1. Nous insistions pour qu'il fasse son travail.
  2. Je ne croyais pas qu'elle puisse le comprendre.
  3. Je craignais que le vieillard ne tombe.
  4. Il valait mieux que l'étudiant relise son propre thème.
  5. Il fallait travailler tous les jours, même si c'était un jour de fête.

**C**　1. Si la France n'avait pas construit des centrales nucléaires, elle n'aurait pas pu réduire ses importations de pétrole.

　　2. Si ce médecin n'était pas mort si jeune, il aurait gagné le prix Nobel.

　　3. Si les employés n'avaient pas fait grève, ils n'auraient pas été renvoyés.

　　4. Nous nous sommes réjouis qu'elle ait voulu passer l'été avec nous.

　　5. Je ne pensais pas que vous ayez tellement souffert.

**D**　1. They saw the king.

　　2. I was born in Baton Rouge.

　　3. You came early.

　　4. I was able to express myself in their language.

　　5. He didn't think that you were going.

　　6. She doubted that we had gotten the letter.

　　7. It would be necessary to speak with them, even if it were only for half an hour.

　　8. "I regret nothing," she said.

　　9. You were lucky.

　　10. We found out the news.

　　11. They were afraid that she had left.

　　12. If you had gone to the party, you would have had a very good time.


# Oral Exercises

## Chapter 1 *The Present Tense of Regular Verbs*

**A**　1. Je finis le travail.
　　2. J'entends un bruit.
　　3. J'obéis toujours.
　　4. Je descends faire les courses.
　　5. Je réfléchis avant d'agir.
　　6. Je rends les livres à la bibliothèque.
　　7. J'applaudis les acteurs.
　　8. J'attends l'autobus.

**B**　1. Vous allumez l'ordinateur.
　　2. Vous téléchargez un programme.
　　3. Vous sauvegardez les documents.
　　4. Vous naviguez sur Internet.
　　5. Vous ouvrez les courriels.
　　6. Vous réussissez à créer un document.
　　7. Vous perdez votre travail.
　　8. Vous répondez aux messages.

**C**　1. Caroline vend sa voiture.
　　2. Caroline perd ses clés.
　　3. Caroline feuillette le journal.
　　4. Caroline célèbre son anniversaire.
　　5. Caroline complète son travail.
　　6. Caroline entend un bruit.
　　7. Caroline choisit un film pour ce soir.
　　8. Caroline attend l'arrivée de son mari.

**D**　1. Nous vous amenons en ville.
　　2. Nous rejetons ces idées extrémistes.
　　3. Nous promenons le chien.
　　4. Nous répétons les nouveaux mots.
　　5. Nous pesons trop.
　　6. Nous préférons le printemps.
　　7. Nous relevons l'entreprise.
　　8. Nous possédons un bon dictionnaire.

**E**　1. Depuis combien de temps est-ce que vous surfez sur le Web?

　　2. Depuis combien de temps est-ce qu'Hélène nettoie la maison?

　　3. Depuis combien de temps est-ce que Lucie et Christine attendent le train?

　　4. Depuis combien de temps est-ce que tu promènes ton chien?

　　5. Depuis combien de temps est-ce que les étudiants téléchargent des programmes?

　　6. Depuis combien de temps est-ce que vous envoyez des courriels?

　　7. Depuis combien de temps est-ce que l'enfant joue dans le jardin?

　　8. Depuis combien de temps est-ce que tu travailles pour cette entreprise?

**F**  1. Ils descendent l'escalier.
2. Elles choisissent un restaurant.
3. Ils entendent la chanson.
4. Elles établissent un système de travail.

5. Ils réussissent à trouver un appartement.
6. Elles finissent le travail.
7. Ils répondent aux messages.
8. Elles interrompent le directeur.

## Chapter 2 Irregular Verbs (Part I)

**A**  1. J'ai sommeil.
2. Je suis de retour.
3. Je fais des randonnées en été.
4. Je prends l'autoroute pour aller à Paris.

5. Je vais au cinéma.
6. Je suis en avance.
7. Je fais acte de présence.
8. J'ai besoin d'une nouvelle voiture.

**B**  1. Il comprend les choses.
2. Il sort ce soir.
3. Il sent la chaleur.
4. Il sert du champagne.

5. Il apprend le français.
6. Il dort à l'hôtel.
7. Il ment au professeur.
8. Il repart en Europe.

**C**  1. Tu avertis les voisins?
2. Tu réussis à comprendre mon français?
3. Quand est-ce que tu pars pour le Canada?
4. Tu crains les conséquences?
5. Où est-ce que tu rejoins le groupe?
6. Tu dors bien?
7. Pourquoi est-ce que tu mens?
8. Combien d'argent est-ce que tu mets à côté?

**D**  1. Nous ne prenons pas de raccourci.
2. Ils n'abattent pas d'arbres.
3. Les enfants ne cueillent pas de fleurs.
4. Il n'apprend pas de langue étrangère.
5. Nous ne craignons pas de désastre.
6. Je ne mets pas d'imperméable.
7. Ils ne servent pas d'hors-d'œuvre.
8. Vous n'accueillez pas d'étudiants français.

**E**  1. Nous prenons une bière.
2. L'étudiant reprend sa place.
3. Tout le monde apprend la nouvelle.
4. Mes cousins font un voyage en Europe.
5. Mon frère et ma sœur vont au bord de la mer.
6. Les employés sont toujours en retard.
7. La population de la ville craint le pire.
8. Le directeur met sa secrétaire à la porte.

**F**  1. Mais non! Il n'a jamais peur.
2. Mais non! Il ne fait jamais de fautes.
3. Mais non! Ils ne font jamais la moue.
4. Mais non! Il ne ment jamais.
5. Mais non! Il ne comprend jamais nos plaisanteries.
6. Mais non! Il n'offre jamais de beaux cadeaux.
7. Mais non! Elle ne bat jamais ses enfants.
8. Mais non! Il ne finit jamais son travail.

## **Chapter 3** Irregular Verbs (Part II)

**A**  1. Tu viens avec nous?
   2. Tu veux de l'eau minérale?
   3. Tu reçois beaucoup de courriels?
   4. Tu conduis lentement en ville?
   5. Tu cours un peu tous les jours?
   6. Tu bois du vin à table?
   7. Tu écris beaucoup de textos?
   8. Tu dis toujours tout ce que tu penses?

**B**  1. Les enfants de Madame Charpentier suivent bien à l'école.
   2. Monsieur Duval ouvre une nouvelle boutique.
   3. Les Roussel conduisent une belle voiture.
   4. Moi, je connais tout le monde ici.
   5. Madame Garnier veut chercher un nouvel appartement.
   6. Le petit Pierre sait nager maintenant.
   7. Les Chevalier lisent le journal en ligne tous les jours.
   8. Martin et Isabelle boivent un verre de vin ensemble.

**C**  1. Philippe doit connaître la Suisse.
   2. Monsieur Lambert doit offrir des cadeaux.
   3. La petite Sandrine doit savoir son numéro de téléphone.
   4. Les touristes doivent suivre leur guide.
   5. Brigitte doit écrire sa thèse.
   6. Vincent doit courir tous les jours.
   7. Timothée et Stéphanie doivent traduire les documents.
   8. Monsieur Lacombe doit convaincre ses clients.

**D**  1. Elles lisent un article.
   2. Ils nous reconduisent après la soirée.
   3. Elles vivent bien maintenant.
   4. Ils écrivent des courriels.
   5. Elles suivent des cours d'informatique.
   6. Elles convainquent les clients.
   7. Ils savent la réponse.
   8. Ils connaissent le quartier.

**E**  1. Je ne sais pas, mais je crois qu'ils veulent connaître la capitale.
   2. Je ne sais pas, mais je crois qu'elle veut suivre la même route.
   3. Je ne sais pas, mais je crois qu'il veut écrire sa thèse.
   4. Je ne sais pas, mais je crois qu'ils veulent construire une piscine.
   5. Je ne sais pas, mais je crois que cette entreprise veut produire des fromages.
   6. Je ne sais pas, mais je crois qu'elle veut vivre mieux qu'avant.

**F**  1. Elle préfère suivre un cours de biologie.
   2. Je n'ose pas dire la vérité.
   3. Vous détestez parler avec votre directeur.
   4. Ils n'aiment pas boire trop de vin.
   5. Elles comptent acheter une nouvelle voiture.
   6. Il ne semble pas comprendre la réponse.
   7. Elle veut aller à la plage.
   8. Ils ne doivent pas manger tant de bonbons.

## Chapter 4 The Imperative

**A**   1. Ouvrez votre ordinateur.
     2. Choisissez un mot de passe.
     3. Lisez vos courriels.
     4. Ne faites pas de coups de téléphone personnels.
     5. Soyez poli avec tout le monde.
     6. N'ayez pas peur de demander des conseils.
     7. Réfléchissez avant d'agir.
     8. Ne sortez pas du bureau avant neuf heures.

**B**   1. Il lui offre la voiture.
     2. Elle leur montre ses peintures.
     3. Nous lui téléphonons.
     4. Je leur enseigne des chansons.
     5. Tu lui rends l'argent.
     6. Je lui dis le secret.
     7. Cet homme lui vole l'ordinateur.
     8. Elle lui ressemble.

**C**   1. Non, elle ne le reçoit pas.
     2. Non, il ne les a pas.
     3. Non, je ne la regarde pas.
     4. Non, je ne compte pas l'acheter.
     5. Non, je ne veux pas le goûter.
     6. Non, ils ne les apprennent pas.
     7. Non, ils ne le mangent pas.
     8. Non, ils ne le finissent pas.

**D**   1. Oui, il le lui envoie.
     2. Oui, ils la lui cachent.
     3. Oui, je les lui apporte.
     4. Oui, elle va le lui demander.
     5. Oui, je veux la leur louer.
     6. Oui, je vais les leur expliquer.
     7. Oui, il la leur prête.
     8. Oui, il le lui donne.

**E**   1. Oui, obéissez-lui.
     2. Oui, annoncez-la.
     3. Oui, dépensez-le.
     4. Oui, oubliez-le.
     5. Oui, photocopiez-le.
     6. Oui, écrivez-leur.
     7. Oui, corrigez-la.
     8. Oui, répondez-leur.

**F**   1. Alors, ne les ouvrons pas.
     2. Alors, ne la mangeons pas.
     3. Alors, ne les remplaçons pas.
     4. Alors, ne l'invitons pas.
     5. Alors, ne lui écrivons pas.
     6. Alors, ne lui téléphonons pas.
     7. Alors, ne le décourageons pas.
     8. Alors, ne la nettoyons pas.

## Chapter 5 The Passé Composé

**A**   1. J'ai préparé le déjeuner.
     2. Tu as vendu ta voiture.
     3. La directrice n'a pas fini son travail.
     4. Ils ont eu une bonne idée.
     5. Elle a été au Canada.
     6. Tout le monde a mangé à midi.
     7. Elle est arrivée en retard.
     8. Il a attendu ses amis.
     9. Vous n'avez pas réfléchi au problème.
   10. Nous sommes sortis avec nos amis.

**B**   1. Les ouvriers ont détruit le vieux bâtiment.
     2. Tu as bu trop de café.
     3. Je n'ai vu personne.
     4. Vous n'êtes jamais venu avec nous.
     5. Paulette a vécu à Paris.
     6. Elles ont appris le vocabulaire.
     7. Le chien n'est pas revenu.
     8. Ils n'ont rien promis.
     9. J'ai suivi cette route jusqu'à la ville.
   10. Il a déçu ses parents.

**C** 1. Quel logiciel est-ce qu'il vous a donné?
2. Sur qui est-ce que vous avez compté?
3. Qu'est-ce qui les intéresse?
4. Combien de documents est-ce qu'ils ont?
5. Comment est-ce qu'elle écrit?
6. De quoi est-ce qu'elles ont besoin?
7. Avec qui est-ce qu'il a parlé?
8. Où est-ce que Claude est allé?

**D** 1. Nous avons travaillé dehors.
2. Il a déjà fini le projet.
3. Tu lui as souvent téléphoné.
4. Elle est peut-être tombée malade.
5. Ils sont vite revenus.
6. Nous l'avons dit exprès.
7. Ils ont beaucoup mangé.
8. Elle est sans doute descendue.

**E** 1. Oui, il l'a dite.
2. Oui, elle l'a mise.
3. Oui, je les ai comprises.
4. Oui, ils l'ont écrite.
5. Oui, ils l'ont construite.
6. Oui, il l'a faite.
7. Oui, elle les a reprises.
8. Oui, il l'a peinte.

**F** 1. La note a été réglée par le client.
2. Ces fromages ont été produits par les paysans.
3. Le marché a été étudié par les consultants.
4. Une nouvelle route a été construite par le gouvernement.
5. Ces ouvriers ont été embauchés par l'entreprise.
6. Des succursales à Marseille ont été ouvertes par la banque.
7. Votre courriel a été reçu par le programmeur.
8. Ces guides ont été appréciés par les touristes.

## Chapter 6 The Imperfect; The Imperfect vs. the Passé Composé

**A** 1. Nous avions une grande maison.
2. Notre ferme était grande.
3. Il y avait des vaches et des chevaux.
4. Mon père travaillait dans les champs.
5. Il conduisait le tracteur.
6. Ma mère cultivait des légumes.
7. J'aidais ma mère dans le jardin.
8. Nous étions heureux.

**B** 1. Il était neuf heures du matin quand vous m'avez téléphoné.
2. Il était midi et demi quand nous sommes sortis du bureau pour déjeuner.
3. Il était deux heures de l'après-midi quand les consultants sont arrivés.
4. Il était deux heures et demi quand la réunion a commencé.
5. Il était cinq heures et quart quand tout le monde est parti.
6. Il était sept heures du soir quand je suis rentré.
7. Il était neuf heures quand nous avons fini de dîner.
8. Il était onze heures pile quand je suis allé au lit.

**C** 1. Il pleuvait quand je suis sorti.
2. Le ciel était couvert quand je suis sorti.
3. Il faisait beau quand je suis sorti.
4. Il neigeait quand je suis sorti.
5. Il faisait chaud quand je suis sorti.
6. Il y avait des éclairs quand je suis sorti.
7. Le temps était à l'orage quand je suis sorti.
8. Il faisait du vent quand je suis sorti.

**D**   1. Depuis combien de temps est-ce que les employés demandaient une augmentation?
2. Depuis combien de temps est-ce que notre ami jouait au golf?
3. Depuis combien de temps est-ce que tu étudiais le russe?
4. Depuis combien de temps est-ce que vous cherchiez un appartement?
5. Depuis combien de temps est-ce que Paul et Christine étaient mariés?
6. Depuis combien de temps est-ce que nous attendions l'avion?
7. Depuis combien de temps est-ce que vous regardiez la télé?
8. Depuis combien de temps est-ce que je cherchais un nouvel emploi?

**E**   1. Non, je n'en doutais pas.
2. Non, elle n'y assistait pas.
3. Non, il n'en parlait pas.
4. Non, il n'y a pas répondu.
5. Non, il n'en a pas été accablé.
6. Non, elle n'y pensait pas souvent.
7. Non, je ne m'en souvenais pas.
8. Non, ils n'y jouaient pas.

**F**   1. Oui, ils lui obéissent.
2. Oui, il en a peur.
3. Oui, j'en ai reçu beaucoup.
4. Oui, ils en reviennent.
5. Oui, elle y fait attention.
6. Oui, nous la connaissons.
7. Oui, il y est resté.
8. Oui, je vais y renoncer.

## Chapter 7 Reflexive Verbs

**A**   1. Il se lève tout de suite.
2. Il se brosse les dents.
3. Il se rase.
4. Il se met en route.
5. Il se dépêche.
6. Il se dirige vers le bureau.
7. Il se réunit avec le directeur.
8. Il s'organise pour la journée.

**B**   1. Ensuite, elle s'habille.
2. Ensuite, elle se peigne.
3. Ensuite, elle se brosse les dents.
4. Ensuite, elle se lave.
5. Ensuite, elle se lave la tête.
6. Ensuite, elle se sèche les cheveux.
7. Ensuite, elle se couche.
8. Ensuite, elle s'endort.

**C**   1. Elle s'est déjà calmée.
2. Ils se sont déjà mis en route.
3. Ils se sont déjà lavé les mains.
4. Ils se sont déjà contactés.
5. Ils se sont déjà donné rendez-vous.
6. Elle s'en est déjà allée.
7. Ils se sont déjà plaints.
8. Il s'en est déjà rendu compte.

**D**   1. Ne te fatigue pas.
2. Couche-toi.
3. Ne t'inquiète pas.
4. Repose-toi.
5. Ne te mets pas debout.
6. Endors-toi.
7. Ne te lève pas.
8. Soigne-toi.

**E**   1. Oui, il me l'a prêté.
2. Oui, il me les a montrées.
3. Oui, il me l'a promise.
4. Oui, il me les a envoyés.
5. Oui, il me l'a emprunté.
6. Oui, il me l'a expliqué.
7. Oui, il me les a communiquées.
8. Oui, il me l'a demandée.

**F**  1. Je vais l'y laisser.
   2. Ils lui en posent.
   3. Je les y ai cherchés.
   4. Je vais leur en envoyer.
   5. Le directeur leur en envoie beaucoup.
   6. Il les y a jetées.
   7. Vous pouvez le lui demander.
   8. Nous les y avons vus.

## **Chapter 8** The Future and the Conditional

**A**  1. Nous finirons le travail.
   2. Quand est-ce que tu viendras?
   3. Je ferai des photocopies.
   4. Il recevra beaucoup de courriels.
   5. Nous jetterons tout ça à la poubelle.
   6. Ils vendront leur maison.
   7. À qui est-ce que tu enverras des cadeaux?
   8. Qu'est-ce qu'il voudra faire?

**B**  1. Chantal ferait des photographies.
   2. Martin et Jean-Claude verraient l'Arc de Triomphe.
   3. Toi, tu achèterais du parfum.
   4. Paulette et Monique iraient voir les châteaux de la Loire.
   5. Joseph ferait une promenade sur les Grands Boulevards.
   6. Tout le monde visiterait le Louvre.
   7. Nous prendrions un bateau-mouche sur la Seine.
   8. On s'amuserait beaucoup.

**C**  1. Je disais que ça finirait mal.
   2. Elle croyait que vous le sauriez.
   3. Nous étions certains que tu réussirais.
   4. Elle pensait que ce produit se vendrait bien.
   5. Je demandais quand nous nous mettrions en route.
   6. On se rendait compte qu'ils ne pourraient pas venir.
   7. Il écrivait qu'il viendrait.
   8. Elles affirmaient que vous voudriez nous voir.

**D**  1. Chantal étudierait le marché.
   2. Maurice et Philippe choisiraient un bureau.
   3. Thérèse et sa sœur chercheraient un associé.
   4. Moi, je travaillerais douze heures par jour.
   5. Marc calculerait les coûts de production.
   6. Pierre emprunterait de l'argent à la banque.
   7. Suzanne embaucherait de bons ouvriers.
   8. Charles et Victor trouveraient des clients.

**E**  1. S'il neige, les enfants voudront sortir.
   2. Si nous nous dépêchons, nous ne serons pas en retard.
   3. Si tu te couches tôt, tu pourras te lever à six heures du matin.
   4. Si on travaille jusqu'à dix heures du soir, on finira le projet.
   5. Si nous travaillons ensemble, le dîner sera prêt.
   6. Si la boulangerie est encore ouverte, j'y achèterai du pain.
   7. Si vous êtes libres, je prendrai des billets de théâtre.
   8. S'il y a un train, Luc reviendra aujourd'hui.

**F**   1. Si Philippe dormait assez, il n'aurait pas sommeil.
    2. Si Stéphane prenait des vitamines, il ne serait pas toujours enrhumé.
    3. Si Christine faisait du vélo, elle aurait de l'énergie.
    4. Si tu mangeais bien, tu ne te sentirais pas malade.
    5. Si Marc ne restait pas toute la journée au bureau, il n'aurait pas mal aux yeux.
    6. Si Aurélie ne travaillait pas trop, elle ne serait pas déprimée.
    7. Si Paul soulevait des poids, il serait musclé.
    8. Si Marie-Laure n'était pas assise toute la journée, elle n'aurait pas mal au dos.

## Chapter 9 Compound Tenses: The Pluperfect; The Future Perfect; The Conditional Perfect

**A**   1. Ma femme avait déjà acheté à manger.
    2. Les enfants avaient déjà fait leurs devoirs.
    3. Les voisins étaient déjà rentrés.
    4. La femme de ménage avait déjà fini son travail.
    5. Elle était déjà partie.
    6. Ma sœur avait déjà téléphoné.
    7. Les enfants avaient déjà commencé à regarder la télé.
    8. Ma fille avait déjà mis la table.

**B**   1. Nous aurons mis des annonces sur les journaux.
    2. Charlotte aura fait une belle vitrine.
    3. Nous aurons reçu la marchandise qu'on va vendre.
    4. Justine aura arrangé la marchandise.
    5. Moi, j'aurai lavé le plancher.
    6. Nos amis auront parlé de l'ouverture à tout le monde.
    7. Nous aurons annoncé des soldes.
    8. Nous serons arrivés au magasin à sept heures du matin.

**C**   1. Nous n'y serions pas allés.               5. Olivier n'y serait pas retourné.
    2. Toi, tu ne l'aurais pas lu.               6. Notre chef ne l'aurait pas résolu.
    3. Vous, vous ne les auriez pas suivis.      7. Mon père ne les aurait pas invités.
    4. Moi, je n'y aurais pas joué.              8. Nous, nous ne l'aurions pas ouvert.

**D**   1. S'il n'était pas rentré tard, il aurait vu les invités.
    2. S'il n'avait pas neigé, nous aurions pu sortir.
    3. S'ils avaient allumé le chauffage, nous n'aurions pas eu froid.
    4. Si elle avait suivi son régime, elle aurait maigri.
    5. S'il avait fait son travail, le directeur ne se serait pas fâché.
    6. Si elle avait lu mon courriel, elle ne se serait pas inquiétée.
    7. Si nous avions fait attention, nous n'aurions pas eu un accident.
    8. Si on lui avait remboursé, elle ne se serait pas plainte.

**E**   1. C'est le logiciel qui est inutile.
    2. C'est le gouvernement qui s'en occupe.
    3. Ce sont les conseillers qui refusent de travailler.
    4. C'est le médecin qui m'a dit de prendre ces vitamines.
    5. Ce sont les petits commerçants qui travaillent tous les jours.
    6. C'est moi qui ai résolu le problème.
    7. Ce sont eux qui ont sommeil.
    8. C'est toi qui as compris cette stratégie.

**F**    1. Ce sont les billets que j'ai achetés.
2. C'est le nouveau programme que le technicien a débogué.
3. C'est le japonais qu'il comprend.
4. C'est une crise économique que nous craignons.
5. C'est cette chanson que nous avons apprise.
6. C'est la salade que j'ai commandée.
7. Ce sont les dossiers que les conseillers ont étudiés.
8. C'est la secrétaire que le chef a licenciée.

## Chapter 10 The Subjunctive (Part I): The Present Subjunctive

**A**    1. Mais il faut qu'elle revienne.
2. Mais il faut qu'il y aille.
3. Mais il faut qu'il le boive.
4. Mais il faut qu'elle les prenne.
5. Mais il faut qu'ils l'apprennent.
6. Mais il faut que vous y réfléchissiez.
7. Mais il faut que vous soyez présents.
8. Mais il faut qu'elle la mette.

**B**    1. Je suis surpris qu'ils ne sachent pas la réponse.
2. Je voudrais que vous fassiez de grands efforts.
3. Je ne permets pas que tu te serves de mon téléphone.
4. Je suis content que vous rangiez vos affaires.
5. Il convient que nous cherchions un appartement.
6. Ce n'est pas la peine que vous le lui disiez.
7. Je préfère que tu viennes avec nous.
8. Il est nécessaire qu'elle s'en aille.

**C**    1. Il n'est pas vrai qu'elle comprenne.
2. Ce n'est pas que je sache déboguer ce programme.
3. Il est douteux qu'il puisse finir son projet.
4. Il est évident que vous avez raison.
5. Je ne suis pas sûr que vous vous en rendiez compte.
6. Je doute que notre voiture soit en panne.
7. Je ne doute pas que nous avons beaucoup à faire.
8. Je nie qu'il ait raison.

**D**    1. Je tiens à ce que les enfants fassent leurs devoirs.
2. Je ne veux pas que tu t'en ailles.
3. Je m'oppose à ce qu'elle soit membre du groupe.
4. Nous consentons à ce qu'il devienne directeur.
5. J'insiste pour qu'il finisse le travail aujourd'hui.
6. Je ne m'attendais pas à ce qu'elle revienne demain.
7. Je veillerai à ce que vous soyez au courant.
8. Je voudrais que tu lui écrives.

**E**    1. C'est à vous que je veux dire quelque chose.
2. C'est à moi qu'on a volé l'ordinateur.
3. C'est au directeur que nous avons montré le compte rendu.
4. C'est à sa sœur qu'elle ressemble.
5. C'est à Mlle Duverger que j'ai donné les documents.
6. C'est aux clients que le vendeur a répondu.
7. C'est à nous qu'il a acheté la voiture.
8. C'est au pharmacien que j'ai demandé un conseil.

**F**  1. Oui, c'est avec Philippe que j'ai joué au golf.
2. Oui, c'est pour sa femme qu'il a acheté ce cadeau.
3. Oui, c'est dans ce tiroir qu'il a trouvé l'argent.
4. Oui, c'est sur la chaise qu'elle a laissé sa serviette.
5. Oui, c'est chez Colette que nous allons nous voir.
6. Oui, c'est au café que je l'ai vu.
7. Oui, c'est en ville qu'il travaille.
8. Oui, c'est au sous-sol qu'on garde les archives.

## Chapter 11  The Subjunctive (Part II): The Subjunctive in Adjective Clauses; The Past Subjunctive; The Subjunctive in Adverb Clauses

**A**  1. Il n'y a personne qui revienne.
2. Il n'y a pas de films qui soient intéressants.
3. Nous ne connaissons personne qui sache écrire en russe.
4. Je n'ai pas de livre qui me plaise.
5. Il n'y a rien qui nous fasse peur.
6. Je ne trouve pas de bureau qui soit assez grand pour l'entreprise.
7. Il n'y a pas de train qui aille à Marseille.
8. Je ne connais personne qui réussisse.

**B**  1. Nous avons besoin d'un conseiller qui connaisse le marché.
2. Je voudrais une secrétaire qui soit très patiente.
3. Ils veulent lancer un produit qui se vende bien.
4. Je cherche un travail qui soit utile à la société.
5. Je cherche un costume qui fasse de l'effet.
6. Je veux un livre qui se lise vite.
7. Il nous faut quelqu'un qui écrive correctement en français.
8. Il a besoin d'un médicament qui fasse maigrir.

**C**  1. Il est possible que l'avion ait décollé.
2. Je doute qu'ils se soient contactés.
3. Je n'approuve pas que tu sois rentré à deux heures du matin.
4. Nous sommes contents que vous vous soyez amusés.
5. Elle est déçue que ses amies soient sorties sans elle.
6. Il est étonnant que tu ne l'aies pas vu.
7. Il est furieux que nous ayons menti.
8. Je regrette que vous ayez eu ce problème.

**D**  1. Nous ne pourrons pas commencer jusqu'à ce que tu finisses ton travail.
2. Ils remettront leur promenade à jeudi de peur qu'il fasse mauvais demain.
3. Discutons le projet avant que le conseiller revienne.
4. Je vous prête mon ordinateur pour que vous puissiez regarder le tableur.
5. Nous ne pourrons pas nous évader sans qu'il le sache.
6. Il ne pourra pas participer aux discussions à moins qu'on le mette au courant.
7. Elle n'est pas d'accord avec vous bien que vous ayez raison.
8. Je suis sûr que vous réussirez pourvu que vous fassiez un grand effort.

**E**    1. À condition qu'il sache programmer.
    2. À condition qu'il soit disponible le samedi.
    3. À condition qu'il comprenne le japonais.
    4. À condition qu'il se fasse comprendre en russe.
    5. À condition qu'il n'ait pas peur de travailler sérieusement.
    6. À condition qu'il devienne un bon compagnon de travail.
    7. À condition qu'il connaisse le marché de nos produits.
    8. À condition qu'il lise toujours ses messages.

**F**    1. À moins qu'il ne revienne pas.
    2. À moins qu'il n'ait pas lu le compte rendu.
    3. À moins qu'il tienne à convoquer la réunion la semaine prochaine.
    4. À moins que les conseillers ne soient pas revenus.
    5. À moins qu'on la remette à vendredi.
    6. À moins que les membres de l'équipe ne soient pas prêts.
    7. À moins que le directeur n'ait pas reçu notre message.
    8. À moins que le président ne soit pas retourné de son voyage.

## Chapter 12 The Present Participle and the Infinitive

**A**    1. Je l'ai vu en arrivant.
    2. Nous l'avons salué en sortant.
    3. L'appétit vient en mangeant.
    4. Le soif s'en va en buvant.
    5. Il a maigri en faisant de l'exercice.
    6. Il s'est cassé la jambe en courant.
    7. Elle regarde la télé en étudiant.
    8. On achète aussi les voisins en achetant un appartement.

**B**    1. Les enfants adorent jouer dans le sable.
    2. Je déteste faire la vaisselle.
    3. Ils préfèrent partir demain.
    4. Nous comptons rentrer avant cinq heures.
    5. Vous voulez faire sa connaissance.
    6. Tu as beau attendre sa réponse.
    7. J'ose vous le dire.
    8. Il espère vous voir au bureau.

**C**    1. Ils viendront nous rendre visite.
    2. Je descends faire les courses.
    3. Les enfants sont montés faire leurs devoirs.
    4. Je sortirai mettre la voiture dans le garage.
    5. Vous rentrerez faire le dîner.
    6. Elles s'en vont travailler à Paris.
    7. Il est revenu faire des photos de la maison.
    8. Tu vas nous aider.

**D**   1. Ces employés s'exercent à parler français.
2. Marie-Claire se consacre à aider les pauvres.
3. Nous nous sommes mis à travailler en équipe.
4. J'hésite à vous le dire.
5. Elle se préparait à partir.
6. Il s'est décidé à nous accompagner.
7. Elle apprendra à utiliser le tableur.
8. Le chef cherchera à nous donner une augmentation.

**E**   1. Elle refuse de changer de travail.
2. Il évite de rencontrer le chef.
3. Il craignait de voir son ancienne fiancée.
4. Vous vous gardez de lui en parler.
5. Elle se repentira de lui dire ce qu'elle pense.
6. Elle a tort de renoncer à son travail.
7. Il a manqué de nous envoyer un courriel.
8. Mon ordinateur s'arrête de fonctionner.

**F**   1. Je m'étonne de vous voir ici.
2. Il se fatigue à faire du sport.
3. Tu risques de faire un scandale.
4. Le directeur a l'intention de l'embaucher.
5. Les enfants s'amusent à regarder la télé.
6. Ils se plaisent à nous ennuyer.
7. Elle pense venir nous voir.
8. Il commence à se fâcher.

# Index

CPSIA information can be obtained
at www.ICGtesting.com
Printed in the USA
LVHW062300250419
615629LV00014B/506/P